Introduction to
INTERNATIONAL
POLITICS

Global Challenges
and Policy Responses

GLENN P. HASTEDT
James Madison University

WILLIAM F. FELICE
Eckerd College

ROWMAN & LITTLEFIELD
Lanham • Boulder • New York • London

Executive Editor: Traci Crowell
Editorial Assistant: Deni Remsberg
Executive Marketing Manager: Amy Whitaker
Interior Designer: Integra

Credits and acknowledgments for material borrowed from other sources, and reproduced with permission, appear on the appropriate page within the text.

Published by Rowman & Littlefield
An imprint of The Rowman & Littlefield Publishing Group, Inc.
4501 Forbes Boulevard, Suite 200, Lanham, Maryland 20706
www.rowman.com

6 Tinworth Street, London SE11 5AL, United Kingdom

British Library Cataloguing in Publication Information Available

Library of Congress Cataloging-in-Publication Data
Names: Hastedt, Glenn P., 1950– author. | Felice, William F., 1950– author.
Title: Introduction to international politics : global challenges and policy responses / Glenn P. Hastedt, William F. Felice.
Description: Lanham : Rowman & Littlefield, [2019] | Includes bibliographical references and index.
Identifiers: LCCN 2019017379 (print) | LCCN 2019021737 (ebook) | ISBN 9781538104927 (electronic) | ISBN 9781538104910 (pbk. : alk. paper)
Subjects: LCSH: International relations. | World politics—1945–1989. | World politics—1989–
Classification: LCC JZ1329.5 (ebook) | LCC JZ1329.5 .H37 2019 (print) | DDC 327—dc23
LC record available at https://lccn.loc.gov/2019017379

∞™ The paper used in this publication meets the minimum requirements of American National Standard for Information Sciences—Permanence of Paper for Printed Library Materials, ANSI/NISO Z39.48–1992.

We dedicate this book to our former
and current students who every day
give us hope for the future.

Brief Contents

Contents

03 THE SOVEREIGNTY CHALLENGE: WHO IS IN CHARGE IN WORLD POLITICS?

04 THE VALUES CHALLENGE: DECIDING WHAT TO DO

07 THE SECURITY CHALLENGE   197

Figures, Tables, and Maps

MAPS

Preface

MAKING SENSE OF INTERNATIONAL POLITICS is never an easy task, but it is especially difficult today. The Cold War period, filled with global conflict and competition between superpowers and firm cooperation among allies, is a distant past. In addition, few now talk of a post–Cold War world dominated by the United States. In today's international system, non-state actors, such as formal international organizations, terrorist groups, multinational corporations, and individuals, are able to exert significant influence over the course of events which can match or exceed that of states. Moreover, to fully understand world affairs, there are an increasing number of states whose foreign policy interests and power must be taken into account. It is not enough to solely focus on what the United States, Russia, or China are doing. Attention must also be given to middle-level and developing states who have the ability to create international problems as well as to cooperate and move forward to address pressing global issues. As if that were not enough, the agenda of international politics continues to expand as the dividing line between domestic and international politics is increasingly blurred and proposed solutions become even more contested with rising nationalist sentiment emerging around the world.

Navigating the complexity of international politics is especially difficult for new students in introductory international relations courses, who are unfamiliar with the language of international politics. It often seems that as soon as one set of ideas is mastered, new material is introduced taking them in a different direction. Compounding this problem is the likelihood that new students will not have an awareness of either the historical perspective into which to place discussions of international politics or the current dynamics at play in studying contemporary issues.

Introduction to International Politics seeks to help students develop a deeper understanding of international affairs and gain the ability to construct informed views about global events and trends. This volume approaches this task in several ways. First, chapters are organized around the theme of "Global Challenges and Policy Responses." This framework helps students focus on key aspects of international politics in order to look beyond the new vocabulary they are learning and focus on policy problems. It also links the discussions and topics in the different chapters into a cohesive whole. Second, we introduce students to the major contemporary theoretical perspectives used by international relations scholars today in a way that links these approaches to past theorizing. Too often, insights from the past get swallowed up and ignored by deep dives into the present. Third, in seeking to bring the past into discussions of the present we also make use of historical case studies to help students appreciate the way in which the past and present are connected without implying that the past determines the future.

Chapter Organization and Structure

This text is organized into four sections. Part I: Foundations of International Politics consists of two chapters that address levels of analysis, history, and theory. Part II: The International System offers two chapters that examine sovereignty and values. Part III: Traditional Global Challenges introduces students to questions of power, war, conflict, and diplomacy in three chapters. Part IV: New Global Challenges introduces students to economic globalization, human rights, and environmental sustainability, also in three chapters. Finally, the concluding chapter discusses the challenges of looking into the future paths that international politics might travel.

Aside from the first and last chapters, those within the main body of the text follow a similar structure. Each chapter begins with a **Historical Perspective** case study to highlight a particular policy challenge in historical context. Near the end of each chapter a **Contemporary Perspective** case study of the same challenge is presented. The two examples are also linked in that they involve the same subject or region. This approach provides students with concrete reference points within which to place the theoretical material, and offers instructors an opportunity to raise additional theoretical issues and make linkages between chapters. The second chapter, which introduces the major theories of international politics, offers an additional case study on the Arctic. It is used to demonstrate how different theoretical perspectives highlight dissimilar aspects in defining a common problem and selecting a response.

Pedagogical Features

Chapters in Parts II–IV also contain a series of three recurring feature boxes that provide critical thinking questions at the end to help students construct informed views about global events and trends. The **Policy Spotlight** presents a policy proposal or analysis to help students bridge the theory-policy gap that plagues much of the writing on international politics. The **Theoretical Spotlight** introduces students to a theoretical piece relevant to the chapter topic or summarizes an argument put forward by a scholar or group of scholars. This box provides students with a more in-depth perspective on international politics theory, as well as a place from which to engage in their own inquiry. Alternatively, it can be used by the instructor as a starting point for discussion.

The **Regional Spotlight** feature places an important facet of the chapter topic into a regional context, offering additional concrete information about the conceptual material presented in the chapters. Over the course of the book all geographic regions are represented.

The final section of each chapter is entitled **Looking to the Future**. It builds on issues raised throughout the chapter, drawing students' attention to three or four critical policy-oriented challenges. It is designed to spark student interest in acute global challenges and provide a platform for discussing and engaging possible solutions. Key terms are bolded throughout the text and defined in a marginal glossary where the terms appear. Learning objectives are provided at the outset of each chapter and a bulleted summary is presented at the end, followed by a list of key terms and critical thinking questions to help students absorb and make sense of the material.

Supplements

Rowman & Littlefield is pleased to offer several resources to qualified adopters of *Introduction to International Politics* and their students that will make teaching and learning from this book even more effective and enjoyable.

- **TEST BANK.** For each chapter in the text, test questions are provided in multiple choice, true-false questions, and essay formats. The test bank is available to adopters for download on the text's catalog page at **textbooks. rowman.com/hastedt-felice**.
- **TESTING SOFTWARE.** This customizable test bank is available either as a Word file or in Respondus 4.0. Respondus 4.0 is a powerful tool for creating and managing exams that can be printed to paper or published directly to the most popular learning management systems. For more information, see: **http://www.respondus.com**.
- **COMPANION WEBSITE.** Accompanying the text is an open-access Companion Website designed to engage students with the material and reinforce what they have learned in the classroom. For each chapter, flashcards and self-quizzes help students master the content and apply that knowledge to real-life situations. Students can access the Companion Website from their computer or mobile device; it can be found at **textbooks.rowman.com/hastedt-felice**.
- **POWERPOINTS.** More than 200 lecture-ready PowerPoint slides provide bulleted talking points for each major section in the text to help instructors guide students through the material. These slides include all of the figures and tables in the textbook in WCAG 2.0-compliant format, as well as embedded video links that may be played in class to supplement any lecture. The PowerPoint slides can be downloaded at **textbooks.rowman. com/hastedt-felice**.
- **EBOOK.** The full-color eBook allows students to access this textbook anytime and anywhere they want. The eBook for *Introduction to International Politics*

includes everything that is in the print edition in vibrant color and features direct links to the Companion Website, where students can access self-quizzes to help test their understanding of the major concepts and terminology in each chapter. The eBook can be purchased at **https://rowman.com/ISBN/9781538104910** or at any other eBook retailer.

Acknowledgments

We wish to thank Rowman & Littlefield Publishers for pursuing the publication of this text. Executive editor Traci Crowell provided exceptional support and guided the manuscript through the various stages in the production process. We also benefited enormously from the helpful feedback and exceptionally skilled editing by copyeditor Karen Trost. We are grateful to Traci and Karen for their professionalism and commitment to this project.

We would also like to thank the following individuals for their valuable input during the development of this manuscript, from the proposal stage to the final book you hold in your hands: Blair Niece (Coastal Carolina University), Crystal Garrett (Georgia State University at Perimeter College), Anip Uppal (Central New Mexico Community College), Brian Urlacher (University of North Dakota), Andrew Kirkpatrick (Christopher Newport University), Leslie Baker (Mississippi State University), Tamra Ortgies-Young (Georgia State University), Austin Trantham (Jacksonville University), Srinivasan Sitaraman (Clark University), Timothy J. White (Xavier University), Jacob Shively (University of West Florida), Nalanda Roy (Georgia Southern University), Donald Inbody (Texas State University), Aaron Karp (Old Dominion University), Jim Zaffiro (Central College), Mike Mayo (St. Petersburg College), M. Joel Voss (The University of Toledo), SimonPeter Gomez (Reinhardt University), Clifton Sherrill (Troy University), David Hunter Walsh (Rutgers University), Danielle Lupton (Colgate University), Ivan Willis Rasmussen (New York University-Shanghai), Sarah Fisher (Emory & Henry College), Harry M. Joiner (Athens State University), Mark Conrad (University of Wisconsin Colleges), Jeffrey Kaplow (College of William & Mary), Kanishkan Sathasivam (Salem State University), Jason Roberts (Quincy College), Lynda K. Barrow (Coe College), Renato Corbetta (University of Alabama at Birmingham), Michael Burch (Eckerd College), Christopher Moore (Bethel College), Mulugeta Agonafer (Spingfield College), Kathleen Barrett (University of West Georgia), Nilay Saiya (State University of New York, Brockport), Augustine E. Ayuk (Clayton State University), Andrea Kent (West Virginia University Technical Institute), Adrien Ratsimbaharison (Benedict College), Janet Adamski (University of Mary Hardin), David Price (Santa Fe Community College, Gainesville), Christi Siver (College of St. Benedict), Joseph Warner (Florida State College at Jacksonville), Daniel McIntosh (Slippery Rock University), Arthur Blaser (Chapman University, Orange County), Baris Kesgin (Elon University), and Andrew Waskey (Dalton State College).

About the Authors

Glenn Hastedt is professor and chair of the justice studies department at James Madison University. He is author of *American Foreign Policy: Past, Present and Future*, 12th edition (2020), editor of *Readings in American Foreign Policy*, 2nd edition (2017), and senior author of *Pathways to Conflict and Cooperation* (2014). Hastedt has served as coeditor of *White House Studies* and has authored articles that have appeared in *Intelligence and National Security, Journal of Intelligence History, Defense Intelligence Journal, International Journal of Intelligence and Counterintelligence*, and *The Journal of Intelligence History* as well as chapters in edited volumes on American foreign policy and intelligence studies.

William F. Felice is professor of political science at Eckerd College in St. Petersburg, Florida. He has won numerous teaching, leadership, and service awards, and was named the 2006 Florida Professor of the Year by the Carnegie Foundation for the Advancement of Teaching. Felice is the author of *The Global New Deal: Human Rights and Public Goods*, 3rd edition (2020), *The Ethics of Interdependence: Global Human Rights and Duties* (2016), and *How Do I Save My Honor? War, Moral Integrity, and Principled Resignation* (2009). He has published numerous articles on the theory and practice of human rights in the *Cambridge Review of International Affairs, Ethics and International Affairs, Human Rights Quarterly, International Affairs, Social Justice*, and other journals. He has served as a trustee on the board of the Carnegie Council for Ethics in International Relations. He was also the past president of the International Ethics Section of the International Studies Association.

▲ Kim Jong-un visits a nuclear site. *Source:* BJ Warnick / KCNA / UPI / Newscom / Alamy Stock Photo

01

THINKING CRITICALLY ABOUT INTERNATIONAL POLITICS

HOW DO YOU MAKE SENSE OUT of **international politics**? On any given day the news presents a bewildering array of stories about the relations among states, international organizations, and non-state actors such as individuals, corporations, terrorist groups, and humanitarian relief organizations. Collectively these interactions form the foundation of international politics. Some stories demonstrate how people and countries can work together to address global problems, while others highlight severe threats from wars, environmental destruction, and political oppression. Among the events and trends introduced in *Introduction to International Politics: Global Challenges and Policy Responses* are the international politics of the Arctic, the conflict in Ukraine, refugee flows, the Ebola outbreak, the Syrian civil war, the North American Free Trade Agreement (NAFTA), globalization, China's growing power, human rights, and protecting the environment. This chapter focuses on introducing key conceptual tools for thinking critically about international politics by focusing on how policy-makers learn from personal experiences, history, and international politics theory.

international politics Relations among states, international organizations, and non-state actors such as individuals, corporations, terrorist groups, and humanitarian relief organizations.

LEARNING OBJECTIVES

Students will be able to:

- Identify the challenges to making sense of international politics.
- Describe key events in the Korean War and negotiations over North Korea's nuclear weapons program.
- Explain how individuals learn from personal experience.
- Identify how individuals can use history to aid in making decisions.
- Explain how theory is used to make sense of international politics.

MAKING SENSE OF INTERNATIONAL POLITICS

Some of the problems raised by events and trends in international politics are believed to have workable solutions. The challenge is to decide among potential solutions and build a consensus to support the chosen solution. For example, representatives from forty-four Allied countries met at Bretton Woods, New Hampshire, in 1944 to lay the foundation for the post-WWII international economic order. Built around fixed exchange rates and free trade, the Bretton Woods Agreement was designed to ensure that the conditions that gave rise to the global economic depression of the 1930s would not reemerge.

Other problems seem to have no permanent or practical solutions. These are often referred to as **wicked problems** because of a lack of clarity about their causes and the inability to determine whether they can be solved or how to go about doing so.[1] Here, the approach is to manage the event or trend to minimize its negative impact on people, states, the international community, and the world. Examples of major wicked problems that exist in international politics today include dealing with climate change, eradicating poverty, defeating terrorism, and ensuring cybersecurity.

One of the most difficult aspects of responding to any challenge in international politics is that problems are not self-contained or isolated like grain in a silo. For example, meeting the challenges presented by terrorism requires moving beyond strictly military solutions to address the issues of promoting economic growth and building democracy. Dealing with climate change also involves multiple issues, not just the economic problems that come readily to mind but military issues as well. Just after the 2016 US presidential election, the Center for Climate & Security, a nonpartisan group of military, national security, homeland security, and intelligence experts, released a report that identified climate change as a significant and direct risk to US military preparedness and strategy.

wicked problems Problems that are difficult or impossible to solve due to their complexity.

The logical starting point for making sense out of events in international politics is to obtain information, typically by answering the five standard newspaper reporter's questions: Who? What? When? Where? Why? For a number of reasons, answering these questions is easier said than done.

First, the amount of information available to policy-makers and analysts has increased dramatically with the development of high-speed and multiple-platform communication technologies. In 1968, after an SR 71 long distance reconnaissance aircraft took twenty minutes to fly over all of North Vietnam, it took five days before the intelligence community had access to the information it had collected. And in 1983, when US forces invaded Grenada to remove a pro-communist government from power, ground troops had to use pay phones to communicate. Today, satellites transmit intelligence information to the ground in real time.

Access to increasingly large amounts of information is not limited to policy-makers. In 2011 the *New York Times* had fifty staff correspondents, twelve reporters who worked primarily for the *International Herald Tribune*, and twenty-five foreign bureau contract writers. Its China bureau alone consisted of six staff correspondents and a contract writer. The *Times* employed forty full-time staffers in Iraq when fighting was winding down. Moreover, the global dimension of traditional print media extends beyond an overseas presence to include a significant overseas readership. In 2015, 92% of digital readers of the British publication the *Economist* resided outside of Great Britain. In that same year, 33% of the digital readers of the *Wall Street Journal* and 25% of *New York Times* digital readers lived outside of the United States.

The global reach of social media is even more pronounced.[2] In 2015, 914 million social media users had at least one foreign connection. That same year Facebook had 1.59 million users worldwide and averaged over one billion daily active users in December 2015 alone. Google processed an estimated 3.5 billion searches per day. YouTube and WhatsApp each had one million users. To put this in context, China's population in 2015 was estimated to be nearly 1.4 billion and the United States had a population of 321 million.

Commercially produced information adds yet another dimension to the overwhelming amount of information available today. In the weeks following the 2018 US–North Korean summit, controversy arose over the extent to which North Korea was dismantling its nuclear weapons capability. Two commercial companies, Digital Globe and Airbus Defense and Space, released satellite images of a North Korean site where space launch vehicles had been assembled.

Second, this information is not all evenly distributed. Significant global information gaps exist. According to former Director of National Intelligence James Clapper, imagery and signals intelligence provide only part of the picture. Information on the ground is needed to bridge the gaps, but the CIA does not have a presence in remote countries in Africa or Asia. In such cases, local governments and their intelligence services are called on to provide information.[3]

The uneven flow of information is evident in media coverage of world affairs. In 2018 the *Washington Post* had twenty-eight foreign correspondents in twenty bureaus: eight in Europe (Berlin, Brussels, Frankfurt, Istanbul, London, Paris, Moscow, and Rome), four in the Middle East (Beirut, Cairo, Jerusalem, and Baghdad), and five in Asia (Beijing, Hong Kong, New Deli, Islamabad, and Tokyo). There was only one in the entire continent of Africa (Nairobi), and two in Latin America (Mexico City and Miami). This imbalanced coverage translates into an uneven flow of information about global events and reflects a combination of considerations: foreign policy (what matters to the United States), economic (where US firms have business interests), and historical-cultural (where US immigrants came from).

In some cases the uneven flow of information reflects domestic political considerations. US-funded media outlets must register as foreign agents in Russia. China began to systematically block and monitor the Internet in 1996, blocking YouTube after unrest in Tibet in 2008 and blocking Facebook and Twitter following the 2009 riots in Xinjiang. In 2016 Freedom House, a nongovernmental organization (NGO) that monitors political freedom and human rights, estimated that a full third of Internet users in sixty-five countries surveyed faced heavy censorship.

signals Clues or pieces of information that are useful in addressing problems.

noise Competing or contradictory information that prevents policy-makers from recognizing signals.

Third, not all information is of equal value in enhancing an understanding of international politics. It is helpful to distinguish between signals and noise. **Signals** are clues or pieces of information that are useful in addressing problems; they identify a danger from or a move or intention by a particular enemy. **Noise** is competing or contradictory information that prevents policy-makers from recognizing signals; it is useless for anticipating an event. This background clutter can occur naturally or be created to deliberately confuse other states. In her analysis of why the United States was caught off guard by the Japanese attack on Pearl Harbor,[4] Roberta Wohlstetter concluded that the United States was surprised not by a lack of signals of an impending attack but because of the large amount of noise that accompanied them.

Finally, the quality of the information must be evaluated using two criteria. The first is the reliability of the source. Is it a trustworthy individual or organization that has a track record of providing good information, or is it hearsay, gossip, or intentionally misleading information provided by a hostile government? The second is accuracy. To what extent is the information consistent with and supported by other information?

These questions are not new. During the Cold War between the United States and the Soviet Union, US intelligence agencies were known to plant a story in one newspaper and then have a contact in another newspaper pick it up and report it as legitimate news. However, they have taken on a new dimension today, as evidenced by the findings of the US intelligence community regarding Russia's use of Twitter and other social media outlets to spread propaganda and disinformation during the 2016 presidential election. The current conflict in Syria between its long-serving government and those seeking to overthrow it is seen by many as the first social media war.[5] Many reporters became victims of the violence, and thus news agencies increasingly came to rely on social media for information. Both the Syrian government and rebel groups actively used social media to promote their stories, raise funds, and influence global public opinion. This can be of great benefit (the US government relied heavily on social media accounts in charging that the Syrian government had used chemical weapons) or a source of disinformation (social media falsely showed government soldiers burying a rebel alive).

As Pearl Harbor demonstrated, the availability of signals does not mean they will be recognized. Distinguishing signals from noise requires observers to listen carefully. The search for insight must be guided by a set of ideas, expectations, and understandings of exactly what drives action in international politics. To varying degrees, policy-makers and analysts rely on personal experience, history, and theories of international politics to make decisions.

KOREA THEN AND NOW

To illustrate how policy-makers and analysts come to under-stand international politics, this section examines two episodes in the complex international politics of the Korean Peninsula (see Map 1.1): the Korean War in the 1950s; and North Korea's current pursuit of nuclear weapons, which former director of national intelligence and head of the CIA Michael Hayden and other government officials identify as a wicked problem with no good answers that has simply been passed along from one administration to another.[6]

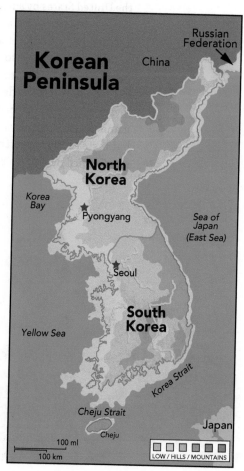

Map 1.1 The Korean Peninsula.

The Korean War

The Korean War has its origin in events that occurred at the end of WWII. At two WWII summit conference meetings the Soviet Union promised it would enter the war against Japan after Germany was defeated. Germany surrendered on May 7, 1945. On August 9, three days after the United States dropped a nuclear bomb on Hiroshima, Russia declared war on Japan, and the next day Soviet military forces entered northern Korea. Five days later, on August 15, Japan surrendered.

It was agreed that Korea would be divided temporarily, with American forces occupying the south and Russian forces in the north and the 38th parallel as the temporary dividing line. After five years Korea was to be reunited into a single country. Tensions both within and between the northern and southern occupation zones as well as growing Cold War tension between the United States and the Soviet Union soon made it clear that reunification was not likely to happen. Confronting a political stalemate on the future of Korea and fearing that North Korean forces could overwhelm South Korea, the United States turned to the United Nations (UN). In September 1947 the UN issued a resolution calling for nationwide elections. North Korea refused, but elections were held in South Korea in May 1948. In August South Korea declared its statehood, and in September North Korea did likewise.

The North Korean ruler was Kim Il-sung. The grandfather of its current leader, he had been placed in that position by the Soviet military in 1945. Soviet forces left North Korea in 1948, and most of the US forces left South Korea in 1949. The departure of these military units did not end tensions between the two nations, and there were numerous and often serious border clashes and military engagements between South Korean forces and communist guerrillas. Events also moved forward on the political front setting the stage for the outbreak of war. In March 1949 Kim Il-sung sought permission from Soviet leader Joseph Stalin to invade South Korea, and in April 1950 he received permission for reasons that are still debated today. In a major public foreign policy address in January 1950, US Secretary of State Dean Acheson defined the US defense perimeter in the Far East with no mention of Korea.

On June 25, 1950, over 100,000 North Korean forces invaded South Korea, catching the United States by surprise. The US response, in turn, appears to have surprised North Korea, which expected a quick victory. The United States responded with both diplomacy *and* the use of force. At an emergency meeting of the UN Security Council, the United States introduced a resolution calling for an immediate cease-fire and the withdrawal of North Korean troops from South Korea. Two days later a resolution was passed calling on UN members to provide whatever assistance was needed to help South Korea repel the invasion and restore peace to the region. The UN also established a unified military command under US leadership. The Soviet Union had the power to veto these resolutions but instead boycotted the meetings to protest the holding of China's seat on the Security Council by Taiwan rather than the People's Republic of China. US President Harry Truman also responded militarily. He sent arms and supplies to South Korea, placed the Seventh Fleet in the Formosa Strait to seal off Taiwan from China, and gave General Douglas MacArthur, Commander of US Forces in the Far East, the authority to provide military assistance to South Korea as head of the Unified Command.

The North Korean invasion was not stopped easily. It was only after a daring military gamble that landed UN forces behind enemy lines at Inchon in September that an effective counterattack was launched. By early October UN forces had crossed the 38th parallel into North Korea. As MacArthur's forces moved northward toward the Chinese border, US goals changed from

Korean War.

Maj. R. V. Spencer / U.S. Department of Defense

protecting South Korea to reunifying Korea. The United States largely ignored signals from China resisting the American troops' approach to its border. Then, as US efforts for a final offensive were under way, 200,000 Chinese troops counterattacked, driving UN forces out of North Korea down to the southern tip of South Korea and forcing MacArthur to make evacuation plans. Ultimately this was not necessary because the tide of battle had shifted in the favor of UN forces, and by March 1951 UN forces had returned to the 38th parallel.

In June 1951 truce talks began, but little progress was made. A truce that ended the fighting was finally signed in July 1953, but nearly seventy years later an official peace treaty has yet to be signed. According to some accounts, President Dwight Eisenhower, who had campaigned on a promise to end the war, threatened China with a nuclear attack unless it convinced North Korea to accept a truce. Other accounts assert that the nuclear weapons threat was never communicated to China.[7]

Nuclear North Korea

North Korean–US relations again made headlines in the early 1990s. This time the issue was nuclear weapons. North Korea made its first steps toward obtaining nuclear capability in the mid-1950s when the Soviet Union began training North Korean scientists, resulting in a 1959 nuclear cooperation agreement. In the 1970s North Korea turned to Pakistan to obtain the necessary resources and technology. With the end of the Cold War North Korean leaders no longer saw Russia or China as firm protectors of their interests and viewed nuclear weapons as a way to increase their ability to defend themselves. They also felt the need to improve relations with the United States. First steps in this direction occurred in a 1992 joint declaration by North and South Korea to denuclearize the Korean peninsula. This was followed by a nuclear safeguard agreement with the International Atomic Energy Agency (IAEA); however, the agreement's requirement that international inspections take place quickly led to confrontations over its terms. It also led to discoveries of "inconsistencies" in North Korea's reporting about its nuclear activities. In response, in 1994 North Korea announced its intention to withdraw from the Nuclear Nonproliferation Treaty (NPT), which it had joined in 1985 as a non-nuclear state.

This worsening situation prompted a series of US–North Korean negotiations that began in June 1993 during the Clinton administration and led to the signing of an Agreed Framework in October 1994. Under its terms North Korea agreed to freeze its nuclear program in return for fuel oil, economic cooperation, the international construction of two proliferation-resistant nuclear reactors, and the promise of improved diplomatic relations with the United States.

The agreement did not end questions about North Korea's ultimate intentions. Evidence pointed to the existence of a covert uranium enrichment program, and in 1998 North Korea tested an intercontinental ballistic missile (ICBM) under the guise of testing a satellite. This stream of activity resulted in the April 2003 Three Party talks among the United States, China, and North Korea, during which North Korea officially acknowledged possession of nuclear weapons. Six rounds of follow-up talks, which included South Korea, Japan, and Russia, continued until 2007. In 2009 talks were officially discontinued following UN Security Council condemnation of a failed North Korean ICBM test.

Political scientist Walter Clemens Jr. characterized the early rounds of the Six Party talks as the United States and North Korea throwing "jokers" into their proposals, guaranteeing rejection.[8] The essence of the US position was that North Korea should accept the rapid dismantling of its nuclear facilities and international inspections, with no guarantee from the United States of improved relations. North Korea countered with a promise to freeze its nuclear program in return for the immediate provision of a significant amount of energy aid.

Eventually two agreements were reached, interrupted by North Korea's first successful testing of a nuclear device in October 2006. In the first agreement on September 15, 2005, North Korea agreed to abandon all nuclear weapons and return to the NPT as soon as possible; the United States confirmed that it had no intention of attacking or invading North Korea; and all participants agreed to promote economic cooperation with North Korea. The second agreement, reached on February 13, 2007, required North Korea to shut down and seal the Yongbyon nuclear facility under international supervision in return for emergency energy assistance and its removal from the US list of state sponsors of terrorism.

By the time Donald Trump became president in 2017, US–North Korean relations had settled into a familiar pattern: the United States ratcheted up economic sanctions, North Korea tested nuclear devices and delivery systems, the UN passed resolutions condemning these tests, and North Korea indicated willingness to enter into talks. Following the US election, this pattern was replaced by a roller coaster alternating threats with expressions of good will.

In April 2017 the United States indicated US openness to talks with North Korea. This position evaporated in August when Trump responded to North Korean criticism of the United States by stating "North Korea best not make any more threats to the United States. ... They will be met with fire and fury that the world has never seen before." North Korea retaliated with a series of ballistic missile threats and its sixth nuclear test, leading Trump to assert that the "Rocket Man is on a suicide mission for himself and his regime." In April 2018 North Korean leader Kim Jong-un agreed to meet with President Trump but then threatened to cancel the summit one month later. On May 25 Trump did cancel it, but then on June 12 the summit was held as scheduled

Nuclear North Korea: Here we see North Korean weapons on display in a parade.

David Guttenfelder / AP Images

in Singapore. After the summit Trump praised his "good relationship" Kim Jong-un, asserting that "we had a fantastic meeting" and declaring that the North Korean nuclear threat was effectively over.

However, post-summit events suggested that the future is looking much like the past. National security advisor John Bolton initially stated that North Korea could dismantle all of its nuclear and biological weapons in a year, but evidence began pointing to continued North Korean nuclear activity. It also became clear that the two sides had different views of what denuclearization meant or how it would be achieved. At the end of 2018 it was generally agreed that the status of North Korean nuclear weapons was just where it was when Trump and Kim Jong-un met in June. A follow-up summit was held in February 2019 but ended abruptly with no agreement as neither side was willing to make compromises on their existing positions.

As noted earlier in the chapter, policy-makers and analysts rely on personal experience, history, and theories of international politics to gather and assess information, evaluate events and trends, and determine how to respond. In the following sections these three sources of insight are applied to the two episodes in the international politics of Korea.

LEARNING FROM PERSONAL EXPERIENCE

Henry Kissinger, who served as national security adviser and secretary of state under Presidents Richard Nixon and Gerald Ford, once commented that "policy-makers live off the intellectual capital they have brought with them to office; they have no time to build more capital."[9] Political scientist Elizabeth Saunders reached a similar conclusion in her study of how presidents shape military interventions, observing that "leaders arrived in office with a set of ideas already in place and held those beliefs before they faced actual crises." She and other researchers characterize such beliefs as "sticky."[10]

Firsthand experiences that occurred early in their careers are particularly valuable sources of beliefs for policy-makers. Once a situation is faced or a decision made for the first time, it establishes a baseline for thinking about issues that leaves a deep and enduring mark. Not necessarily related to international politics, these earlier experiences may include successful strategies or positions taken on issues that led to winning elections or a desirable outcome in non-political professional undertakings.

In her study Saunders found that some presidents defined a threat as domestic and others defined it as a foreign policy issue. Internal threats resulted in US efforts to reshape the domestic structure of the countries involved. External threats simply sought to change another country's foreign policy. For example, Dwight Eisenhower's perception of threat was externally oriented. During WWII, in making plans to invade North Africa, he stated "the sooner I can get rid of all these questions that are outside the military in scope, the happier I will be."

In contrast, John F. Kennedy consistently focused on the domestic roots of threats. Early in his career he argued for reductions in US foreign aid, indicating that the United States should not try to raise the standard of living of "people all over the globe who might be subject to the lure of communism." After a 1951 trip to Asia he reversed his position, indicating that cutting nonmilitary aid would be a "tremendous mistake" and asserting that "communism cannot be met effectively by merely the force of arms. It is the people themselves that must be led to reject it."

Personal Experiences and Policy-Making Toward Korea

A variety of personal experiences shaped Harry Truman's response to North Korea's attack on the South. As a senator Truman had voted to support neutrality legislation and was against global involvement by the United States, but that changed with Pearl Harbor, an event that left him filled with guilt and shame about his earlier position.[11] When Greece was torn apart by civil war in 1947, amidst fears that a victory by pro-Soviet communist forces might lead to communist victories throughout the region, Great Britain informed the United States that for financial reasons it could no longer provide Greece with protection. In response, Truman issued the Truman Doctrine, which committed the United States to stopping communist aggression. The Truman Doctrine is seen as the turning point from isolationism to Cold War containment of the Soviet Union in US foreign policy. In formulating this policy, Truman identified Korea as the Greece of the Far East.[12] After the 1947 Moscow Conference Truman wrote this to Secretary of State James Byrnes: "[T]here is no doubt in my mind that Russia intends an invasion of Turkey and the seizure of the Black Sea Straits to the Mediterranean. ... Only one language do they understand—how many divisions have you? I do not think we should play compromise any longer."[13]

Personal experiences also influenced the approaches of Bill Clinton, George W. Bush, and Donald Trump to dealing with North Korea's growing nuclear capability, but in a very different way. Although their experiences differ greatly, what unites them is a personalization of diplomacy. For them, US–North Korean relations were more about relationships among leaders than about underlying forces. This perspective is not unique. Personal relations are the core rationale for holding summit conferences; face-to-face contact gives leaders a chance to break through the historical and institutional obstacles that can make reaching agreements difficult.

Referencing negotiations to end the North Korean nuclear program, Bill Clinton notes in his memoirs that "based on previous experience, I was unwilling to trust North Korea and would leave sanctions hanging until we received official confirmation of North Korea's change in policy."[14] George Bush was more explicit, telling reporter Bob Woodward that "I loathe Kim Jong-il. I've got a visceral reaction to this guy. ... Maybe it's my religion, but I feel passionate about this."[15] According to biographer Jean Edward Smith, this comment was consistent with Bush's approach to foreign policy. For Bush foreign policy was an exercise in morality, and information played a secondary role.

Smith recounts one meeting when, in speaking about CIA intelligence briefs, Bush said "I wish those [*****] would put things just point-blank to me. ... I get a half book telling me about the history of North Korea. I don't do nuance."[16] From the outset of his presidency Donald Trump has demonstrated lack of interest in delving into the details of foreign policy issues prior to summit meetings. He instead relies on his experience as a business negotiator to provide the foundation for his foreign policy. His preference is for one-on-one negotiations with little support from professional diplomats, military officials or other experts, leaving it to them to follow through on the agreements he negotiates.

The importance of personal and societal experiences is not limited to US politics. In a meeting planning a response to the 1989 pro-democracy movement, Chinese leader Deng Xiaoping asserted that the protesters' demands were "altogether the same stuff as what the rebels did during the Cultural Revolution. All they want is to create chaos."[17] Vladimir Putin has been particularly adept at drawing on the collective memory of Russians in justifying his foreign policy. In a speech to Russian officials about the annexation of Crimea following the 2014 military conflict with Ukraine, Putin asserted, "Crimea has always been an integral part of Russia in the hearts and minds of people." At a public rally on Red Square he stated, "After a long, hard and exhaustive journey at sea, Crimea and Sevastopol are returning to their home harbor to the native shores, to the home port of Russia."[18]

The influences of personal and societal experiences are also evident in North Korean decision-making. Kim Il-sung, who led the North Korean invasion, had a strong military background, having engaged in guerrilla wars against the Japanese occupation of Korea in the 1930s and 1940s. His son, Kim Jong-il, lacked any true military experience. Described as a spoiled son who dabbled in political philosophy, he had to invent a military reputation and advance the creation of a strong military and the development of nuclear weapons to legitimize his rule, transforming himself into a "respected and beloved general."[19]

LEARNING FROM HISTORY

History is a valuable resource for policy-makers confronting unexpected or new situations, as well as situations with large information gaps. However, turning to history for insights about the present has its own problems. One problem is that history is not set in stone; it is constantly being revisited and reinterpreted.

Prominent **revisionist histories** include those about WWI and WWII. For example, the Versailles Peace Treaty that ended WWI identified Germany as responsible for the war, but later revisionist histories suggested that most European governments had come to feel that war was either inevitable or a solution to domestic problems. Traditional accounts lay blame for WWII squarely on Germany and Japan, but some revisionist accounts argue that overly aggressive US economic policies forced Japan to enter the war. Traditional accounts also identify the bombing of Hiroshima and Nagasaki as

revisionist history Reinterpretation of the orthodox manner in which events have been explained and evaluated.

necessary to end WWII without an invasion of Japan, but revisionist accounts argue that it was a signal to Russia about US military power. More recent examples of conflicting accounts include those about the Vietnam War and the Iraq War.

A second problem with learning from history is information overload. There may be too much history to grasp in the short period of time allotted to policy-makers, who face very real decision deadlines. *Usable history*, history that appears to relate directly to the problem at hand, is more important. Often this translates into events and consequences. Hitler invaded Poland. Communist rule collapsed in Russia. The Shah of Iran was overthrown. Genocide took place in Rwanda. Left out of usable history are earlier policy-makers' perceptions: how the situation was defined, why it occurred, the extent to which accidents and luck influenced the outcome, and costs.

In practical terms, policy-makers who wish to use history to understand the present must decide which past events are relevant. Among the most frequently used are **generational events** such as such as Pearl Harbor, Vietnam, and 9/11. In contrast to firsthand personal experiences, which leave their mark in the memory of individuals, generational events have a profound impact on a society's collective memory.

In looking to the past for insights, policy-makers engage in *analogical reasoning*, making comparisons between events in order to identify key points of similarity. Political scientist Yuen Foong Khong identifies six ways in which analogies help policy-makers make decisions:[20]

<aside>
generational events Events that have a profound impact on the collective memory of a society, even for those who do not experience them personally.
</aside>

- Assist in defining the nature of the current situation.
- Help assess the stakes involved.
- Provide options.
- Predict the chances of success.
- Evaluate the moral rightness of options.
- Provide warning about associated dangers.

Despite these potential benefits, most observers assert that learning from the past does not earn passing grades. "Munich" is a generational event most frequently used to illustrate this point. Under the terms of the WWI peace agreement, Germany was to demilitarize its territory along the River Rhine, making it difficult to threaten neighbors or start another war. In 1936 Hitler began to ignore the letter and spirit of this agreement, sending troops into the Rhineland and then demanding the right to annex the Sudetenland, the ethnically German portion of Czechoslovakia. The 1938 Munich Conference, involving French, British, and German leaders, considered this demand. Rather than challenging Hitler, they agreed to allow him to proceed. British Prime Minister Neville Chamberlain characterized the agreement as creating the basis for "peace in our time." Sadly, it was not to be. In 1939 Germany and Russia signed a secret nonaggression agreement to divide territory along their borders between them. This agreement held until 1941 when Hitler invaded Poland. France and Great Britain responded by declaring war.

The universal lesson drawn from Munich is that hostile states cannot and should not be appeased through diplomatic dialogues. Appeasement will only embolden them to undertake further and even more threatening military action. This lesson was invoked by US policy-makers in the decision-making processes that led to the Korean War, the support of France's efforts to hold onto its colonies in southeast Asia, the Vietnam War, the provision of aid to the Contras battling the Sandinistas in Nicaragua, and the Iraq War. Research suggests that this conclusion is overstated. Appeasement succeeds or fails depending on a number of factors, including the identity of the aggressor, the issue being contested, and the options open to the state considering appeasement.[21]

A second criticism of learning from history is that all too often leaders use historical lessons to justify and promote policy decisions that have already been made rather than to make policy. A case in point is the use of the post-WWII occupation of Germany and Japan by the George W. Bush administration in discussing the rebuilding of Iraq following the removal of Saddam Hussein from power. "America has made and kept this commitment before. ... [A]fter defeating enemies, we did not leave behind occupying armies, we left constitutions and parliaments."[22]

An example of effective learning from history comes from the resolution of the Cuban Missile Crisis. In October 1962, after the United States discovered that the Soviet Union was secretly placing offensive nuclear missiles in Cuba, the Kennedy administration demanded that they be withdrawn. Some called for an air strike against the missile sites without warning, but Kennedy rejected that approach to avoid creating a Pearl Harbor in reverse, with the United States as the attacker that started a global war. Instead, he imposed a naval blockade around Cuba to stop the shipment of additional missiles and threatened additional military action if the existing missiles were not removed.

Learning from History and Policy-Making Toward Korea

A closer examination of the Korean War reveals that policy-makers turned to the past in formulating a response to the North Korean invasion, which in turn became the source of analogies for later US military action. These events demonstrate how various states and individuals can interpret history differently.

President Truman drew heavily on lessons of the past in responding to the North Korean invasion. Characterized as a devoted student of history, Truman later observed that its lessons offered clear guidance as to the "right principles" for action. He compared the North Korean attack to German, Italian, and Japanese aggression leading up to WWII. In his memoirs he wrote: "I recalled some earlier instances: Manchuria, Ethiopia, Austria, I remembered how each time that democracies failed to act it had encouraged the aggressors to keep going ahead ... If this was allowed to go unchallenged it would mean a third world war ..."[23]

Differences in reading the past also played a major role once the Korean War was underway. Neither Truman nor MacArthur expected China to intervene militarily in the Korean War because of what Truman referred to, just prior to the Chinese counterattack, as the "long-standing American friendship for the people of China."[24] As political scientist John Stoessinger notes, "Truman and MacArthur perceived a China that no longer existed."[25] The communist Chinese officials in power did not see the United States as a friend but as the inheritor of Japan's imperialist position in Asia. To this end the Chinese saw invasion of South Korea as a logical policy option.

Still another misperception based on history lay in MacArthur's assessment of Chinese military power. Instead of viewing China as a military equal, MacArthur viewed it in what Stoessinger describes as paternalistic and contemptuous terms.[26] MacArthur equated the well-disciplined communist Chinese soldiers of 1950 with the demoralized Nationalist Chinese soldiers allied with the United States who were defeated in 1948. On the other side, Chinese propaganda treated the United States as a paper tiger that could easily be defeated.

A fundamental lesson drawn by policy-makers from the Korean War was that it represented an example of "communism at work," with North Korea, Russia, and China as co-conspirators. A State Department White Paper about the conflict between North and South Vietnam stressed that "North Vietnam's commitment to seize control of the South is no less total than was the commitment of the regime in North Korea in 1950." In a 1965 speech Assistant Secretary of State for Far Eastern Affairs William Bundy summarized the lessons of the Korean War for US foreign policy toward South Vietnam in the following terms:[27]

- Aggression of any sort must be met early and head on or it will have to be met later and in tougher circumstances.
- A defense line in Asia, stated in terms of island perimeter, did not adequately define our vital interest.
- [A] power vacuum was an invitation to aggression ... there must be a demonstrated willingness both to assist and intervene if necessary.

Not all agreed with using the Korean War analogy as a key to making decisions about Vietnam. Most prominent among them was Under Secretary of State George Ball, who had worked extensively with France early in his career. In 1964 he wrote a memo entitled *South Vietnam Is Not Korea*. In it he made five points.[28]

- The United States was fighting in Korea under a UN mandate. No such mandate exists in Vietnam. The US presence is ... at the request of the South Vietnamese government and is part of its commitment to the SEATO (Southeast Asia Treaty Organization).
- UN forces in South Korea numbered up to 53,000 troops from fifty-three countries. The United States is fighting alone in South Vietnam.
- The South Korean government was stable. The South Vietnamese government is not.
- South Koreans had been at peace since the end of WWII. The South Vietnamese have been fighting for almost twenty years against the French colonial government and now North Vietnam.
- The Korean War started with a massive invasion. The war in South Vietnam is a domestic insurgency with external help from North Vietnam.

Preliminary efforts to identify how much learning from the past took place in negotiating an end to the North Korean nuclear program have identified errors and omissions rather than successes. Historian Bruce Cumings observes that a major impediment to learning from the past is the lack of contextual understanding of North Korean interests and policies. He asserts that US policy-makers and commentators have tended to analyze North Korea through the lens of Soviet behavior.[29] Along similar lines Michael Hayden, who served in South Korea as an intelligence officer, argues that there has been widespread ignorance among policy-makers about three key concepts central to the governing of North Korea: *Junce,* self-reliance, *Songun,* putting the military first, and *Byungjin,* the simultaneous development of nuclear power and the economy.[30] Perhaps nowhere was a lack of historical context more evident than when National Security Advisor John Bolton indicated that North Korea's denuclearization would end the same way as Libya's. Libyan denuclearization involved not only giving up its nuclear weapons program, but also NATO air attacks against Gadhafi and the capture and killing of Gadhafi by his opponents.

Given the serious consequences to contemporary international politics problems of misinterpretations of the past, one of the challenges is how to go about developing a better understanding of history. Francis Gavin has proposed five concepts that should be used to guide the search for lessons from the past:[31]

1. **Vertical history. Vertical history** is the sequence of events that preceded the event under study. The origins of an event should be traced back to its root causes and its development highlighted. This basic format is used in the overview of the Korean War presented earlier in this chapter, but a more complete vertical history would go back much further. It would include the First Sino-Japanese War (1894–95), which ended Chinese domination over Korea and led to the establishment of the Korean Empire, and the Russo-Japanese War (1904–05), which resulted in Japan making Korea a protectorate and then annexing it in 1910 following adoption of the Japan-Korea Annexation Treaty.

   vertical history The sequence of events that preceded the event being examined.

2. **Horizontal history. Horizontal history** is composed of events that occur at the same time as or relatively close to the event under study. What else was happening in the world as this event was unfolding? Rarely does a major historical event develop in isolation. Interconnections among events should be established both as they occurred and as policy-makers perceived them. Figure 1.1 provides an overview of key global events that make up part of the horizontal history of the Korean War.

   horizontal history Events that occur at the same time as or relatively close to the event being examined.

3. **Chronological proportionality.** Gavin warns against fixation on "big events" that make the front pages of newspapers and the neglect of less sensational events and trends whose impact can be even more significant over time.

4. **Unintended consequences.** Not everything goes as planned. In learning lessons from the past it is important to understand which consequences were intended and which were not and to identify the warning signs of unintended consequences.

5. **Recognize when policy has little impact.** When does history suggest that it is appropriate to do nothing?

Figure 1.1 Horizontal Korean War Dateline.

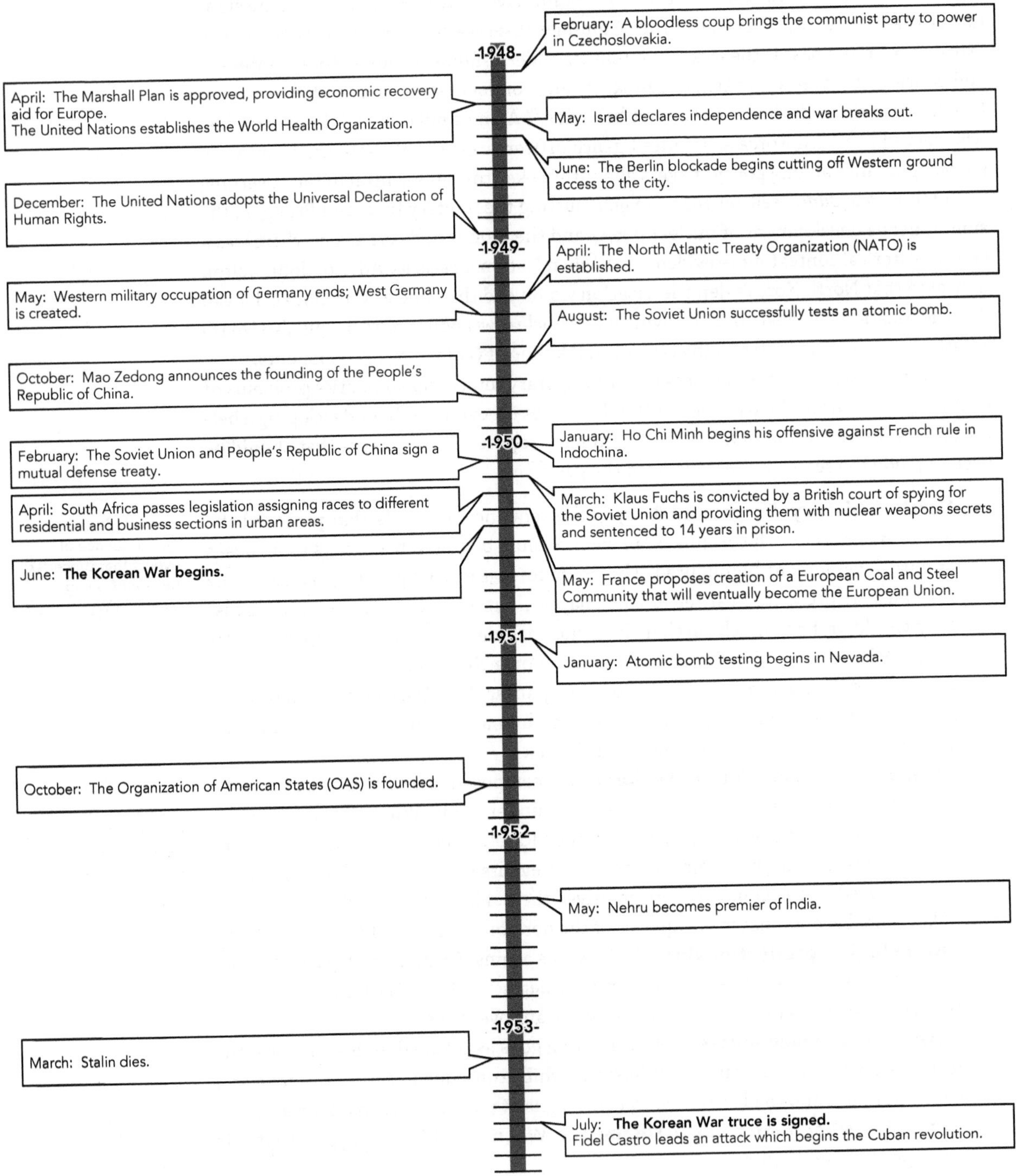

-1948-

February: A bloodless coup brings the communist party to power in Czechoslovakia.

April: The Marshall Plan is approved, providing economic recovery aid for Europe.
The United Nations establishes the World Health Organization.

May: Israel declares independence and war breaks out.

June: The Berlin blockade begins cutting off Western ground access to the city.

December: The United Nations adopts the Universal Declaration of Human Rights.

-1949-

April: The North Atlantic Treaty Organization (NATO) is established.

May: Western military occupation of Germany ends; West Germany is created.

August: The Soviet Union successfully tests an atomic bomb.

October: Mao Zedong announces the founding of the People's Republic of China.

-1950-

January: Ho Chi Minh begins his offensive against French rule in Indochina.

February: The Soviet Union and People's Republic of China sign a mutual defense treaty.

March: Klaus Fuchs is convicted by a British court of spying for the Soviet Union and providing them with nuclear weapons secrets and sentenced to 14 years in prison.

April: South Africa passes legislation assigning races to different residential and business sections in urban areas.

June: **The Korean War begins.**

May: France proposes creation of a European Coal and Steel Community that will eventually become the European Union.

-1951-

January: Atomic bomb testing begins in Nevada.

October: The Organization of American States (OAS) is founded.

-1952-

May: Nehru becomes premier of India.

-1953-

March: Stalin dies.

July: **The Korean War truce is signed.**
Fidel Castro leads an attack which begins the Cuban revolution.

LEARNING FROM THEORY

In addition to personal experiences and drawing analogies from the past a third approach to making sense out of international politics is to organize investigations around **theory**, a set of general principles used to explain, predict, and describe a class of events. Theories are mental maps that that go beyond the limits of intuition and help to avoid the dangers of making hurried and impulsive judgments about how the past relates to the present. They direct attention to the key features and underlying forces in international politics. In this sense theories simplify international politics by stressing some aspects and downplaying others. Because of disagreement about key features and underlying forces, there are multiple theories of international politics.

> **theory** A set of general principles used to explain, predict, and describe a class of events.

Five of the most common theories are realism, liberalism, economic structuralism, constructivism and feminism. Brief descriptions are included here; for a more complete discussion of each theory see Chapter 2. Realism views international politics as a struggle for power carried out by states under anarchic conditions; according to this view, the enduring nature of the global struggle for power makes it possible to anticipate foreign policy outcomes and consequences. Liberalism rejects the inevitability of conflict among states, instead emphasizing democratic government, free trade, and the creation of international organizations as bases for cooperation. Economic structuralism defines the pursuit of wealth as the driving force in domestic and international politics; this pursuit has led to imperialism and global class conflict. Constructivism rejects the existence of permanent patterns and instead sees change as constant, focusing on contextual analysis to determine the meaning of events and ideas. Feminism considers the study and practice of international politics rooted in gender-based ideas and polices and seeks to make women more visible and to incorporate feminist perspectives.

Despite their differences in focus, all of these theories can be used to perform three important tasks in studying international politics.

1. Theories provide a framework for describing events and trends in a consistent and concise fashion.
2. They can be used to explain international politics, allowing us to move beyond identifying **correlations** to establish **causation**. Two or more factors may be correlated, or appear together repeatedly, such as democracy and prosperous economies or war and sudden changes in the global distribution of power, but this does not mean that one led to the other. Establishment of causation requires one factor to produce another.
3. Theories can be used to make predictions about the future. Confidence in an understanding of the causes of past and present events and trends allows calculations about how the future will unfold when these patterns reappear.

> **correlation** Close links in time or location between two events.

> **causation** An act, event, or process that produces an effect.

Research **methodology** guides the use of theories of international politics. Theoretical investigations can be carried out qualitatively or quantitatively. *Qualitative research methodologies* rely on primary sources such as newspaper and media accounts, government

> **methodology** A set of rules, procedures, and principles used for studying a topic.

documents, memoirs, and interviews to reconstruct events and trends. One example of qualitative research is the case study. Case studies may focus on a single event or country or evaluate an event across time or countries. The Korean War has been studied as a single event and in comparison with other wars. Political scientist Glenn Paige broke down his study of the Korean War into separate case studies of the days leading up the US decision on how to respond.[32] One important, sometimes thorny question in carrying out a case study is "When did the event begin, and when did it end?" The Korean War began with the invasion in June 1950; an armistice ending hostilities was signed in July 1953, but there is still no peace treaty today. Are the Arab-Israeli military conflicts (discussed in Chapter 7) a single case study or several related cases? The same issue confronts analysis of the fight against terrorism.

Quantitative research methodologies emphasize the collection of objective data and its statistical analysis. According to this research strategy, a true understanding of a topic is best achieved not through the convincing argument of one researcher but through the ability of other researchers to replicate a study and achieve the same results. Replication requires exactness and transparency in data collection, coding, and analysis.

Research can be cast in positivist or post-positivist terms. *Positivism* assumes that it is possible to find the correct answer to the research question. Both qualitative and quantitative research strategists have traditionally believed this to be the case and only differ on the best approach. *Post-positivism* rejects this position, asserting that all knowledge is contextual and depends on perspective. According to this view, finding a correct answer is impossible because there is no universal shared experience. In addition, as experiences change the correct answer will change as well. The goal of post-positivist research is not to find "truth" but to promote a dialogue and unearth hidden assumptions and distortions in commonly accepted accounts of international politics. Of the theories introduced earlier in this section, constructivism and feminism are most closely associated with post-positivist research. Realism, liberalism, and economic structuralism are associated with positivism.

Political scientist Robert Cox suggests another distinction, separating theories into problem-solving and **critical theory**.[33] Problem-solving theory "takes the world as it finds it." A problem-solving approach to international politics has the objective of overcoming problems so that the international system will work better. Rather than accept the world as it is, critical theory asks, "How did the international system reach its current condition?" Critical theory's primary orientation is not problem solving but transformation of the international system into an alternative world order.

critical theory Social theory that takes as its starting point the need to critique and change established social and political systems rather than understand them.

Theory and Policy-Making Toward Korea

levels of analysis The focal points (individual, societal, state, or global) that can be used to study international politics.

One of the most important differences among theories of international politics is that they direct attention to different **levels of analysis**. Each level is made up of a set of variables or explanatory factors that can be grouped together and operate at the same point or location. Three levels of analysis are most frequently used in studying

Figure 1.2 Three Levels of Analysis in International Politics.

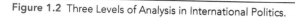
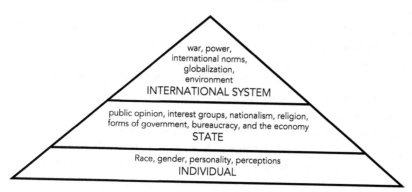

international politics, and they are often visualized as a pyramid: individual level, state level, and international system level (see Figure 1.2). There is no one-to-one relationship between theories and levels of analysis. Some theories, such as realism, operate almost exclusively on one level of analysis (the international system level). Others emphasize factors at multiple levels. For example, liberalism considers the international system and the state level.

The base of the pyramid, the individual level of analysis, includes explanatory factors such as race, gender, personality, and perceptions. Debate continues about why Stalin initially did not give permission to Kim Il-sung for an invasion of South Korea and then changed his mind.[34] In March 1949 Kim Il-sung travelled to Moscow to obtain Soviet support for the invasion, but evidence suggests that it was not until April 1950 that he received Stalin's approval. Was the change of heart due to changes in the global distribution of power (the third level of analysis) or to personality and perceptions? The discussion of the Korean cases up to this point suggests that perceptions and beliefs did play important roles in US decision-making regarding the Korean War. Identifying these events as cases and placing them in a theoretical context could allow development of accurate and reliable generalizations about the nature of perceptions and situations in which they matter. Elizabeth Saunders' case study of US military intervention introduced earlier in the chapter is an example of using theories in the context of case studies.

The center of the pyramid, the state level of analysis, includes public opinion, interest groups, nationalism, religion, forms of government, bureaucracy, and the economy. In writing about Truman's decision to send US troops into North Korea once the tide of battle had turned, biographer Robert Dallek comments that "domestic political considerations were not absent from Truman's thinking." Public opinion and looming congressional mid-term elections were of particular relevance (64% of the American public wanted to continue fighting to push North Korean forces back across the 38th parallel and have them surrender). With elections only two months away, failure to defeat North Korea politically and militarily would greatly aid Republican candidates.[35]

Domestic concerns also surfaced in dealings with North Korea by the Clinton and George W. Bush administrations. In 1996 plans were in place for Clinton to travel to North Korea for a presidential summit with North Korean leader Kim Jong-il. Expectations, like those for the more recent Trump–Kim Jung-un summit, were that better relations between the two countries could be established and the North Korean nuclear threat could come to an end. The summit never happened, because objections were raised about the appropriateness of a summit meeting involving a lame duck president whose successor had a different foreign policy agenda. These differences were made clear in early March 2001, only three months into the Bush presidency; Secretary of State Colin Powell indicated that the administration planned to "pick up where President Clinton and his administration left off" in engaging North Korea on nuclear matters. This statement had not been cleared with President Bush and the next day Powell backtracked, saying that the administration would hold a full review of the US relationship with North Korea and that negotiations were not imminent.

Bureaucratic and institutional conflicts led Truman to remove General Douglas MacArthur from his position as commanding officer of US troops in Korea in 1951, after MacArthur made public statements contradicting official US policy. Placing domestic, bureaucratic, and institutional concerns in the context of state-level theorizing provides the opportunity for more confident generalizations about the role of such considerations in international politics, projections for when domestic level influences might arise, and steps that might be taken to minimize or eliminate their influence.

The top of the pyramid, the international-system level of analysis, includes the presence (or absence) of war, the distribution of power, international norms, the extent of globalization, and the state of the environment. Throughout the two events in Korea's history that we have discussed, the importance of such factors is evident in the links to earlier conflicts made by policy-makers. In the case of the Korean War, the dominant reference points were WWII and the beginning of the Cold War. In trying to curb North Korea's nuclear capability, the Trump administration offered denuclearization of Libya as a positive historical reference point, but North Korean leaders viewed that event very differently. The question remains whether, from a theoretical point of view, perception at the individual level or distribution of power in the form of nuclear proliferation at the international-system level is the better level of analysis for understanding this wicked problem.

North Korean–South Korean leaders meeting.

BJ Warnick / KCNA / UPI / Newscom / Alamy Stock Photo

USING CHALLENGES AND RESPONSES TO MAKE SENSE OF INTERNATIONAL POLITICS

Two basic truths emerge from this overview of the attempt to make sense of international politics. First, neither policy-makers nor scholars can escape the challenges presented by complex events and trends and the need to manage information about them. Second, they need each other: Policy-makers need scholars to provide insight into their policy challenges. Scholars must obtain important pieces of information from policy-makers to provide a complete picture of the topics they are seeking to describe, explain, and predict. Working separately, they are likely to create incomplete and perhaps conflicting pictures of important contemporary policy challenges and possible responses.

Policy-makers and scholars recognize this mutual dependence, but finding common ground is easier said than done. They work under different time constraints; they are not always interested in the same dimensions or aspects of an issue; and the consequences of their decisions are very different. Not surprisingly, scholars and policy-makers often talk past one another, coming together only in after-the-fact analyses of a policy. This often puts policy-makers on the defensive in explaining why a policy initiative failed or an event was not anticipated. This long-standing challenge in international politics was raised many years ago by Alexander George. In *Bridging the Gap*, an examination of US strategies toward Iraq in the late twentieth century, George called for greater communication between academic scholars and practitioners.[36]

Introduction to International Politics: Global Challenges and Policy Responses also seeks to bridge the gap by linking theories, history, and policy in an organized way to help you get behind the headlines and develop informed opinions about today's international politics challenges and possible responses. In Part One, this chapter and Chapter 2 lay the foundations for studying international politics by examining the roles of history and theory. Part Two (Chapters 3 and 4) examines the international system with an emphasis on sovereignty and values. Part Three (Chapters 5, 6, and 7) introduces traditional global challenges by looking at power, war, conflict, and diplomacy. Part Four (Chapters 8, 9, and 10) introduces newer global challenges, focusing on economic globalization, human rights, and environmental sustainability. Concluding, Chapter 11 discusses ways in which you can think about the future and introduces possible future challenges you may face.

Summary

- Several obstacles exist to obtaining the information needed to analyze international politics, including quantity, availability, unevenness of flow, quality, and usefulness.
- Since the end of WWII, Korea has emerged twice as a major challenge in international politics, first, during the Korean War in the 1950s; second, when North Korea became a site of nuclear proliferation, which remains a wicked problem today.

- Firsthand personal experiences, especially those experienced early in their careers, are especially important in guiding policy-makers in international politics decision-making.
- Policy-makers can learn from both vertical and horizontal history, but past events should be examined closely when making contemporary decisions, as they are subject to revision.
- Theories, including realism, liberalism, economic structuralism, constructivism, and feminism, consist of general principles used to explain, predict, and describe a class of events. Used at different levels of analysis, they help direct attention to key features and underlying forces of international politics.
- Insights by both policy-makers and scholars are needed to construct a complete picture of the topics they are seeking to describe, explain, and predict.

Key Terms

Causation *(17)*
Correlation *(17)*
Critical theory *(18)*
Generational events *(12)*
Horizontal history *(15)*
International politics *(1)*
Levels of analysis *(18)*

Methodology *(17)*
Noise *(4)*
Revisionist history *(11)*
Signals *(4)*
Theory *(17)*
Vertical history *(15)*
Wicked problems *(2)*

Critical Thinking Questions

1. Rank the information obstacles to making sense of international politics in order of importance from highest to lowest, and then explain your ranking.

2. Which is the more significant event for future studies of international politics: the Korean War or current negotiations over North Korea's nuclear weapons program? Explain your answer.

3. Is it bad for policy-makers to rely on personal experience in making decisions? Why or why not?

4. Which generational events are of most importance to policy-makers today who seek to learn from history, and why?

5. Which of the three levels of analysis is most important for studying international politics, and why?

6. Does history or theory matter more in identifying important international politics challenges and formulating responses? Explain your answer.

Practice and Review Online
http://textbooks.rowman.com/hastedt-felice

▲ Canada kicks off Arctic patrol program. *Source:* Guenterguni / iStock

02

THE THEORY CHALLENGE

AFTER THE 9/11 TERRORIST ATTACKS many commentators were critical of the US intelligence community for not "connecting the dots" to see the attacks coming. This is easier said than done. Events are not self-interpreting. Dots can be connected in many different ways, each of which has different implications for international relations. Analysts and policy rely on theories to help them analyze issues and connect the dots.

This chapter introduces five major theories used to study international politics: realism, liberalism, economic structuralism, constructivism, and feminism. Each presents a different way to identify the connections between the dots and interpret their meaning. After highlighting their key features, each one will be used to analyze the Arctic. Once a seldom-studied area on the fringes of international politics, the Arctic is now being recognized as a major area of international competition and cooperation.

To frame the theoretical discussion, the chapter begins by examining the fall of the Berlin Wall, which symbolized the Cold War conflict between Russia and the United States. Its fall marked the end of the Cold War and came as a surprise to adherents of realism and liberalism, the dominant theories of the day, leading analysts to look for alternative theoretical perspectives. The chapter ends by applying theory to key features of the 2014

Ukrainian crisis, which some commentators see as the possible beginning of a new cold war. As with the end of the Cold War and the events of 9/11, the dots leading up to the Ukrainian conflict were not widely connected; disagreement still exists over why it happened.

LEARNING OBJECTIVES

Students will be able to:

- Discuss why the Berlin Wall was an important symbol of the Cold War.
- Identify the key assumptions and varieties of realism.
- Discuss the importance of democracy and free trade to liberalism.
- Contrast the assumptions of economic structuralism with realism and liberalism.
- Define constructivism and identify its key assumptions.
- Distinguish between the different schools of thought within feminism.
- Apply the theoretical perspectives introduced in this chapter to the Arctic.
- Discus why the Ukraine is considered by some as the starting point of a new cold war.

HISTORICAL PERSPECTIVE:
The Fall of the Berlin Wall

In a series of summit conferences in the closing months of WWII the leaders of the Soviet Union, Great Britain, France, and the United States decided to divide Germany into four occupation zones, each administered by one of the four victorious states. Because Berlin, Germany's capital, was deep in the middle of the Soviet zone, it was also divided into four zones. The occupation of Berlin began in July 1945. By 1948, in the face of rising tensions between the Soviet Union and the United States and its European allies, the Soviet Union announced that the three Western powers no longer had a right of access to Berlin. Effectively, this denied the Western-ruled sectors of Berlin access to food, fuel, and other material. The West responded with a massive airlift that lasted 324 days and provided West Berlin with more than 2.3 million tons of supplies. The Berlin blockade was lifted in May 1949 after it became clear that the Western powers were not going to abandon West Berlin and that the blockade had failed.

A new Berlin crisis erupted in 1958, rooted in the massive exodus of citizens of East Germany (the Russian occupation zone) through Berlin to West Germany (the combined British, French and US occupation zones). An estimated 150,000 East Germans fled each year since the division of Germany into occupation zones. Soviet Premier Nikita Khrushchev set a six-month ultimatum for talks on the future of Germany and Berlin. If negotiations were not complete by the deadline, the Soviet Union would recognize the government of East Germany and turn over control of East Berlin to it, putting an end to any possible reunification of Germany. Even though no talks were held, Khrushchev did not carry through with this threat.

In 1961 Khrushchev made new demands for talks on the future of Germany and Berlin. In July, following a summit meeting with Khrushchev, President Kennedy pushed back, asking Congress for additional funding for the American military presence in West Berlin. The following month Khrushchev authorized East Germany to close the border and begin construction of a barbed wire and concrete wall that divided Berlin in half. In June 1963 Kennedy travelled to Berlin and reaffirmed the US commitment to West Berlin by declaring in a speech "I am a Berliner." With the passage of time the Berlin Wall became an increasingly long and imposing barrier; it eventually spanned some 96 miles, and the addition of mesh fencing and barbed wire caused it to rise to a height of 12 feet. More than 5,000 East Germans still managed to cross the Berlin Wall by going over it or under it, and more than 170 died trying to do so.

The Berlin Wall continued to serve as a symbol of the Cold War over the next several decades, as evidenced by President Ronald Reagan's 1987 challenge to Soviet leader Mikhail Gorbachev to "tear down that wall." The fall of the Berlin Wall was not far off. In June of 1989 Solidarity, a group opposed to communist party rule that was founded in Polish shipyards in 1980, won an election in Poland and set off a wave of protests throughout much of communist-ruled Eastern Europe. This also spurred a new mass exodus of citizens fleeing East Germany for the West through neighboring communist states that were now opening their borders. On November 9, 1989, the East German government announced that citizens would now be free to cross its borders to the West. Destruction of the Berlin Wall began that day as "wall peckers" began to tear it down stone by stone, and that weekend more than two million residents of East Berlin crossed into West Berlin. On June 13, 1990, the East German government began the official teardown, and in October East and West Germany reunited into the single country of Germany for the first time since the end of World War II. The following year, in December 1991, the Soviet Union officially came to an end. With virtually no warning and without a direct military confrontation, the conflict that had gone on for some forty years had ended. The Cold War was over.

Jose Giribas / Süddeutsche Zeitung Photo / Alamy Stock Photo

The Berlin Wall served as the Cold War dividing line separating East and West Berlin.

This was not the way that the leading theories used to study international politics anticipated it ending. The surprise ending of the Cold War led scholars to reexamine the assumptions on which their theories were based and how to evaluate the Cold War. For example, long-time Cold War scholar John Gaddis argued that the Cold War period should not be seen as a period of conflict but as "the long peace."[1] Other scholars turned to new theoretical perspectives as the basis for studying international politics. The following five sections introduce the major theoretical perspectives used today.

REALISM

realism A classic perspective for studying international politics that starts from the assumption that it is a struggle for power carried out by states under anarchic conditions.

Realism is one of the most dominant schools of thought used to study international politics.[2] Rather than a single theory of world politics, realism is better seen as a broad umbrella covering several different theoretical perspectives. Their common foundation emphasizes to a varying degree the role of power in international politics, the central position of the state, and the lack of central authority in the international system.

Hans Morgenthau published *Politics among Nations* in 1948 and is widely considered to be the founding voice of realism, but its intellectual roots reach much farther back in time.[3] Elements can be found in the writings of Thucydides (400 BC), Machiavelli (1469–1557), and Thomas Hobbes (1588–1679). Central to Thucydides' analysis of the Peloponnesian War, which detailed the struggle for dominance between Athens and Sparta, was the argument that war was inevitable due to Athens's rising power and the fear it produced in Sparta. Machiavelli's sixteenth-century writings presented a pessimistic view of human nature and stressed the centrality of power as a force shaping human behavior. Born just after Machiavelli died, Hobbes wrote of the necessity of creating strong governments to maintain order in an anarchic world.

Morgenthau saw international politics as structured around a set of forces that remain constant over time. Foremost is the idea that the struggle for power is central to international politics. States are the key actors in this global struggle and are seen as largely autonomous actors positioned to construct foreign policy in a rational manner consistent with the national interest. The enduring nature of the global struggle for power also makes it possible to accurately anticipate the outcomes and consequences of different foreign policies. In sum, for Morgenthau, states "think and act in terms of interests defined as power."[4] Doing so allows them to protect the national interest and prevents them from adopting policies that will produce harmful results.

Peace requires states to follow their own narrowly defined national interests instead of definitions built around abstract moral principles or global ambitions. This does not make states indifferent to moral or ethical principles, but it does place boundaries on their influence on foreign policy. States must distinguish what is desirable from what is possible. For Morgenthau, a rational foreign policy is one that minimizes risks and maximizes benefits, bringing together the moral principle of caution and the political requirement of success.

The positive response to Morgenthau's analysis owed much to the perceived failings of post-WWI US foreign policy as outlined in Woodrow Wilson's 14 Points, which called for creating the League of Nations, ending colonialism and secret diplomacy, increasing self-determination, and implementing arms control. World events did not unfold in the expected fashion. The United States did not join the League of Nations, and the Washington Naval Conference—intended to reduce the size of navies—failed to stop a naval arms race. Colonialism did not end, and Hitler came to power in Germany. According to one line of analysis, the onset of WWII was due to the failure of policy-makers to properly implement the policies that Wilson had advanced at the end of WWI. In another view, held by a group that identified themselves as realists, the policies themselves were fundamentally flawed. This group referred to the first group as idealists.[5]

Following Morgenthau's lead, early realists (today referred to as classical realists) emphasized the role of human nature in making foreign policy decisions. In their eyes, human nature was inherently selfish and driven to acquire power. The drive to acquire power and autonomous foreign policy decisions by policy-makers were seen as the central features of international politics.

As the Cold War progressed, a competing theoretical perspective began to emerge within realism. *Neorealism* argued that the key factor influencing foreign policy decisions was the structure of the international system. Although not free from disagreement, neorealism is the dominant realist school of thought today.

In emphasizing the structure of the international system neorealists build on what they perceive to be its three core characteristics:

- **Lack of central authority**. The international system lacks a central authority capable of creating and maintaining order. It is highly decentralized and competitive, a condition commonly referred to by neorealists as *anarchy*.
- **Need for state security**. Within this anarchic international system each state is responsible for providing for its own security. States cannot blindly rely on international law, international organizations, or other countries for their security. The international system is a self-help system, and the only avenue open to states to provide for their own security is through the acquisition of power.
- **Changing distribution of power**. The distribution of state power in the international system is not fixed. It changes over time as states gain power and lose power. As a result the policies states follow to protect their national interests must also change. A policy that protects or advances the national interest in one distribution of power will not necessarily do so in another. It may leave the state in a dangerous position. The most commonly discussed distributions of international power are a *unipolar system* in which one state is more powerful than all others, a *bipolar system* in which there are two powerful states, and a *multipolar system* in which there are five or more powerful states.

One point of disagreement among neorealists is what type of distribution of power is most likely to lead to international stability and the absence of major wars. One theoretical perspective, called the *balance of power*, argues that stability and peace are most likely to be realized when there is a relatively even distribution of power among the most powerful states in the international system, so that no state can achieve dominance over all of the others.[6] The most powerful states will recognize this and limit their definition of the national interest to maintaining the status quo. This entails preventing others from rising up and upsetting the balance of power or allowing any one state to gain a significant advantage. Challenging this view, the *hegemonic theory perspective*[7] holds that stability is best realized when a single powerful state (a *hegemon*) exists. Because it sits atop the international power hierarchy, the hegemon uses its power to maintain order by countering the power of challengers and providing assistance to those states facing problems that could cause international instability. The erosion of its power weakens the ability of a hegemonic state to carry out these functions. Should no state replace it, the international system would slide into a period of heighted competition for power.

There is also disagreement about the strategic purpose of power. Kenneth Waltz was the first to lay out the principles of neorealism; early neorealists led by Waltz embraced a *defensive realism perspective*.[8] According to this view, the fundamental purpose of power is to protect states from threats. A competing school of thought, referred to as *offensive realism*,[9] holds that the structure of the international system creates powerful incentives for states to constantly explore ways of acquiring power at the expense of other states, with the ultimate goal of becoming the hegemon.

Idealism did not end with the rise in influence of realism. Especially in the United States it continued to be a prominent viewpoint used for studying international politics, and its influence can be seen in liberalism; realism and liberalism remain the two major theoretical perspectives in use today.

LIBERALISM

liberalism A perspective for studying international politics which holds that states are capable of acting rationally in international politics in pursuing their national interests; emphasizes democratic government and free trade as the bases for cooperation.

The long-standing competing perspective to realism is **liberalism**, the idea that states are capable of acting rationally in international politics in pursuing their national interests. Liberalism emphasizes democratic government and free trade as establishing the basis for cooperation. It too has a long scholarly history and is characterized by numerous internal divisions.[10] Early liberal theorists focused heavily on the organization of domestic society, from which they drew implications for the operation of the international system. They adopted what some refer to as an "inside-out" perspective on international politics.[11]

Two aspects of domestic society are of special interest to liberalism. The first dates back to the time of the American Revolution when Adam Smith (1776) published *The Wealth of Nations*. Smith argued that economies work best when left free of government interference. He called for a rejection of mercantilism, which emphasized conducting international trade for the purpose of making the state stronger. In Smith's view the "hidden hand" of free economic competition led to increased efficiency and greater wealth and lessened economic conflicts. Richard Cobden, in *England, Ireland and America, by a Manchester Manufacturer* (1836), echoed Smith's argument in the early nineteenth century. He too called for rejecting mercantilism and suggested replacing it with a policy of free trade. Free trade would help lay the foundation for peace because properly organized trade (i.e., trade that was carried out without government interference) would be mutually beneficial to all involved and would promote peaceful cooperation among societies in contrast to the competition and conflict promoted by mercantilism.

The second aspect of domestic society important to classical liberalism is the form of government. In his classic work *Perpetual Peace* (1795) Immanuel Kant argued that the only justifiable and universal form of government was republican government, one in which governmental power is constrained by a constitution and the rule of law.[12] These constraints establish a political environment in which individual citizens are free, equal, and able to engage in rational thought. In Kant's view Republican states were "peace producers" because in them "the consent of the citizens is required to decide whether or not war is declared [and] it is very natural that they will have great hesitation in embarking on the road to war.

There was nothing automatic in moving from the condition of perpetual war that Kant saw as inherent in the logic of balance of power to perpetual peace. Republican states first had to move the rule of law and republican principles onto the international stage and make them universal to check the aggressive tendencies of rulers and lay the foundation for creating a community of peaceful states.

The contemporary adaptation of this inside-out political accounting of state behavior in international politics is democratic peace theory, which will be examined more closely in the Policy Spotlight feature in Chapter 4. Advanced by Michael Doyle in 1983, this theory holds that democratic states do not go to war with other democratic states.[13] Advocates of democratic peace theory vary in terms of whether greater emphasis is given to the existence of liberal institutions within states or the presence of liberal cultural values. In either case it is recognized that war between democracies and authoritarian states remains possible. Realizing global peace requires increasing the number of democracies in the world. As their number increases, the potential for war decreases.

In contrast to classical liberalism's inside-out perspective in explaining state behavior, *neoliberal institutionalism,* like neorealism, emphasizes the structure of the international system as the dominant explanatory force in international politics. Unlike neorealism, however, it does not see states as locked into an unending struggle for power. It shares with classical liberalism the belief that, under the proper conditions, cooperation is possible. The key development in achieving cooperation among states is the creation of international organizations. This happens in response to the states' increased *interdependence,* or situations of reciprocal effects. The actions of one state inevitably affect the actions of other states. The most important aspect of interdependence is that states cannot act alone but must rely upon others to achieve their foreign policy goals. International organizations promote international peace because they serve as a reliable source of the information that can help states overcome uncertainties about cooperation. Past positive cooperative efforts by international organizations in solving technical and political global problems also promote trust.

Interdependence does not bring about an end to power politics, but it does transform views about power. It limits the range of problems for which military power is a viable option by exposing states to military, economic, or political alternative strategies.

THEORY SPOTLIGHT

Prisoner's Dilemma

International cooperation is not easy. One branch of international politics, game theory, is particularly concerned with the dynamics of cooperation. It applies principles of logical reasoning and mathematics to understanding situations in which cooperation is essential because neither side can control the outcome alone. Game theory builds its analyses around the assumption that, to pursue their goals and protect their interests, individuals will select the option that holds the least risk to their position, not the one that promises the most gain. This is referred to as the *minimax strategy* because it minimizes the maximum damage. The simplified hypothetical situations of game theory can be used as models for cooperation in real-life international political situations.

One of the most famous game theory models is the *prisoner's dilemma*. It focuses on the tension that often exists between what is desirable from an individual perspective and what is desirable from a group perspective. Individual rationality may lead to an undesirable group outcome. In the prisoners' dilemma game, two burglary suspects are placed in different rooms so they cannot communicate with one another. Prosecutors have enough evidence to convict them of possessing stolen goods, but not enough to convict them of burglary. Each is told they are being offered the same set of options. If both remain silent and neither confesses to the break in, then both will get light sentences for possession of stolen goods. If one confesses to the break in and turns state evidence while the other remains silent, the one who confesses will go free and the other will get a lengthy jail sentence. If both confess to the burglary they will both get medium length prison sentences.

The dilemma facing the prisoners is straightforward and is illustrated in Figure 2.1. The numbers represent the preferred order of choices (1–4) with the choices for prisoner A listed first in each box. From a collective perspective, the best outcome is achieved by remaining silent. But the potential costs of doing so are great. If your partner confesses in order to go free (the best individual outcome), remaining silent condemns you to a lengthy prison term (the worst individual outcome). Minimizing the worst individual outcome requires that you confess.

Interdependence is not always equal, however. Some states may be heavily dependent on other states and others far less so. Some states are more sensitive to changes in interdependence, needing to adjust their policies as the pattern changes or perhaps unable to adapt, as the changes may be too difficult and expensive to make. The existence of asymmetries in interdependence give rise to bargaining power over the terms of cooperation within international organizations. The International Monetary Fund (IMF) does not make decisions based on a one-country–one-vote formula but relies on a weighted voting system based on the amount of money a country contributes to the IMF. As a result, the United States has 16.5% of the vote and Japan has 6.1%.

The Theory Spotlight highlights one of the most enduring cooperation challenges in international politics, the prisoner's dilemma. Based on game theory, it demonstrates how individual rationality may not produce on outcome that is best for all.

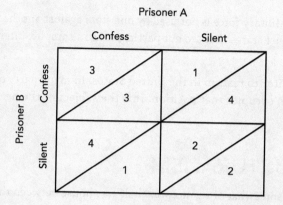

Figure 2.1 The Prisoner's Dilemma.

Assuming that both prisoners follow this same logic, both will confess.

One example of a prisoner's dilemma is an arms race. Two states locked in an arms race face similar choices: disarm or build weapons. The preferable collective outcome is disarmament, since building and maintaining weapons are expensive. But if one state disarms and the other does not, the disarmed state faces a significantly increased security threat from the state that continues to build weapons. In order to minimize the maximum danger, both states will continue to build weapons.

For realists, the prisoner's dilemma is simply a fact of life that must be considered in all international interactions. Liberalists are not as willing to accept the outcome of the prisoner's dilemma as inevitable. They see the inability to communicate and the possibility of only two outcomes as inaccurate reflections of the reality of international politics. They view states as having the potential to build trust over time because they are engaged in playing repeated games with other states, not just one. A constructivist would take exception to the fixed image of distrust that is central to the prisoner's dilemma game and hold out the possibility for the two conflicting sides to redefine their overall relationship, thus creating new payoff structures and new types of cooperation.

Think about It

1. How would economic structuralists and feminists evaluate the prisoner's dilemma as a tool for thinking about international cooperation?

2. Are there international politics policy areas where the prisoner's dilemma scenario does not apply?

In 1977 Robert Keohane and Joseph Nye proposed an ideal type of international system, *complex interdependence*, in which the power focus of realism was replaced by the bargaining focus of interdependence.[14] In contrast to interdependence, which they saw as evolving naturally, complex interdependence was deliberately created by states. It has three defining characteristics:

1. **Multiple channels of interstate, transgovernmental and transnational relations between societies**. *Transgovernmental relations* refers to interactions between equivalent bureaucratic entities, such as interactions between the Treasury Department of the United States and the German treasury department. *Transnational relations* refer to interactions among civil, society, and nongovernmental organizations.

2. **Absence of issue hierarchy**. The distinction between domestic and foreign issues is blurred, and military issues do not dominate economic, human rights, or environmental issues.

3. **Absence of military force**. Military force is not used by one state against another. It may, however, be used against states that are not participating in complex interdependence arrangements.

Liberalism is the primary competitor to realism in the United States. In many parts of the world economic structuralism occupies that position. It is the subject of the next section.

ECONOMIC STRUCTURALISM

economic structuralism A perspective that draws heavily on Marxism and emphasizes the pursuit of wealth in international politics and the exploitive relations it creates.

Economic structuralism sits in somewhat of a conceptual half-way house between the first two theories discussed in this chapter (realism and liberalism) and the two yet to come, constructivism and feminism. It shares with realism and liberalism the belief that there are clearly identifiable underlying forces driving international politics, but it disagrees about what those forces are. Economic structuralism defines the driving force in both domestic and international politics as the pursuit of wealth, not power.[15] It also shares with the latter two theories a critical perspective on the study of international politics. Rather than accept international politics as an objective and value-neutral undertaking, a critical perspective on international politics asks the following questions: How did its policies, practices, and ideas come about? Whom do they benefit and harm? How might they change? As Robert Cox put it, "theory is always for someone and for some purpose."[16]

Two of the most significant voices most associated with economic structuralism are Karl Marx and Vladimir Lenin. They held that the driving force in both domestic and international politics was the unequal relationship between economic classes and the resulting conflict between them. Domestic societies are not made up of equal people engaged in productive work. They are organized in a hierarchical fashion, with those few at the top who are in control of key resources and means of production (the bourgeoisie) exploiting those beneath them (the proletariat) by not providing them with a fair compensation for the work they do.

This division is not permanent. It can change, because one of the key features of maturing economic systems is the increased intensity of class conflict. In capitalist economic systems there is a growing contradiction between the large amounts of goods being produced and the inability of lower classes to buy these goods due to low wages; this combination reduces profits. Ultimately this deepening class conflict results in a transformation of the economic system and the establishment of a socialist economic system.

Economic structuralists predicted that socialism would emerge first in Europe, the location of the most advanced capitalist systems. This did not happen. A series of largely democratic and nationalist political revolutions arose in Europe in 1848, targeting the continued rule of monarchies, but they did not lead to the anticipated downfall of capitalism and replacement by socialism. The opposite soon happened. Capitalism was strengthened by a new wave of colonialism in the 1870s, which provided the bourgeoisie with new markets, access to additional resources, and cheap labor. According to Lenin, the higher profits that resulted from colonialism undermined and held off the impending socialist revolution by allowing capitalists to "buy off" disgruntled workers through pay raises without lowering their profits.

Lenin attributed this new wave of colonialization to a policy of imperialism and argued that it represented the highest stage of capitalism. Under imperialism, he anticipated the formation of international monopolistic capitalist associations that would divide and share the world but offer only the temporary survival of capitalism. Like Marx, Lenin continued to view capitalism's inevitable tensions as leading to its revolutionary downfall, but he revised Marx's view of where the revolution would begin: in the poorer countries being exploited. Lenin also anticipated that imperialism would lead to war among the leading capitalist states. As long as there were new territories to be colonized, the potential for conflict among capitalist nations was limited. Once the supply of new territories ran out, the only way to acquire additional cheap labor, inexpensive natural resources, and new markets would be to take them from another capitalist state.

Economic structuralism never attracted the level of following of realism and liberalism. Politics played an important role. The Soviet Union, founded in 1917 by a communist revolution led by Lenin, was largely isolated from the capitalist West between WWI and WWII. After WWII the Soviet Union and the United States became locked in a cold war, which ended in 1989 with the fall of the Berlin Wall and the collapse of the Soviet Union, as described in the opening to this chapter. These events led to talk of the triumph of liberal democracy over communism and the end of ideological conflict that were captured in Francis Fukuyama's essay "The End of History," further reducing interest in a theoretical perspective that emphasized the centrality of class conflict and the inherent weakness of capitalism.[17]

Economic structuralism was not without its followers. Those most attracted to it were found in Latin America, Africa, and Asia, areas that economic structuralism identified as having been exploited the most by capitalism. The post-WWII era brought political independence but did little to change the backward economic status of these areas. Global economic stratification remained a reality. Imperialism by the sword gave way to neoimperialism by multinational corporations.

Two important lines of analysis grew out of economic structuralist thinking. One is *world system theory*, which divided the world and the states within it into three regions: core, periphery and semi-periphery.[18] Relations between the core and periphery were seen as exploitative and undermined the ability of the periphery to engage in meaningful economic and political development. A second is *dependency theory*.[19] It too sees international politics as divided into different regions but also stresses the limited independent economic and political development potential of poor countries. Originating among Latin American scholars in the 1950s, Latin American dependency theory gained supporters throughout the developing world in the 1960s.

CONSTRUCTIVISM

constructivism A perspective for studying international politics that emphasizes contextual analysis and the need to determine the meaning of events and ideas from the setting in which they take place.

Constructivism is a relatively new perspective used to study international politics. It is defined as a perspective that emphasizes contextual analysis and the need to determine the meaning of events and ideas from the setting in which they take place. Originating in the early 1980s, it began to attract a significant number of supporters with the failure of realism and liberalism to anticipate the end of the Cold War. The constructivist approach parts company from those perspectives in a number of important ways.[20] First, it sees change as a constant feature of international politics. Neither the structure of the international system nor state (or international organization or NGO) foreign policies are immutable. Second, norms, ideas, beliefs, and values take center stage in this type of analysis.

Constructivism seeks to understand how the value preferences and interests that underlie policy decisions are formed and translated into policies. This directs constructivist analysis in three directions. The first is to investigate how identities are formed; how do individuals determine who they are and what they value? Constructivism looks to gender, race, class, ethnicity, and nationalism to understand the origin of attitudes, beliefs, and values.

The second area of constructivist inquiry is an examination of the social process through which ideas are shared, challenged, refined, and ultimately embraced by a society and how they shape its identity. Individual interactions and reactions to ideas are just as important to constructivism as the ideas themselves.

The third direction of investigation arises from these first two: the interactions among individuals, societies, and the international system. This is best summed up by an observation made by Alexander Wendt in 1992: "Anarchy is what states make of it."[21] From the perspective of constructivism, anarchy does not have a fixed definition. It is not an objective term, nor does it have a constant and fixed impact on foreign policy and the operation of the international system. The impact of anarchy depends upon the choices made by policy-makers, which are rooted in the values, norms, and ideas they hold. They can interpret anarchy as (1) always requiring states to acquire more power, (2) providing an opportunity for cooperation, or (3) a temporary and minor global condition of little significance.

The same line of reasoning applies to the definition of and importance assigned to other central concepts in the study of international politics. Who is an enemy and who is a friend? What is power? Is power the ability to get your way through military force (realism), the ability to get your way through bargaining, negotiation, and writing rules (liberalism), or the ability to acquire wealth (economic structuralism)? A constructivist would respond that it depends and that the answer could change over time. It depends on such factors as the particular situation, the extent to which ethical questions related to justice and community are considered, the priority placed on efficiency, the willingness to pay the costs, and how success is defined.

Emphasis on different investigative directions result in several different schools of constructivist thought.[22] A common criticism is that constructivism is not a theory of international politics like realism, liberalism, or economic structuralism, which view international politics as unchanging and revolving around fixed patterns of interaction. Even many constructivists agree that it is not a theory per se and reject the idea of a general theory of international politics because in their view ideas are more important than objective conditions within states or the international system. Constructivism is often presented instead as a general approach for implementing social change.

A related concern is that constructivism lacks a normative and prescriptive component. It is a valuable tool for understanding how perceptions of the international system evolve and why policies look the way they do, but it is unable to provide guidance on how to construct policy to deal with the challenges and opportunities states face or to identify the goals they should embrace. Constructivism is not alone in emphasizing the need to break loose from the dominant realist and liberal international politics theories and the importance of perceptions. Feminism makes the same point and is the subject of the next section.

FEMINISM

Just like the other frameworks introduced in this chapter, **feminist theory** contains multiple pathways and points of emphasis in studying international politics.[23] What unites them is a shared commitment to making women more visible in international politics and highlighting hidden assumptions about the role that gender plays. Feminist theory has repeatedly encountered two prevalent myths: "Divisions and differences assigned by gender are either 'god-given' or 'natural' and therefore out of the realm of political analysis," and the idea that "gender has nothing to do with international politics and events."[24]

An important first step toward unmasking these myths is drawing a distinction between sex and gender. *Sex* is a biological concept grounded in genetics and anatomical characteristics. *Gender* is a socially and culturally defined concept that is learned. Typically this learning process identifies masculine and feminine traits, characteristics, and outlooks in oppositional terms. Masculinity is typically identified with bravery, power, assertiveness, control, and domination. Femininity is usually identified with softness, caring, passivity, weakness, and comfort.

Feminist empiricism has most directly addressed the problem of invisibility by asking the question "where are the women?" Part of the answer involves documenting the worldwide underrepresentation of women in government and private sector positions that influence the conduct of foreign policy and structure of the international system. Another part goes beyond numbers to address the more complex question of what would

feminist theory A perspective that takes as its point of departure the gendered nature of political phenomena and the need to explicitly take gender into account in the analysis of international politics.

change if women were more visible. Feminist theory is divided into two perspectives on this point. *Difference feminists* assert that increasing the number of women in prominent international politics positions will lead to different policy outcomes and has the potential to change the nature of the international system. *Liberal feminists*, on the other hand, do not consider that women's perspective will necessarily be different from that of men; they argue, rather, that increased visibility of women is critical because it adds to the size and scope of the skill set of those making decisions.

Another aspect of the "where are the women?" question centers on the impact of international politics on women. The literature of international politics focuses heavily on the consequences of large-scale actions such as war, economic sanctions, international trade and finance, international conferences, and humanitarian assistance, seldom making a distinction among the consequences for men, women, or other groups in society. Instead, society-wide or global analyses are more common. Consider the consequences of war, particularly for landmine survivors. While many international agreements make specific references to gender equality issues and provide aid for women and children who are victims of landmines, the on-the-ground reality is quite different. The International Red Cross notes that, in many countries, female casualties often go unreported and injured females do not have equal access to medical facilities and treatment options. Women are often directed to home-based remedies. Even when they have access to treatment centers, the activities and programs are often male oriented.[25]

Two related perspectives, *standpoint feminism* and *postmodern feminism,* directly address the hidden assumptions about gender that are found in the language and imagery used to analyze international politics and conduct foreign policy. One of the most fundamental assumptions in international politics is that its language (including terms such as the national interest, power, anarchy, the state, peace, justice, and interdependence)

Women landmine survivors in Mozambique.

© Fellipe Abreu

and fundamental ideas transcend gender. Adherents of standpoint feminism and postmodern feminism assert that this is not the case; instead, the terms used to define the reality of international politics and the meaning given to them are determined by individual experiences, and the experiences of men and women in international politics have been quite different. The impact of gender is also exhibited in the way that academics write about international politics because, for a long period of time, this field was dominated by men.

Consider the concept of the state. The model for the modern state comes from ancient Greece. Feminist Rebecca Grant states that it was created as part of "the transition from societies based on kinship to the domination of patriarchal units like the male-headed family."[26] With the development of the state two sets of social relations were created: (1) the public sphere centered on the roles of citizen and soldier; and (2) the private sphere centered on the family and home. Because the state was the product of male thinking, state power was conceived of in masculine terms with an emphasis on power and control.

Standpoint feminists seek to give greater voice to women *because* their experiences are different and provide a broader lens through which to study and practice international politics. This lens does not prioritize the public over the private sphere. For example, questions of human rights would be expanded beyond political participation to include economic, health care, environmental, and social rights. Policies would be formulated or conceptualized in terms of empowerment as well as control.

Postmodern feminism is equally critical of the gendered nature of the language and practice of international politics. It parts company with standpoint feminism by stressing the impossibility of establishing a true and permanent masculine or feminine definition of concepts related to international politics. From this perspective all such definitions and perspectives are partial and arbitrary, a product of the interaction with gender of such factors as power and self-interest. Postmodern feminism seeks to deconstruct international relations theory so that the meanings of concepts and understanding of events are not assumed to be natural or taken for granted. This perspective seeks to explore, unravel, and evaluate the historical and contemporary contexts in which the understanding of key concepts are developed and applied to formulate policy.

Theories of international politics help us understand problems and formulate policies. They differ from each other in what aspects of the problem they highlight and how what policies they advocate. These differences come into clear focus in looking at how the five theories just discussed evaluate the policy challenges found today in the Arctic.

APPLYING THEORIES TO THE ARCTIC

The Arctic is a region of the world that has been rediscovered and redefined in recent decades. Once a peripheral region whose fate could be safely left in the hands of low ranking diplomats and bureaucrats, it now commands the attention of heads of government of major powers, international organizations, businesses, and civil society groups. For example, in April 2019 Russian President Vladimir Putin announced a major new program to build new ports and other facilities in the region as well as expand its nuclear icebreaker fleet. It also had just completed a modernization of its military based across the polar region. So how should the Arctic be studied? This section answers this question by applying the five broad theoretical perspectives introduced in this chapter. Let's begin with a brief overview of the Arctic to provide context.[27]

What Is the Arctic?

Three features of the Arctic are important to understanding the emerging role of this region in world politics. First, the Arctic lacks both a geographic and political center. It even lacks an agreed-upon geographic definition. Most commonly the Arctic is defined as the global region north of the Arctic Circle at a latitude of 66.34 degrees North. It is largely an ice-covered ocean surrounded by several continents. The land mass of the Arctic includes a large portion of Greenland (a self-governing part of Denmark); the Spitsbergen peninsula (belonging to Norway); and parts of Finland, Sweden, Iceland, Russia, Canada, and the United States. The Arctic Zone of the Russian Federation (AZRF) covers one half of the Arctic's territory, some nine million square miles.

Second, no single factor has attracted states to the Arctic. Russians entered Siberia in the sixteenth century in pursuit of the fur trade. Through their possession of Canada, the British turned to the Arctic in hopes of finding a route to China in the 1500s that would not only reduce travel time but allow them to avoid the powerful Portuguese and Spanish navies patrolling the warm water oceans; this sea route to the Pacific Ocean through the Arctic Ocean, called the Northwest Passage, extends along the northern coast of North America via waterways through the Canadian Arctic Archipelago. The United States became an Arctic power with the purchase of Alaska from Russia in 1867.

Today the most often-cited factors attracting states to the Arctic are its potentially valuable natural resources and the dangers of global warming. While the exact date varies, scientists predict relatively ice-free summers and an ice-free Arctic Ocean to be the Arctic norm by 2040. The 2018 annual Arctic Report Card produced by the National Oceanic and Atmospheric administration concluded that the oldest and thickest Arctic ice declined by 95% over the past three decades.

The consequences of global warming in the Arctic include shifting vegetation patterns, cultural losses, threats to animal populations, food supply problems, and increased pollution. Arctic global warming is also linked to a rising number of extreme weather events in Russia, the United States, and Europe. Where some see dangers from global warming, others see the potential for economic

Map 2.1 Map of the Arctic Ocean Including Parts of the Hudson Bay, with Borders Determined by the International Hydrographic Organization.

gain. Shrinking glaciers will expose once ice-covered land that may be rich in energy resources and mineral deposits. It will also open up shipping lanes to year-round travel.

The third defining characteristic of the Arctic is its indigenous population. As of 2013, it was home to approximately four million people. This figure combines the indigenous population, whose roots go back thousands of years, and the nonindigenous population, who moved into the region largely in search of jobs. Estimates from 1910 placed the total Arctic population at less than 300,000. The most politically significant indigenous population in the Arctic then and now is the Inuit, who live in Canada, Russia, Greenland (Denmark), and the United States. Current estimates place the number of Inuits at 160,000.

Applying Realism

As you have already learned, realism focuses on states pursuing their national interest in a competitive and anarchic international system in which self-help and the acquisition of power are key concepts. Realism focuses on the dynamics of military competition in the Arctic. The Policy Spotlight brings into focus that not all conflicts are the same. It presents three different conflict situations states find themselves in: fights, games, and debates. All three may emerge over time in the Arctic.

The primary benefit of the Arctic to states along its perimeter was a wall of security that sealed them off from a northern attack. With the onset of the Cold War, the Arctic became a primary route through which air and missile attacks might occur, a concern shared by both the Soviet Union and the United States. The use of submarines was also made easier. Some 5,000 miles were saved by sending submarines covertly to the Pacific through Arctic waters rather than public passage through the Panama Canal.

The importance of the Arctic to national security declined with the end of the Cold War, but it has resurfaced over the past decade as polar states, most notably Russia, have demonstrated a renewed interest in the military dimension of Arctic interactions. Even among realists, disagreement exists about how to interpret the Russian militarization in the Arctic. Some see it as a return to a more normal level of military activity to be expected from a major global power intent on protecting its borders. Others view it as an unwarranted military buildup that must be countered and an escalation in the probability of war in the region.[28]

A number of official Russian government documents containing statements about Russia's Arctic policy since Vladimir Putin first assumed the presidency in 2000 point to an increased military interest in the region. They include the following:[29]

- *Foundations of the State Policy of the Russian Federation in the Arctic for the Period until 2020 and Beyond.* This document, approved by Russian President Dmitry Medvedev in 2008, simultaneously defined the Arctic as a region for peaceful cooperation and a region of military security that demands careful attention to the modernization and buildup of Russian military capabilities.

POLICY SPOTLIGHT

Fights, Games, Debates

Not all conflicts work according to the same inner logic. One of the greatest policy challenges states face is understanding the type of conflict situation they are in and adopting appropriate strategies to deal with it. During the height of the Cold War, Anatol Rapoport identified three basic types of conflicts: fights, games, and debates.[30]

Fights are conflict situations in which both sides seem to be on "automatic pilot." The conflict is driven forward by a series of moves and countermoves. Often this sequence results in a *conflict spiral*: the conflict gets increasingly severe as each side responds to the actions of the other. Without finding a way of breaking the action-reaction cycle, the ultimate outcome is war. Reversing this escalatory pattern can be a difficult and drawn-out process. Leadership changes, economic exhaustion, and fear are the most often-cited factors stimulating the search for an escape. The series of Arab-Israeli wars, terrorist and counterterrorist attacks, and the trade wars of the 1930s (when countries raised—and re-raised—tariffs in an attempt to protect their economies) are examples of fights.

Games are conflict situations governed by the rules of rationality. Like fights, games can lead to the defeat of one side, but in international politics they more commonly involve situations with the goal of a mutually agreed-upon outcome. In a game each side attempts to anticipate the opponent's next move and plot its strategy accordingly so that its core goals are protected and realized at an acceptable cost. Arms control negotiations, financial bailouts of states, and global and regional trade agreements can be seen as driven by the logic of games. The Theory Spotlight on game theory goes into more detail on the dynamics of games in international politics.

Debates focus on resolving differences by converting an opponent to your point of view. They involve controlling how a problem is defined, which sets limits on the range of action and the types of policies that are permissible both in the present and future. The language of a debate also influences how victory or success is determined. International human rights policy and global environmental policy are generally formulated through debate.

International conflicts are not necessarily defined by one form of conflict. A conflict may contain elements of all three, but not necessarily in the same place, and its inner logic may change over time. And determining to what extent fights, games, or debates are driving a conflict is not easy in areas such as cyber conflict, where much disagreement exists regarding

- *Foreign Policy Concept of the Russian Federation.* This document, approved by Putin in 2016, discusses the principles that govern Russian foreign policy toward other Arctic states. At its core is the belief that Russia is once again a Great Power; as such, Russian foreign policy must seek to "consolidate Russia's position as a center of influence." Speaking specifically of the Arctic, the document states that Russia wishes to "promote peace, stability and constructive international cooperation" in the region but goes on to assert that it will "be firm in countering any attempts to introduce elements of political or military confrontation in the Arctic."

A number of policy initiatives have been implemented or proposed in line with the more aggressive aspects of Russia's strategic statements.

Photo by Hossein Heidarpour

Iranian President Hassan Rouhani and Head of the Atomic Energy Organization of Iran (AEOI) Ali Akbar Salehi in Bushehr Nuclear Plant.

of the North Korean regime, including its right to pursue nuclear capability. Shortly after the 2018 Olympic Games ended, a shift in the dynamics of this conflict took shape. North Korea and the United States agreed to enter into talks. The fights and debates seem to have receded, replaced by the logic of games.

The dynamics of fights, games, and debates are also evident in US-Iran nuclear relations. Initially this conflict largely took the form of a debate in the United Nations, which passed a series of resolutions calling on Iran to halt its nuclear program. Iran refused. The negotiation of the 2015 Joint Comprehensive Plan of Action (JCPOA) between the United States and other powers had the characteristics of a game, as both sides bargained over its terms. The Trump administration's decision in 2018 to withdraw from JCPOA and imposition of an escalating set of sanctions on Iran, and Iran's counter moves to develop its nuclear program, can be characterized as a fight.

which defensive and offensive strategies to use and even how to define cyber war.

Consider the nuclear weapons conflict between the United States and North Korea during the early part of the Trump administration, which was discussed in Chapter 1. At the outset its underlying dynamics reflected the workings of fights and debates. A series of North Korean nuclear tests occurred in rapid succession, followed by escalating threats of military action by the United States. Simultaneously taking place was a highly charged debate between North Korea and the United States over the legitimacy

Think about It

1. Identify one current international politics problem that is a fight; one that is a game; one that is a debate; and one that has characteristics of more than one type of conflict.

2. Which theoretical perspective is most helpful for understanding each of these types of conflicts?

- **Renewal of its submarine fleet**. At present, seven submarines are being updated and plans call for introducing a new generation of nuclear powered ballistic missile submarines.

- **Reorganization of conventional forces**. All conventional forces in the Arctic Zone of the Russian Federation (AZRF) were combined into an Arctic Group of Forces under the direction of a Joint Strategic Command in 2015. A second Arctic Brigade was created in the aftermath of the Ukraine crisis.

- **Creation of new military divisions**. Two new Arctic coastal divisions are being created. They will be equipped to conduct anti-assault, anti-sabotage and anti-aircraft defensive operations. Additionally 20 border guard stations are to be built along the Russian Arctic coastline.

- **Missile tests**. In 2018 the Russian Northern Fleet carried out a drill in which it responded to a simulated air attack by firing anti-aircraft missiles.
- **New icebreakers**. In 2017 Russia introduced its first new icebreaker in 30 years. Icebreakers are vital for economic reasons. Without them it is impossible to keep the northern waterways open all year. They are also valuable for military purposes, as Russian icebreakers are designed to carry cruise missiles.

Applying Liberalism

Like realism, liberalism acknowledges the role that war and the preparation for war have played in international politics, but it does not see anarchy as a persistent condition. According to this perspective, states and their leaders can cooperate once the proper conditions and mechanisms are in place. From the perspective of liberalism, a major challenge facing proponents of Arctic cooperation is creating a unifying center force that will allow them to cooperate more efficiently and effectively. Doing so requires answering five questions that Douglas Nord raises in his study of Arctic cooperation.[31]

- *Who is to govern?* Is Arctic governance limited to Arctic states, or can non-Arctic states such as China become full participating members? What native groups should be represented, and what governance role should they play?
- *What is to be governed?* Historically the focus was on environmental protection and sustainable development. Should military national security issues be added to the list?
- *Where is governance to take place?* Should the focus of Arctic governance be on land-based issues or extend to maritime boundary issues and ownership of deep-sea mineral assets?
- *How is governance to function?* Should it focus on promoting awareness of the issues facing the Arctic, or should it adopt the role of setting standards and enforcing them?
- *Why is regional governance necessary?* Is it inward looking, providing information about conditions, options, and best practices to those in the Arctic, or is it to provide a platform for the Arctic voice to be heard in global deliberations?

Movement toward the creation of an international governing structure for the Arctic only began in the late 1980s. In a speech in Murmansk on October 1, 1987, Soviet head of state Mikhail Gorbachev outlined agendas for military security and nonmilitary cooperation in the Arctic. He called for denuclearization of the Arctic, naval arms control, and the development of confidence-building measures and proposed cooperation in developing natural resources/energy, coordinating scientific research, and coordinating the protection of the environment. He also called for a change in Soviet policy to allow indigenous people within the Soviet Union to attend international meetings of Arctic peoples.

The impact of Gorbachev's speech on Arctic governance were mixed. His military security agenda was met with skepticism and produced little meaningful diplomatic activity. In contrast, his calls for cooperation in the areas of environment, science, and natural resources led to the creation of the Arctic Environmental Protection Strategy (AEPS) in June 1991. This nonbinding agreement was signed by Canada, the United States, Denmark, Finland, Iceland, Norway, Sweden, and the Soviet Union. Signatories to the agreement pledged to preserve the environmental quality and natural resources of the Arctic environment and to meet the needs and traditions of the Arctic native peoples. This meeting was considered historic, in part because three indigenous peoples' groups attended as observers and were designated as permanent participants, the first time this had occurred in an international agreement between states.

Since the AEPS was established, a number of additional instruments of regional cooperation have been created. They exist alongside of the Law of the Sea Treaty, which has a global application; its history is outlined in the Regional Spotlight feature in Chapter 7.

The Arctic Council. Established in 1996 it absorbed the AEPS. A number of contentious issues divided its founding members. One was the scope of the Council's concern. The United States was adamant that the Council's focus should be narrowly restricted to environmental issues and rejected proposals that extended its jurisdiction to include military security issues or development issues. Russia shared the US objection to any discussions on a common security approach. A second divisive issue was the official status of the Arctic Council. The United States insisted that it be an arena for political discussion—a forum for exchanging views—without power to make decisions or take legally binding action.

The Arctic Five. This is a second dimension of Arctic cooperation, embedded within the Arctic Council. This association of nations, comprised of the United States, Russia, Denmark, Norway, and Canada, met in Ilulissat, Greenland, in 2008 to discuss the future of Arctic governance. Their final statement, known as the Ilulissat Declaration, began by asserting that their sovereignty, sovereign rights, and jurisdiction of the Arctic Ocean put them in a unique position to address the possibilities and challenges facing the region. It went on to assert that "We therefore see no need to develop a new comprehensive international legal regime to govern the Arctic Ocean."

Arctic Peoples Conference and Inuit Circumpolar Conference. A third dimension of Arctic cooperation centers on treatment of its indigenous population and control over natural resources and land rights, two issues at the heart of an even larger one—self-determination. These concerns have shaped pan-Inuit cooperation across national boundaries and were, in turn, shaped by the discovery of oil in the Arctic. Oil was discovered in Arctic Alaska in 1957. By 1963, 1,000 indigenous people from twenty-four Alaskan villages had petitioned for a land freeze in the state until issues of native rights were resolved. The Inuit of the North Slope of Prudhoe Bay, where oil was discovered, soon organized the Arctic Slope Native Association and laid claim to over 88,000 square miles of traditional Inuit hunting land. The political organization of indigenous people took on an international dimension in 1973 when the first Arctic Peoples Conference was held in Copenhagen, Denmark. In 1977 the first Inuit Circumpolar Conference (ICC) was held.

Northern Forum. Officially established in 1991, the Northern Forum is comprised of subnational and regional governments. Among its founding members from eight northern countries were representatives from China, Japan, and the Republic of Korea, giving the Northern Forum a more extensive political and geographic scope than the Arctic Council. The Northern Forum has become increasingly identified with Russian subnational governments located in the Arctic. Among the problems facing this group are a lack of clearly defined objectives and the inability to define such key terms such as "Northern peoples" and "common challenge."

Applying Economic Structuralism

Recall that, from the vantage point of economic structuralism, international politics is about the pursuit of wealth and profits by individuals whose position in society allows them to control the state. Nothing better captures the economic structuralism perspective than the announcement by President Donald Trump's Secretary of the Interior before an audience of oil producers meeting in Anchorage in May 2017 that Alaska "is open for business!" and Putin's 2019 announcement that Russia will increase the amount of cargo it ships through the Arctic from twenty million metric tons in 2018 to eighty million in 2025.

Evidence supporting his claim was hard to refute. That same month the Environmental Protection Agency approved a proposed gold mine in Bristol Bay. One month earlier Trump had signed an executive order allowing oil drilling in the Arctic waters under US jurisdiction. And in December of 2017 the Senate voted to open up the 30,000 square mile National Wildlife Refuge to oil and gas drilling. Estimates predicted the discovery of 7.7 billion barrels of oil. The United States is not alone in viewing the Arctic as a source of future wealth. In August 2007 Russia made the highly symbolic act of planting its flag 14,000 feet below the North Pole using mini-submarines. Canada also claims this territory, and it responded by stating "This isn't the fifteenth century. You can't go around the world and just plant flags and say 'we're claiming this territory'."[32]

The potential to provide immense profits for corporations and individuals is significant and has created an Arctic gold rush.[33] Nineteen geological basins within the Arctic contain oil reserves; only about half of them have been explored. The US Geological Survey estimates that 13% of the world's undiscovered conventional oil reserves and 31% of the undiscovered natural gas reserves can be found in the Arctic. By 2012 Shell Oil had spent over $4 billion on Arctic oil exploration without drilling a single well. Russia's energy reserves are believed to account for 52% of the Arctic total. The Arctic also possesses an abundance of other mineral resources. The exact amount and value of these resources are subject to debate, because they are located in portions of the Arctic that are difficult to access and exploit. Within Russia, more than seven hundred different minerals have been found on the Kola Peninsula, including large reserves of nickel-copper ores, phosphate, bauxite, alumina, rare metals, titanium, construction materials, and semi-precious stones. Exploration for key metals is also competitive. Greenland has issued over a hundred exploration permits, and recently a consortium paid $590 million for a large iron ore deposit in the Arctic.

Melting Arctic sea ice has raised the possibility of increased shipping at reduced costs, further accelerating the race for resources. The most favorable route is the Northern Sea Route along the Siberian coast. It holds the potential for reducing the shipping time between Europe and East Asia by one-third and providing access to foreign markets at considerably reduced costs. The principal alternative shipping route goes through the Suez Canal and is 40% longer in distance. It is estimated that insurance premiums, along with ransoms and other disruptions to shipping, currently cost shipping companies $7–12 billion per year.

Ideas about how to make the Arctic an even more profitable region for entrepreneurial activity are currently being proposed. A Finnish corporate executive has suggested creating a Pan-Arctic Free Trade Zone to establish strong market connections within the region and ensure market access for investors. He has also called for greater use of public-private partnerships to finance new Arctic initiatives. His most intriguing proposal was the development of an Uber Icebreaker fleet. Rather than have individual countries build their own, expensive icebreaker fleets, he has recommended construction of a rental fleet of icebreakers that states could contract as needed. In conclusion he proclaimed, "Business is multinational. Let's make it pan-Arctic."[34]

Applying Constructivism

Constructivism directs attention to how images and selected policies of international politics are shaped by experiences and interactions with others. These images and policies are not fixed but change over time as experiences change and dialogues evolve.

At the outset of this discussion, the Arctic was defined as the land and sea area north of the Arctic Circle which is located at 66.34 degrees north latitude (see Map 2.1). Constructivists would reject this definition, asserting that "the Arctic is what you make of it." Many definitions of the Arctic exist and are based on factors such as average temperature, the northern tree line, the amount of permafrost on land, the extent of sea ice on the ocean, and administrative boundaries. Others make a distinction between the "high Arctic," the colder parts of the Arctic near the North Pole, and the "low Arctic," which is less cold and further from the North Pole.

The selected definition reflects both personal experience and the outcome of dialogues with others about what constitutes the Arctic. It will change over time as more and more "non-Arctic" states seek to establish a presence there. Foremost among these is China, which in 2018 unveiled its Polar Silk Road initiative.[35] Just as the Silk Road connected China with Europe as a land route across Asia, the Polar Silk Road will connect China with Europe and the Middle East through shipping lanes opened by global warming. Promising to work with Arctic states and indigenous peoples, China plans to develop oil, gas, mineral, and tourism resources, among others.

One of the first points constructivists would make is the extent to which discussions of the Arctic are organized around historical images and romantic myths. A second point is that the dominant images of the Arctic are created by outsiders. The Arctic is routinely portrayed as either a frozen wasteland or a pristine wilderness inhabited by polar bears and indigenous people embracing a traditional lifestyle. As one commentator noted what is missing is a depiction of the Arctic as "home" for animals or people.[36] Concern for the impact of climate change has altered this picture to some degree, but much of the same imagery continues and hides an evolving Arctic reality.

Today indigenous people are a minority in all parts of the Arctic except those belonging to Canada and Greenland. Data suggest that while hunting and fishing remain important sources of food for indigenous people, nontraditional foods are increasingly becoming chief sources of nutrition. In addition, significant economic changes have occurred as increasing numbers of indigenous communities are becoming structured around a mixture of traditional economic activities and wage employment.

Constructivists would also highlight the dominance of self-serving imagery advanced by business people and investors about the economic future of the Arctic. Most notably, the potential environmental problems created by harvesting the Arctic's natural resources are recognized, but they are presented as technical problems that can be solved in a scientific and value neutral fashion. Their impact on different groups within society are downplayed, as is the question of who pays to minimize or fix the damage. A case in point is the rhetoric about the Northern Sea Route becoming a year-round northern Suez Canal, which will compete with, and perhaps overtake, the Suez and Panama Canals. Viewed strictly in terms of mileage, the argument that the Northern Sea Route will cut shipping time through the Suez Canal by twenty days is sound; when placed in the context of broader economic and geographic considerations, however, such as the unpredictability of ice conditions and the uncertain impact of oil spills in high-latitude, cold-ocean environments, the argument weakens considerably.

Constructivism emphasizes the importance of context for understanding international politics. One important implication of constructivist analysis is that there may exist other "poles" beyond the Arctic and Antarctic. The Regional Spotlight feature introduces a possible Third Pole.

Applying Feminism

A starting point for feminist analysis of the Arctic is the idea that women are invisible in spite of the fact that in 2007 women and children made up almost 70% of the Inuit population. Arctic policy debates focus almost exclusively on regional-level economic development, climate change, environmental pollution, and national security issues and not on gender issues. When the discussion moves down to a more personal level, there is little acknowledgment of differences in impact on women and men or of the complex nature of gender relations in the Arctic; in Inuit society gender is "situational and contextual" rather than "fixed and binary."[37] For example, in 2000 an estimated 80%

of Inuit men engaged in harvesting fish and game, which is not surprising, but 63% of Inuit women did so as well. Education rates also break from traditional stereotypes. In 1999 43% Nunavut women graduated from secondary school compared to 27% of men.

One of the most complex and pressing issues related to differential gender impact is the forced resettlement of Inuit communities due to changing environmental conditions. Resettlement has separated men from their traditional roles as hunters and compelled them to adapt a different identity and assume a different place in society, which has created emotional problems such as alcoholism. Some feminists argue that women, whose traditional role is in the home, should be better able to adapt to their new life. However, data show that Inuit women are more likely to become homeless and that domestic violence against women and children is on the rise in many areas within the Arctic.

Standpoint feminism points to the role that women have played in promoting health in the Arctic. Arctic women have held a different perspective on environmental pollution from that of men. Because of their traditional role as health care providers for their families, women had been especially sensitive to problems related to contamination of food products in situations ranging from harvesting fish and game to breast feeding.

From both the feminist and constructivist perspectives, the vocabulary of political analysis is not value neutral but, rather, serves as a source of power for those who define terms. Of central importance to feminism is bringing attention to the gendered nature of the language and imagery used to discuss problems and define relationships. One area of feminist investigation is the language used by the Arctic Council to frame human development issues. A recent study highlighted three key concepts: strength of community, vulnerability, and the need for adaptation.[38]

- **Strength of community**. Community is portrayed by the Arctic Council as the unit through which human development takes place. It is also the means of organizing and exercising power in the Arctic. Arctic communities are pictured as harmonious groups of united individuals who share traditional values. This portrayal of the community as the centerpiece of Arctic human development overlooks divisions within communities, including conditions such as the large-scale outmigration of young and educated women, who seek human development with a different reference point.
- **Vulnerability**. While communities are viewed as a source of strength, individuals and households are portrayed as vulnerable by the Council. The vocabulary employed to discuss vulnerabilities is heavily science oriented and depicts them as objective and preexisting. However, vulnerabilities vary and are perceived differently depending on an individual's place in the community. The scientific view also hides the impact of factors such as law, politics, education, and culture.
- **Need for adaptation**. The position of the Council is that individuals and entire Arctic communities must be willing to change their behavior patterns and practices to better cope with the challenges they face. Feminist critics argue that the emphasis on adaptation downgrades efforts to change or reverse the conditions that create vulnerabilities and that much of the reporting on adaptation highlights failures rather than successes: alcoholism, suicide rates, and domestic violence. Like vulnerability,

REGIONAL SPOTLIGHT

The Third Pole

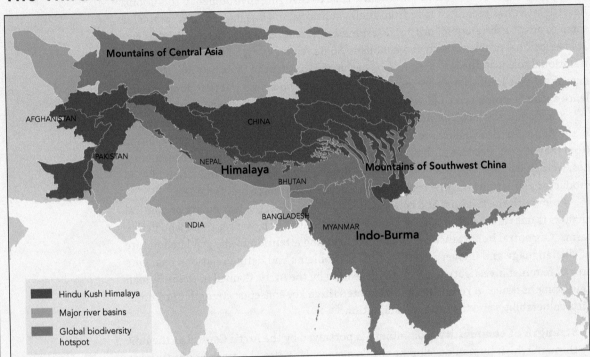

Map 2.2 The Third Pole.

Most world maps have two poles, one north and one south. The land and water mass surrounding the North Pole is the Arctic region discussed extensively in this chapter. That surrounding the South Pole, the Antarctic, makes up about 20% of the southern hemisphere. The land mass of Antarctica is almost twice the size of Australia and 98% of it is covered in ice. It lacks an indigenous population. Seven states claim ownership of parts of the Antarctic, and since 1959 the region has been governed by an international treaty. Antarctica suffers from many of the same environmental problems currently

adaptation is pictured as a gender-neutral process, ignoring the socially constructed nature of gender roles and the importance of traditional Arctic culture.

Using different theoretical perspectives to examine a policy issue is valuable because it provides alternative viewpoints for understanding international politics issues, but doing so is no guarantee against surprises. As was noted at the outset of this chapter, the end of the Cold War caught most observers by surprise. The chapter closes by looking at a more recent surprise: the Ukrainian conflict of 2014.

experienced by the Arctic. Most notably, in 2018 scientists announced that 10% of Antarctica's coastal glaciers are retreating and the sea level is rising.

Today, increasing attention is being paid to "the Third Pole," the snow-covered Hindu-Kush Himalayan (HKH) mountain region that sits atop the Tibetan Plateau. Covering some five million sq km, it stretches from Afghanistan in the west to China in the east and crosses over Pakistan, Nepal, India, Bangladesh, Bhutan, and Myanmar. It contains an estimated 46,000 glaciers. The HKH Mountains are the origins of ten of Asia's largest freshwater systems, including the Mekong, Yellow, Yangtze, Ganges, Indus, and Brahmaputra rivers. Taken together, the drainage basins from these rivers cover an area the size of Brazil. An estimated 120 million people depend on these waters for irrigation of farmland, and some 1.3 billion people (20%) of the world's population rely on them in some way for food, water, and energy.

The Third Pole historically has been susceptible to major ecological disturbances such as windstorms, wildfires, and droughts. About 15% of the world's major twentieth-century earthquakes (magnitude 8 or higher) took place here. In 2012 cloud bursts in the Third Pole led to flash floods that killed over 5,000 people. Climate change has added another dimension to the geographic vulnerability of the region. Since 2005 the speed at which the Third Pole glaciers are melting has nearly doubled, and over 500 small glaciers have disappeared completely. Urbanization and economic development are other ecological problems facing the Third Pole. The increased use of coal burners and the pollution from car exhaust systems have resulted in the settling of dust on the glaciers, causing them to absorb rather than reflect the sun's rays and accelerating the melting rate.

Recent studies report that the Third Pole is already in a state of crisis.[39] One of the challenges facing those trying to assess the dangers is the lack of data. Only recently have systematic studies been undertaken, and many uncertainties remain. A major concern related to global warming is whether precipitation in the HKH Mountains takes the form of snow or rain, but satellites cannot tell the difference between solid and liquid water.

Compounding the scientific and technological problems of identifying the threats to the Third Pole are the political problems of formulating policies to address them. Government responses are described as crisis oriented and carried out in "silos" that frustrate both national and regional planning. Concerns are also raised about the lack of local level involvement in formulating responses. Feminists highlight the plight of the poor, indigenous peoples and women; they are among those most affected by Third Pole environmental crises but have little or no voice in decision-making.[40]

Think about It

1. What factors justify thinking of this region as a Third Pole? What factors would lead you to reject this idea? Which of the two arguments is most persuasive?

2. Rank order the theoretical perspectives introduced in this chapter in terms of their value for thinking about the future of the Third Pole.

A CONTEMPORARY PERSPECTIVE ON THEORY:
The Ukraine

The Ukraine became an independent state with the collapse of the Soviet Union in 1991. During the Cold War it had been an important contributor to the Soviet economy and the location of a significant portion of the Soviet nuclear force. In addition, the Crimea, a territory that the Soviet Union put under Ukrainian control in 1954, was home to the Black Sea fleet.

Photo by Mstyslav Chernov

Protesters fighting government forces on Maidan Nezalezhnosti in Kiev on February 18, 2014.

After independence, the Ukraine adopted a foreign policy of neutrality to preserve its Cold War role as a buffer zone between the Soviet Union and Western Europe. Ukrainian interest in signing a free trade agreement with the European Union (EU) fueled doubts within Russia about the new nation's future neutrality. In September 2013 Russia warned the Ukraine of dire economic consequences if it went ahead with this agreement. In November Viktor Yanukovych, the pro-Russian president of the Ukraine, announced that he would not sign the agreement negotiated by his predecessor but would instead pursue closer economic ties with Russia. That decision set off a series of often violent street protests, which in February 2014 resulted in the removal of Yanukovych from power; he ultimately fled to Russia.

Within days of his ousting, disguised Russian ground forces along with pro-Russian Ukrainian militia took control of the Crimean Peninsula, a strategically important region for projecting Russia's naval power. In mid-March the Crimean regional assembly voted to secede from the Ukraine and become part of Russia. On March 21 Russian President Vladimir Putin made the reunion official.

The military confrontation between the Ukraine and Russian backed anti-government forces quickly moved to the Donbass region of Ukraine along the Russian border, which is home to many ethnic Russians. Anti-Ukrainian government protesters took to the streets in pro-Russian demonstrations in early March, followed by an uprising against the Ukraine government. While publicly led by local pro-Russian Ukrainian militia, the uprising was universally considered to be organized and staffed by Russian forces. Ukrainian military forces entered the region and appeared to be the verge of quashing this uprising when a Russian-led counter offensive began. In early August a convoy of Russian military vehicles and Russian volunteer soldiers "on vacation" crossed into the Donbass region. Pro-Russian separatist leaders claimed to have 3,000–4,000 Russian troops fighting alongside them. NATO referred to this activity as an "incursion" and not an "invasion." Russia's official position was that the military activity was being carried out by Ukrainian separatists.

Cease-fire agreements negotiated in 2014 quickly broke down. Sporadic fighting continues today, as does the political stalemate over the future of Donbass. Tensions increased significantly in November 2018 when Russia seized three Ukrainian naval vessels in the first direct military conflict between the two countries. A 2003 agreement between Russia and Ukraine had guaranteed free passage through the waterway, a narrow stretch of water separating the Black and Azov Seas, over which both countries claim to have sovereignty.

For many observers the Ukrainian conflict signals a return of Cold War international politics. As with the end of the twentieth-century Cold War, the theoretical perspectives introduced in this chapter provide different interpretations of the origin of the Ukrainian conflict. For realists, the conflict began because of failure by the United States to understand the strategic importance of the Ukraine as a buffer zone for Russian security interests. Liberalism highlights the underdeveloped nature of Russian democracy, which allowed Putin to pursue an aggressive foreign policy without any effective constraints. Economic structuralists would characterize the conflict as involving two capitalist core areas (the EU and Russia) over a periphery (the Ukraine) that each wished to deny to the other and exploit for its own economic advantage. Constructivists would note how much of the language of the conflict, such as references to the Ukraine as a state and the Ukrainian people, was artificial and disconnected from the historical reality that the Ukraine was a multiethnic state that had a history of being both independent and part of larger political units at various times. Feminism directs attention to the invisibility of women in the analysis of the conflict and the masculine nature of the narrative, which provides an incomplete and biased account of the conflict by framing the issue as a contest of power, states' rights, and prestige.

Summary

- Events are not self-interpreting. Theory is needed to "connect the dots" between them in order to respond to challenges effectively.

- The fall of the Berlin Wall was unexpected and symbolized the end of the Cold War.

- Realism emphasizes the anarchic nature of the international system and the central role of power and the state in international politics.

- Liberalism emphasizes the ability of states to cooperate if the proper conditions are in place, including democracy, free trade, international organizations, and arms control.

- Economic structuralism views international politics as an arena characterized by exploitation, in which individuals compete in the pursuit of wealth.

- Constructivism rejects the notion that international politics are driven by an unchanging set of underlying forces. It emphasizes the role of perceptions and social interactions in defining problems and solutions.

- Feminism seeks to make women more visible and highlight the role that gender plays in international politics.

- The Arctic is a complex region. Each theoretical perspective offers a different lens through which contemporary Arctic issues can be analyzed. Realism emphasizes military competition, liberalism points out cooperative efforts, economic structuralism stresses competition for resources, constructivism highlights the changing nature of the Arctic, and feminism identifies gender bias in language and policy.

- The continuing conflict in Ukraine is seen by many as the start of a new cold war–era. Opinions about its origins differ as widely as the theoretical perspectives used to analyze them.

Key Terms

Constructivism *(36)*
Economic structuralism *(34)*
Feminist theory *(37)*

Liberalism *(30)*
Realism *(28)*

Critical Thinking Questions

1. Are there international conflicts today that have real or symbolic Berlin Walls?

2. Can realism promote meaningful peace, or must it lead to conflict and war?

3. Is liberalism based on global ideas on how to build cooperation or on Western ideas?

4. Must capitalism be exploitive, or can it reform itself and lead to international and domestic peace?

5. Is it possible for constructivism to serve as a guide in policy-making? How would it do so?

6. Which of the versions of feminism presented is most useful for studying international politics? Why?

7. Which of the theoretical perspectives presented offers the most insight into studying the Arctic today? Which will be most useful in ten years?

8. Is the Ukrainian crisis a fight, game, or debate? Explain your answer.

Practice and Review Online
http://textbooks.rowman.com/hastedt-felice

▲ Thousands march in demonstration over the proposed British exit from the European Union (Brexit).
Source: Mark Kerrison / Alamy Live News / Alamy Stock Photo

03

THE SOVEREIGNTY CHALLENGE: WHO IS IN CHARGE IN WORLD POLITICS?

AT THE CENTER OF THE SOVEREIGNTY CHALLENGE is determining "who is in charge" in international politics. The traditional answer is states, especially the most powerful ones. This answer is rooted in the principle of sovereignty established by the Treaty of Westphalia in 1648, which ended the Thirty Years War in Central Europe. This war began as a conflict between Protestant and Catholic states. By the time the Thirty Years War ended it ended it had become a war between European great powers. Some eight million people died as a result of the fighting. Among the many issues fought over was the role of religion and the church in politics. The result of these debates was agreement that state rulers—not the Catholic Church—should determine how to manage religious matters within their countries. In time this principle of **sovereignty**, the idea that states control their own affairs without outside interference, would be extended to all domestic and foreign issues. Today many question whether this interpretation, which gives states the leading position in international politics, is still valid.[1] The growth in the number and importance of international nongovernmental organizations as well as the spread and deepening of globalization are used to support the argument for a revised definition of sovereignty.

sovereignty The principle that no authority exists above the state; states decide what goals to pursue and how to pursue them.

This chapter opens by tracing the development of the European Union (EU) from its beginnings in the 1950s through its formal establishment. The next three sections introduce the major types of actors in international politics: states, international organizations, and non-state actors. Coverage then turns to how to respond to three sovereignty challenges: redefining sovereignty, reforming the United Nations Security Council, and bringing greater coordination to international cooperation. The chapter concludes by revisiting the EU and the challenge presented to it by Brexit (British exit).

LEARNING OBJECTIVES

Students will be able to:

- Recognize the ways in which sovereignty was strengthened and weakened in Europe by the development of the European Union.

- Identify the different categories used to distinguish between states and describe the role these types of states play in international politics.

- Understand the differences among types of international organization and the resources international organizations possess that make them important actors in international politics.

- Explain why non-state actors are important actors in international politics and evaluate their impact on states and international organizations.

- Assess the role that concerns about sovereignty have played in the controversy over Brexit.

- Understand key challenges to sovereignty that may exist in the future and strategies that have been proposed for responding to these challenges.

HISTORICAL PERSPECTIVE:
From the Common Market to the European Union

Two world wars in the space of fifty years convinced many in Europe that positive steps had to be taken to ensure that there would not be another one. In May 1950 French Foreign Minister Robert Schuman proposed that France and West Germany place their coal and steel industries under a common authority that would have the power to set production quotas, transportation costs, and other measures to prevent unfair competition. The choice of coal and steel was deliberate. The two countries had a long history of competing for control of the Saar and Rhine regions in which these industries were concentrated. In 1951 Belgium, Italy, Luxembourg, and the Netherlands joined with France and West Germany to create the *European Coal and Steel Community*. In December 1950 France made another international proposal: the establishment of a European Defense Community that would include a single integrated European army. Behind this French initiative was the perceived need for (and fear of) German rearmament because of the outbreak of the Korean War. The proposal failed to gain the necessary support from the members of the European Coal and Steel Community.

In 1955 new efforts were undertaken to bring greater unity in Europe. An international agreement created *a European Atomic Energy Community* and a *European Economic Community (EEC)* (better known as the *Common Market*). The Common Market began in 1957 with great success, leading other West European states to seek membership. It reduced trade barriers between member countries and established common economic policies. Great Britain applied for membership in 1961, but French President Charles de Gaulle vetoed its membership for fear that British membership would reduce French influence in EEC decision-making and would also provide the United States, a strong British ally, with a means of influencing EEC policy.

Map 3.1 Six Original Members of the European Coal and Steel Community (ECSC).

In 1965 members of the Common Market agreed to merge these three organizations into a single institution called the *European Community (EC)* that would be governed by a single Council of Ministers and a bureaucratic administrative body. Great Britain applied for membership again in 1967 but nothing came of it. It wasn't until 1973 that Great Britain, along with Ireland and Denmark, became members of the European Community. One reason France ceased opposing Great Britain's admission was that West Germany and its strong economy were now viewed as the primary threat. Great Britain was now seen as a potential ally that could weaken Germany's influence.

In 1986 the passage of the Single European Act was yet another step forward in creating the *European Union* (EU). The goal was to create a European market with greater economic and social cohesion. The Act set December 1992 as the date for the accomplishment of over 280 detailed changes, including measures designed to achieve monetary union. Not all EC countries supported these changes. In 1988 the most vocal opponent, British Prime Minister Margaret Thatcher, asserted that "to try and suppress nationhood and concentrate power at the centre of a European conglomerate would be highly damaging."

The final step forward to European Union began in 1991 with negotiations that led to the signing of the Maastricht Treaty in 1993. This treaty added two new pillars to the economic focus of European cooperation: (1) justice and home affairs and (2) foreign

POLICY SPOTLIGHT

When Is a State a State?

At what point does a state come into existence? Consider the case of West Germany. After WWII Germany was divided into four occupation zones. In 1949 the French, British, and US zones were united into the Federal Republic of Germany (West Germany). In 1954 West Germany joined NATO. In 1955 the occupation of West Germany officially ended, and in 1957 it helped establish the European Coal and Steel Community. In 1973 West Germany was admitted to the United Nations (UN). When exactly did West Germany become a state?

Two different approaches have been used to answer this question. One is that a state becomes a state when it is recognized by other states. The second defines statehood in terms of characteristics. The 1933 Montevideo Convention defines a state as having (1) a permanent population (2) a defined

territory, (3) a government, and (4) the capacity to enter into relations with other states. Neither of these approaches is without problems or is followed consistently.

As an economically advanced country and a potentially important ally against the Soviet Union, West Germany was fortunate, and few hesitated to call it a state. Not all countries are so lucky. They may be condemned to a type of global no man's land in which their ability to participate in international organizations and meetings, sign agreements, and receive international monetary assistance is severely limited.

A case in point is Palestine. It is recognized by over 130 states, but it is not a state by most accounts. In 1974 the UN General Assembly passed a resolution recognizing the right of the Palestinian policy and security policy. As a result of the Maastricht Treaty, European citizenship was granted to citizens of all member countries. Another significant policy decision was a blueprint and timeline for establishing a single currency. Ratification of the Maastricht Treaty was complex, involving a combination of public votes, parliamentary votes, and court decisions. Approval was achieved only after agreement that, under certain circumstances, EU members could "opt out" of participating in a EU policy. Denmark and Great Britain both opted out of the final stage of monetary union in January 1999, when the euro became a real currency and national currencies disappeared.

STATES

The concept of sovereignty implies a high degree of equality among states. While true in an official or ceremonial sense, this is not really the case. States are born unequal. Some are better able to protect themselves from foreign interference and can impose their will on others through the use of force and other policy instruments. The inherent inequality of states leads commentators and policy makers to think of states as grouped into different categories. Among the most common are great powers, middle powers, and fragile states. Regardless of the category to which a state is assigned, an assumption

David Coulson / iStock

Taiwanese military forces in training for combat.

people to self-determination and sovereignty in Palestine. In 2011 Palestine applied for but failed to gain membership in the UN. Further complicating the case for Palestinian statehood is the lack of agreed-upon boundaries.

A second example is Taiwan. Both Taiwan and mainland China (the People's Republic of China, PRC)

claim to be the only government of all of China. When the United States established diplomatic relations with the PRC in 1979, it had to end relations and all treaties with the Taiwanese government. The PRC took its seat at the UN. Only about twenty countries have full diplomatic relations with Taiwan.

What about ISIS (the Islamic State of Iraq and Syria)? Most observers define it as a terrorist group, but when it controlled territory in Syria, had a significant military capability, controlled the local economy and lines of communication, and funded its own operations, others referred to it as a pseudo state.[2] Becoming a state was certainly its ultimate objective: to establish a *caliphate*, a state governed by Sharia.

Think about It

1. What is the most important defining characteristic of a state?

2. How much do states matter today?

is being made that it is in fact a state. But when is a state a state? That question is taken up in the Policy Spotlight.

Great Powers

great powers States that possess the ability to use their military, economic, and political resources to influence events on a global scale.

Sitting at the top of the hierarchy of states are those referred to as **great powers**. There is no single set of characteristics identifying what makes a county a great power,[3] but two are generally cited:

1. **The ability to influence the policies of other states**. Influence is usually defined in terms of military power. No agreement exists as to how much power or what type of power is required. Some say a great power is one that can fight a major war, while others characterize it as one that can defend itself against all others even when they are united.
2. **The ability to influence international political issues in most of the world**. This ability sets great powers apart from middle powers whose ability to influence political, military, and economic issues far beyond their borders is limited.

Some identify a third characteristic of a great power: recognition and treatment of a country as a great power by other states in the international system. Most importantly, the state must be recognized as a great power by other great powers. Until then it remains a rising challenger demanding a larger voice in world affairs.

In the 1800s great power status was all but reserved for European empires that possessed large armies and navies and ruled over colonial territories in Africa and Asia. The two world wars in the twentieth century and the advent of nuclear weapons effectively reduced the number of great powers to two: the United States and Soviet Union. With the fall of communism and the breakup of the Soviet Union in 1989, many considered the United States to be the world's only great power.

A major point of debate today is whether China (and perhaps Russia) should be considered a great power. The question is an important one from the perspective of *offensive realism*, which sees the pursuit of power and security as the primary motivating forces in shaping a state's foreign policy. Offensive realism argues that "Great Powers are primed for offense."[4] Rarely are great powers content with the power status quo. They fear other great powers and rising challengers. Great powers are always looking for opportunities to gain more power or reduce the power of others. Other states share these concerns, but great powers are far less constrained by the structure of the international system from taking offensive action to accomplish their foreign policy goals.

Great powers are not mindless aggressors. They attempt to weigh the costs and benefits of aggressive action. When the potential costs of offensive action are too high, great powers seek out other ways of protecting and advancing their power against real and potential challengers.[5] Among the options are deterrence, containment, and working with other states to establish a balance of power in the international system. Each of these options will be taken up in more depth in later chapters.

Middle Powers

A few steps down the ladder from great powers are **middle powers**. By definition, middle powers are states that have limited ability to influence the distribution of power in a region but can defend their interests and influence the policy positions of more powerful states.[6] Middle powers are not newcomers to international politics. Today as in the past they have been largely overshadowed by great powers and major powers such as Great Britain, France, Germany, and Japan and, while possessing significant amounts of global political influence, lack the ability to act alone militarily or economically to defend their national interests. During the Cold War, middle powers largely fell into two categories:

1. Countries supportive of one of the great powers. Canada and Australia were prominent middle powers allied with the United States; whereas, until the Sino-Soviet split in 1960, China was a loyal supporter of the Soviet Union.
2. States seeking to remove themselves from Cold War politics. The vehicle selected to accomplish this goal was the nonaligned movement. The foundations for this movement were laid in a 1956 meeting attended by Yugoslavia, India, Indonesia, and Ghana. Officially the nonaligned movement continues to exist today and includes over a hundred member states.

The end of the Cold War and the growth of globalization have brought new attention to middle powers and increased their degree of involvement in international politics. No longer are they largely passive, either generally supporting the actions and positions of the great powers or trying to distance themselves from them. Middle powers actively promote and protect their own interests, especially on foreign policy issues related to economic development such as trade and climate policy. Increasingly, middle powers are also acting in concert with other states. Examples of small-scale, limited, or issue-specific cooperation initiatives include: BRICS (Brazil, Russia, India, China, and South Africa), MIKTA (Mexico, Indonesia, Republic of Korea, Turkey, and Australia), and CIVETS (Columbia, Indonesia, Vietnam, Egypt, Turkey, and South Africa). The primary forum for cooperation among larger numbers of middle powers is the Group of Twenty (G-20) created in 1999. At G-20 meetings high-level government officials and central bank governors from the world's major economies meet to exchange views on global economic issues. Following the 2008 global financial crisis, the G-20 replaced the Group of Seven (G-7; Canada, France, Germany, Italy, Japan, the United Kingdom, and the United States) as the central forum for such discussions.

The rise of the middle powers presents a number of challenges to the great powers and major powers. Two of these are particularly difficult to accommodate:[7]

1. Not all of the middle powers share the belief that the current international order is just. Many see it as a system built around Western values forced on the rest of the world by Western-dominated international institutions. These middle powers want global policy decisions to better reflect their own values and desire a greater role in the operation of international institutions.

2. Many middle powers reject the notion of limits to state sovereignty that justify international intervention in domestic affairs. This is especially true of areas such as economic policy, human rights, and environmental policy, where middle states view the great powers states as seeking to impose their own standards and transfer the cost of global policy reforms to the middle powers.

One limitation on the ability of middle powers to cooperate with one another is differing political and economic circumstances. A case in point is BRICS.[8] Brazil, Russia, India, China, and South Africa share many key economic characteristics. They have large populations, expanding domestic markets, and adequate labor reserves, and they have undergone impressive growth spurts. They are also seen as regional leaders in undertaking military modernization programs. Yet their efforts at presenting a united front have often been limited to holding summit meetings and issuing press releases pledging unity and highlighting the failures of other powers.

Economic and national security considerations contribute greatly to this limited ability to forge common policy. All five BRICS are in competition to attract foreign investments. Brazil and India tend to focus on domestic markets to generate growth. The Chinese economy has prospered by stressing exports, a policy that has harmed domestic producers in Brazil, India, and South America. In the military sphere BRICS have created a Defense Council largely at the urging of Russia, which sees BRICS as an additional counterweight to the North Atlantic Treaty Organization (NATO). India, South Africa, and China are reluctant to embrace military cooperation, so little has been accomplished in this sphere other than joint statements on cybersecurity.

Fragile States

fragile states States that struggle to control violence, lack accountable government institutions, and have little economic stability, making them especially vulnerable to social, economic, and political shocks.

No label attached to states is more contested than that of **fragile states**, with the possible exception of the term which it replaced: failed states.[9] The term failed states came into widespread use in the 1990s after the Cold War ended. During the Cold War the United States and the Soviet Union routinely helped support governments with financial aid and military assistance to ensure that they did not fall under the influence of their opponent through a coup, domestic uprising, or civil war. With the end of the Cold War and the fall of the Soviet Union, these states were no longer the object of superpower competition. Economic aid and military assistance did not end completely, but there was no longer the same sense of urgency. Renewed attention was paid to failed states when it became clear that domestic protest movements, terrorism, and civil wars had the potential to escalate into destabilizing regional conflicts.

Early definitions identified failed states as countries that were unable to function as independent states or those in which basic governing duties were not being performed. Among those identified as failed states were the Ivory Coast, the Democratic Republic of the Congo, Sudan, Iraq, and Somalia.

Consistent with the constructivist perspective on international politics, three objections were often raised when identifying states unable to respond to significant government challenges as failed states:

1. The term "failed state" reflected Western political and philosophical biases about what was considered a "successful state."
2. This bias led to "'cookie cutter'" solutions to the problems faced by failed states instead of taking into account their historical experiences or the nature of the problems they faced. Simply identifying them as failed states led to a one-solution-fits-all mindset.
3. The concept of a failed state implied that the idea of a given country was a failure. Critics argued that attention should instead be directed at individual policy-makers, who often put the pursuit of personal wealth and power above the interests of their country.

These criticisms led many to move away from the concept of a failed state toward characterization as a fragile state.[10] Typically there is no single qualification. Instead, the annual Fragile State Index created by the Fund for Peace (see Table 3.1) identifies four common dimensions of state fragility:

- The loss of physical control of its territory or a monopoly on the legitimate use of force.
- The erosion of legitimate authority to make collective decisions.
- An inability to provide reasonable public services.
- The inability to interact with other states as a full member of the international community.

Of the 178 countries examined in 2017, the five most fragile states were (1) South Sudan, (2) Somalia, (3) the Central African Republic, (4) Yemen, and (5) a tie between Sudan and Syria. The five least fragile states were (1) Finland, (2) Norway, (3) Switzerland, (4) Denmark and (5) Sweden.[11]

All states regardless of their power standing sometimes find it is difficult if not impossible to act alone to achieve their goals. In these situations they may turn to international organizations for help. But international organizations are not simply tools of member states. They have their own goals and interests to protect and may have the power resources to act on their own.

INTERNATIONAL ORGANIZATIONS

International organizations are institutions formed by states in which states retain sovereignty. For a long time the ability of states to retain sovereignty relegated international organizations to something of a second-class status in international politics. They were viewed as institutions that help states achieve shared foreign policy goals

international organizations Formal institutions created by states to better realize common goals; final political power and authority reside with the member states.

TABLE 3.1	The World's Most Fragile States	
2017	2015	2010*
1. South Sudan	1. South Sudan	1. Somalia
2. Somalia	2. Somalia	2. Chad
3. Central African Republic	3. Central African Republic	3. Sudan
4. Yemen	4. Sudan	4. Zimbabwe
5. Syria (tie)	5. Democratic Republic of Congo	5. Democratic Republic of Congo
6. Sudan (tie)	6. Chad	6. Afghanistan
7. Democratic Republic of Congo	7. Yemen	7. Iraq
8. Chad	8. Syria	8. Central African Republic
9. Afghanistan	9. Afghanistan	9. Guinea
10. Iraq	10. Guinea	10. Pakistan

*In 2010 this listing of countries was referred to as the Failed State Index.

but have little power or authority to act. Important early examples of international organizations that fit this description are the International Telegraphic Union (1865), the Universal Postal Union (1874), and the International Labor Organization (1930).

This view is changing. Member states still retain sovereignty, but it is increasingly recognized that international organizations often do have the power and authority to influence state behavior and change international norms in three ways:[12]

1. They offer a forum for harmonizing policies. Standardizing rules, procedures, technical requirements, health and safety policies, and other areas of common interest reduces the level of foreign intrusion into states, decreases the political and financial costs of globalization, and allows states to move forward in modifying policies from a common base.

2. International organizations sort through the abundance of information that exists today and allow states to quickly and economically obtain the expertise and skills necessary to operate in a globalized setting.

3. International organizations can serve as a mechanism of enforcement. Most commonly this function is accomplished through a strategy of "naming and shaming," in which state violations of commonly accepted international policies and standards are publicly identified and criticized.

The number of international organizations has grown dramatically over the past century. Just prior to the outbreak of WWI there were 49 international organizations. In 1951 there were 123. By 2015 that number had grown to 273. Behind these numbers is a great deal of variation. At a most basic level, international organizations can be distinguished from one another on the basis of two dimensions: membership and range:

- **Membership**. Some international organizations have universal membership, so all states are eligible to join (although they may have to meet membership requirements and conditions). Membership in others is limited, typically to certain regions.
- **Range**. Some international organizations focus on a small number of challenges, examining one or only a few policy areas. The agendas of others cover a wide range of policy problems.

Combinations of these two dimensions result in four basic types of international organizations: Universal membership and general-purpose organizations (the United Nations); universal membership and limited purpose (the World Trade Organization); limited membership and general purpose (the African Union); and limited membership and limited purpose (NATO). Regardless of the organization's form, questions of state sovereignty are ever present. The Theory Spotlight provides an overview of strategies advanced by integration theory for addressing this issue. The rest of this section introduces several of the most significant international organizations and their roles in international politics.

The United Nations

With 193 members, the **United Nations (UN)** is the world's largest and most widely recognized international governmental organization (IGO). Its agenda covers virtually the entire spectrum of contemporary problems facing states, as well as those problems that have endured for generations. The UN's most prominent functions are maintaining peace and security, promoting human rights, furthering economic development, protecting the environment, and responding to humanitarian crises.[13]

The UN is not the first effort at creating an international organization with universal membership that is focused on maintaining global peace and security. The League of Nations was created in 1921 at the Paris Peace Conference that ended WWI. Its peace-promoting efforts were centered on two principles: respect for the territorial integrity and political independence of other states, and collective security. According to the League of Nations, an act of aggression by one state against another was considered an act of aggression against all. All members of the League of Nations were expected to collectively counter this aggression through means such as economic sanctions and—if necessary—military action.

The League of Nations failed to prevent a breakdown of the international order in the 1930s and stop the onset of WWII. Two points of weakness in its organization and operation attracted the attention of the states that created the UN:

- **The "empty chair problem."** The League was unable to get key states to join and remain members. The United States never joined. The Soviet Union did not join until

United Nations
(UN) An international
organization founded
in 1945 that provides
a forum for members
to discuss shared
concerns and under
certain circumstances
take action to address
global problems.

THEORY SPOTLIGHT

Integration Theory

The relationship between states and international organizations is fraught with potential problems. From a realist perspective, states continue to be the dominant actors in international politics. They join international organizations to promote their interests but retain sovereignty to avoid being forced to adopt policies that are not in their national interest. From a liberal perspective, international organizations are important actors in their own right. Not only do they help states achieve their goals, but they have the power to guide the direction of international politics down a more cooperative path. So it is vital that strong international organizations be created and that states participate in them. Because the economic structuralism perspective holds that states are controlled by capitalists and pursue wealth it sees international organizations as exploitive and used to perpetuate states' global dominance.

These different perspectives on the relationship between states and international organizations raise two questions. First, what is the best way to bring together separate states under a common authority? Second, how much authority should be given to the larger organization? Should it be an international organization in which states retain sovereignty or a supranational organization that requires states to give up all or part of their sovereignty? The EU, a supranational organization, is universally considered to be the most successful regional economic organization. From the outset, many saw the ultimate objective of European cooperation as the creation of a United States of Europe.

Integration theory proposes several strategic options for how to effectively bring states together into a larger political unit.

- **Federalism.** This approach starts with the premise that some form of political unity must precede economic, social, and cultural integration. Only a frontal assault on state sovereignty will provide the momentum needed to overcome states' inevitable resistance to loss of power to a larger political unit, make it possible to create a common culture, and provide economic benefits that will promote cooperation.
- **Functionalism.** This approach gives priority to economic integration. Rather than create a larger

1934 and was expelled in 1939. Germany was a member from 1926 to 1933. Japan withdrew from the League in 1933. Italy left in 1937.

- **The concept of collective security**. For a collective security system to work, the aggressor must be identified in a timely fashion and all states must respond in an agreed-upon manner regardless of the identity of the aggressor. Neither requirement is easily met. Aggression is not always clear cut nor is it always carried out by military means. Terrorism and cyber-attacks are cases in point. States do not view all other states in equal terms. Some are allies; some are enemies. In addition, policy-makers are often reluctant to commit themselves in advance to an automatic response. Prudence dictates caution and an exit strategy.

The UN Charter was signed in San Francisco on June 25, 1945. The United Nations formally came into existence in October after all five permanent members of the Security Council and one-half of the other 51 founding members ratified the agreement. The UN

Ton Koene / Alamy Stock Photo

A political protest at an EU summit meeting.

areas to be integrated because of their political or economic importance and ability to create spillover (bring additional economic areas forward to be integrated).

The EU has travelled a neofunctionalist path that began with the creation of the European Coal and Steel Community (ECSC) by six states as a way to avoid the outbreak of another war in Europe and moved forward to the signing of the Maastricht Treaty and the creation of a continent-wide currency. However, challenges remain. In terms of federalism, the EU has created only "one-half of a house." There is a common currency but not a common banking system. In terms of neofunctionalism, elites may have transferred their loyalties to the EU, but many citizens remain nationalists.

political unit from scratch, functionalism seeks to make sovereignty irrelevant by involving states' economies in a cooperative series of economic ventures that they will find it difficult if not impossible to escape. The ultimate goal is not a larger state but the creation of a web of regional and international organizations.

- **Neofunctionalism**. This option differs from functionalism in two ways: (1) It seeks to create a larger political unit, leading some to describe it as federalism in functionalist clothing. (2) Where functionalism sees integration as the natural result of the interaction of economic activities, neofunctionalism deliberately identifies economic

Think about It

1. Which of the three theories presented here (realism, liberalism, and economic structuralism) best captures the relationship between states and international organizations?
2. Which of the three options presented here (federalism, functionalism, and neofunctionalism) is most likely to succeed?

is not just a single organization. It is a complex system made up of different types of organizations that are assigned different tasks and have different operating procedures (see Figure 3.1). A helpful approach to understanding the UN system is to break it down into three different United Nations:[14]

1. The first UN is the most visible part of the UN system. Here, member states exercise their sovereignty to protect their own interests and act together to promote the global interest. It is a political arena.
2. The second UN is the bureaucratic core of the UN. It is made up of the operating institutions of the UN such as the Economic and Social Council, the International Court of Justice, and the secretariat.
3. The third UN is the least visible; it cannot be found on UN organizational charts and is not officially part of the UN. This UN is made up of nongovernmental organizations, multinational corporations, individuals, independent commissions, and

Figure 3.1 United Nations Organizational Chart.

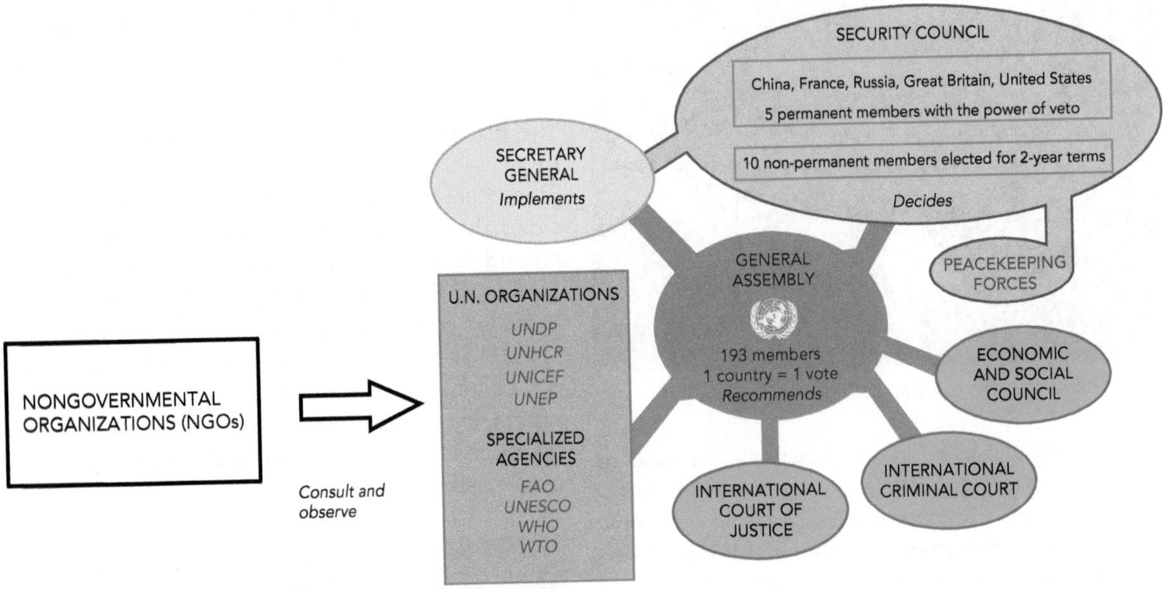

others. Members of the third UN lobby the first and second UNs to adopt policies they favor, provide expertise and information for policy decisions, and sometimes act as subcontractors for the UN in carrying out policy decisions. Some 4,000 NGOs currently have observer or consultative status with the UN, which allows them to participate in international conferences. The General Assembly and Security Council have also granted observer status and informal access through consultative groups to a limited number of nongovernmental organizations (NGOs).

NGOs will be discussed in the next section on non-state actors. This section concentrates on the first and second UNs.

The two core institutions of the first UN are the General Assembly and the Security Council. The General Assembly is the legislative body of the UN to which all member states belong and in which each has a single vote. The General Assembly is not free to do as it wishes. The UN Charter restricts it from making decisions that are binding on members, it cannot make any recommendations on issues that are before the Security Council, and it cannot intervene in the domestic affairs of member states. The General Assembly expresses its position on issues in one of three ways:

1. It may pass a resolution that calls upon members to adopt certain policies. One of the most controversial UN resolutions is Resolution 242 that condemns Zionism and likens it to racism.
2. It can pass a declaration, or statement of principle. Among the most notable declarations was the 1948 Declaration on Human Rights and the 1976 Declaration on the New International Economic Order.

3. It can pass a convention or international agreement that then goes to member governments for ratification. One of the UN's more significant conventions was the 1996 Comprehensive Test Ban Treaty.

According to the UN charter, the Security Council has jurisdiction over economic and military sanctions, but it must rely on UN members to enforce its decisions. The Security Council has representatives from fifteen states, five of which (the P-5) are permanent members and have veto power: the United States, Russia, China, France, and Great Britain. These states were the "winners" in WWII. Granting them veto power effectively removes the UN from collective security activities; it guarantees that the UN cannot create economic or military actions that can be used against these five states. Disputes among them are to be settled outside the UN. The remaining states are elected for a two-year term. The seats are allocated to different geographic regions with the understanding that states from these regions will select the delegates; the General Assembly is expected to recognize their choices and vote for their seating on the Security Council.

Some 41,000 professionals and support staff work in the UN Secretariat in New York City and around the world, forming the foundation on which the second UN is built. The second UN does far more than simply administer policies determined by the first UN. It also acts independently to influence member states and global policy positions. At the top of the bureaucracy of the second UN is the Secretary General. The first two Secretaries General—Trygve Lie of Norway, and Dag Hammarskjold of Sweden—came from neural European states. Since then they have come from non-European developing countries. Nominated by the Security Council and approved by the General Assembly, the Secretary General may serve two five-year terms. The UN Charter places the Secretary General in a challenging role. On the one hand, he or she is authorized to bring to the attention of the Security Council "any matter" that may threaten the maintenance of international peace and security. On the other hand, she or he must retain the support of the five permanent members of the Security Council. In 1996 the United States opposed the reelection of Boutros Boutros-Ghali as Secretary General, so Kofi Annan was elected to the position instead. As one commentator notes, the permanent members of the Security Council have clearly preferred someone who is more of a secretary who takes orders than a general who gives them.

The Economic and Social Council (ECOSOC) is another key bureaucratic actor in the second UN. Established in 1945 with eighteen members, its governing body now includes representatives from fifty-four states. As in the Security Council, seats are apportioned on a regional basis and elected by the General Assembly. ECOSOC has dual roles: (1) a forum for discussing pressing international economic and social issues; and (2) coordinator of the activities of UN agencies and organizations operating in the areas of social, health, economic, and human rights policies. The ECOSOC acts primarily through decisions and resolutions that are nonbinding on member states and specialized agencies.

The ECOSOC faces a daunting task. Most directly under its control are a series of regional and functional commissions and councils, including the Commission on the Status of Women and the Economic Commission for Africa. It is also expected to coordinate autonomous organizations such as the United Nations Children's Fund (UNICEF), the UN High Commissioner for Refugees (UNHCR), the World Food Council, and the United Nations Conference on Trade and Development (UNCTAD). Even further removed from its immediate control are specialized UN agencies with membership that is technically independent of UN membership, including the World Health Organization (WHO), the United Nations Educational, Scientific, and Cultural Organization (UNESCO), and the International Monetary Fund (IMF).

The International Court of Justice (ICJ) is another important organization of the second UN. It developed from the similarly named Court of International Justice that was established by the League of Nations in 1921, which was never formally part of the League. Because the ICJ is part of the UN system, member states are automatically granted membership. The ICJ is composed of fifteen judges elected for nine-year terms by votes of the Security Council and the General Assembly. A state has the right to add a justice if it is part of a case being heard and there is not a judge from its country seated on the court.

The ICJ has two main roles: (1) it is the constitutional court of the UN; (2) it is a place where states can take their disputes to be settled. ICJ decisions are nonbinding. States voluntarily take issues to the ICJ and abide by its decisions. In a break with the US experience where the Supreme Court cannot issue advisory opinions, the ICJ can be asked to do so. From 1946 to 2015, 161 cases were brought to the ICJ. Twenty-six times it was asked for an advisory opinion. In a much publicized 2008 case, Serbia asked the ICJ to provide an advisory opinion on the legality of Kosovo's unilateral declaration of independence. Not long after the fall of the Soviet Union, Yugoslavia began to disintegrate. Serbia was the last remaining part of Yugoslavia and sought to prevent Kosovo from becoming an independent state. The resulting civil war ended only after a NATO intervention in response to acts of genocide committed by Serbia against Kosovars. In 2010 the ICJ concluded that Kosovo's declaration of independence did not violate international law, but the court sidestepped the more fundamental questions of sovereignty and self-determination presented in the case.

The International Monetary Fund (IMF)

The UN was not the only international organization created after WWII. A set of more specialized international organizations were created that were designed to prevent a reoccurrence of the breakdown in the international economic system that led to the Great Depression of the 1930s. Instead of working together to overcome their economic problems, states adopted a "beggar-thy-neighbor" mindset in which they sought to protect themselves by adopting protectionist policies that caused people in other countries to suffer. At a meeting in Bretton Woods, New Hampshire in 1944 forty-four countries came together and created the **International Monetary Fund (IMF)** and the International Bank for Reconstruction and Development (IBRD) which became known as the World Bank (see next section). A third organization, the International Trade

International Monetary Fund (IMF) An international organization that has primary responsibility for monetary stability.

Organization (ITO), was proposed but never came into existence due to opposition from the US Congress. Today, the World Trade Organization (WTO) plays the role the ITO had been intended to fulfill. A more in-depth discussion of the WTO's role in international relations can be found in Chapter 8.

The IMF was established with the primary goal of stabilizing the international monetary system by coordinating exchange rates and serving as the source of short-term loans for states with balance of payments problems. A *balance of payment problem* exists when a state consistently imports more goods than it exports, creating a deficit. Correcting the problem may require revaluation of currency, a move that not only affects the price of the goods being bought and sold in that country but also holds the potential for undermining international trade. If revaluation occurs too often, businesses would not be sure of the value of the currencies they were using to buy and sell goods.

Over time the IMF's role in preventing the breakdown of the international economic system has changed. A key factor prompting this change was states' accumulation of long-term debts that they had little if any hope of paying off. This raised the possibility of state bankruptcies and loan defaults. If this happened with any frequency, the large international banks that provided the loans might also go bankrupt. The IMF became both a mediator in negotiations between countries and banks on repayment terms and a source of emergency bailout funds. States had to comply with certain conditions in order to receive these loans, including the removal of government subsidies, the opening of markets to equal competition among foreign and local firms, privatization of state-owned firms, and cuts in government spending. Collectively these efforts were known as structural adjustment policies. They became a major point of conflict between the IMF and rich countries that provided the IMF with funds and the countries receiving financial aid.

The IMF includes 189 member states. Traditionally the managing director of the IMF has been from Europe, while the head of the World Bank has been from the United States. Developing countries led by the BRICS have called for change. Most of the money the IMF lends is provided by member countries. The amount is assigned on the basis of a quota system that reflects the state's relative size in the world economy. In 2016 this system provided the IMF with some $668 billion. That year the largest borrowers were Portugal, Greece, the Ukraine, and Pakistan. Voting in the IMF is largely based on the same quota system, with the number of votes based on size. Currently, the six countries with the most votes are the United States (16.73%), Japan (6.23%), China (6.16%), Germany (5.39%), France (4.09%), and the United Kingdom (4.09%). All other states have less than 4% of the vote each.

The World Bank

In contrast to the IMF's primary focus (stabilizing the international economic order), the focus of the International Bank for Reconstruction and Development (IBRD) or **World Bank** has been economic growth. The World Bank's current mission statement is to end extreme poverty and build shared prosperity. Its efforts have been marked by successes,

World Bank An international organization designed to provide states with an additional source of development funds beyond those that private banks could provide; also known as the International Bank for Reconstruction and Development (IBRD).

failures, and much controversy. Initially the World Bank's efforts were directed at rebuilding the war-torn economies of Europe. That challenge proved to be beyond its capacity. The primary recovery program for Europe became a US bilateral foreign aid program, popularly known as the Marshall Plan, in which the United States provided funding for recovery plans drawn up by European states.

In the 1960s the World Bank's focus shifted to promoting economic development outside Europe in what was then often referred to as the Third World. The initial emphasis was on funding large-scale infrastructure development projects such as airports and power plants. Such projects were seen as the foundations on which economic growth would take place, but governments in poor countries could not afford them. These governments' inability to deliver the promised economic growth, along with the continuing widespread poverty in these states, pressured the World Bank to alter its approach to emphasis on basic human needs. In the late 1970s its efforts were redirected toward providing better access to education, health care, and other public services as part of a *basic needs strategy*.

More recently, in 2016 the World Bank along with the IMF shifted its focus again; today it advocates policies designed to promote free market economies in a reaction to the Brexit vote (discussed in the Contemporary Perspective section at the end of this chapter) and the strong calls for protectionism that arose in the US presidential election. All 193 members of the UN are also members of the World Bank. Technically it is one of five lending agencies that collectively make up the World Bank Group. The World Bank's lending focus is on developing and transitioning countries. A second organization within the Group, the International Development Association, concentrates on proving aid to poorer countries that do not qualify for IBRD loans. The other three lending agencies concentrate on activities such as providing private firms with risk insurance and dispute resolution services to encourage them to invest in developing countries.

The World Bank shares many of the same operating principles as the IMF. Both rely heavily on money contributed by member states, but the World Bank also obtains money through international financial markets just like a government or business firm. Both have a weighted voting system based on financial contributions. In 2016 the six countries with the highest percentage of votes were the United States (16.28%), Japan (7.02%), China (4.53%), Germany (4.11%), the United Kingdom (3.85%), and France (3.85%). Both the World Bank and the IMF require the approval of a supermajority of 85% of the total votes to change the voting shares of member states, effectively giving the United States a veto over any change in voting power.

The World Trade Organization (WTO)

World Trade Organization (WTO) An international organization that has primary responsibility for managing international trade relations by establishing international rules for trade.

The third major universal-member economic international organization is the **World Trade Organization (WTO)**. An International Trade Organization (ITO) was proposed as part of the Bretton Woods system, and its charter was drawn up at a meeting in Havana in 1947–48. Concerned with protecting US sovereignty and control over trade policy, the US Congress never ratified the agreement, but it did ratify the *General Agreement on Trade and Tariffs (GATT)*. GATT was transformed from a temporary framework into the WTO, a permanent organization with the stated goal of reducing barriers to international trade. It did so through a series of eight negotiating rounds that spanned almost five decades, from 1947 to 1994.

GATT's ability to promote global free trade declined over time for two reasons:

1. **Decreasing importance of tariff barriers**. Nontariff barriers such as environmental and safety standards became an increasingly greater threat to free trade as rich countries relied on them heavily to protect domestic industries. GATT was unsuccessful in eliminating these nontariff barriers.

2. **Focus on manufactured goods**. Agreements could not be reached on trade in agricultural products or services, which were an increasingly vital part of global trade.

In 1995, as part of an agreement to address these issues, the World Trade Organization was established.

Since 2016, 164 countries have belonged to the WTO. The highest WTO decision-making body is the General Council. The WTO characterizes itself as providing a forum in which states can come together and formulate international trade policy. It follows the precedent set by GATT; decisions are made by consensus agreement, not by voting. Should a consensus prove to be beyond reach, the WTO conducts a vote based on a one-country–one-vote principle. The WTO also acts as a mediator to resolve disputes between states. Should mediation prove unsuccessful, the case is sent to the Dispute Settlement Body where a binding decision is made. Of the more than 500 cases that have been brought forward by states, the Dispute Resolution Board has issued some 350 rulings. The country judged to be in violation of WTO rules is expected to revise its policy or offer compensation. If it does not do so, the harmed state is allowed to take retaliatory action.

Regional Organizations

The immediate post-WWII period gave birth not only to important universal membership international organizations, but also prompted the emergence of regional organizations.[15] Three types of regional organizations have come to play significant roles in international relations:

1. **Regional security organizations**. The North Atlantic Treaty Organization (NATO) was established in 1949 and brought together the United States and its West European allies (for more on NATO, see Chapter 5). The Warsaw Pact was established in 1955 and was composed of the Soviet Union and its East European satellite states.

REGIONAL SPOTLIGHT

Association of Southeast Asian Nations (ASEAN)

Map 3.2 Map of Southeast Asia.

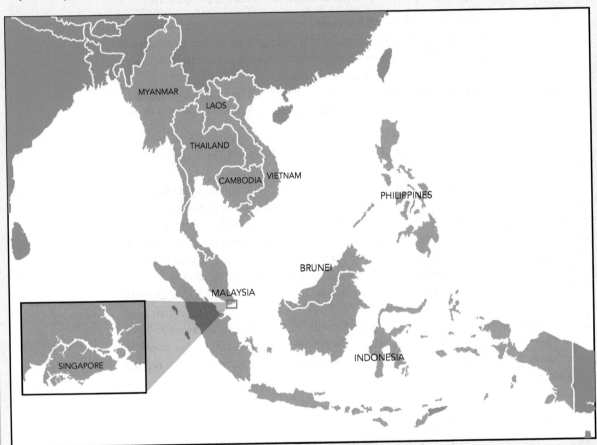

A notable non-European regional international organization is the Association of Southeast Asian Nations (ASEAN). Formed in 1967, it brought together five states (Indonesia, Malaysia, the Philippines, Singapore, and Thailand) to promote economic, political, and security cooperation. By the end of the 1990s its membership had doubled to ten with the addition of Brunei, Vietnam, Laos, Myanmar, and Cambodia.

As none of the founding members were regional military or economic powers, ASEAN remained on

Photo by Gunawan Kartapranata

The flags of the ASEAN member states in Jakarta, Indonesia.

the sidelines of Asian regional politics for much of its early history. It was not until the end of the Vietnam War and the end of the Cold War that ASEAN started to exercise a noticeable voice in the region. In 1976 the five ASEAN members signed a Treaty of Amity and Cooperation. In 1992 ASEAN created a regional free trade bloc among its members (the ASEAN Free Trade Area). In 1995 its members created a nuclear-free zone. ASEAN entered into an agreement with China, Japan, and South Korea in 1997 to create a consultative group known as ASEAN + 3 to promote greater economic cooperation in Asia. In 2005 ASEAN + 3 was expanded to ASEAN + 6 with the addition of as Australia, India, and New Zealand to the consultative group. Significantly, ASEAN + 6 emerged as part of the first East Asia Summit, held in 2005. ASEAN acts as host for this summit, which includes Russia and the United States as participants. At the second East Asian Summit held in 2006 the ASEAN + 6 group began to move forward in its efforts to create a Regional Comprehensive Economic Partnership (RCEP) that would unite members in an Asian free trade zone.

ASEAN's expanded focus has not been without controversy. Three issues stand out:

1. **China's aggressive policy in the South China Sea**. China, Brunei, Malaysia, Vietnam, and the Philippines all hold conflicting sovereignty claims over parts of the South China Sea.
2. **Human rights**. Some member states, including the Philippines, Cambodia, and Myanmar, have carried out repressive human rights policies against their own citizens.
3. **Free trade**. India would be a major force in the RCEP, but it has been reluctant to engage in across-the-board tariff reductions.

Two factors are often cited as complicating ASEAN's ability to respond to these and other policy challenges. The first is its decision-making model, which stresses informal consultations, avoiding positions that embarrass other members, and nonconflictual problem solving. While some see this as consistent with Asian cultural norms, others see it as driving ASEAN to adopt lowest-common-denominator policies that have little chance of succeeding. The second factor is that, in contrast to forward-looking European regionalism, ASEAN regionalism is reactionary. Major steps are taken only in response to regional crises. ASEAN was created in response to the Vietnam War, ASEAN + 3 was created in response to the Asian currency crisis, and RCEP was initiated in response to the US-sponsored Trans Pacific Partnership. This reactive approach limits ASEAN's ability to formulate creative policy initiatives.

Think about It

1. What should be the goal of regionalism? Can reactive regionalism succeed in bringing this about?
2. Which of the three issues areas where conflict exists presents the greatest challenge to reactive regionalism?

2. **Regional economic organizations**. The most important example, again found in Europe, is the Common Market (EU). Its origin was chronicled in the opening to this chapter.

3. **Multipurpose institutions**. Prominent examples include the Organization of American States (OAS; founded in 1948), the Organization of African Unity (OAU; founded in 1963 but disbanded and replaced by the African Union in 2002), and the League of Arab States (also known as the Arab League; founded in 1945). These three multipurpose regional organizations have had varied histories. The United States has dominated the OAS and used it as a foreign policy instrument to keep communism out of Latin America. The OAU and Arab League might be best described as tools of the weak in the world of the strong as they seek to bring domestic and international stability into parts of the world market disrupted by superpower intervention and weak state governments.[16] Another important regional organization is theAssociation of Southeast Asian Nations (ASEAN). Its history and development are presented in the Regional Spotlight.

The movement away from intense competition toward détente between the United States and Soviet Union during the Cold War and the subsequent collapse of the Soviet Union and end of the Cold War spurred another round of regional organizational growth. More specialized regional organizations have emerged, such as the Economic Community of West Africa (ECOWAS), the Southern Common Market (MERCOSUR), the Southern African Development Community (SADC), and the Organization for Security and Cooperation in Europe (OSCE). In addition, multipurpose regional organizations have expanded. The principal concern of the African Union and its predecessor the OAU was economic development issues, but it now devotes increasing attention to resolving regional military conflicts. The OAS has become actively involved in protecting human rights and promoting democracy. ASEAN has taken an active role in peacekeeping efforts, most notably in Cambodia. Specialized regional organizations are also going down this path. The OSCE has added a conflict prevention focus to its original agenda, which centered on arms control and human rights.

In the past international politics was dominated by states acting alone, in combination with other states, or through international organizations. Today, another type of actor is important: non-state actors. By definition, they are individuals or groups that act outside of the formal control of governments.

NON-STATE ACTORS

A wide variety of non-state actors are now active in international politics. In this section three of the most prominent non-state actors are highlighted: nongovernmental organizations, multinational corporations, and terrorist groups. All three have the ability to influence the outcome of events in international politics.

Nongovernmental Organizations (NGOs)

Even more invisible than international and regional organizations in traditional think-ing about international politics are **nongovernmental organizations (NGOs)**, which are private, independent, not-for-profit organizations. Like other international organi-zations, NGOs have increased dramatically in number, from 170 on the eve of WWI, to 832 in 1951, to more than 3,200 today. NGOs are particularly active in four broad policy areas: humanitarian affairs, human rights, conflict resolution, and development.[17] Each type of NGO faces serious dilemmas in carrying out its activities.

> **Nongovernmental organizations (NGOs)** Voluntary, nonprofit organizations that operate indepen-dently of governments with the general pur-pose of bringing about progressive changes in international politics.

The activities of humanitarian NGOs can be grouped into two broad areas: humanitarian relief and recovery assistance. Humanitarian relief efforts are pictured as short-term, emergency operations that are nonpolitical in nature. The mission is to save lives. Recovery relief is seen as a long-term undertaking in which political consid-erations play a large role. Decisions must be made about how to spend funds and what projects to pursue. Traditionally, relief and recovery are seen as two very distinct policy areas, but in reality they are closely related. Decisions made in short term humanitar-ian relief undertakings often have serious long-term consequences for recovery policy. For example, giving aid to all who enter refugee camps potentially provides support both for those fleeing a conflict and for those who were carrying out the violence. As a result, refugee camps risk becoming militarized, and the good intentions of NGO work-ers become suspect.

A dilemma faced in the second area of NGO activity, promoting and protecting basic human rights, is the relationship between peace and justice. Peace entails an end to vio-lence, but justice requires more than that. It requires identifying what happened and who was responsible, and ultimately bringing together all those affected. Pursuing jus-tice greatly complicates the peace-building process and its goal of ending violence, but it may be necessary in order for peace to last.

Those NGOs involved in conflict resolution, either as mediators in an ongoing conflict or as promoters of preventive measures to stop the outbreak of violence, face disagreement about their degree of involvement in conflict resolution. Superfi-cial involvement may prevent valuable conflict resolution skills from being brought to bear and allow ongoing tension to fester. Overly deep involvement may undercut the authority and legitimacy of existing political institutions, undermining their long-term ability to govern and raising the possibility of short-term backlashes against the NGOs.

NGOs involved in development seek to bring about political, economic, and social change by adopting one of three roles:

1. Implementers of change that mobilize resources and provide people with the neces-sary goods and services to bring about change.
2. Catalysts of change that inspire change by providing new approaches to development.
3. Partners of change that work with individuals, other NGOs, international organiza-tions, and governments to promote change.

No matter which role they adopt, the ultimate challenge facing these types of NGOs is answering the following question: development for whom?

Regardless of the primary nature of their activity in international relations, NGOs face a common set of issues, two of which stand out:

- **Accountability**. At least in theory, governments are accountable to citizens and international organizations are accountable to states. To whom are NGOs accountable?
- **Expectations**. There was once a tendency to view NGOs as miracle workers able to achieve goals and objectives beyond the reach of states and international organizations, but this is no longer the case. Concerns about expectations move in two different directions: (1) The actions of NGOs may be questioned because they are seen as little more than instruments of neo-imperialism, imposing Western values on non-Western states and undermining local values. (2) Although NGOs may be well-intentioned, some question whether they do more harm than good.[18]

Multinational Corporations (MNCs)

multinational corporations (MNCs) Business firms that are head-quartered in one country but have sales, production, research, or resource extraction activities in others.

Multinational corporations (MNCs) businesses that control assets (manufacturing plants, mines, sales offices, investment offices, etc.) in two or more countries, also play an important role in international politics today. MNCs are not a new phenomenon. Their roots can be traced back to private business operations as the Hudson Bay Company, the Portuguese Mozambique Company, and the Dutch East India Company. The concessions granted by governments to these businesses often gave them significant powers. Its 1602 Charter authorized the Dutch East India Company to seize foreign ships, coin money, and establish colonies.

In 2017 the top ten Global 500 companies ranked by overall revenue are shown in Table 3.2. Approximately 75% of the Fortune Global 500 identify one of the following as their home country: the United States, China, Japan, France, Germany, and Great Britain. With some 6,370 retail outlets in twenty-six countries, Walmart International accounts for just over 25% of Walmart's profits. Of the approximately 4,000 Walmarts in Latin America, about 2,400 of them are in Mexico. State Grid, an electric company owned by the Chinese government, came into existence in 2002. It is the largest utility

TABLE 3.2 Top Ten Global 500 Companies (by Revenue)	
1. Walmart (United States)	6. Volkswagen (Germany)
2. State Grid (China)	7. Royal Dutch Shell (Netherlands)
3. Sinopec Group (China)	8. Berkshire Hathaway (United States)
4. China National Petroleum	9. Apple (United States)
5. Toyota (Japan)	10. Exxon Mobil (United States)

company in the world; in 2007 it won the rights to run the Philippines power grid until 2058, and it owns portions of three power grids in Australia.

The Global 500 rankings illustrate how quickly the fate of an MNC can change. Chevron, General Motors, Phillips 66, and Ford were all in the top ten in 2015. Exxon Mobil was second. Berkshire Hathaway was fourth in 2015, fell off the top ten list in 2016, and climbed back onto the list in 2017. BP did not make the top ten in 2015, it was tenth in 2016, and it fell off the list again in 2017. Changes in ranking also provide a great deal of information about the changing nature of the global economy. As measured by the UN Conference on Trade and Development in 1990, 75% of the investments of the top one hundred MNCs were in the manufacturing sector, 14% were in services, and 11% were in agriculture. In 2015 the split was 55% manufacturing, 34% services, and 11% agriculture.[19]

From a strictly economic perspective, the primary motivating factor behind the global involvement of MNCs is the pursuit of profit, which can take them in two directions:

1. Searching for markets to sell their goods and services or to acquire raw materials and natural resources.
2. Holding down transportation and production costs by setting up assembly facilities outside of the home state of the MNC that bring together raw materials and component parts before a product is sent to its ultimate destination for marketing.

The pursuit of profit by MNCs creates a dilemma for states. While MNCs bring added revenue and jobs, they also decrease control of the domestic marketplace. This may take the form of MNC pressure on the governments to adjust property rights, patent laws, labor practices, tax laws, or environmental regulations. MNCs may also urge governments to adjust their foreign policies by removing economic sanctions against states with which they seek to do business or to use military force to protect the MNCs' investments.

MNCs may also be motivated by other factors, especially when they are owned or heavily supported by governments, as has been the case with many Russian and Chinese firms. The primary goal of these MNCs can be access to new technologies, either through the acquisition of foreign companies or participation in foreign markets where these technologies are available. Under such circumstances an MNC is likely to be viewed more as a threat than as a stimulus to economic growth. A contemporary example is Huwei, a Chinese telecommunications company which sells products and services in more than 170 countries. The US has identified it as a significant national security threat and has tried to pressure allies not to allow Huawei to build their 5G networks.

Even when there are no direct connections between MNCs and their home governments, the firms can be viewed with suspicion and distrust by host states. The principal concern here is a long-standing one that predates globalization. MNCs are seen as agents of capitalism and Western values that will distort or destroy the culture, society, and political vales of the host country. Dependency theory takes the threat posed by MNCs one step further, arguing that the end result of capitalism's capture of underdeveloped areas is not economic growth but perpetual subjugation and exploitation of the periphery by capitalist core areas. According to this view, the colonial holdings that the major powers of the world historically used to rule over the periphery have been replaced by MNCs and communication technologies, which perpetuate a system of neocolonial dominance.

Terrorist Groups

terrorism Violence employed for purposes of political intimidation and the achievement of political goals.

Terrorism means different things to different people. The definition used here is that **terrorism** is violence for purposes of political gain. Viewed in this way, terrorism is not linked to a specific ideology or strategy. It can be carried out in a variety of ways and for a variety of purposes. It is also not limited to acts by non-state actors. This definition allows acts of violence by governments against their own citizens to be categorized as terrorism. This expansive view is not universal; most accounts of international terrorism focus largely on non-state actors and treat violence by governments against citizens as domestic politics and violations of human rights. It also can be applied to government agencies such as in 2019 when the Trump Administration designated Iran's Revolutionary Guard a foreign terrorist group. The more limited perspective on terrorist groups as non-state actors will be used here.

Before examining these issues it is important to understand that terrorism is not an exclusively modern phenomenon. Today's international system is experiencing the fourth wave of terrorism since the beginning of the twentieth century. Each of the preceding three waves lasted a generation. If that pattern continues, today's fourth wave of terrorism will not subside until around 2025. The first wave, associated with anarchism, began in Russia as a response to political and economic reforms undertaken by the Tsar. The second wave of terrorism had an anticolonial focus; it began in the 1920s and ended in the 1960s. Among the major second-wave terrorist movements were the Irish Republican Army (IRA), the Irgun that sought to create an independent Israel, and the National Liberation Front in Algeria. The third wave, set in motion by the Vietnam War, was made up of Marxist groups who opposed the war and separatist forces such as the Palestine Liberation Organization who sought self-determination for minorities that they felt were trapped inside larger states. Today's fourth wave dates back to 1979 and has two defining characteristics: (1) rooted in Islam, it has a religious base; (2) it embraces strategies that produce mass casualties. Earlier waves of terrorism focused largely on assassinating key individuals or the symbolic killing of relatively small numbers of individuals.

Terrorist groups have proven to be highly adaptive organizations with varying internal structures and relationships with governments.[20] The relationship between terrorist groups and governments takes one of three different patterns:

- **Non-state supported**. These terrorist groups operate autonomously and receive no significant support from any government.
- **State supported**. These groups generally operate independently but do receive support from one or more governments.

- **State directed**. These groups act on behalf of governments, from whom they receive significant intelligence, logistical, and operational support but no official contact.

The internal structures of terrorist groups have changed and evolved over time. Like those active today, early terrorist groups were also organized into small groups of individuals that were referred to as cells. Within the broader terrorist organization cells were linked together in a hierarchical fashion and operated with little to no contact with other cells in order to protect the larger terrorist organization against infiltration. The cells were expected to carry out their orders with little freedom to decide how and when to act. Terrorist groups using this traditional hierarchical cell structure include the Irish Republican Army, the Red Brigades in Italy, the Palestine Liberation Organization, and the ETA (a Basque separatist group).

More recently, terrorist groups began organizing themselves in a less hierarchical fashion to provide their cells with greater autonomy and flexibility in carrying out the goals of the terrorist group leadership. For example, Al Qaeda is organized in a series of concentric circles. At the core is Al Qaeda central, its senior leadership. The next circle includes Al Qaeda affiliates, groups associated with Al Qaeda that operate in different countries and locales, largely in Africa and the Middle East. Prominent examples include Al Qaeda in the Arabian Peninsula (AQAP), Al Qaeda in the Islamic Maghreb (AQIM), Al Shahab in East Africa, and smaller groups in Afghanistan. The third circle is comprised of Al Qaeda locals, often referred to as lone wolves or wolf packs. These individuals or groups have little or no direct connection with Al Qaeda but are drawn to its ideology and practices. At one point Al Qaeda had more than 1,000 pages of training manuals, global training camps, and a library of training videos, but these individuals did not receive instructions from Al Qaeda in terms of specific terrorist targets or projects.

Today it appears that another form of organization is emerging, in which the central leadership of terrorist groups act more as "inspirational commanders" than as tacticians or strategists. This most recent organizational pattern is sometimes referred to as *devolution*.[21] The core terrorist leadership group largely serves as a gateway for extremists to find others who share their cause. This organizational model stresses the role of social media in information-sharing and in its ability to bring like-minded individuals together in small groups to advance local causes. Over time these local groups become more and more detached from and more conspiratorial in nature than the group that inspired them. In the end these lone wolves or wolf packs may or may not invoke the name of the larger terrorist group in carrying out their terrorist acts. For governments the end result is just as challenging as more conventional organizations. These micro-targets are capable of having a macro-impact.

Regardless of their structure or affiliation, terrorist groups have tended to pursue a limited set of goals.[22] Three are especially important for international politics:

1. **Regime change**. Bringing a new government to power is a goal frequently pursued by Marxist groups.

2. **Territorial change**. Here the goal is for a portion of the state to secede to become a new state or part of another state. The Tamil Tigers seek to gain independence for the Tamil areas of Sri Lanka. Kurdish groups seek to unite Kurdish sections of several Middle East states into a single Kurdistan.
3. **Foreign policy change**. The primary goal of Al Qaeda is to end US support for Israel.

CONTEMPORARY PERSPECTIVE:
Leaving the EU: Brexit

By 2007 membership in the European Union (EU) had grown from the original six states that made up the European Economic Community to twenty-eight states, a testament to the economic success of the EU. However, growth also brought increased challenges to European unity as member countries became increasingly diverse in their size, level of economic development, historical backgrounds, social and cultural traditions, and political systems. The most recent of these challenges and the most threatening to the future of the European Union is Brexit, Great Britain leaving the European Union.

British Prime Minister David Cameron had promised a referendum on EU membership in 2013 as part of a strategy to quiet Conservative Party members of Parliament who had become increasingly vocal in their opposition to EU membership and to counter

Map 3.3 Current Twenty-Eight-Member European Union.

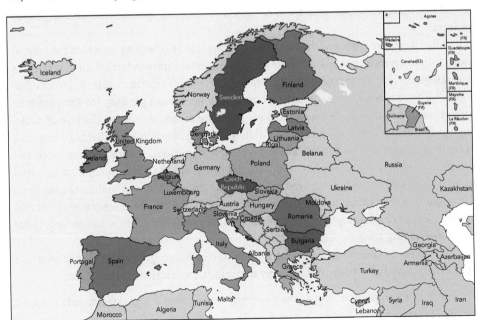

the growing influence of the right-wing anti-EU UK Independence Party. In a national referendum in June 2016 52% of British voters supported British exit from the EU (Brexit). Commentators described this unexpected result as a "seismic event." Cameron resigned the following day. His successor, Theresa May, promised to abide by the outcome and arrange for Brexit.

The Brexit vote revealed the existence of a divided British society. Support was strongest among older voters, working-class voters, the economically disadvantaged, and those who had left school without a diploma. As one observer put it, Brexit supporters lived in areas where jobs are hard to find, easy to lose, and badly paid; where affordable housing is scarce. Those opposed to Brexit tended to be young and highly educated who valued the ability to travel freely throughout the EU.

No country has ever left the EU. In March 2017 Prime Minister May set in motion a two-year deadline to negotiate Brexit before Great Britain's exit officially was set to take place on March 29, 2019. The first EU summit on establishing guidelines for exit was held the following month, and British-EU Brexit talks began two months later, in June 2017. For both sides the central issue was whether to push for a hard or soft Brexit. Under a hard exit Great Britain would unilaterally leave the EU. It would depart from the single EU market and retake full national control over its laws, borders, and immigration policy. Under a soft exit Great Britain would remain in some EU activities but not others. EU negotiators faced their own dilemmas about how to move forward. Fears existed that providing Britain with too soft an exit would lead other states to set up "copy-cat" referendums to exit the EU altogether or as a means of gaining leverage over EU decision-making.

In November 2018 details of the Brexit agreement that had been under negotiation for almost two years were made public, setting off a political crisis that led to postponing the Brexit vote in Parliament scheduled for December. Nearly 600 pages in length, the soft exit agreement that was described in media reports as a half-in–half-out version of Brexit. It established (1) the post-Brexit rights of EU citizens in Great Britain and of British citizens on the continent, (2) a financial settlement with the EU to meet agreed commitments, and (3) keeping in place a border-free frontier between the Republic of Ireland and Northern Ireland. Additionally a backstop agreement or insurance plan was reached which comes into effect if a free trade agreement is not finalized within a two-year transition period after Brexit. It would keep Great Britain in the European customs union, and Northern Ireland would abide by all EU economic regulations.

The political battle over Brexit reached new heights as 2018 drew to a close. Two cabinet members, including the foreign secretary, resigned; the House of Commons held May's government in contempt of Parliament for failing to provide it with all of the information available on the Brexit agreement; and May survived a Conservative Party no-confidence vote by a 200–117 margin. Further complicating the outcome of the political debate in Great Britain was the advisory decision of the European Union's highest court that Great Britain could unilaterally reverse its decision to leave the EU.

March 29, 2019, came and went with no decision on how to proceed. May lost three exit strategy votes in parliament. After the third vote the EU extended the departure date to May 22. It scheduled a summit meeting to review the situation and gave Great Britain until April 12 to present a plan for leaving the EU. At that meeting it extended the Brexit deadline until October 31, 2019.

Brexit was not the first sovereignty challenge to face the EU, nor is it likely to be the last to surface in international politics. In 2009 the EU faced the possibility of Grexit (Greece exit). Greece faced a financial crisis that raised the prospect that it might default on its loans and be forced to leave the EU if it did not receive financial help from the EU. Other examples of sovereignty challenges include the Spanish province of Catalonia, which voted for independence in 2017, as did the Kurds in an oil rich region of Iraq the same year.[23]

LOOKING TO THE FUTURE

This section highlights three sovereignty challenges and responses that may play important roles in international relations in the future: the definition of sovereignty; the perceived need to reform the UN Security Council; and the need to increase the efficiency of cooperation among the large number of actors in international politics.

Toward a "New Sovereignty"

For centuries the concept of sovereignty has been the foundation for conducting international politics. It allowed a clear definition of states as autonomous actors whose decisions were not to be determined beyond their borders by states or other actors. Such actors may threaten, offer rewards and promises, or use other overt means to influence decisions, but only the state's own government has internationally recognized decision-making power.

The representative of China speaks during a session of the UN Security Council.

Luiz Rampelotto / EuropaNewswire / Dpa picture alliance / Alamy Stock Photo

Is this approach to conducting international politics still appropriate in an era of globalization? Anne-Marie Slaughter and other international relations scholars argue that it is not.[24] They call for moving away from viewing sovereignty as the power to be autonomous and act without the interference of others toward the capacity to participate in international collaborative efforts and influence decisions.

Two aspects of globalization are seen as particularly important to this revised definition:

1. It is increasingly impossible for states to accomplish both foreign policy and domestic policy goals without the cooperation of other states. It is ineffective to try and act alone to promote economic growth, control immigration, protect the environment, or end the arms race.
2. It is increasingly impossible to stop other countries from interfering in a state's decision making process. One example is Russian hacking in the 2016 US presidential election. It has also become clear that domestic socioeconomic and political conditions in one state may create serious harm for other states. These include terrorism, mass famine, natural disasters, disease epidemics, and civil wars. Cooperation with other states to stop interference or to interfere collectively in another state has become a foreign policy necessity.

Moving to a new definition of sovereignty will not end debate over what it means to be sovereign. One of the most fundamental tensions in the traditional view of sovereignty is the distinction between sovereignty as a legal concept and sovereignty as a practical matter. The principle of sovereignty implies that all states are equal in their autonomy, but in reality states are unequal in practice. Some states possess more of the military power required for autonomy. According to the revised definition, sovereignty resides in the process of cooperation among states, but not all states are equally capable of such cooperation. Some states possess more of the power resources needed to cooperate with other states to achieve their goals.

Reforming the UN Security Council

The changing nature of international politics has produced increasing pressure to reform the UN Security Council and make it more representative of the changing power structure in international politics and more attuned to regional perspectives. Two broad approaches have been proposed: alterations in membership and changes in veto power.

Several proposals have been put forward to change the members of the Security Council:

- Expand the number of permanent members. Most often mentioned are the Group of 4: Brazil, Germany, India, and Japan.
- Add more seats, increasing Security Council membership to as many as twenty-four. The new seats would be distributed on a regional basis to Africa, the Asia-Pacific, Europe, and the Americas.
- Give some states semi-permanent status.
- Allocate some Security Council seats on the basis of religion.

A second approach focuses on limiting the types of issues on which the P-5 can use their veto power. From 1946 to 2015 a total of 274 vetoes were cast. Russia (including the former Soviet Union) has exercised its veto power most frequently at 131 times. The United States did not exercise its veto power until the 1970s but has now done so 83 times.

Most frequently the United States has used its veto on resolutions related to the Middle East and the Arab-Israeli conflict. By 1955 Russia had used its veto 83 times to prevent UN action that harmed its interests in the early stages of the Cold War. Most recently, Russia, along with China, has used its veto on multiple occasions to prevent the UN from adopting resolutions on Syria.

One proposal for limiting the P-5's veto power, put forward by France in 2001 and still being negotiated, calls for banning a veto on issues involving mass-atrocity crimes. Almost seventy countries have expressed support for this proposal. Garth Evans, a former member of the Australian Parliament, identified a number of key elements that would be needed for this reform to be adopted:[25]

1. **Agreement on the definition of a mass atrocity crime**. A definition that is either too broad or too narrow would undermine the proposal.
2. **Verification**. There must be some way to verify that a mass-atrocity crime has taken place.
3. **Trigger mechanism**. There must be some agreed-upon mechanism to indicate that the P-5 could not exercise its veto, such as a vote by the General Assembly with support from all regions.
4. **Override**. Members of the P-5 would have to be given the right to use a veto if they felt their national interests were at stake. Evans suggests that, while possible, the use of a veto under such circumstances would be at significant political cost to the P-5 member.

The "Cherry-Picking" Problem

The increasing proliferation of global international organizations, regional international organizations, nongovernmental organizations, and multinational corporations presents the international community with a dilemma. On the one hand, this provides greater avenues for cooperation among international actors and makes it possible for more and more states to participate in cooperative efforts. The great powers would no longer be the only states in a position to organize and influence international politics. All of this is consistent with the idea of a new definition of sovereignty.

On other hand, it may actually make international cooperation more difficult. Instead of promoting cooperation, the constant creation of new platforms may merely result in an epidemic of cherry picking where states deliberately pick and choose ways to cooperate that benefit them the most and ignore others. There seems to always be another global or regional international organization, nongovernmental organization, or multinational organization seeking cooperation on a particular goal; if not, one can be created. International actors frustrated by one set of partners can always form another cooperative venture.

Related to the cherry-picking problem is the problem of responsibility. With so many actors involved in human rights, who is responsible for preventing human rights violations? Who among all of the actors is responsible for financing economic growth? Cooperation is far from automatic. Personalities, financial constraints, jurisdictional disputes, and policy disagreements are ever present and not easily overcome.

It is not always easy to tell whether cooperative ventures are really promoting cooperation or just adding another layer of complexity in seeking solutions to common problems. A frequently cited example is the UN Global Compact. Created in 1999, this information-sharing and discussion forum brings together global companies, labor organizations, national governments, civil society organizations, and cities to promote solutions to problems in the fields of human rights, the environment, labor, and corruption. Some 8,000 companies participate in the Compact. Advocates see it as an effective means of bringing together multinational corporations, which are often viewed as valuing profit over goals such as sustainable development. Critics argue that, because the compact is only a discussion forum and lacks any monitoring or enforcement powers, multinational companies can use it largely for public relations purposes, a strategy also known as "bluewash." In it MNCs take credit for global partnerships with international organizations that help create a positive image of them as good global citizens without really taking actions that help those in need.

One solution to the cherry-picking problem is for international and regional organizations to create regional centers that would bring together their expertise along with that of key nongovernmental organizations and multinational corporations.[26] Responsibilities could be shared, and activities could be coordinated from this enhanced platform. The centers would be positioned to study regional problems, distribute information in the region and across regions, and engage in activities such as early warning, promotion of regional economic growth, conflict mediation, and humanitarian assistance. The creation of regional centers would not end the problem of the proliferation of organizations but, if successful, it would privilege some over others, reducing the appeal of cherry picking.

Summary

- The growing importance of international organizations and nongovernmental actors has led many to question how sovereignty should be defined.
- The path from the Common Market to the European Union was marked by frequent tensions between states and international organizations.
- States are unequal and play different roles in international politics.
- International organizations are used by states to protect and promote their own interests but are also capable of acting independently from them to influence international politics.
- Three important types of non-state actors that are capable of influencing international politics are nongovernmental organizations, multinational corporations, and terrorist groups.

- Three important sovereignty challenges and responses involve the definition of sovereignty, reforms to the UN Security Council, and improvements in the basis for international cooperation.
- The current sovereignty challenges facing the EU in Grexit and Brexit illustrate the continuing tension between state sovereignty and international cooperation.

Key Terms

Fragile states *(64)*
Great powers *(62)*
International Monetary Fund (IMF) *(72)*
International organizations *(65)*
Middle powers *(63)*
Multinational corporations (MNCs) *(80)*

Nongovernmental organizations (NGOs) *(79)*
Sovereignty *(57)*
Terrorism *(82)*
United Nations (UN) *(67)*
World Bank *(73)*
World Trade Organization (WTO) *(74)*

Critical Thinking Questions

1. Was the effort to create the EU worth it? Did it create peace and prosperity in Europe?

2. Which of the labels used to define states is more important in international politics today: great powers or fragile states?

3. Are international organizations best seen as tools of their members or as independent actors?

4. Which of the non-state actors is most important for each of the following: realists, liberals, and economic structuralists?

5. Has the end point of European Union been reached?

6. Identify a future sovereignty challenge not discussed and suggest a response.

Practice and Review Online
http://textbooks.rowman.com/hastedt-felice

▲ People come out on the streets to assess the damage after a bombing in Homs, Syria. *Source:* Anas Alkharboutli / Picture-alliance / Dpa / AP Images

04

THE VALUES
CHALLENGE:
DECIDING WHAT
TO DO

POLITICAL SCIENTIST DAVID EASTON PROPOSED what has become one of the most enduring definitions of *politics*: the authoritative allocation of values.[1] What these values are and whose interests they serve continue to be debated. The standard answer in international relations is that the primary values are those that serve the national interest. Others argue that this answer does not rank the human interest or the global interest highly enough. To begin the examination of the role of values in international relations, this chapter opens with a review of the history of the Nansen Passport, one of the earliest attempts to address the question of how to respond to an international refugee crisis. The Nansen Passport highlights the inherent tensions found in refugee policy and many other areas of international politics: how to reconcile the conflicting claims to rights and responsibilities put forward by individuals in need and governments as well as establish a meaningful role and voice for the international community in setting standards.

With that historical perspective in mind, the definitions of the national, human, and global interest are examined. The chapter then turns to the ways in which societal and global influences can affect the definition of the national interest, along with an overview of the policy-making steps involved in moving from an idea to adopting a policy to evaluating that policy. Then it discusses the current situation of Syrian refugees fleeing to Europe and the problem of responding to refugee flows. The chapter then looks to the future by describing two challenges international actors face in defining their interests and some of the suggested responses, as well as the issues analysts face in studying how values are incorporated into foreign policies.

LEARNING OBJECTIVES

Students will be able to:

- Explain the conflict over values at the center of the disagreement over how to address the problem of Russian refugees that led to the Nansen Passport.
- Define the three basic categories of international politics values: the national interest, the human interest, and the global interest.
- Understand the underlying dynamics of two-level game policy-making in international politics.
- Compare and contrast the influence and roles of voting, interest groups, social movements, and the media on policy-making.
- Compare and contrast the influence of foreign lobbying and transnational advisory networks on policy-making.
- Identify the five steps that comprise the policy-making process.
- Understand the continuing role that values conflicts play in international refugee policy-making.
- Evaluate the potential contribution of three responses to the values challenge: finding the global voice, harmonizing interests, and picking a decision-making model.

HISTORICAL PERSPECTIVE:
The Nansen Passport

In November 1917 civil war erupted in Russia between the Bolsheviks (the Reds) and a loose alliance of monarchists, capitalists, and socialists referred to as the Whites. The Reds were led by Vladimir Lenin; the previous month Lenin had seized power from a provisional government created in February of 1917 when Tsar Nicholas II resigned, ending nearly two centuries of rule by the Russian monarchy. The Whites opposed the establishment of a communist state proposed by Lenin. The civil war continued until 1922 when the Reds triumphed and established the Union of Soviet Socialist Republics (USSR). The Russian civil war is widely considered to be the world's most deadly civil

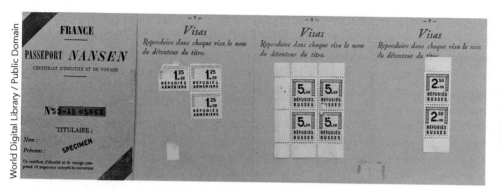

World Digital Library / Public Domain

The Nansen Passport was an international passport created in 1922 by the League of Nations that allowed people to cross borders in search of work and not be deported.

war. An estimated one-and-a-half million soldiers were killed and some eight million civilians died from armed attacks, famine, and disease. Another one to two million Russians, most of them affiliated with the Whites, fled the country, becoming refugees.

In April 1920, just three months after its founding, the League of Nations tasked Fridtjof Nansen to organize a repatriation program for approximately 500,000 people who had fled their homelands as a result of WWI. Nansen headed Norway's delegation to the League of Nations. As he searched for avenues to return these refugees to their homelands, Nansen accepted another assignment. In February 1921 the International Committee of the Red Cross (ICRC) contacted the League of Nations about the frightful living conditions and lack of legal protection of some 800,000 Russian refugees. In August 1921 Nansen became the League of Nation's High Commissioner for Russian Refugees, and his mandate was later extended to cover other refugee crises in Europe.

Nansen faced a complex set of obstacles. The Soviet government did not join the League of Nations, seeing it as a tool of capitalism. This perception was reinforced by the support given to the White forces by the United States, Great Britain, and other Western powers. Western nations also showed little interest in providing funds to help refugees because there had been little recovery from WWI's damage to their own economies. For many Russian refugees repatriation was not a viable option. Few desired to return, fearing political persecution and imprisonment. The Soviet government insisted on screening those seeking repatriation and blocked refugees deemed objectionable from returning. Finally, Lenin had revoked the Russian citizenship of those who had fled during the Russian civil war.

In the face of these obstacles, Nansen came to the conclusion that the solution to helping Russian refugees centered on their ability to travel and find work. Travel across international borders was all but impossible, since in a very real sense these Russians were "stateless." In March 1922 Nansen proposed that the League of Nations create an international passport that would allow its holder the right to cross borders in search of work and not be deported; this became known as the Nansen Passport. In July of 1922 sixteen states adopted the Nansen Passport at a League of Nations conference. More than fifty states eventually signed on and, over time, some 450,000 Nansen Passports were issued.[2]

Nansen did not receive a great deal of financial or political support from the League of Nations for his efforts, and he complained publicly about the discrimination facing the refugees. Countries were less interested in protecting refugees than in supporting their freedom of movement as a form of burden sharing. With the freedom to cross borders, no one country would have to bear the cost of supporting refugees who were unable to return home.

Among Nansen's actions was a 1928 agreement allowing the High Commissioner of Refugees' office to certify the status of individuals as refugees. This removed individual countries from involvement in this decision and enabled the direct involvement of an international organization in protecting human rights. Nansen also secured financial aid by issuing annual passport stamps to refugees who could afford payment. In 1922 Nansen was awarded the Nobel Peace Prize for his efforts.

During the 1930s the Nansen Passport system was overtaken by events. An increasing number of European states devised schemes to avoid giving asylum to Jews who were seeking to flee Germany. More broadly, aid to refugees was not seen as a humanitarian good; instead, refugees were perceived as unwanted economic migrants in an era of depression and high unemployment.

The Nansen Passport highlights a common situation inherent in international politics: no one set of values drives decisions; conflict between different values is always present. Two points of tension arose here. The first was the tension between the conflicting claims to rights and responsibilities put forward by governments versus individuals in need. The second was the challenge of establishing a meaningful role and voice for the international community in determining common values in a world dominated by states.

INTERNATIONAL POLITICS VALUES

While disagreement over what values should drive international politics is ever present, it generally centers on which of three different perspectives should be given priority. The first holds that the interests of states should be valued most highly. The second believes that the interests of individuals should guide decision-making. The third places greatest emphasis on the global interest. Each of these three perspectives is discussed below.

National Interest

It is hard to imagine an important foreign policy statement made by a government official in which frequent and impassioned reference is not made to "the national interest." The concept of the national interest is rarely defined. Instead, its meaning and importance to making foreign policy is taken for granted. Considerable disagreement exists over how to define the national interest. This section begins by examining the concept of national interest and then introduces its two major competitors as guides to foreign policy-making: the human interest and the global interest.

The classic statement on the national interest was put forward by Hans Morgenthau when he stated that "the national interest of peace-loving nations can only be defined in terms of national security, and national security must be defined in terms of national territory and its institutions." Thus defined, national interest is pursued, Morgenthau argued, by increasing one's own power relative to that of other nations.[3]

Interpretation of Morgenthau's statement has been the source of ongoing debate. Is the national interest an objective guide to action or a subjective call to action? If interpreted as an objective guide to action, foreign policies should flow logically from the national interest. This approach would not necessarily end debate over what to do or not do because policy-makers might misinterpret developments or lack enough information to make a judgment about the true meaning of a situation and its relevance to the national interest.

On the other hand, those who see the national interest as a subjective call to action argue that the concept is fundamentally ambiguous. According to this view, foreign policy should advance the interests of the state and not individuals, groups, or humanity as a whole; beyond that it explains very little. From this perspective the primary usefulness to policy-makers of the national interest is not in guiding action but in mobilizing the public to support a policy by rallying around the flag and putting differences aside. In either case, the concept of the national interest would provide a benchmark to use in decision-making.

A second debate is whether the national interest is fixed or evolving and changing over time. One example which illustrates the tension between these two positions. A September 1999 speech by UN Secretary General Kofi Annan addressed this issue in his annual report to the General Assembly. In it he asserted that "state sovereignty, in its most basic sense, is being redefined by the forces of globalization and international cooperation." He called for members of the UN to adopt "a new, more broadly defined, more widely conceived definition of national interest in the new century."[4] This call was met with a hostile reaction.

A third debate is over whether the national interest is best defined strictly in terms of zero-sum national security and power considerations or whether it should be expanded to include values, beliefs, and other foreign policy goals. Numerous frameworks have been used to prioritize foreign policy goals. Morgenthau used two categories: (1) interests that are indispensable for the national survival and (2) those that are desirable but should be pursued only under favorable circumstances. Today, frameworks tend to distinguish among three categories: (1) core objectives, (2) middle-range goals, and (3) long-term goals.[5]

The case for a narrow definition rests heavily on cost considerations. One of the great dangers of a broad definition of national security, according to those opposed to it, is *mission creep*, a situation where the goals and objectives of an organization keep expanding. This is common in peacekeeping operations where military forces take on responsibilities that were once carried out by diplomats and those working for humanitarian organizations. Since all foreign policy goals are costly, adding more goals to the list of national interest goals will mean that the pursuit of some true national security goals will be put off and delayed.

Supporters of the adoption of a broader definition of the **national interest** present the counter argument that security is itself a value. By only focusing on security, other important values are too easily ignored. Foremost among them are nonmilitary concerns such as environmental, health, democratization, and poverty issues. The addition of such concerns shifts attention away from the interests of the state to include the human interest of individuals and the global community.[6]

national interest The fundamental goals and objectives of a state's foreign policy; typically including physical survival, economic well-being, and preservation of the form of government.

Human Interest

human interest Values that promote the human condition; presented as an alternative to the national interest, which seeks to promote the global standing of states.

It is argued that changing the value focus from states to people, or the **human interest**, is necessary because the dynamics of international politics are far different today than in 1648 when the Treaty of Westphalia, which established the principle of state sovereignty, was signed. In today's international politics, intrastate violence and civil wars are far more common than wars between states, placing ever increasing numbers of individuals at risk. In addition, globalization has greatly reduced the ability of governments to control their country's economic fate without the cooperation of other states, international organizations, and multinational corporations.

The inability of states to provide for the security and well-being of individuals led to a 1994 United Nations Human Development Report that drew attention to the need to promote **human security** on a global scale.[7] The UN report defined human security as "safety from chronic threats such as hunger, diseases and repression, as well as protection from sudden and harmful disruptions in the patters of daily life." As defined in this way, human security has a more narrow focus than does the concept of the human interest. Human security is intended to form a bridge that unites traditional concerns for economic development and human rights and goes beyond them. Economic development should remove barriers preventing individuals from expanding their life choices and improve access to basic needs. In contrast, human security is more pessimistic, focusing on the downside risks that accompany economic development: discrimination, exposure to diseases, and harsh working conditions. From a human security perspective human rights are largely defined in legal terms and provide guidance on how human security can be safeguarded and advanced. Human security identifies those freedoms that need to be promoted and safeguarded. Seven different types of human security threats have been identified. They are listed in Table 4.1 along with examples of each.

human security Protecting individuals from situations of fear and want; considered to be more focused in its perspective on international politics than human interest.

As a broad and overarching concept, human security contains a number of potentially conflicting elements, three of which are the most crucial:

1. Should the primary emphasis be on "freedom from fear" or "freedom from want"? Advocates of the "freedom from fear" perspective advocate a focus on protecting individuals from becoming the victims of violence through such measures as emergency assistance, conflict resolution programs, and peace building. The "freedom from want" perspective calls for a broader, more holistic approach that focuses on development and environmental issues. These two perspectives are divided by differing judgments about what is feasible and necessary as well as the strictness of the definition of human security.

2. Which is better: a top-down or bottom-up approach to human security? A top-down approach, a more protection-oriented definition of human security, emphasizes motivating states, nongovernmental actors, and international organizations to take proactive steps to help individuals in situations such as natural disasters, health epidemics, and military conflicts. The bottom-up approach, an empowerment-oriented definition of human security, emphasizes developing the strength and flexibility of

TABLE 4.1	Human Security Threats
Type of Security	Examples of Main Threats
Economic security	Persistent poverty, unemployment
Food security	Hunger, famine
Health security	Deadly infectious diseases, unsafe food, malnutrition, lack of access to basic health care
Environmental security	Environmental degradation, resource depletion, natural disasters, pollution
Personal security	Physical violence, crime, terrorism, domestic violence, child labor
Community security	Inter-ethnic, religious and other identity-based tensions
Political security	Political repression, human rights abuses

Source: *Human Security in Theory and Practice* (New York: Human Security Unit, United Nations, 2009), 6.

individuals and communities in the face of challenges so that they can respond with choices that improve their lives.

3. Should the focus of human security be helping individuals deal with widespread pervasive ongoing problems or severe sporadic events? For example, in the case of health security should the emphasis be on vaccination against common diseases such as tuberculosis or policy-making to deal with the outburst of an Ebola epidemic? With regard to climate security, the decision would be whether to emphasize coping with long-term droughts or preparing for the onset of a sudden typhoon or flash flood.

Global Interest

Trying to determine what is in the **global interest** can be even more challenging than defining the national interest or the human interest. Until relatively recently little systematic attention was paid to the possibility of the existence of a global interest or its weight in foreign policy decision-making. The traditional way of thinking about the national interest was that it was different from, and in opposition to, the global interest; each state possessed its own national interest that competed with those of other states. The global interest was somewhat of a remainder or leftover; its content was vague and its importance to states was considered minimal.

This characterization of the global interest was not shared by all. In 1962 Arnold Wolfers called upon states to recognize the importance of **milieu goals**.[8] He defined the *milieu* as the conditions of the environment in which states pursue their more narrowly defined national interests. He noted that peace is not a condition possessed by any one state but is essential to the achievement of the security and prosperity of all states. Peace is a condition of the global environment, and it takes at least two states to make

global interest Goals that are in the interests of all states or benefit the international system as a whole.

milieu goals Foreign policy goals that shape the global context in which all states act.

it happen. Wolfers recognized that costs were involved in pursuing milieu goals and that some states might see themselves as losers in the process of creating a beneficial global environment. Conceding that some milieu goals may be in the national interest of countries other than one's own, he argued that this did not make them any less important. Achieving national interest goals requires a supportive global environment which, in turn, often requires cooperation among states.

Historically, there is evidence that at least some states adopted Wolfers' outlook. In the nineteenth century Great Britain promoted an open international economic system that would ensure the freedom of the seas. After WWII the United States spearheaded the creation of an international monetary system in which the US dollar was "as good as gold." In both of these cases, Great Britain and the United States benefitted by creating a supportive global milieu, which allowed other states to achieve their national interest goals. These cases also highlight a potential danger of pursing milieu goals. Both Great Britain and the United States experienced increasing costs in maintaining this milieu overtime and stopped supporting the freedom of the seas and

 THEORY SPOTLIGHT

The Global Community and Global Justice

One of the most problematic issues that must be addressed by theories of international politics in deciding what values to place at the center of foreign policy is that of justice. Is it superior to security and economic prosperity as the primary goal of policy? And justice for whom: individuals, states, or the global community? The focus here is on global justice. No single definition of global justice exists. Some stress procedural questions in judging whether an action or decision is just, while others focus on outcomes. Nor is there agreement on how to weigh the importance of justice compared to other goals such as security. Answering such questions about global justice is particularly challenging because it involves considerations of the interactions among human, national, and global interests in the global community. This feature highlights the relationship between definitions of the global community and global justice. There are three broad conceptions of the global community, each of which carries a different set of implications for global justice:[10]

1. **Statist perspective**. The first global community is defined as a community of states. This perspective fits comfortably with the traditional realist perspective that a state is sovereign and has supreme power and authority within its boundaries. However, it goes somewhat beyond realism in arguing that while no power exists above states, states share common interests that lead them to develop an informal set of rules governing their behavior. This has the effect of creating a global community. Concerns about individual justice, justice as applied to people, are secondary to how states treat one another.

2. **Universalistic or cosmopolitan perspective**. Individuals, not states, are the foundation of the global community. This perspective asserts that there is a single definition of justice that applies to all people. In this view state boundaries have little moral significance; they are artificial and do not establish boundary points for definitions of justice. In addition, cultural factors and political

the international monetary system as these costs rose and international conditions changed.

While the milieu perspective directs attention to the importance of a positive global environment, it still defines the global interest in terms of its contributions to national interests. A second perspective on the global interest directs attention away from a focus on states to the needs of the international system itself. Central to this perspective are environmental considerations such as pollution, the destruction of natural resources, and global warming. This second perspective is often identified with the term *ecopolitics* or a politics of the planet earth.[9] It calls for a shift in thinking from treating the earth's resources as unlimited assets to be used to advance particular interests to viewing them as inherently limited and requiring preservation. Some refer to this change as moving from a "cowboy economics" perspective, where open lands are to be used at will, to a "spaceship earth" perspective where the survival of the whole must take precedence over the use of resources for personal gain. One particularly important dimension of the global interest is the concept of global justice. It is the subject of the Theory Spotlight feature.

YanC / istock

The rule of law is central to the concept of justice. In the arena of international politics it is a highly debated concept.

differences are not central to the single definition of justice. A true definition of justice is universal and transcends state boundaries. It is the responsibility of states to protect and promote the universal definition of justice within their borders.

3. **Communitarian perspective**. According to this perspective, the concept of justice only gains meaning when placed in the context of a community, and the dominant communities in international politics continues to be states.

As such, definitions of justice, rights, and responsibilities are formulated and enforced within state boundaries. The key to global justice is how states define justice. When states respect the rights of individuals and the rights of other states, global justice and peace are possible.

An important distinction between the cosmopolitan and communitarian perspectives involves the responsibility to correct violations of justice. Since holders of the communitarian viewpoint continue to see the state as the central actor in international politics, they are hesitant to intervene and compel states to change their justice policies. According to the cosmopolitan perspective, such interventions are necessary and there is far less reluctance to undertake them.

Think about It

1. How would you define global justice? Can global justice as you defined it ever be achieved?

2. What is the proper relationship between global justice and national security?

A TWO-LEVEL GAME

Recognizing that a values debate exists in international politics has important implications for our understanding of how values become the basis for policy. Most of all it requires that we are sensitive to wide variety of voices that can influence policy decisions. Robert Putnam captured the essence of this point by asserting that in creating their policies government officials operate within the logic of a **two-level game**.[11] They simultaneously have to win the support of other states and win the support of domestic political groups. This may not be easily accomplished. The North American Free Trade Agreement (NAFTA) and the proposed Trans Pacific Partnership both provoked strong political backlashes in the United States as did Cold War nuclear arms control agreements with the Soviet Union and more recently with Iran. British membership in the European Union, which is discussed in Chapter 3, also became a long-running point of controversy.

two-level game The need for policy-makers to simultaneously direct their attention to the domestic political context in which they operate as well as the international context for policies to succeed.

The problem Putnam highlighted, the need to gain the support both of domestic political forces and external actors, is not unique to states. It exists in varying forms for all international politics actors. Chapter 3 noted that the UN can best be seen as made up of three different UNs which exist simultaneously. Our discussion of conference diplomacy, which is often sponsored by international organizations, will emphasize the role that voting blocks and coalitions play in making decisions.

Non-state actors do not escape the two-level game challenge. A case in point is the adoption of the Sullivan Principles by General Motors (GM). In 1977 GM was the largest employer of blacks in South Africa. Under pressure from Reverend Leon Sullivan, who sat on its Board of Directors, General Motors agreed to a policy that included non-segregated eating and working facilities, equal pay for all employees, fair treatment of all employees, and increasing the number of blacks in management positions. The Sullivan principles met with mixed success. (Sullivan himself later repudiated these principles in disappointment over what had been achieved.) Over a hundred US MNCs adopted them, but apartheid continued. Providers of humanitarian aid face the simultaneous challenge of establishing a positive working relationship in dealing with the government of the state within which they operate and satisfying the needs of their home office whose operation largely revolves around fundraising activities and gaining contracts from international organizations and donor states.

The different ways in which societal voices influence decision-making have been studied most thoroughly in the field of foreign policy analysis, once generally referred to as comparative foreign policy. The following section introduces the major societal voices. The section that comes after it examines global influences on foreign policy-making.

SOCIETAL INFLUENCES ON FOREIGN POLICY-MAKING

This section examines three of the most prominent societal voices examined in foreign policy analysis: voting, participation in interest groups, and participation in social movements. Another important societal voice, the role of the media, will also be explored.

Voting

In thinking about how individuals form their views on policy issues, attention is almost always directed at voting and elections. However, the ability of voting to promote or hinder foreign policy initiatives tends to be limited by several factors. One is the infrequency of voting opportunities. A second is that domestic issues generally overshadow foreign policy issues in the minds of voters, reducing the likelihood that voting results are closely tied to foreign policy issues or sending mixed signals about their importance. As a result, policy-makers may not feel it politically necessary to adjust foreign policy in a specific direction.

In the 2006 US midterm elections Republicans lost control of the House and Senate in what was widely interpreted to be a protest vote against increased deployment of troops in the Iraq War. Instead of beginning a troop withdrawal in line with a recommendation made by an independent commission set up to examine options, George W. Bush adopted a policy change advocated by the American Enterprise Institute think tank, which was favored by few in his administration. This policy option, which involved increasing the number of troops sent to the Middle East, came to be known as the surge.

Referendums, direct votes on policy issues, are a means of getting around some of the limitations of exercising influence through voting in elections. Almost fifty referendums have been held in European countries on matters from membership in the European Union (EU) or its forerunners to specific policies such as adopting the euro. The yes/no structure of a referendum clarifies what the public wants but does not dictate the structure of the resulting foreign policy. For example, in 2016, Great Britain voted by a slim majority through a referendum to leave the EU, an action popularly referred to as Brexit. (In 1975 a referendum had supported the British government's decision to join the EU.) The 2016 referendum did not specify when or under what terms Great Britain would leave the EU. One year later negotiations to bring Brexit about began, and controversy over terms and timeline continues.

Interest Groups

Interest groups are sets of people working together for a shared cause. There are two different types of interest groups related to foreign policy issues. *Special interest groups* designate those groups whose cause advances the interests of group members rather than society as a whole. The most prominent foreign policy interest groups are organized around economic interests, ethnicity, and religion. *Public interest groups* seek to advance foreign policy ideas that directly impact society as a whole as their primary areas of concern.

interest group A set of people working together for a shared cause.

SPECIAL INTEREST GROUPS

Because special interest groups vary along many dimensions, they do not wield a uniform level of influence over foreign policy decisions. Some interest groups operate outside of the governmental structure. They exert their influence through such actions as supporting candidates for office, lobbying elected government officials and bureaucrats, and acting as watchdogs to alert interest group members to relevant policy decisions. Other interest groups are closely tied to the government through patronage, formal affiliation with political parties, or by including group members with important government positions.

Special interest groups tend to operate in single policy areas called *silos*, and rarely venture into others. The more that one group can dominate a policy silo, the greater will be its influence on policy. Take trade policy, for example. Multiple interest groups often compete with one another in trying to influence policy, which makes the influence of any single interest group uncertain. Farmers tend to favor protectionist policies that either restrict the amount or raise the cost of foreign food products that can enter domestic markets. Manufacturers and business interests such as banking and investments prefer free trade; their primary interest is gaining access to foreign markets and raw materials and reducing production costs by establishing overseas production facilities.

Special interest lobbying is not unique to democracies. A study of domestic Chinese firms, foreign firms, and trade associations found that that over 90% of the companies surveyed regularly engaged with the government, participating in legislative or administrative hearings, supporting scholarly policy research, providing written policy information to government officials, submitting articles to the media, running training sessions for journalists, and hosting banquets.[12]

It is important to note that the ability of special interest groups to shape foreign policy decisions is not without its critics. This criticism is loudest and most intense regarding what is commonly called the military-industrial complex, a term coined by C. Wright Mills in 1956. President Dwight Eisenhower used this term in his farewell address, in which he warned against the military-industrial complex's excessive and unjustified influence over American foreign policy as well as the dangers of misplaced power.[13] The principal argument is that defense policy is dominated by a concentrated group of professional soldiers, government officials, and defense industry officials; out of a shared common interest in high levels of defense spending and a large military establishment, this group advocates a definition of national security that presumes a hostile and conflict-filled world, demanding in consequence an aggressive and interventionist foreign policy. A prime example of military-industrial complex lobbying is the F-35 combat fighter. This is one of the Department of Defense's most expensive weapons programs, with a cumulative cost of $1.5 trillion. Lockheed Martin, the prime force behind the F-35, maintains thirty-five lobbyists to make its case, including former defense department officials and a member of the Joint Chiefs of Staff. To support its case Lockheed claims that 125,000 people work on the F-35 in 46 states, providing tremendous support to the US economy.

PUBLIC INTEREST GROUPS

Public interest groups are especially active in advancing foreign policy ideas in the areas of human rights, environmental protection, international development, health promotion, and conflict prevention. One problem these interest groups face is that for the most part the issues they promote have historically been defined as *low foreign policy areas*, issues that do not directly threaten national security. In contrast, those that directly threaten national security are referred to as *high foreign policy areas*. Low foreign policy areas do not demand immediate action or the attention of high-level policy-makers and can be handled in routine fashion by lower-level officials. A second problem is that, unlike special interest groups that operate both inside and outside of official government circles, public interest groups generally voice their foreign policy ideas from outside the government, which more often than not puts them in the position of criticizing rather than supporting existing foreign policy.

Similar in some respects to public interest groups, public policy research organizations more commonly referred to as **think tanks** cover a wide variety of ideological and political viewpoints and voice opinions on the conduct of foreign policy. The differences are in how they promote their values. Public interest groups target both policy-makers and the broader public, but think tanks focus more heavily on influencing policy-makers. Think tanks may also be more closely tied to governments and thus able to work within the system. They may be government funded and include individuals who hold or have held government positions. Box 4.1 includes a list of foreign policy think tanks and research institutions utilized by the Policy Planning Staff at the US State Department.

think tanks Policy or research institutes that conduct research on policy problems and make policy recommendations.

Social Movements

Participation in social movements is yet another way in which individuals may act collectively to shape the ideas that drive foreign policy. In contrast to special and public interest groups, which tend to be stable and long-standing formal associations, social movements are composed of loosely connected individuals united by a common purpose. The values that social movements advocate vary widely in ideology and the degree to which they promote fundamental foreign policy changes, advocate incremental reforms, or seek to preserve the status quo.

Social movements do not just happen. They progress through a life cycle that begins when a sufficient number of people become upset with a policy or system of government.[14] As unrest ferments and deepens, the connections among individuals become stronger and the movement becomes more organized and focused on specific leaders and demands. Increasing numbers of supporters and expanding areas of activity such as protests and rallies lead to a more formal organizational structure capable of coordinating and maximizing political resources. At the end of the cycle, social movements begin to lose their energy. This may result from a variety of factors including achievement of goals, co-optation into public interest groups, internal disputes, or protest fatigue.

The most politically consequential social movement of the past decade took place in North Africa and the Middle East. Referred to by various names, it is most often identified as the Arab Spring. The Arab Spring began in Tunisia on December 17, 2010, when a street vendor whose produce had just been confiscated by police set himself on

Box 4.1 Foreign Policy Think Tanks and Research Institutions

One of the functions of the Policy Planning Staff at the US State Department is to act as a liaison to think tanks and research institutions. The following is a partial listing in alphabetical order of those they have found to be particularly useful. The list does not represent an official endorsement or approval by the US State Department of any website, product, service, or opinion found on any of these sites.

- American Enterprise Institute for Public Policy Research
- Arms Control Association
- Atlantic Council of the United States
- The Brookings Institution
- Canadian Institute of Strategic Studies
- Carnegie Endowment for International Peace
- The Cato Institute
- Center for Strategic and International Studies
- Centre d'Etudes et de Recherches Internationales (Center for International Studies and Research)
- Clingendael (Netherlands Institutes of International Relations)
- Council on Foreign Relations
- Deutsche Gesellschaft für Auswärtige Politik (German Council on Foreign Relations)
- Federation of American Scientists
- Freedom House
- Henry L. Stimson Center
- The Heritage Foundation
- Institut Français des Relations Internationales (French Institute of International Relations)
- Institute for International Economics
- International Centre for Trade and Sustainable Development
- International Institute for Strategic Studies
- New America Foundation
- RAND
- Royal Institute of International Affairs (Chatham House)
- Stiftung Wissenschaft und Politik (German Institute for International and Security Affairs)
- Stockholm International Peace Research Institute (SIPRI)
- Woodrow Wilson International Center for Scholars
- World Economic Forum
- United States Institute of Peace

fire. Violent street protests followed; within a month the government fell and its president went into exile after ruling for twenty-three years. Shortly afterward, eighteen days of protests in Egypt led to the resignation of President Hosni Mubarak after his thirty years in power. Syria, Yemen, and Iraq also experienced significant Arab Spring protests, and lesser protests took place in over a dozen North African and Middle Eastern states.

The protests did not appear out of thin air. Mounting discontent had been reflected in labor protests, food strikes, and anti-corruption protests. As these issues suggest, the Arab Spring was not directly about foreign policy, but was driven by domestic political and economic issues. However, global and regional foreign policy consequences quickly followed. In Egypt the Muslim Brotherhood's candidate won the presidency, only to be forced out of office by continued mass protests and a military coup in 2013. In Libya anti-Gaddafi protests contributed to the increased violence cited as justification for UN imposition of a no-fly zone and for the bombing of pro-Gaddafi forces by the United States and its allies. Government repression and attacks

Arnaud Martinez / Alamy Stock Photo

In 2011 a series of anti-government protests that came to be known as the Arab Spring spread across Northern Africa and the Middle East.

against anti-government demonstrators helped fuel Syria's civil war. In Yemen demonstration protests would bring down the government, but three years later its successor was overthrown, setting off a civil war backed on opposing sides by Saudi Arabia and Iran. By December 2012 the energy of the Arab Spring had largely been extinguished. As this record suggests, there was no single end to the Arab Spring. In some cases protests led to changes in government. In other cases it led to counter-violence by government supporters, foreign intervention, and civil war. And in yet other cases the protests produced minor changes or faded from the political scene having failed to achieve meaningful changes.

The Media and Foreign Policy

Reporting by newspapers and television have long been the starting point for thinking about the influence of the media on foreign policy. With the increased and increasing prominence of social media, a far more complex situation exists today.

There is a long-standing central question about foreign policy reporting by newspapers and television in democratic systems: where do they get their information? The first two answers that come to mind are reporters on the scene and policy-makers. Due to declining budgets, rising costs, and competition from other media sources, overseas reporters are a dying breed. From 1998 to 2010 eighteen newspapers and two newspaper chains in the United States closed all of their overseas offices. In 2014 ABC News announced that it would close most of its eleven foreign bureaus. From 2008 to 2013 CBS News closed nine foreign news bureaus, including those in Moscow, Paris, Baghdad, Tel Aviv, and Hong Kong.

The drawback to relying on policy-makers as a source of information is that they are not neutral. Information must be "framed" or placed in context in order to be meaningful.[15] Many events are not self-interpreting and do not carry obvious meaning. What does the change in the value of the Chinese currency mean? Why does it matter if Russian troops are moving toward the Ukraine? What is the significance of a terrorist attack on Paris? Policy-makers frame their answers to these questions in terms of certain values, policies, or definitions of the national interest. In democracies the starting point for obtaining information is from statements by presidents, prime ministers, and high-level cabinet officials. There is no guarantee that policy makers will be successful in framing foreign policy news. Policy frames that do not resonate with the public can result in loss of control over the story. In such cases "the CNN effect" takes over; policy-makers become reactive, responding to never-ending "breaking news" stories presented by the media 24/7. When presidents control the frame of the policy debate/news story, they have few problems with the CNN effect. But when they do not, they are constantly responding to stories, trying to justify their position and show that they are in charge.

While the media as a whole relies heavily on the same official sources for its foreign policy information, not all media sources will report a foreign policy story in the same fashion either within a country or in different countries.

An evaluation of almost 1,900 articles on the 2011 Libyan civil war in over a hundred daily newspapers from around the world revealed that news coverage by papers in democratic countries was more frequent and diverse than that in nondemocratic systems. Coverage from nondemocratic country newspapers was found to have a status quo bias and focused more on the violent action of rebels. In contrast, coverage by democratic country newspapers focused more on protest movements and government repression. Distinctions also depended on media ownership and circulation. Independent family-owned newspapers in democratic countries were more likely to report on the Libyan crisis and adopted a hard news perspective that was often critical of the policy of their country's government. Hard news reporting on Libya was also more likely in large circulation newspapers.[16]

Relying on social media for foreign policy news does not eliminate issues associated with framing or uneven coverage. A study of the use of social media in the Syrian civil war found that YouTube videos, Facebook posts, and Twitter accounts of the conflict typically were constructed for the purpose of framing the conflict, not for providing information, especially regarding images of violence.[17] This study also found that Arab- and English-language postings focused on different issues and that, over time, Arab social media postings tended to become more narrowly focused to appeal to like-minded religious, political, or ethnic audiences.

Evidence collected by US intelligence agencies, research firms, and major technology companies concerning Russian involvement in the 2016 presidential election highlights an additional dimension to the role of social media in shaping values. As noted in a report by a research project: "social media has gone from being the natural infrastructure for sharing collective grievances and coordinating civic engagement to being a computational tool for social control manipulated by ... politicians in democracies and dictatorships alike."[18]

GLOBAL INFLUENCES ON FOREIGN POLICY-MAKING

In today's globalized world, it is important to recognize that global voices may also be active in trying to shape policy-makers' calculations about the domestic consequences of a decision. To capture this influence, this section highlights the activities of interest groups and advocacy networks operating internationally.

Foreign Lobbying

A wide variety of global political actors engage in lobbying foreign governments and societal groups to adjust policies that bear (either directly or indirectly) on foreign policy concerns. In the United States an obvious target for foreign lobbying is Congress and a primary area of concern is arms sales. Just prior to President Donald Trump's visit, Saudi Arabia added three new lobbying firms to the three it hired after Trump's election. One of these is composed of former Trump advisors and will earn $5.4 million for one year's work. Saudi Arabia also employs the Podesta group, which has close ties to the Democratic Party. In March 2017 the Podesta Group sent pro-Saudi material to hundreds of congressional staffers and Middle East policy analysts to bolster the case for arms sales to Saudi Arabia in the face of Congressional criticism of its human rights policy. Late in the Obama administration an Iranian opposition group, Mujahedin-e-Khalq (MEK), successfully lobbied the State Department to drop its formal designation as a terrorist group. Among its loudest supporters were two former CIA directors and a former head of the FBI. Washington think tanks have also been the target of foreign lobbying. Japan recruited the Brookings Institution to bolster support for the Trans Pacific Partnership agreement with a $1.1 million contract. In 2014 another Washington think tank, the Center for Strategic and International Studies, identified thirteen foreign governments from which it had received donations, including Germany and China.

Foreign lobbying is not always welcomed. In 2012 Russia passed a "Foreign Agent Law" requiring all independent groups that receive foreign funding and engage in political activity to register with the government as foreign agents. Among those groups targeted are Amnesty International, Human Rights Watch, and Transparency International. In India over 11,000 nongovernmental organizations (NGOs), including some nonprofit public health organizations that had received money from the Gates Foundation, are prohibited from accepting funding from foreign donors on the grounds that the NGOs use some of this money to lobby the government.

Transnational Advocacy Networks

Global values are also able to influence foreign policy choices through the operation of **transnational advocacy networks (TANs)**, groups of activists from around the world who are linked together to promote change in policy issues that cross state boundaries. By doing so, they effectively blur the traditional boundary line between domestic politics and international politics.

TANs bring together a wide variety of political actors including domestic interest groups, international and regional government organizations, social movements, foundations, trade unions, churches, and international nongovernmental organizations. Transnational advocacy groups are organized around ideas and values.[19] Environmental protection, human rights, health, and women's rights are policy areas in which transnational advocacy groups have been very active.

TAN group members are linked together through use of multiple communication channels that promote the flow of information and mobilize members into action. Transnational advocacy groups are not new; they were active in the anti-slavery movement leading up to the US Civil War. What has changed is the global scope and speed of communication systems today.

As a force in policy-making, transnational advocacy groups make it difficult for governments to control information. They provide an avenue for injecting new ideas into the policy making process and serve as watchdogs evaluating the manner in which government policies are implemented. Prior to the 1992 Earth Summit in Rio de Janeiro, transnational advocacy groups influenced the formulation of government positions. During the 1975 Helsinki Accords, the Soviet Union made a political commitment to improving human rights conditions as part of an agreement to improve its relations with the United States and Western Europe. TANs played key roles in verifying that the Soviet Union was meeting its commitments by monitoring Soviet human rights actions and making their findings public. Transnational advocacy groups operate most freely in democratic societies but can also reach into more authoritarian systems by what is sometimes called the boomerang effect.[20] When the voices of domestic public interest groups are silenced or ignored by the government, transnational advocacy group can pressure the government beyond the nation's borders.

International governmental organizations (IGOs) are another important influence on formulating national values, both as members of transnational advocacy networks and as international actors in their own right. This is especially true for those that are part of the UN system. As was noted in Chapter 3, many IGOs have played important roles in shaping global and national thinking about such issues as human security, environmental protection, women's rights, and development.

The success of transnational advocacy groups in shaping policy has involved a lot of hard work. These groups have succeeded in getting the United States and European states to include human rights standards as part of their loan programs. TANs have also prompted the World Bank to include environmental evaluation reports as part of its loan process but have been less successful in getting the United States and European states to do so.

transnational advocacy networks (TANs) Groups of activists from around the world who are linked together to promote change in policy issues that cross state boundaries.

THE PATHWAY FROM IDEAS TO POLICY

Embracing a definition of the national interest, human interest, and global interest is not the same as making it the basis for the conduct of foreign policy by states and other actors in international politics. Change is not easy. Simply moving from one definition of the national, human, or global interest to another will provoke opposition. Once an idea does become the basis for action, vested political, societal, and organizational interests are created that makes change difficult.

Steps in the Policy-Making Process

For ideas to become policy, a challenging pathway must be successfully traveled. This section charts that pathway and breaks the **policy-making process** into five steps. Not every policy decision will progress through all five stages in the same way. Policy debates may move almost immediately to the decision-making stage during a crisis, but trade policy discussions may crawl through the five stages at a drastically slower pace.

policy-making process The steps that a policy proposal must pass through in order to move from an idea to a formal policy; they include getting on the political agenda, formulating a policy option, making a decision, implementing the decision, and evaluating the decision.

GETTING VALUES ONTO THE FOREIGN POLICY AGENDA

There is no shortage of ideas about what should be done about foreign policy challenges. The first step is to get serious attention for the idea as a policy option, or securing it a place on the foreign policy agenda. Advocates of change can reside either inside or outside of government. The George W. Bush administration led a highly orchestrated campaign for going to war with Iraq. Calls for ending the Vietnam War and nuclear disarmament originated largely in American society. The difficulties of overcoming the influence of entrenched interests that support the status quo often mean that a sudden, unexpected and game-changing shock or international crisis such as Pearl Harbor, the 9/11 terrorist attacks, the fall of the Soviet Union, or financial crises must occur to provide a window of opportunity for a new—or not so new—idea to reach the policy agenda.

FORMULATING A POLICY

Once an idea is on the policy agenda, the second step is to formulate and advance a foreign policy built on it. A political coalition must be formed to generate a formal policy proposal that embodies the favored value and is capable of securing political support in subsequent steps. Joe Hagan has proposed three alternative political strategies that are employed in constructing foreign policy coalitions:[21]

1. A strategy of *accommodation* emphasizes bargaining and avoiding controversy.
2. Using the second strategy, *mobilization*, leaders make heavy use of nationalist and patriotic themes in an attempt to divert attention from any controversial aspects of the policy proposal and at the same time highlight their ability to lead.
3. Leaders using the third strategy of *insulation* seek to contain or limit opposition by suppressing it, co-opting it by making concessions, or—if possible—simply ignoring it.

MAKING A DECISION

The third step in building a foreign policy is the decision on what to do:

- Should the proposed policy be adopted?
- Should it be modified (and if so, how)?
- Should it be rejected in favor of continuing the current policy?

rational actor model
A model of decision-making that is based on the assumption of informed choice in which all options are known and evaluated, and the option selected is the one most likely to realize the desired goal at a reasonable cost.

Commentators have constructed a number of decision-making models in order to better understand how this step works. The one that has been employed the longest is the **rational actor model**. The basic elements of this decision-making process are as follows: (1) goals are clearly stated and ranked in order of preference, (2) all options are considered, (3) the consequences of each option are assessed, and (4) a value-maximizing choice is made. In carrying out these calculations, the state is seen as being unitary, responding with one voice to the challenges and opportunities confronting it. With a unitary rational actor there is no need to take into consideration such factors as domestic politics or personalities in trying to understand why a policy was selected.

The rational actor model is attractive because it places few informational demands on the observer. You do not need to know about the intricacies of North Korean politics, the personalities of its leaders, or details about the operation of its military forces to understand or predict the policies it adopts. You can accurately predict the policy by carrying out this type of situational analysis. The rational actor model is held to be inadequate because too much is left out. Policy-makers often pursue multiple and vaguely defined goals or proceed without a full understanding of their consequences.

One alternative is to emphasize individual characteristics or traits that might govern a policy-maker's decision making. There are many ways to place individuals at the center of the policy-making process. An early study of individual decision-making found that certain personality traits were related to aggressiveness (such as the need to manipulate and control others), and others were associated with conciliatory behavior (such as the need to build and establish friendly relations). Another factor that could affect a policy-makers' decision is their perception of the stakes involved. According to **prospect theory**, policy-makers are more likely to take risks in trying to defend something they already possess than in trying to achieve a new objective.[22]

prospect theory
A theory of decision-making that assumes individuals value losses and gains differently; they are more like to take risks to prevent possible losses than they are to seek potential gains.

Prospect theory divides decision-making into two phases. In the first phase, known as the editing or framing phase, individuals identify and define the policy options available. The objective is not to consider all options in a conscious and deliberate way but to simplify the evaluation of choices that is carried out in the second phase. Especially influential in this editing process is how options are presented or framed. Experimental evidence suggests that policy-makers are often not aware of the influence of these considerations. Among the most influential framing factors are the expectations, values, and habits of decision-makers as well as such apparently trivial factors as the order in which policy options are presented and the language used by advisors in presenting them. For example, a controlled lab experiment presented individuals with policy options on how to respond to a health disaster. One policy was presented in terms of the number of people who would live. The other option was presented in terms of the number who would die. Even though the numbers were identical, routinely the preferred policy was that defined in terms of survivors.

The second phase is the evaluation phase. Here the options are evaluated in terms of their impact from a specific reference point rather than in terms of their overall value impact. The status quo often serves as a reference point during stable times, while hopes and aspirations are reference points in rapidly changing times. A number of important implications follow from the use of a reference point as the basis for making calculations about what policy to adopt. The most frequently cited is that individuals tend to be risk-averse in pursuing policy gains but are inclined to accept risks when seeking to protect positions or values they already possess. Falling into this category are President Jimmy Carter's decision to go ahead with the failed effort to rescue hostages in Iran and Nikita Khrushchev's decision to send nuclear weapons to Cuba in an effort to preserve Fidel Castro's rule (a decision that led to the Cuban Missile Crisis). This presents a major challenge to studies of international politics, since identifying a policy-maker's reference point is not easy. Political scientist Jack Levy raises this point with regard to Saddam Hussein after Iraq's invasion of Kuwait. Did he resist US and UN demands to leave Kuwait because for him this was the new status quo, or did he resist because he continued to view regional politics from the point of view of the old status quo, a situation he rejected as unacceptable?[23]

Many models of individual decision-making emphasize the role of beliefs as key to shaping decisions. Beliefs are considered as screens that allow policy-makers to take in certain information and remove conflicting information from view. One way in which beliefs influence policy is through the creation of an individual's operational code,[24] which consists of two parts: (1) beliefs about the nature of other states and the nature of international politics and (2) beliefs about what constitutes a proper response to a foreign policy challenge.

Another policy-making model focuses on the dynamics of small-group decision-making. The most important small groups in foreign policy-making are those that formulate responses to an international crisis. Small groups are seen as important for understanding the decision-making process, because they often produce strong in-group pressures on members to bow to the group's decision. This pressure produces a "deterioration of mental efficiency, reality testing, and moral judgment" that increases the likelihood of the group's making a potentially defective decision. Irving Janis coined the term **groupthink** to capture this phenomenon.[25] Groupthink is a tendency that can be avoided. One tactic is to have someone in the group act as a devil's advocate, advancing ideas or policy options not seriously being considered. The problem here is that devil's advocates are most effective when they argue positions they believe in. When the arguments become routine or part of standard operating procedures they lose their ability to shape decision-making.

The **bureaucratic politics model** is the one most frequently used for studying decision-making on policy issues such as arms control, trade, and environmental policies

groupthink A key concept in small-group decision-making that holds that internal pressures for group consensus leads to a deterioration of rationality and morality.

bureaucratic politics model A perspective on policy-making that emphasizes the central role played by bureaucratic factors such as bargaining, vested interests, and standard operating procedures in formulating policies.

that involve large numbers of participants and proceed slowly over time. Politics rather than rationality is seen as dominating the decision-making process, because decision-making power is shared and because people see problems differently depending on their position in the bureaucracy. Not everyone in the government participates in a particular policy-making bargaining "game." Policy-makers are linked together by lines of authority, decision-making rules, and budgetary constraints. Together they create action channels that confer power on some and deny it to others. The typical end result of bureaucratic politics bargaining is that the agreed-upon policy will not differ greatly from the existing policy. The inflexible and blunt nature of organizational routines, often referred to as standard operating procedures, make administrative feasibility a key consideration in deciding which policy to adopt and limiting dramatic changes to existing policy.

IMPLEMENTING THE DECISION

The fourth step in the policy making process is determining how to implement the selected policy. In the vast majority of cases foreign policy is implemented through government institutions. The key foreign policy instruments available to states are highlighted in Chapter 5. What is important to note here is that states occasionally rely on individuals and nongovernmental bodies to carry out their foreign policy initiatives. This tends to happen when one country lacks diplomatic relations with another and needs a third party to act as a communication channel or arbitrator of disputes. For example, Pope Francis played the role of mediator and power broker in helping to restore diplomatic relations between the United States and Cuba. Such an arrangement can also occur when relations are so bad that both sides seek the help of a third party; US Secretary of State Henry Kissinger flew back and forth between Israel, Syria, and Egypt in what came to be known as shuttle diplomacy to produce a peace agreement regarding the Yom Kippur War. On October 6, 1973, Syria and Egypt launched a successful surprise attack on Israel. Israeli forces managed to regroup and counterattack, retaking lost territory and capturing new ones. A ceasefire took effect on October 25.

EVALUATING THE DECISION

The fifth and final step on the path from idea to foreign policy is policy evaluation. Judging whether a particular foreign policy is a success or a failure is not an easy task, for several reasons. Most fundamentally, any given policy is likely to contain a number of different goals. Victory in war is not only intended to bring peace but also involves creating stability, government alliances, and perhaps democracy. Similarly, foreign aid programs generally are expected to bring about not only national economic development but also greater income equality, improved governance, and reduced civil strife. Another challenge in the evaluation stage is the existence of multiple standards to measure success and failure. The two most frequently used reflect the dual motivations driving policy-makers in constructing foreign policy: achieving goals and retaining political power. The pursuit of goals leads to objective technical evaluations of accomplishments and their degree of efficiency. The standard of retaining power leads to evaluations based on the amount of support for the policy from important political groups.

Not only is change not easy but it is not always successful or without controversy. The Policy Spotlight feature highlights one such policy and its consequence: the democratic peace.

CONTEMPORARY PERSPECTIVE:
The Refugee Flow into Europe

Refugee crises are still with us. So too are the challenges Nansen faced in providing assistance to refugees. According to the office of the United Nations High Commissioner for Refugees (UNHCR), twenty people worldwide were forced to flee their homes every minute in 2016 due to persecution, violence, or human rights violations. While some remain within their home country, others flee abroad and are considered refugees. In 2017 there were 17.2 million refugees (not counting 5.3 million Palestinian refugees). In addition, there were 10 million *stateless people*, individuals who have been denied a nationality. Developing countries host 84% of the world's refugees (about 14.5 million people). Turkey, Pakistan, Lebanon, Iran, Uganda, and Ethiopia host the largest numbers

Emilio Morenatti / AP Images

Migrants jumping into the Mediterranean Sea in order to be rescued.

POLICY SPOTLIGHT

The Democratic Peace

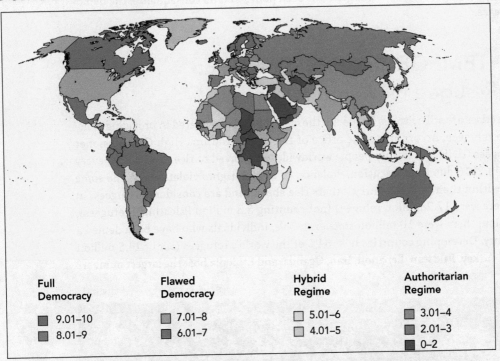

Full Democracy
■ 9.01–10
■ 8.01–9

Flawed Democracy
■ 7.01–8
■ 6.01–7

Hybrid Regime
□ 5.01–6
□ 4.01–5

Authoritarian Regime
■ 3.01–4
■ 2.01–3
■ 0–2

Map 4.1 Democracy Map.

Notes:

Full democracies: countries where civil liberties and basic political freedoms are respected and reinforced by a political culture built on democratic principles. A governmental system of checks and balances and an independent judiciary exists.

Flawed democracies: countries that have fair and free elections and where basic civil liberties are honored but that also experience low levels of participation in politics and issues in the functioning of governance.

Hybrid regimes: countries that combine characteristics of democracy and authoritarianism. Elections are irregular and not fair and free. Governments lack independent judiciaries, are plagued by widespread corruption, place constraints on the media, and harass political opponents.

Authoritarian regimes: countries where an independent civil society is largely absent. Elections are not fair and free and the media tend to be state-owned or controlled by groups associated with the ruling regime. Governments are ruled by an elite group which operates beyond the control of the public.

of refugees. In response to the refugee crisis, several commentators have called for a revival of the Nansen Passport. One argued that "without a renewed effort to give refugees a chance at legitimate migration, world governments will make their own populations less secure" and that "the current crisis is rooted in our global institutions' failure to learn from either the negative or positive experiences of the past."[27]

One of the most enduring questions in international relations is "why do states go to war?" It can be answered many ways. One of the most intriguing approaches is to reverse the question and ask "why do states *not* go to war?" Many answer that it is because they are democracies, an idea that has become known as **democratic peace theory**.[26] Two reasons are generally given for why democracies are peaceful:

democratic peace theory Theory asserting that democracies do not fight wars against other democracies.

1. The social norms associated with democracy emphasize respecting basic rights, negotiation, and compromise.
2. Democratic political institutions are able to control aggressive leaders and hold them accountable for their actions.

Democratic peace theory has far-reaching policy implications. If democracies promote global peace, then building democracies becomes a foreign policy goal that advances the national, human, and global interest. But how good a guide to foreign policy is the democratic peace argument? Should authoritarian regimes be removed from power through war? Is this an acceptable reason to go to war, or is the democratic peace theory just a convenient rationale for promoting the national interest (as some argue was the case with the Iraq War)?

The initial version of the democratic peace theory asserted that democracies were more peaceful than authoritarian regimes, but research has not supported this view. The claim today is that democracies do not go to war against other democracies but may go to war against authoritarian regimes. Overall, the evidence supports this position, but several important challenges have been raised:

- **The definition of a democracy.** No single agreed-upon definition exists. Is it enough that periodic elections are held, or must freedom of speech, religion, and assembly also exist?
- **The definition of war.** Must war be declared? Must there be a certain number of military casualties?
- **The relationship between democracies and war.** For all of the attention they receive, wars are relatively rare events in the history of international politics, as are democracies. Might the relationship between them be spurious and due to chance?

Evidence shows that, while established democracies do not go to war with other democracies, new democracies have a greater tendency to go to war than either more established democracies or established authoritarian regimes. So creating democracies may increase the likelihood of war in the short run. If the foreign policy goal is peace, it might be preferable to leave an authoritarian regime that is willing for the most part to play by the rules of the game in power. This is just part of the foreign policy dilemma facing the United States in its relations with China.

Think about It

1. Is it better to push democratization or work with China to create a stable international system? Explain your answer.
2. What characteristics of a democratic system are most likely to produce war rather than peace? How likely is this to happen?

In 2016 more than 30% of all refugees came from Syria where they were fleeing a protracted civil war. Ongoing conflicts in Afghanistan, South Sudan, and Somalia also produced large numbers. Of Turkey's 2.8 million refugees, 2.7 million came from Syria. Many of those fleeing sought *asylum* (international protection) in Europe. In 2016 European Union (EU) states received more than 1.2 million first-time asylum requests. As the pressure increased on smaller European countries and those located close to Syria, a number of them took steps to close off their borders. Hungary built a razor-wire barrier on its borders with Serbia and Croatia. Austria erected a fence along its border with Slovenia and stationed troops there. Only eighty refugees per day were allowed to seek asylum in Austria; an additional 3,200 were permitted to pass through each day on their way to other destinations. With land routes increasingly blocked, the primary pathway out of the Middle East, North Africa, and Syria was by sea. In 2015 the International Organization for Migration estimated that over one million refugees travelled by sea and some 35,000 by land. The sea voyage is neither inexpensive nor safe. In 2016 over 4,600 refugees died at sea, and the likelihood of dying was estimated to be one in eighty-eight. A rubber boat from Turkey to Greece could cost $1,000.

Largely overlooked in the massive outpouring of refugees from Syria into Europe is the ongoing problem of protracted refugees. A *protracted refugee situation* is one in which 25,000 or more refugees of the same nationality have been in exile for five consecutive years in the same asylum country. In 2016 it was estimated that two-thirds of all refugees (11.6 million) were in protracted refugee situations, over four million of whom had been in this situation for twenty years or more. While the largest number of protracted refugee situations are in Africa, those in Afghanistan, Pakistan, and Iran involve the largest number of people. Most Syrian refugees are not yet considered to be in a protracted refugee situation.

The EU's response to the refugee crisis has been marked by internal disagreements over how to proceed, criticism from international human rights groups, and pressure from international organizations and other countries to take more forceful action. In 2016 the UN and the United States both organized conferences to call attention to the refugee crisis in Europe, but neither met with much success. The draft document circulated at the UN meeting was characterized by Amnesty International as "a wasted critical opportunity."[28] Only eighteen of twenty-eight EU member states participated in the US meeting, with key EU leaders calling for greater border controls and reducing refugee movement within Europe.

Four aspects of the EU's handling of the refugee crisis have received a great deal of attention and criticism:

1. The EU placed greater emphasis on stabilizing the situation and reducing the scope of the problem than on protecting human rights and outsourcing responsibility for refugees. The EU pursued agreements with countries from which refugees originated to reduce these flows by improved patrolling of territorial waters (Libya) or facilitating their return (Afghanistan).

2. EU policy unevenly and unfairly placed responsibility for managing the refugee flow. Under the Dublin System, the country in which refugees first arrive bears the primary responsibility for the asylum seekers regardless of their final destination.

3. Many objected to a 2016 EU-Turkey agreement in which Turkey would receive billions of euros in aid and other concessions from the EU in return for accepting all asylum seekers who travelled through Turkey to Greece by sea.
4. The EU failed to develop a viable resettlement plan. The EU-Turkey agreement contained a controversial resettlement provision that linked the number of Syrian refugees in Greece who were sent back to Turkey with the number of new Syrian refugees leaving Turkey for other EU states. More broadly, in 2015 EU members agreed on a plan to resettle 22,500 recognized refugees in the next two years, but only some 10,000 refugees were resettled, and nine EU countries failed to resettle any refugees.

Refugee arrivals by land and sea into Europe have declined significantly since their height in 2015, but the challenges remain. In 2017 EU countries granted protection to more than 538,000 people, 25% below 2016. A key issue is sea arrivals and the lack of a collaborative and well-managed response by the EU. In 2018 an estimated 139,300 people crossed the Mediterranean; almost 3,000 died or are missing. The overall refugee flow is expected to continue because its root causes of poverty, human rights violations, and conflict continue. Nigeria, Mali, Niger, and Cameroon have been identified as states where these conditions exist and might generate significant sea-based refugee flows into Europe by sea in the coming years. Ongoing and developing tensions in the Middle East are expected to produce continued land-based flows of refugees into Europe.

Refugees are not the only people who find it necessary to flee their homes. Internally displaced people (IDPs) are another large group. The key difference between them is that refugees cross international borders whereas IDPs remain within their home countries. The Regional Spotlight feature focuses on IDPs in Africa.

It is clear that debates over what values ought to guide the foreign policies of states, international organizations, and non-state actors will always play a major role in international politics. The following section examines three of the major challenges facing the selection of values and possible responses.

LOOKING TO THE FUTURE

This section highlights three salient challenges that are likely to be key to resolving the value conflicts in international politics in regard to refugees and IDPs in the future. The first two deal with concrete problems: finding the global voice and harmonizing interests. The third will help deals with studying and better understanding how values are translated into policy.

Finding the Global Voice

One of the challenges in defining the global interest is determining who speaks for the global community. Most frequently the search for a global voice leads to the

REGIONAL SPOTLIGHT

Internally Displaced People in Africa

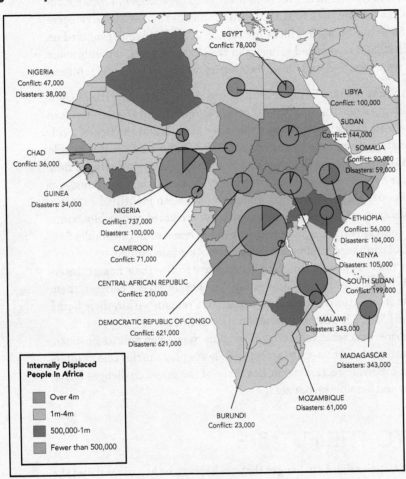

Map 4.2 Map of Africa Highlighting the Numbers and Locations of Internally Displaced People.

Internally displaced people (IDPs) are individuals who have been forced to flee their homes but remain in their home country rather than crossing an international border. As such, they are not considered refugees or migrants and are not protected in any way by international law. In 2016 31.1 million new displacements were recorded in 125 countries. This amounts to one new displacement every second. The most common reasons IDPs flee their homes are conflicts, violence, and natural disasters. In 2016 natural disasters produced 24.2 million new displacements. A report by the Norwegian Refugee Council calculated that a further 6.9 million people were internally displaced by conflict and violence in 2016. The total number of IDPs displaced by violence or conflict worldwide is 40.3 million, double the number from the year 2000. According to the United Nations Refugee Agency, the number of refugees during the same time period was 15.6 million.

A large column of internally displaced people moving across the Democratic Republic of the Congo in 2016.

The IDP situation in Africa is highlighted here because one of the major international agreements on IDPs is the 2009 Kampala Convention sponsored by the African Union. This agreement establishes obligations for members to protect and aid IDPs who have been displaced by armed conflicts. Beyond this initiative little has been done to address the plight of IDPs. At the May 2016 World Humanitarian Summit UN Secretary General Ban Ki-moon urged that new attention be given to IDPs with the goal of reducing their number by 50% by the year 2030. A few months after the summit his call seemed forgotten. The final statement of the September 2016 UN conference on refugees and migrants contained only one reference to IDPs, calling for action to prevent IDPs from becoming refugees.

Viewed in global terms, the largest number of new IDPs created by conflict situations occurred in sub-Saharan Africa. The single largest source of conflict-driven IDPs was the Democratic Republic of the Congo, which had over 900,000 new IDPs in 2007, a 50% increase from the year before. Nigeria, Ethiopia, and South Sudan also ranked in the top ten. The primary cause of the large number of IDPs in Nigeria was the conflict between Boko Haram and opposing government forces, a situation that was often compounded by near-famine conditions. The Nigerian situation also highlighted a dilemma faced by many IDPs (and returning refugees): Some 1 million Nigerians returned in 2016 to find that their homes and towns had been destroyed and little security existed, so they remained displaced.

From 2013 to 2016 one in four people in South Sudan had been forced to leave their homes. Almost 1.9 million of these were classified as IDPs; the majority were women and children. A situation common to IDPs in South Sudan and other countries is *circular displacement*. Displaced people are forced to move within a country several times in search of food and safety and then cross the border and become refugees, only to return again and repeat the cycle. Complicating the challenge South Sudan faces in providing food and security to its over 400,000 IDPs is that it houses nearly 300,000 refugees from neighboring countries.

Two-thirds of all natural disaster–driven IDPs in 2016 were found in the Pacific and East Asia. No African state ranked in the top ten in the number of IDPs displaced because of natural disasters in 2016, but that did not mean Africa avoided serious consequences. Heavy rains and flooding followed a period of severe drought and food shortages, displacing 300,000 people in Ethiopia. Flooding later in 2016 displaced 123,000 people in Sudan including some 1,700 whose homes in displacement camps were destroyed.

One of the major challenges faced by those seeking to help IDPs is the lack of data. Many experts believe that the number of IDPs in Africa due to natural disasters is under-reported as the numbers focus primarily on sudden and short-term disasters. It is commonly believed that the numbers would be significantly higher if population movements resulting from long-term drought conditions and food shortages were better documented. Similarly, the number of IDPs does not include forced displacements or evictions such as happened to over 266,000 people in Zimbabwe in 2016 or those who were displaced by the Ebola epidemic in West Africa from 2013 to 2016.

Think about It

1. Should IDPs be protected by international law? Should they be treated the same as refugees?

2. What steps can be taken to break the link between natural disasters and IDPs?

formation of international organizations such as the United Nations, the World Trade Organization, or the International Monetary Fund. While never considered to be strong, their voices seem to be especially weak today, leading many to worry about the ability of the global community to respond effectively to problems such as terrorism, refugee flows, climate degradation, nuclear proliferation, poverty, and the spread of diseases.

Political scientist Michael Mazarr concludes that this search is misdirected.[29] He argues that attention should instead be directed at more loosely organized collections of states and nongovernmental organizations that view themselves as a de facto global community. They work together to accomplish common goals, not out of altruism but out of a sense of self-interest stemming from shared and overlapping values. Mazarr identifies some forty-four states that are members of what he characterizes as the global guiding coalition (see Table 4.2).

The member nations in this coalition are largely but not exclusively democracies. They actively participate in a wide variety of international economic and security organizations, support international principles of nonaggression, and promote the peaceful settlement of disputes. Their formal state-to-state interactions are supported by the relatively free flow of information and the activities of multinational corporations, professional groups, and humanitarian organizations. As a group, the members of the guiding coalition are *order-producing states, countries committed to preserving the existing global*

TABLE 4.2 Membership in the Global Guiding Coalition		
Argentina	Iceland	Romania
Australia	India	Saudi Arabia
Austria	Indonesia	Singapore
Belgium	Ireland	Slovak Republic
Brazil	Italy	South Africa
Canada	Japan	South Korea
Chile	Luxemburg	Spain
Colombia	Malaysia	Sweden
Czech Republic	Mexico	Switzerland
Denmark	Netherlands	Thailand
Finland	New Zealand	Turkey
France	Norway	United Kingdom
Germany	Peru	United Arab Emirates
Greece	Poland	United States
Hungary	Portugal	

Source: Michael Mazarr, "Preserving the Post-War Order," *Washington Quarterly* 40 (2017): 34.

order or status quo, countries who share a commitment to territorial nonaggression, economic integration and stable global markets, and collective action.

Harmonizing Interests

As you have already learned, standard accounts of national, human, and global interests more often than not picture them in opposition to one another. So pursuing one means rejecting the others. One of the major challenges facing policy-makers is to move discussions of the definitions of values and interests into a less conflictual context. One strategy is to think of national, human, and global interests as nested on top of one another. Rather than being in conflict, these interests build on one another in a positive fashion to produce policies that advance all three.

The most important recent attempt to unify national, human, and global interests is the concept of **responsibility to protect (R2P)**.[30] According to R2P it is the state's responsibility to protect its population from genocide, war crimes, ethnic cleansing, and crimes against humanity, and the international community is responsible for helping states accomplish this. When a state cannot safeguard its population, the international community must take decisive and timely action. One of the most significant features of R2P is that it adds a new layer of responsibility to states without challenging state sovereignty. No longer are states responsible only for protecting their own interests; they are also responsible for protecting human interests. R2P portrays the international community as providing assistance without challenging sovereignty.

The immediate stimulus for R2P was the failure of states and the international community to respond to the 1994 genocide in Rwanda, which resulted in the deaths of more than a million people, along with the policy of ethnic cleansing that took place in the former Yugoslavia (most prominently in Bosnia, Serbia, and Kosovo), which resulted in the deaths of over a hundred thousand people. In the wake of these large-scale violations of human rights, Canada sponsored an International Commission on Intervention and State Sovereignty (ICISS).

The concept of responsibility to protect was put forward in the course of the ICISS deliberations. Its report identified R2P as consisting of four parts, two of which have already been identified: (1) primary responsibility of states to protect their populations from mass atrocities; and (2) the responsibility of the international community to aid states in this task. The report identified two further responsibilities of the international community: (3) prevention of mass atrocities; and (4) assistance in rebuilding affected societies in which mass atrocities have occurred. The ICISS report met with a mixed response at the United Nations. The United States, Russia, and China all raised objections as did smaller states, expressing concerns that R2P needed to respect territorial sovereignty. Ultimately R2P was approved by the UN with the qualification that references to the international community's responsibility to prevent and rebuild were dropped and that any intervention had to be authorized by the Security Council.

responsibility to protect (R2P) A global principle that reverses the traditional emphasis on sovereignty away from the right of states to act as they choose to require states to take responsibility for the welfare of their citizens in such areas as crimes against humanity, genocide, ethnic cleansing, and war crimes.

R2P is very much a work in progress. The best-known case in which R2P was invoked is the bombing of Libya that removed Muammar Gaddafi from power. This example highlights both the positive and negative features of R2P in its present form. On March 17, 2011, the UN Security Council passed Resolution 1973 approving a no-fly zone over Libya to protect civilians from attacks that might lead to crimes against humanity. The resolution authorized UN members to act through regional organizations to take all steps necessary to protect civilians. Ten countries voted yes, and five (Germany, Russia, China, India and Brazil) abstained. Two days later the North Atlantic Treaty Organization (NATO) began military action in Libya through conventional air strikes, cruise missile strikes, and a naval blockade. Gaddafi was killed on October 20 and the NATO mission officially ended on October 31. The positives of the Libyan R2P were the demonstrated ability of the international community to act and the removal of Gaddafi from power. More negatively, some felt that military action was taken too quickly after the UN resolution, arguing that it did not reflect a concern for human rights but a desire to use R2P as a cover for traditional national interest concerns. The domestic unrest that occurred in the wake of Gaddafi's ousting is seen as supporting the need for international aid in rebuilding a society, one of the parts of the original R2P that was dropped from the UN version.

Selecting a Decision-Making Model

A constant source of frustration for those who study international politics is understanding the process through which values are translated into policy, particularly step three, making a decision. Several models of decision-making have been presented: the rational actor, the personalities and perceptions of policy-makers, and small-group and bureaucratic politics models. The challenge is to select the model that is most helpful to explaining, predicting, and evaluating the process through which a particular decision is made.

A number of different standards can be applied in selecting the most helpful decision-making model. One is the amount of information required. The bureaucratic politics model requires a great deal of information. The rational actor model is much more helpful if little information is available. Second, different models are most helpful for different policy challenges. Because international crises are fast moving, policy-makers often utilize small-group decision-making and individual-centered models. Trade, environmental, and arms control policies tend to take a long time to work their way through the decision-making process, so bureaucratic politics models are frequently used to evaluate them.

One strategy is to use more than one model in studying a foreign policy decision. The model used changes depending on the step being evaluated. One such approach is the **poliheuristic model**.[31] This two-stage model of decision-making combines elements of

poliheuristic model
A two-stage model of decision-making in which policy-makers eliminate policy options on the basis of their beliefs in the first stage and conduct a more precise and reasoned evaluation of the merits of the remaining policy options in the second stage.

the rational actor model and individual-centered models that emphasize perception and reasoning. In the first stage, policy-makers simplify the decision they face by eliminating policy options on the basis of their beliefs about what is more highly valued and what might be "good enough." In the second stage they conduct a more precise and reasoned evaluation of the merits of the remaining policy options.

Summary

- Politics can be defined as the authoritative allocation of values.
- The Nansen Passport illustrates the challenge of reconciling human, national, and global interests.
- Foreign policy values focus on agreement and disagreement about the definitions of human, national, and global interests.
- Policy-making is a two-level game in which societal interests and the interests of international actors must be balanced.
- There are four major categories of societal influences on foreign policy making within states: (1) voting, (2) interest groups, (3) social movements, and (4) the media.
- Lobbying and transnational advocacy groups are two ways in which global voices influence foreign policy-making within states.
- The five majors steps in the policy-making process are (1) getting on the foreign policy agenda, (2) formulating a policy, (3) making a decision, (4) implementing the decision, and (5) evaluating the decision.
- Among the most significant value challenges are (1) finding a global voice, (2) harmonizing interests, and (3) selecting a decision-making model.
- The contemporary refugee crisis in Europe highlights the conflict among human, national, and global interests.
- Looking to the future, challenges including finding the global voice, harmonizing interests, and achieving a better understanding of how values are translated into policy.

Key Terms

Bureaucratic politics model *(113)*
Democratic peace theory *(117)*
Global interest *(99)*
Groupthink *(113)*
Human interest *(98)*
Human security *(98)*
Interest group *(103)*
Milieu goals *(99)*
National interest *(97)*

Policy-making process *(111)*
Poliheuristic model *(124)*
Prospect theory *(112)*
Rational actor model *(112)*
Responsibility to protect (R2P) *(123)*
Think tanks *(105)*
Transnational advocacy networks (TANs) *(110)*
Two-level game *(102)*

Critical Thinking Questions

1. Should a universal or global citizenship passport be created today?

2. Select a contemporary problem and discuss to what extent national, human, and global interests are present.

3. Rank in order of importance the *domestic* influences on selecting the values that guide foreign policy making. Justify your ranking.

4. Rank in order of importance the *global* influences on selecting the values that guide foreign policy-making. Justify your ranking.

5. Which of the steps in the pathway to policy is the most important? Explain your answer.

6. Would a Nansen Passport be helpful in dealing with the contemporary refugee problem in Europe?

7. Is it necessary to harmonize interests in addressing problems in international politics?

Practice and Review Online
http://textbooks.rowman.com/hastedt-felice

▲ An AIM-7 Sparrow medium-range air-to-air missile being fired from an F-15 Eagle aircraft. *Source:* US Air Force

05

THE POWER CHALLENGE:
THE ABILITY TO ACT

IN DISCUSSIONS OF INTERNATIONAL RELATIONS, **power** is the ability to influence and determine the actions of others. It is viewed in a number of different ways. Some stress that power is a resource. Others emphasize that power is a relationship or a means to an end. All agree that power is necessary to achieve foreign policy goals. One challenge policy-makers face is deciding what type of power is needed and how to acquire it. Power is not equally usable in all cases. The same military, diplomatic, or economic instrument of power cannot be used with equal effectiveness against all states or in all types of conflict situations. In addition, the foundations of power change over time. For example, because technological change has a tremendous impact on power, it serves as the focal point in the chapter-opening Historical Perspective and chapter-closing Contemporary Perspective sections. Still another challenge facing policy-makers is deciding when to use power and when to exercise restraint. Using power has its costs. Rather than advance the national interest, the exercise of power may not only fail to solve the problem it was intended to but create new ones.

The chapter also examines the nature of power in international relations, the newest form of power (cyberpower), the range of foreign

power The ability to influence and determine the actions of others; can be viewed as a resource one possesses, a relationship, or a means to an end.

policy instruments available to decision makers who use power to carry out foreign policy decisions, and responses to three of the main policy challenges facing those decision-makers in using power. The final section examines one of the most controversial contemporary uses of air power: armed drones. Let's begin with one of the earliest attempts to anticipate and understand the role of power: the wartime use of airplanes for strategic bombing.

LEARNING OBJECTIVES

Students will be able to:

- Explain how the debate over strategic bombing relates to the concept of power.

- Identify the sources and types of power and the difficulties in measuring and using it.

- Explain how cyberpower can be used in international relations.

- Describe how the different foreign policy instruments are used to develop and exercise power.

- Explain how technology can change the world's view of the use of power.

- Identify the policy responses to the three major challenges that states face when acquiring and using power.

HISTORICAL PERSPECTIVE:
The Case for Strategic Bombing

In 1921, three years after WWI ended, the Italian Ministry of War published a book called *The Command of Air*. Its author, Giulio Douhet, would come to be widely recognized as one of the founding theorists of air warfare.[1] Somewhat surprisingly, Douhet was trained as an infantry officer and never flew. He argued that future wars would be won or lost on how well the participating militaries had incorporated new technologies into their war plans. Technology was moving forward at a rapid pace when Douhet made his argument in 1921. The Wright Brothers flew the first airplane in December of 1903. Italy built its first dirigible in 1905 and flew its first plane in 1908. Three years later Italy became the first country to fly a plane in combat during the Italo-Turkish War in which Italian forces took control of much of Libya from Turkey. For most military strategists the dirigible was the airpower weapon of choice, with the primary mission of reconnaissance. Douhet disagreed, advocating the massing of airplanes for high-altitude strikes against decisive targets. In an argument that would become central to his thinking about the use of air power, Douhet identified the economic and administrative centers of the adversary rather than traditional front-line combat areas as these targets. His forceful and insistent advocacy of massed air power brought him into conflict with leading figures in the Italian military. After complaining to members of Italy's parliament that the general staff had misused airpower and was following a flawed ground offense strategy, he was court-martialed in 1916 and spent one year in prison.

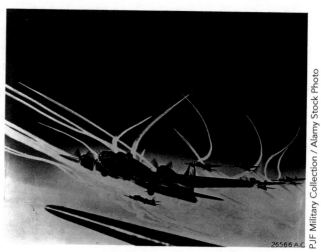

The Command of the Air, published in 1921 by Giulio Douhet, was one of the first books to examine the offensive and defensive use of air weapons.

Four assumptions formed the core of Douhet's argument:

1. Strategic bombing changed the character of war. It could no longer be assumed that bombing will be limited to contested military space; targeting economic and administrative centers put everyone—soldiers and civilians alike—at risk.
2. The central strategic principle in this new era of warfare was to deliver maximum damage against the adversary as quickly as possible. Surprise attack and preemption were essential to victory.
3. Traumatizing and crushing civilians by large-scale bombing will cripple an adversary's ability to fight. As Douhet wrote, "for military results it is much more important to destroy a railroad station, a bakery, a war plant...or any other behind-the-scenes objective than to strafe or bomb a trench. The result[s] are immeasurably greater in breaking morale...and spread terror and panic."
4. There is no effective defense against airpower.

Douhet's analysis of the future of airpower and modern warfare has been both embraced as prophetic and challenged as fundamentally flawed. One of those positively influenced by Douhet's views was Billy Mitchell, widely considered to be the father of the US Air Force. Mitchell similarly advocated a policy of strategic bombing with a heavy emphasis on civilian population centers, but he was less convinced of the invincibility of airpower. Like Douhet's, Mitchell's aggressive promotion of air power put him at odds with others in the military and government, leading to his court-martial for insubordination.

Later critics point to three significant flaws in Douhet's analysis:

1. Air power is not invincible. Anti-aircraft weapons and missile defense systems can limit the ability of aircraft to accomplish their missions.
2. Douhet overestimated the potential of large-scale bombing to destroy civilian morale. During WWII Hitler's attacks on London did not produce public demands that Great Britain sign a peace agreement. Similarly, US bombings of German military and industrial targets and the fire bombings of Dresden, Leipzig, and Hamburg did not lead to Germany's surrender.

3. Douhet ignored one of the oldest principles of warfare: war is a continuation of politics by other means. According to the constructivist and liberal theoretical perspectives, international relations are about values as much as they are about power. One of the most notable trends in the development of global values is the notion that civilians should not be made military targets. The targeting policy advocated by Douhet is no longer held to be acceptable without challenge. It is routinely condemned or must be justified. A notable case in point came as WWII ended when President Truman stated "The world will note that the first atomic bomb was dropped on Hiroshima, a military base... we wished to avoid insofar as possible the killing of civilians."[2] The evolutionary process of establishing a global consensus on the legitimacy of engaging in military practices that result in civilian casualties has not ended. Debate continues in military circles about the proper boundaries between military and civilian targets.[3]

This disagreement over the role of air power in a state's ability to achieve its objectives was not the first time that a debate occurred over the impact of technology in international politics. It is a long-standing point of controversy that continues today as commentators debate the value of drone technology, a topic taken up in the Contemporary Perspective on Power section near the end of the chapter.

One of the most famous debates took place at the turn of the twentieth century between American naval historian Thomas Mahan and British geographer Sir Halford Mackinder. Both agreed that control over oceans was the key to global dominance. They disagreed on how this was best achieved. Mahan's reading of the future was that, from a technological perspective, it would resemble the past. Control over the oceans required a strong naval force. Continental powers with strong military competitors on their borders could not afford to build large navies. States whose borders were protected by water, including Great Britain, Japan, and the United States, would be the dominant powers. Mackinder countered that land-bound states were likely to dominate because developments in railroad technology and weapons development gave them the ability to move large numbers of forces across land quickly and securely. This would allow them to outmaneuver and overpower states relying on naval power. For Mackinder, Russia was the state in the best position to take advantage of these technological developments.

Technology is not the only factor that influences the ability of states to act. In order to fully understand why power is crucial to international relations, it is important to recognize and appreciate that power is a multidimensional concept and that it has to be studied from a variety of perspectives. This chapter identifies four aspects of power that are of particular importance to its role in international relations: (1) sources of power, (2) types of power, (3) the difficulty of measuring power, and (4) the challenge of using power.

THE MANY SOURCES OF POWER

Only a moment's reflection is needed to realize that the list of factors that affect a state's power is lengthy and potentially endless. In addition to technology, which is covered in the Historical Perspective section, national will, political capacity, wealth, geography, populations, and natural resources are among the most frequently cited resources. This section provides a brief overview of each of them.

National Will

Sometimes referred to as national unity, *national will* is the existence of a socially accepted sense of purpose behind a foreign policy. Where national will is strong, the public is willing to make and accept sacrifices in the name of promoting foreign policy goals. Where it is weak or lacking, societies are deeply divided over what are proper foreign policy goals and the appropriate means to achieve them. Under such conditions foreign policy may lack consistency and a central purpose. It will take on an ad hoc quality, bouncing from policy to policy and from strong policy initiatives to inaction in the face of crises. A strong national will was seen as a key element of Israel's power base in fighting the Arab-Israeli wars of the 1950s, 1960s, and 1970s. One of the major consequences of the Vietnam War is seen to be the loss of an American national will to take the lead in keeping order in the international system, a feeling captured in President Donald Trump's campaign slogans of "America First" and "Make American Great Again." From the perspective of many, one of the major challenges facing the international community today is to create a strong sense of global will to counter terrorism and address pressing humanitarian problems.

Political Capacity

Political capacity refers to the ability of state institutions to formulate and implement policy. It is commonly seen as having two dimensions. The first is the ability of legislatures, executive branches, and the bureaucracy to act together in a coherent fashion. Gridlocked legislatures, presidents or prime ministers unable to construct a foreign policy agenda, or bureaucracies that constantly seem at odds over implementing policy are all seen as undermining a state's political capacity. The second dimension of political capacity refers to the ability of the state to resist pressures from interest groups, political parties, and other societal actors in formulating and implementing policy. To the extent that states are "captured" by these political forces, state capacity is threatened. Political capacity is an important element in identifying strong and fragile states, a subject that was taken up in Chapter 3.

Wealth

A state's wealth always has been an important contributor to a state's power. Traditionally, wealth is defined in terms of a state's *gross national product (GNP)*: the total value of goods and services produced by its firms at home or abroad. The greater a state's wealth, the better it is able to construct an industrial and technological base capable of producing modern military weapons. Without this ability, a state's military establishment would stand on a hollow foundation that could not withstand the challenges of a lengthy conflict or multiple wars. This narrow perspective on wealth as a source of power because of its ability to support military operations is now joined by one that emphasizes the importance of wealth as contributing to the construction of vibrant societies. This is accomplished through strong education systems, cultural pluralism, the promotion of technological change, and the development of democracy, all of which are important foundations of state power outside of the military arena.

Geography

Geography is valued as a power resource because size, *topography* (the physical features of a country), location, and climate play key roles in defining and responding to national security threats. Consider Russia. Even stripped of much of the territory held by the old Soviet Union, Russia remains the world's largest state, with a territory of almost 6.6 million sq. miles.

Throughout its history, Russia has used its large size and its climate to its advantage. A century apart, both Hitler and Napoleon met defeat as their invading armies marched deep into Russia only to confront cold harsh Russian winters. By a quirk of fate, Russia was also made vulnerable to attack from Europe by the absence of any natural barriers—such as mountains—to block an invading army. This was one of the factors that led to Stalin's interest in surrounding the Soviet Union with East European satellite states after WWII.

Another example is Israel. With an area of only some 8,000 sq. miles, this country has faced a different security challenge. Lacking the luxury of trading land for time to defeat an aggressor, Israel has repeatedly engaged in offensive military actions to push perceived military threats from its borders, including opposing armies and terrorist groups. Examples include the 1948 Arab-Israeli War, the 1956 Suez Crisis, the 1967 Arab-Israeli War, and the 1982 Lebanon War, as well as smaller military incursions into Palestinian territories and neighboring countries.

Population

A large population is valued because it provides the foundation for a large military as well as a large work force to produce the goods and materials that create national wealth and military hardware. However, power cannot be built on population alone. The make-up of the population is also important. A population dominated by the elderly or by children is a potential drain on state power, as neither group contributes to the production of wealth or the size of a military, yet they both consume resources. Japan stands out as an example. *The CIA World Factbook* calculates that 27.8% of the Japanese population is aged sixty-five and over. At the opposite end of the age continuum is Iran; 23.65% of its population is aged fourteen and under. Large populations that lack education or other vital workplace skills limit a state's ability to create power. An estimated 54% of Canada's population aged twenty-five to sixty-four have completed tertiary (college) education, as have 42% of Great Britain's population. At the other extreme, only 7% of South Africa's population and 14% of Brazil's population in this same age group have completed their college educations.[4] An ethnically divided population can also undercut a state's power base. While few states possess ethnically homogeneous populations, some states face ongoing tensions between different ethnic groups that weaken state power by creating conditions ranging from civil wars to political stalemates. The ethnic conflicts that have received the most global attention over the past decades because of their high level of violence are those in the Balkans, the Sudan, Iraq, Rwanda, Chechnya, and Darfur.

Natural Resources

Oil is one of the natural resources most important to power. From a consumer perspective, the power potential of oil is fully evident in the surge in oil prices that accompanied the Organization of Petroleum Exporting Countries (OPEC)–led oil embargo of the early 1970s and a second wave of price hikes in 1980. Before the 1973 OPEC oil embargo, the price of oil was $1.80 per barrel. It rose to $11.67 after the embargo began and skyrocketed to over $30 per barrel in 1980. Oil-producing countries gained great wealth from these price increases, but they also experienced a reality quite different than expected. The incoming funds were unable to help them develop an industrial or commercial base independent of oil production. Most of the money was invested abroad or used to purchase the loyalty of key individuals and groups. The result of this continued dependence on oil hit home when the price of oil plummeted to $16 per barrel in 1986. Oil dependency for sellers remains a problem today. In 2017 it became widely recognized that, with the large increase in US shale oil production, OPEC is no longer in control of global oil prices the way it once was. The mixed blessing of oil is one example of the resource curse. Natural resources simultaneously provide great wealth and undermine a country's efforts to develop. The resource curse will be examined more fully in Chapter 8 in the examination of global economic challenges.

It is often assumed that the more power resources a state possesses, the more likely it is to win wars. Yet having lots of power resources is not enough to guarantee victory. Powerful states often lose wars. The Policy Spotlight discusses why this happens.

THE MANY TYPES OF POWER

Different types of power address different challenges. The nature of the challenge, foreign policy goals, location, the amount of time available to act, the identity of the other actors, and the stakes involved all affect potential responses and require different types of power. In this section two different characterizations of power are examined. The first is power over outcomes and power over the rules of the game. The second is the difference between hard power and soft power.

POLICY SPOTLIGHT

Why Powerful States Lose Wars

The flags of what are commonly considered to be the most powerful global and regional states in the world today.

Wars between strong and weak states are often referred to as asymmetric conflicts, due to large differences in power resources and military strategies. It is generally taken for granted that strong states, those with greater military power resources, will defeat weaker states in a war. This is not always the case, however. Understanding why strong states lose wars to weaker states requires answering two questions.

How often do more powerful states lose wars? The data here are mixed.[5] One study found that from thirty wars took place from 1816 to 1965 and strong states won all but nine of them. Another study published in 2000 concluded that weaker states came out ahead in 41% of all wars. One explanation for these different findings is that researchers often use different time frames, define war differently, and define winning differently.

What causes a more powerful state to lose a war? No one reason is agreed upon by all. Most would argue that the failure of a strong state to triumph in war is the result of a combination of factors. A common

Power over Outcomes and Power Over "Rules of the Game"

A distinction is often made between two different types of power. The first is the power to determine the outcome or content of a specific decision such as the content of an international trade agreement, imposing an economic boycott, and preventing a country from developing nuclear weapons or selling weapons to another country. The second type of power is the ability to establish "the rules of the game," the procedures and values that guide the decision-making process. This type of power is seen in the ability to create and operate international organizations such as the United Nations (UN) or the World Trade Organization (WTO), or it may take the form of leading by example and setting international norms regarding the proper way to address global challenges. Such challenges include the provision of humanitarian aid after a natural disaster or the provision of relief for refugees.

Power over specific outcomes and power over the rules of the game are not mutually exclusive. A state may possess either, both, or neither. Negotiating an international climate or trade agreement involves both types of power. Power over specific outcomes starting point is to argue that the strong state adopted the wrong strategy in fighting the war. If this is the case the key question becomes: why was the strategy adopted? Answers to this question are often sought by using the types of decision-making models presented in Chapter 4.

Another reason lies with the nature of victory in war. Clausewitz observed that while battles can be analyzed in terms of "self-contained contests of military power...the final outcome of wars depends upon a much wider range of factors." He singled out the impact of domestic politics as particularly important. This line of thinking has led many to conclude that the strong lose wars because their citizens become war weary and tired of the human and monetary price of the war. Strong states do not lose on the battlefield but decide to stop fighting.

One variation on this argument holds that it is not the actual cost of a war so much as whether the cost of a war is higher than was expected. A second variation has to do with the nature of the objectives sought by the strong state. Here the distinction is between non-transformative and transformative goals. An example would be simply replacing one leader with another and trying to create a democracy where none existed. Non-transformative goals can be achieved by battlefield victories where strong states are unlikely to lose. Transformative goals require getting the population of the weaker state to agree with the goals of the stronger state and work toward achieving them, neither of which is not easily achieved using military power alone.

Think about It

1. Are strong states more likely or less likely to lose wars today than in the past? Why? What has changed?
2. What steps might a strong state take to avoid losing a war?

comes into play when making decisions about issues related to the goals of the agreement, such as deciding whether to require rich countries to provide poor countries with financial assistance and specifying the conditions under which such aid is given. Power over the rules of the game is exercised when participants determine whether the terms of the agreement are legally binding (or merely recommended); identify procedures for treaty violations, revisions, or exit; or decide what type of information must be provided by those signing the treaty.

Power over the rules of the game is central to the liberal perspective on international relations. It is of special interest to states for a number of reasons:

1. Looking into the future is not easy. Circumstances may change, allies may become enemies, and/or new issues may arise. Structural power provides a platform for managing future issues and events.
2. Determining the outcome of specific issues depends on how many states are involved and their respective levels of power. Structural power can provide a less expensive way to achieve goals.

3. The rules of the game created by structural power are not neutral. Because they reflect the values and positions of those powerful enough to create them and have a potentially long lifespan, they can provide benefits to the states that created them even if the power of those states declines.

Hard and Soft Power

Joseph Nye asserts that foreign policy options can be visualized as a continuum of choices, each of which requires different power resources[6] (see Figure 5.1). At one end of the continuum is co-optation, in which you are able to manipulate opponents into coming over to your side. Attraction, in which your policies serve as a magnet bringing other countries over to your side because they agree with you, is next on the continuum, and agenda setting falls toward the middle. All of these are forms of soft power. **Soft power** is the power of persuasion using information, culture, values, and ideas to accomplish foreign policy goals. Nye identifies three primary sources of soft power for a state as its culture, political values, and foreign policy.

soft power The power of persuasion using information, culture, values, and ideas to accomplish foreign policy goals.

Next along the continuum are foreign policies based on inducements or incentives (such as bribes and the provision of military and economic assistance) and foreign policies based on coercion, in which sanctions and force are used to convince others to act in the desired manner. At the far end of the continuum, the desired outcomes are imposed on others by foreign policies based on command. Inducements, coercion, and command rely on **hard power**, power with roots primarily in military and economic capabilities.

hard power The power of coercion and command to accomplish foreign policy goals, generally by employing military and economic means.

Hard power is the traditional view of power in international relations. Associated with realism, this view considers power to be something you possess and compete with other states to acquire. In the extreme, this competition takes on the character of a zero-sum struggle. The more military or economic coercive and command power a state has, the less that others will have. Soft power tends to be associated with liberalism, constructivism, and feminism.

Soft power is considered important to the successful conduct of foreign policy by those who see the replacement of the traditional hierarchy of hard-power states by a networked structure of states and non-state actors that values coordinated action to address global challenges. In addition, some argue for the existence of a *global public.*

Figure 5.1 Power Continuum.

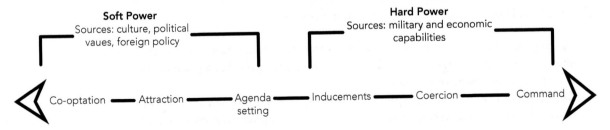

According to this view, the combination of the rapid spread of information through the Internet and related communication systems has democratized information and created the foundation for an activist and informed global citizenry. This global public requires the use of soft power to accomplish foreign policy goals.

Although described as a continuum, hard and soft power should not be viewed as polar opposites. What matters is how power resources are used. Victory in war is largely the result of the ability of one military to defeat another, which requires hard power. Yet this victory may generate soft power if it leads to the creation of new ideas, attracting other states to the victor's values and in the process changing definitions of acceptable behavior in international relations and/or creating new international institutions. For example, after WWII the United Nations was created, along with a series of international economic bodies including the International Monetary Fund and the World Bank, and the goals of promoting human rights and democracy emerged on the global agenda. All of these efforts reflected the values of the United States. In contrast, soft power did not follow victory in WWI. The League of Nations floundered when the United States refused to join, American isolationist sentiment grew stronger, right-wing political parties came to power in Europe, and the global economic depression created deep divisions among countries.

THE DIFFICULTY OF MEASURING POWER

Given the range of factors that contribute to a state's hard and soft power capabilities, it is not surprising that measuring power is difficult. One way in which governments and scholars have sought to measure state power is by creating a *power index*, an equation that identifies the key elements of power and relates them to one another through addition, subtraction, division, and multiplication to produce an overall power rating. Creating a power index requires clarity about the factors that contribute to state power. For example, if you identify the level of military spending as a factor in determining a state's power, you need to decide if this should be calculated by looking at the total amount spent annually, the percentage of the total government budget, or the percentage of the gross national product. Likewise, if the size of the military is considered an ingredient in state power, do you measure this by counting the number of active duty personnel, or do you include military reservists, border police, and other units?

Two examples of the measurement of power using a power index that reflect thinking about power in two different countries are the Global Power Index created by the US National Intelligence Council and the Comprehensive National Power (CNP) Index created by the Chinese military. The focus of these examples is not the specific measures used but identification of the ingredients thought to be of importance.

- *Global Power Index.* Every four years the US National Intelligence Council produces a *Global Trends* report that provides a strategic assessment of key global uncertainties and trends and their implications for the future. The first report, published in 1997, sought to help policy-makers think about what the world might look like in 2010.

The most recent *Global Trends* report, produced in 2017, highlighted global issues and trends that might dominate world politics in 2035.[7] To construct its analysis of the future, the National Intelligence Council created a Global Power Index. The initial version had four hard power resources: gross domestic product (GDP), population size, military spending, and technology. More recently, this list has expanded to include soft power resources relevant to twenty-first century power: health, education, and governance. The new index gave a different picture of emerging global power trends. The original index projected that China's power would equal that of the United States in 2030. The updated power index indicates that China will be 4–5 percentage points below the United States. Both versions of the index expect that developing world countries will overtake most of the developed world by the year 2030.

- *Comprehensive National Power (CNP) Index.* The need for a comprehensive measure of China's comparative power was first voiced by Deng Xiaoping, the most powerful political figure in China from 1978 until his retirement in 1989. The task of constructing a Comprehensive National Power (CNP) assessment was undertaken by a

THEORY SPOTLIGHT

Measuring Soft Power

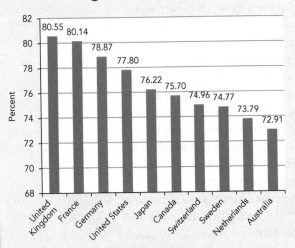

Figure 5.2 The 2018 Portland Soft Power 30 Index.

Theories are sets of ideas and principles that provide us with a framework for studying international politics. Testing theories requires that we have clear and precise measures of their key concepts. This is easier said than done. This feature takes up the challenge of defining soft power so that it can be tested. Just like hard power, soft power is a multidimensional concept requiring equal precision in its conceptualization and use in the study of international relations. One of the first attempts to create a soft power index was constructed in 2015 by Portland Communications, a British public relations and political consulting firm. Its Soft Power 30 Index has been revised in subsequent years.[9]

The Portland Soft Power 30 Index uses Joseph Nye's definition and three key primary sources of soft power (political values, culture, and foreign policy) to create six objective sub-indices to measure a state's soft power. The six objective data categories, along with a short list of indicators used for each, are as follows:

- Culture (total number of international tourists, size of the music market, number of films appearing in major film festivals).

number of different institutions, so there is no single CNP assessment. One CNP index, created by a branch of the People's Liberation Army called the Academy of Military Science,[8] constructed four different power "subsystems": (1) material or hard power, (2) spirit or soft power, (3) coordinated power (such as leadership and lines of command), and (4) environmental factors. Using this index, the Academy of Military Science study concluded that the United States would remain as the most powerful state until 2020. China was found to rank fifth in 2000 but was expected to be second in 2020.

The fact that different power indices produce different power rankings highlights both the difficulty of measuring power and the value of creating an index. Power indexes are valuable because they require critical thinking about power. Instead of speaking in general terms about one state being more powerful than another, indexes promote dialogue about the nature of power. The resulting clarity sets the stage for the formation of focused and critical policies related to power.

- Digital (Facebook followers, number of Internet users per thousand inhabitants, mobile phones per hundred inhabitants).
- Education (number of top global universities, gross tertiary education [university] enrollment rates, number of international students).
- Engagement (total overseas development aid, membership in international organizations, number of environmental treaties).
- Enterprise (global patents filed, foreign direct investment/GDP, Heritage Economic Freedom score, Global Innovation Index score).
- Government (Human Development Index, Freedom House score, Press Freedom Index).

As you have already learned, one of the major features distinguishing soft power from hard power is that it cannot be truly possessed by states. Because it is the power of attraction, it depends as much, if not more so, on how others view the political values, culture, and foreign policy of a particular country. To better understand this important characteristic of soft power, the Portland Soft Power 30 index commissioned a set of polling questions that were asked of 10,500 people in twenty-five countries. Questions on a wide range of subjects included identification of technology products and luxury goods produced, cuisine of other countries, contributions to global culture, and trust in the approach of other countries to global affairs.

The top ten soft power states in the 2018 Portland Soft Power 30 Index are shown in Figure 5.2. China came in at twenty-seventh (51.85), and Russia was ranked twenty-eighth (51.10). In the previous year China had been ranked twenty-fifth and Russia twenty-sixth.

The soft power index confirms the perceived domination of Western political values and culture in thinking about soft power and raises questions about the extent to which a definition of soft power rooted in Western values (or of those from any single region) can effectively function as a source of attraction in a globalized world.

Think about It

1. What indicator or measure would you add to the soft power index to make it more complete? Why?

2. How does a measure like the Portland Soft Power 30 Index hurt a developing country like India?

Constructing an index is not unique to the study of power. Indexes are frequently used to measure changes in an attempt to understand other complex subjects in international relations. Other important indexes include the Human Development Index, the Corruption Perceptions Index, the Freedom in the World Index, the Rule of Law Index, and the Environmental Performance Index. Although hard power is easier to measure, it is just as important to measure soft power; see the Theory Spotlight for ways to measure soft power.

THE CHALLENGE OF USING POWER

Using power is not without its problems. A distinction is commonly made between the amounts of power possessed in the abstract or on paper (*latent power*) and the amount of power that can actually be used to influence outcomes (*actualized power*). Inevitably, a certain amount of leakage occurs when moving from one to the other.

Studies of the use of military power throughout the years have described the challenges in moving from latent military power to actualized military power. Carl von Clausewitz, a Prussian military officer who fought against French forces during the French Revolution and the Napoleonic Wars, wrote that in war "everything is very simple but the simplest things are difficult."[10] Two reasons for this are "fog" and "friction." Fog is a metaphor for the inherent uncertainty in gaining complete and accurate information about a situation so that correct decisions can be made. Friction refers to the idea that unforeseen problems will inevitably arise when military power is used. Clausewitz stressed that, while breakdowns in the execution of military plans (such as a delay in positioning troops, misinterpretation of orders, or late arrival of supplies) may be small, the consequences of friction are cumulative and can have potentially dire political consequences and may even result in military defeat. For example, a US bombing mission in May 2017 against a target in Mosul, Syria, killed an estimated 140 people. This was not the intent. The United States dropped a 500lb. bomb on a building to kill to ISIS fighters on the roof. Instead it caused the building to collapse, killing those in it. Others outside the building were killed by debris. Air attacks were halted for two weeks as investigators reviewed some 700 hours of footage taken by jets trying to determine what went wrong.

The movement from latent to actualized power also affects economic power, including the use of economic sanctions. States are often unable to prevent sanction-busting behavior by other states and by multinational corporations who provide the target state with the resources it needs to withstand the sanctions' economic impact.[11] For example, from 2006–2017 eleven rounds of UN sanctions were applied against North Korea because of its missile testing program, but its leaders took advantage of numerous loopholes:

- North Korea has dodged banking sanctions by using front companies that, while they appear to be independent companies, are really controlled by North Korea.
- Many North Korean garment firms produce clothing with "made in China" labels.
- North Korea earns some $1.1 billion each year selling coal to China and $70 million per year allowing China to fish in its territorial waters. China has argued that doing so

does not violate UN sanctions, since ending these transactions would hurt ordinary people and not North Korea's military programs.

Soft power has its own transformation costs. In a sense they are of a different kind since two of the three sources of soft power—culture and political values—are not possessed by a state in the same way as hard power resources. States have tried to control or project soft power, however. During the cold war the United States did so through Radio Free Europe and Voice of America radio broadcasts into the Soviet Union and East Europe. The US Information Agency was created in 1953 to help spread American values and culture. A charge frequently leveled at such soft power instruments is that they engage in propaganda and their reporting is not necessarily truthful. With the explosion of global communication systems and 24/7 news coverage, controlling the images of the United States that are seen by citizens of other countries has become much more difficult. More often than not, today's governments find themselves placed in a reactive position, trying to correct false information or engage in damage control when problems stemming from the use of hard power or domestic government policies have provoked a public outcry abroad.

CYBERPOWER

The newest form of power is **cyberpower**, information used in order to inflict harm, persuade, or more generally gain an advantage over an adversary.[12] Among its most significant characteristics is the inability of major powers such as Russia, China, and the United States to monopolize or dominate it. Cyberpower can be exercised by individuals, non-state actors ranging from terrorist groups to reform-minded civil society organizations, and far less powerful states. Vietnam, North Korea, Iran, and Israel have all been linked to significant cyberattacks in the recent past.

cyberpower
Information used in order to inflict harm, persuade, or more generally gain an advantage over an adversary.

Unlike traditional military technologies, which achieve their objectives through the physical destruction of a target, cyberpower achieves its objectives by temporarily capturing its target and providing it with misleading or false information that reduces its ability to function properly. Entry into computer systems can be achieved in any number of ways ranging from weaknesses in computer operating systems, to organizational security lapses, to individual carelessness. Given the wide range of actors who can engage in cyberattacks, one of the major challenges of cyber foreign policy is to determine which attacks qualify as security challenges and which are better classified as mischief, protest, criminal, or profiteering attacks, or some combination of them, such as the ransomware attacks that crippled thousands of computer systems worldwide in 2017.

The first and most significant military use of cyberpower occurred in 2010 when the United States and Israel partnered on a cyberattack designed to cripple Iran's efforts to obtain nuclear capability. Work on the project began in 2007, partly as an effort by the United States to convince Israel that war with Iran was not the only way to avert Iran's becoming a nuclear power. Five different organizations in Iran were targeted, but the Natanz nuclear enrichment facility was the primary focus of the attack. After obtaining knowledge of the codes within the computers' operating systems from Siemens (the company that built them), the Stuxnet virus issued instruction to the computers controlling the uranium enrichment centrifuges to change their speeds, causing them to break. About 30,000 IP addresses were infected, resulting in a 30% loss of Natanz's operational capacity.

One of the most fundamental challenges facing policy-makers in using cyberpower is developing an effective cybersecurity strategy. As you learned in Chapter 1, policy-makers often look to the past for guidance in solving new problems. In the case of cybersecurity threats, this approach has led some commentators to warn of cyber Pearl Harbors and cyber 9/11s. As symbolically powerful as these two surprise attacks were, they do not provide a basis for developing a coherent strategic framework for thinking about cyberpower. An approach that has been used more frequently involves employing the language and logic that has governed military planning about the use of nuclear weapons. Many argue that, like the development of nuclear weapons, cyberpower will usher in a new age of military strategy and will redefine global power relations. This line of thinking has led to creation of cyberattack ladders that organize possible cyberattacks from the most minor to the most significant. These ladders are built on the concept of a nuclear escalation ladder that was popularized by Herman Kahn in the 1960s.[13] An example of a cyberattack ladder is presented in Figure 5.3.

Although the historical analogy with nuclear weapons is tempting on the surface, there are a number of differences between nuclear power and cyberpower. The first and most obvious difference is that nuclear weapons are immensely destructive in their own right. In contrast, cyberpower cannot destroy buildings or kill people in an instant. Secondly, nuclear technology and the associated defensive and offensive strategies have changed and developed over time. For example, nuclear weapons were seen initially as an offensive force, but over time their role has become one of defense and deterrence. Today cyberoffense appears to hold the advantage, but that may change as well. Uncertainty exists over how long offensive cyberattacks can retain their advantage over defensive measures.

The Stuxnet attack on Iran's nuclear facilities described earlier is a case in point. Initial evaluations of the attack in the West were positive, as the attack was credited with having damaged key aspects of Iran's nuclear program. Gradually doubts were raised about its effectiveness. International Atomic Energy Agency inspections suggested that Iran was able to move quickly to overcome these setbacks despite international economic sanctions limiting its access to nuclear material. Further doubt about the game-changing nature of cyberattacks comes from indications that the United States wanted to use a version of Stuxnet against North Korea, which failed due to an inability to infect North Korean computer networks. Cyberattacks have also proven ineffective in efforts to end terrorism. One year after the United States mounted a cyberoffensive against ISIS computers, ISIS terrorist attacks against Great Britain and Iran still took place. Terrorists use computer technology more for recruitment and propaganda than for organizing attacks. Much of their technology is commonplace and can easily be reestablished following an attack.[14]

A third and related complication in using nuclear strategic logic is that the key to the success of deterrence is the ability to identify whom to retaliate against if deterrence

Figure 5.3 Cyberthreat Escalation Ladder.

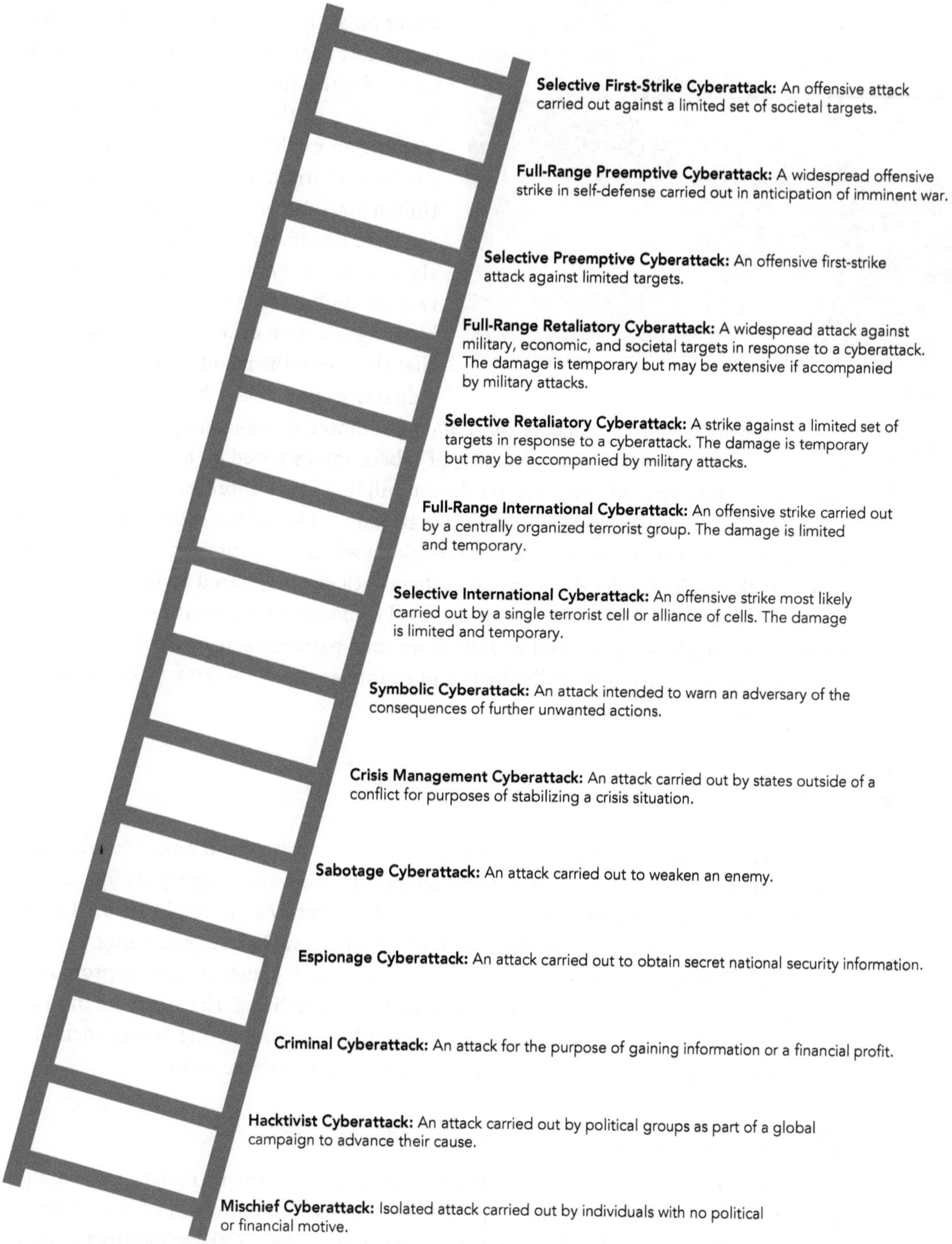

Selective First-Strike Cyberattack: An offensive attack carried out against a limited set of societal targets.

Full-Range Preemptive Cyberattack: A widespread offensive strike in self-defense carried out in anticipation of imminent war.

Selective Preemptive Cyberattack: An offensive first-strike attack against limited targets.

Full-Range Retaliatory Cyberattack: A widespread attack against military, economic, and societal targets in response to a cyberattack. The damage is temporary but may be extensive if accompanied by military attacks.

Selective Retaliatory Cyberattack: A strike against a limited set of targets in response to a cyberattack. The damage is temporary but may be accompanied by military attacks.

Full-Range International Cyberattack: An offensive strike carried out by a centrally organized terrorist group. The damage is limited and temporary.

Selective International Cyberattack: An offensive strike most likely carried out by a single terrorist cell or alliance of cells. The damage is limited and temporary.

Symbolic Cyberattack: An attack intended to warn an adversary of the consequences of further unwanted actions.

Crisis Management Cyberattack: An attack carried out by states outside of a conflict for purposes of stabilizing a crisis situation.

Sabotage Cyberattack: An attack carried out to weaken an enemy.

Espionage Cyberattack: An attack carried out to obtain secret national security information.

Criminal Cyberattack: An attack for the purpose of gaining information or a financial profit.

Hacktivist Cyberattack: An attack carried out by political groups as part of a global campaign to advance their cause.

Mischief Cyberattack: Isolated attack carried out by individuals with no political or financial motive.

Ebrahim Norouzi / AP Images

Computers at Iran's Bushehr nuclear plant, which was a Stuxnet target.

fails. The inability to identify a cyberattacker quickly and with certainty casts some doubt on applying the logic of nuclear deterrence to cyberattacks. Without the ability to identify the aggressor with certainty (analogous to the fog of war), any retaliatory action might prove to be incorrect. In the case of Stuxnet, neither Israel nor the United States accepted responsibility for the attacks against Iran. Similarly, China, Russia, and North Korea have routinely denied responsibility for cyberattacks, either by blaming them on other states or asserting that they were the result of actions by individual citizens and not the government.

Conceptual problems such as these have prompted some leading commentators on cyberconflict to call for the rethinking of cyberstrategy based on a nuclear weapons conceptual framework. Martin Libicki calls for building a new approach to cyberconflict around the rules used to fight crime rather than wars.[15] Like crime, cyberattacks cannot be stopped; they will not go away or end. Hacking will be a continuing threat. What is needed is threefold: (1) development of a cyberattack strategy based on improved security rather than the use of violence as a standard response; (2) international norms that define cyberattacks as illegal and wrong rather than patriotic acts or playful undertakings; and (3) recognition by individuals and countries that cyberattacks will result in swift and severe punishment.

INSTRUMENTS OF POWER

In practical terms the translation from latent power to actualized power involves the employment of specific instruments of foreign policy. This section highlights four important foreign policy instruments that can be used separately or in combination: (1) the military, (2) economics, (3) diplomacy, and (4) covert action. Before proceeding, a caveat is in order. Different states employ different foreign policy instruments in promoting their interests, and not all states are created equal. In addition, there is little international agreement on how to best address the challenges confronting states, including how to defeat terrorism, protect human rights, or ensure national security.

The Military as an Instrument of Power

Discussions of the military as an instrument of power and the formulation of foreign policy have several different starting points. Some focus on the area in which a military operation will take place (land, sea, air, outer space, and cyber). Others identify the tasks that the military needs to be prepared to undertake. There are five broad approaches to the use of the military as an instrument of power:

1. **Homeland defense**. Although the related term of *homeland security* only came into popular usage in the United States after the 9/11 terrorist attacks, protecting a state's borders from foreign attacks (and by extension its independence and sovereignty) has long been the primary mission of the military. The 9/11 attacks, along with subsequent terrorist attacks around the world including Paris, London, and Tehran, expanded the notion of what constituted homeland defense. In addition to the threat of an armed invasion, violent acts within a country that could be considered acts of war must also be considered.

2. **Combat operations**. Combat operations can take several different forms. At one extreme they involve the use of nuclear weapons during war as the United States did in Hiroshima and Nagasaki in the concluding phase of WWII. Although US nuclear strategy now uses them in a deterrent role, nuclear weapons can still be used as part of wartime military operations. Israeli war plans in the 1967 Arab-Israeli War called for a "doomsday operation," detonation of a demonstration nuclear blast if it appeared that Israel would lose the war.[16] At the other end of the continuum are hybrid wars, such as that fought in the Ukraine and the 2006 war between Israel and Hezbollah. **Hybrid war** combines elements of conventional warfare, irregular warfare, and cyberpower to create a highly flexible and resilient fighting posture that can adapt readily to changed circumstances. Combining multiple forms of warfare in a single conflict is not a new military strategy; what has changed is the integration of nonmilitary instruments such as social media.

   hybrid war A form of warfare that combines elements of conventional warfare, irregular warfare, and cyberwarfare to create a highly flexible and resilient fighting posture that can adapt readily to changed circumstances.

3. **Internal foreign defense**. These operations involve the use of military force against terrorist operations or rebellions supported by outside powers. More generally referred to as *counterinsurgency operations*, internal foreign defense emphasizes the provision of weapons, training, and advice for the military forces of the host country but may include direct involvement in fighting terrorist or rebel forces as well. It brings military forces into close contact with foreign populations. Winning the hearts and minds of the public replaces winning the battle as a primary objective. Recently, the United States has engaged in internal foreign defense operations in Syria, where it has partnered with Syrian Democratic Forces and in Iraq, where it has helped train and organize Iraqi counterterrorism forces.

4. **Peacekeeping and stabilization missions**. These military operations occur after fighting has ended. As such, their focus is not on defeating an enemy per se but on helping create a domestic security environment in which progress can be made toward the establishment of a new government and the undertaking of needed political, social, and economic reforms. Early in the post-Cold War period peacekeeping and stabilization missions were largely identified with United Nations operations such as those established to create buffers between Israel and Arab forces in 1956 and 1973 and most recently in the Sudan in 2007. Today, individual states are also

heavily involved in them. One of the leading peacekeeping and stabilization states is Canada. Numbered among the missions it has undertaken are reinforcing police reform efforts in the Ukraine, supporting the implementation of the Colombian peace plan, carrying out stabilizing operations in Mali, and providing assistance to Afghan security and defense forces.

5. **Force projection**. This catch-all category includes the ability to conduct raids and rescue operations, carry out military strikes, demonstrate force through military exercises, enforce sanctions, and guarantee freedom of the seas. What unites these military operations is that they are generally carried out in response to developing crisis situations or during an ongoing military conflict where the nature of the military challenge is still in its early developing stages. Today there are two regions where major force projection activities are taking place. The first is the South China Sea. Here, the United States and China have each carried out a series of naval operations and instituted changes in military strategy designed to highlight their ability to dispatch significant naval forces to the region on short notice. The second is the Arctic where Russia has built up its naval capabilities in anticipation of further warming and competition over northern sea lanes.

Diplomacy as an Instrument of Power

diplomacy The practice of fostering relationships around the world in order to resolve issues and advance interests.

Diplomacy is both a long-established tool of exercising power and an evolving one. Henry Kissinger presents a traditional definition. He defines **diplomacy** as "the art of relating states to each other by agreement rather than by the exercise of force."[17] Diplomatic

Alexander Zemlianichenko / AP Images

Russian military might on display during a parade of the armed forces.

success requires credibility, the building of trust, and perseverance. A more contemporary definition of diplomacy is put forward by the US State department which defines diplomacy as "a complex and often challenging practice of fostering relationships around the world in order to resolve issues and advance interests."[18]

Today diplomacy operates in multiple dimensions, three of which stand out:

1. Traditional state-to-state diplomacy is now complemented by diplomatic initiatives directed at foreign publics, known as *public diplomacy*. The primary objective of public diplomacy is not to solve a problem or manage relations but to provide information to the citizens of other states that presents a more sympathetic and supportive image. For example, a country's economic achievements, its cultural history, or its involvement in global disaster-relief operations could be highlighted. In carrying out this mission, public diplomacy seeks to distance itself from charges of engaging in propaganda by stressing the truthfulness and objectivity of the information being provided.

2. Diplomatic initiatives are carried out in a greater variety of ways. Face-to-face meetings on the part of ambassadors or other government representatives are no longer the only form of diplomacy. A considerable amount of diplomacy is carried out through computer and online communications. The primary use of such digital diplomacy is in the area of public diplomacy. Approximately 190 countries and more than 4,000 embassies and ambassadors currently have some type of Twitter account. Social media accounts operated by the US State Department include Facebook, Pinterest, Twitter, Instagram, and YouTube.[19]

3. Diplomacy is now organized around the specific type of foreign policy challenge being addressed; it is no longer a one-size-fits-all undertaking. Examples of such tailored diplomacy include natural disaster diplomacy, coercive diplomacy, environmental diplomacy, humanitarian diplomacy, preventive diplomacy, and health diplomacy.

Finally, diplomacy is no longer monopolized by state departments and foreign ministries. The expanded range of issues involving diplomacy has been accompanied by an expansion in bureaucratic units ranging from the military and treasury departments to commerce and agriculture. In the area of US health diplomacy, the Department of Health and Human Services, the Department of Defense, and the Agency for International Development have at one point or another assigned health attachés to US embassies in China, Brazil, Switzerland, South Africa, India, Vietnam, Indonesia, Ethiopia, Afghanistan, and Iraq.[20]

Economics as an Instrument of Power

Discussions about the role of economic factors such as currency value, foreign trade balance, and the health of the job market take place largely in the context of globalization in which the starting point for analysis is the ability of economic factors to help create a more prosperous world economy for all. This is the approach that we will follow in Chapter 7. Here, the focus is on the role of five dimensions of economic policy in promoting the national interests of states: (1) foreign trade, (2) foreign investment, (3) monetary policy, (4) economic sanctions, and (5) economic aid.[21]

A wide variety of specific tools can be used to construct a state's foreign trade policy. The overall goal is to influence the export and import of goods and services to promote the national interest. This can be done both by rewarding other states and by punishing them. Among the trade policies used are setting tariff levels (taxes charged on goods coming into a country) and establishing or removing trade restrictions such as quotas (the numerical limit on how much of a product can be imported) and embargoes (the refusal to sell a product to another country).

Foreign direct investments (FDI) involve the purchase of financial interests in a foreign company in order to gain a high degree of control. Advanced technology and natural resource companies are key targets of FDI. Common policy tools used to encourage FDI in a state include providing subsidized loans to investors and granting of tax credits. States can also try to stop FDI in their country by such means as *expropriation* (seizing ownership of property), freezing company bank accounts, and imposing limits on when and how foreign companies can enter key markets such as computers, oil, or transportation.

Foreign monetary policy refers to actions that affect the inflation rate, interest rate, and international exchange rate of money in a particular country with an eye toward promoting foreign policy and national security goals.[22] For example, during his presidential campaign Donald Trump repeatedly asserted that China was a currency manipulator with the goal of driving down the value of Chinese currency in order to increase exports. Early in his presidency he did an abrupt about face and changed his position, stating that the Chinese were not currency manipulators.

Economic sanctions are "the deliberate withdrawal of normal trade or financial relations for foreign policy purposes."[23] They are intended to bring about specific changes in a targeted country and are removed when the changes take place. The reasons for imposing sanctions vary widely. Iran has been the target of US sanctions for its pursuit of nuclear weapons and support of international terrorism. President Jimmy Carter imposed sanctions on Iran in 1979 after the US embassy was seized and sixty-six American diplomats were taken hostage. The United States placed sanctions on Cuba in 1960 after Cuba nationalized US property. In 1996 the United States threatened economic sanctions against any country that provided Cuba with foreign aid. As the Cuban example indicates, traditionally sanctions were directed at hurting the entire economy of a targeted state. Dissatisfaction with the limited success rate of these sanctions and a concern for the welfare of the citizens in the targeted state led to the adoption of *smart sanctions*. These are sanctions targeted at the leadership of the state, such as seizing their bank accounts or properties in other states and refusing to grant them entry visas to travel abroad.

Economic assistance can take the form of loans (which must be paid back) or grants (which are not repaid). Loans and grants provided as economic assistance by one country to another are collectively referred to as *bilateral aid*. Loans and grants can be used for purposes including defense, economic development, improving governance and building democracy, and support for humanitarian projects. Often bilateral aid comes with strings attached in terms of the types of projects the money can support or where the money is spent. For example, a grant may require funds to be spent on goods produced in the donor state. To minimize such influences, aid recipients often turn to international

Danny Lawson / EMPPL PA Wire / AP Images

Iran's oil and natural gas industry, once a source of strength, has become a target of US economic sanctions.

organizations such as the World Bank and the International Monetary Fund for assistance. However, these entities also have rules about how funds can be spent and, to a great extent, these rules are written by the same donor countries that provide bilateral aid.

Covert Action as an Instrument of Power

Attempts to further the interest of one state by secretly altering the internal balance of power in another state are referred to as **covert action**. The tendency is to equate covert action with secret offensive military action, but in practice it covers a much broader range of activity. Covert action can be carried out using military, economic, or political instruments to accomplish offensive or defensive goals.[24] Covert action is used not only by the United States but also by Great Britain, West Germany, Israel, South Africa, France, Chile, China, and the Soviet Union/Russia, to just name a few.

The most common form of covert action involves providing clandestine (secret) support for individuals and organizations such as political parties, newspapers, labor unions, and religious groups. For example, between 1948 and 1968 the Central Intelligence Agency (CIA) secretly spent over $65 million in Italy in support of pro–United States politicians, national leaders, and newspapers. Secret support can also be given to the security and intelligence services of another country. For example, according to Bob Woodward's history of the CIA, *VEIL: the Secret Wars of the CIA*, these operations each cost between $300,000 and $1 million. Among those countries receiving this aid were Chad, Pakistan, the Philippines, and Lebanon.[25]

covert action An attempt to further the interest of one state by secretly altering the internal balance of power in another state.

REGIONAL SPOTLIGHT

Russia's Military Power and Strategy

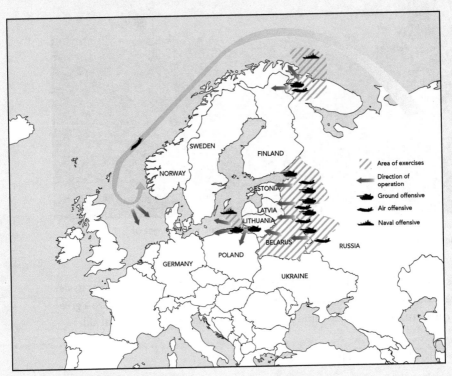

Map 5.1 Zapad 2017.

In the post–Cold War era the primary focus of global concerns with military confrontations shifted from conflicts growing out of the US-Soviet tensions to those involving terrorism and internal political strife. Russian involvement in the 2014 Ukrainian conflict, which was highlighted in the Contemporary Perspective section of Chapter 2, brought renewed attention to Russian military power. Its involvement in the Syrian civil war, where it redeployed elite units from the Ukraine and sent a naval fleet to Syria in support of Syrian President Bashar al-Assad, as well as its links to that government's reported use of chemical weapons, provided additional support to the view that Russia had reemerged as a prominent military power in international politics.

At the conventional level one of the most visible signs of Russia's renewed embrace of military power is found in the recent scale of its annual military exercises. Officially these exercises are designed to enhance Russian security and prepare its troops and commanders. Two are especially noteworthy. Zapad 2017 (Russian for "west") was officially defined as a military exercise involving fewer than 13,000 troops, a level below that at which by international agreement the United States and its allies could send in observers. Western estimates placed the number as approaching 100,000. The military exercise was organized around a simulated attack by a fictional country and two fictional allies that sought

Russian President Putin observes an explosion during the Zapad exercise.

to create an opening between Russia and Belarus. Russian troops stationed in the Arctic Far East, the Black Sea, and Georgia participated in the exercise, as did warships, submarines, fighter jets, air defense, Special Forces, and nuclear capable missiles. The second military exercise of note was Vostok 2018 (Russian for "east"). Some 300,000 Russian troops took part in it, along with military units from China and Mongolia. An estimated 36,000 tanks, armored personal carriers and other military vehicles were involved, along with over 1,000 aircraft, drones, and helicopters, and 80 naval vessels. Part of the exercise focused on large-scale airstrikes and countering cruise missile attacks. Another part included military operations in the Sea of Japan, Bering Sea and Okhotsk Sea.

At the nuclear level concern has focused on Russia's escalate-to-deescalate nuclear strategy and pursuit of low-yield nuclear weapons to implement it. During the Cold War the most feared scenarios involved large-scale nuclear strikes by Russia and the United States. The highly destructive nature of such a conflict led to viewing the central use of nuclear weapons as one of deterring war. The end of the Cold War altered this thinking. Nuclear weapons now came to be seen largely in political terms as providing prestige and status but holding little value for fighting small wars or countering terrorism.

This changed with the 1998 Kosovo Conflict and the 2003 Iraq War. In these wars the United States demonstrated a highly sophisticated precision offensive conventional weapons capability that produced only minimal amounts of collateral damage. Lacking any ability to counter such attacks, Russia put forward a new defensive military strategy for fighting a conventional war. It emphasized the role of using nuclear weapons to inflict "tailored damage" in order to deter a conventional attack and to prevent any further escalation of an ongoing conventional military conflict. This strategic doctrine left open the question of whether such nuclear strikes would involve only battlefield-oriented low-yield nuclear weapons or would include long-range strike capabilities. Russia's new nuclear doctrine was initially portrayed as a stopgap measure to compensate for the lack of an effective counter to the US capability but in 2010 became a permanent part of Russian strategy. To demonstrate Russia's commitment to the escalate-to-deescalate strategy all Russian military exercises since 2000 have included a nuclear component. Russia has also developed a new generation of long-range sea- and air-launched nuclear missiles, precision-guided gravity bombs, and short-range ballistic and cruise missiles.

As will be discussed in Chapter 7, one consequence to this military buildup plus the US response, which was to begin strengthening its low-yield nuclear capability, was the termination of the Intermediate Nuclear Force Treaty in 2019. This agreement had banned land-based ballistic missiles, cruise missiles, and short- and long-term missile launchers.

Think about It

1. What are the dangers of an escalate-to-deescalate strategy? Are they greater than its benefits? Why or why not?

2. Since the Zapad and Vostok military exercises were defined as defensive, should they be seen as threatening peace in Europe or Asia? Explain your answer.

Another form of covert action was presented in the discussion of soft power: propaganda. As you have already learned, transmission of propaganda ranges from radio broadcasts, to placing articles in newspapers with the help of journalists, to circulation of rumors and misinformation via social media and other Internet tools. This form of covert action is at the heart of the controversy over Russia's efforts to influence the outcome of the 2016 presidential election. Covert action can also take place in the economic arena. Attempts range from disruption of economic activity by physically or electronically disabling energy or communication technologies, to undermining the ability of states to obtain needed resources, to sabotaging products, or to creating major economic disruptions through crop destruction or alterations to the environment.

The riskiest forms of covert action are covert paramilitary operations that provide secret military assistance and guidance to foreign military forces and organizations for the purpose of bringing down an adversary, or even assassinating foreign leaders. Such actions are not always successful. In the final analysis, for states aspiring to great power status the most valued type of power remains military power, as is highlighted in the Regional Spotlight which reviews Russian military power and strategy.

CONTEMPORARY PERSPECTIVE:
Armed Drones

While Douhet's post-WWI debate over the ability of armed aircraft to change the nature of warfare is now history, the debate over the ability of technology to change the world's view of military power and its use continues. The most important issue today is the use of armed drones. For some, this technology has ushered in a new era of warfare, especially when the enemy is a terrorist group. For others it is just another weapon. And for still others it is a potentially dangerous weapon that is as "addictive as catnip" to policymakers, which can lead to its overuse.[26]

Typically classified as either Unmanned Aerial Vehicles (UAVs) or Remotely Piloted Aerial Systems (RPAS), drones come in many sizes and can be used for a wide range of purposes, from gathering intelligence through surveillance, communication intercepts, and reconnaissance flights to providing close tactical support for combat troops, to delivering precision missile strikes against hostile forces or persons. Of particular value is drones' ability to patrol an area for up to twenty-four hours at a time. The two primary armed drones employed by the US military in strikes against suspected terrorist leaders are the Predator and the Reaper.

From a technological and strategic point of view, armed drones are not radically new technologies, but the evolution of existing weapons. During WWII US Army Air Force General "Hap" Arnold had B-17 and B-24 bombers restructured into remotely piloted aircraft. Sounding very much like Douhet, Arnold speculated that "the next war may be fought by airplanes with no men in them at all."[27] The United States began using drones for reconnaissance purposes in the 1950s, and the idea of using them to destroy targets has been part of every drone research and development initiative for six decades.[28]

US MQ-9 Reaper unmanned aircraft firing a drone.

As in Douhet's thinking about air power, nothing is clear about the future impact of drone technology on the ability for fight and win wars.[29] Working against future successes is the reality that the United States does not have a monopoly on the use of armed drones. In 2016 over a dozen countries including Great Britain, Israel, China, and Iran also possessed armed drones. In that same year Pakistan, Turkey, Russia, and India were moving to create their own armed drone production facilities. European and Asian states are moving forward on a cooperative venture for the same purpose. Non-state actors have also used armed drones to further their agendas, often transforming over-the-counter commercial drone products. These groups include ISIS, Houthi rebels in Yemen, and Hezbollah. Libyan rebels, Kurdish forces, and Colombian and Mexican drug cartels have all employed drones for reconnaissance purposes. In spite of the proliferation of state and non-state acquisition of drones, drone technology is complex, involving the integration of sophisticated communication systems, access to satellite bandwidth, and computer technology. Together these considerations place significant obstacles in the way of their effective use.[30]

The United States is the principal user of armed drones today. Observers estimate that the United States operates drone bases in at least twelve countries including Afghanistan, Ethiopia, Kuwait, Niger, Turkey, the Philippines, Yemen, and Saudi Arabia. In 2001 following the 9/11 attacks George W. Bush was the first to employ drones against terrorists as part of his strategy for defeating al-Qaeda. By the time he left office, more than fifty drone strikes had taken place.

During the Obama administration drone strikes increased significantly in number and many were carried out against a new target, ISIS (Islamic State of Iraq and Syria).[31] According to a 2017 account, Obama approved over 540 drone strikes in non-battlefield areas including Yemen, Somalia, and Pakistan. Mid-way through Obama's first term in office, drone strikes were occurring at a rate of one every four days, compared to one every forty days under Bush. By early June 2013 Obama had authorized 309 strikes in Pakistan that killed between 2,021 and 3,350 people along with an estimated 56 leaders of terrorist groups. One in every three drone strikes killed a militant leader under Bush, compared to only 13% under Obama.

Far fewer drone strikes occurred late in the Obama administration. In 2016 there were only thirty-eight drone strikes in Yemen and three in Pakistan. One factor was growing negative public reaction to attacks in which non-terrorists were killed. A December 2013 attack on a Yemeni wedding procession killed twelve and wounded fifteen. The official US position was that those present were members of Al Qaeda in the Arabian Peninsula, but military and local government officials in Yemen called the attack a mistake. A 2013 YouGov poll showed that while 60% of Americans supported drone strikes against terrorists, 52% opposed attacks that kill civilians.[32] Another contributing factor to reducing the number of these attacks were changes in the authorization of armed drone strikes. Initially Obama asserted that they could only be used if it was impossible to capture an individual who was moving forward in a plot against the United States. This policy gave way to a broader authorization of "signature strikes," in which drone strikes were allowed to take place if a pattern of suspicious activity consistent with the behavior of terrorists was observed. By the time his administration ended, Obama had again placed tighter restrictions on the use of armed drones, including the requirement of "near certainty" that no civilians would be harmed in strikes outside the war zone.

With the beginning of the Trump presidency the pendulum swung back toward a greater use of armed drones. Obama had transferred authority to carry out drone strikes to the military, but Trump returned this power to the CIA, a move that reduced the possibility of obtaining information on these strikes. In 2019 he signed an executive order ending the policy of reporting on civilian casualties in drone strikes. Parts of Yemen and Somalia are now defined as "areas of active hostilities," giving the military greater latitude in using armed drone strikes. In 2018 a substantial drop occurred in drone strikes, a shift explained by observers as due to the changing tempo and needs of US counterterrorism policy. An overview of recent US drone strikes is found in Figure 5.4.

Along with cybertechnology, which was discussed earlier in this chapter, the use and control of drones in international politics promises to be a major challenge that states and other international actors must address. These are not the only challenges on the horizon. The final section of the chapter introduces three additional factors that complicate the future ability of actors to achieve their goals.

LOOKING TO THE FUTURE

The complex nature of power places many obstacles in the path of states seeking to achieve their goals using foreign policy instruments. This section highlights three major future challenges that states will face in acquiring and using power—the Tool Box Syndrome, grand strategy, and red lines in the sand—as well as the policy responses to each of these challenges.

Figure 5.4 Drone and Air Strikes, 2016–2018.

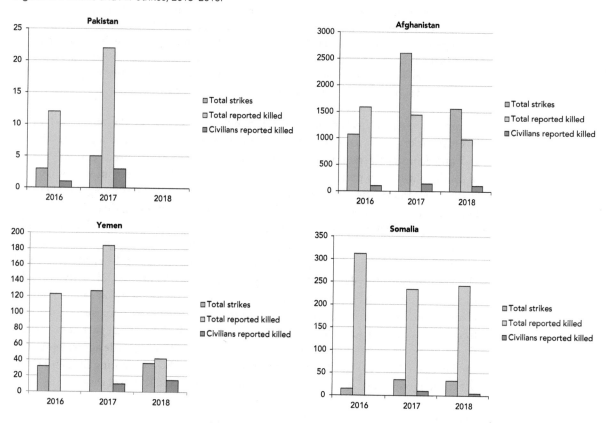

Escaping from the "Tool Box Syndrome"

As the old saying goes, "if all you have in your tool box is a hammer, every problem looks like a nail." The primary target of this critique today is an imbalance in the use of power: the overuse of military power and the underuse of soft power. The primary user of the military hammer in the world today is the United States, but excessive reliance on military power is nothing new. Back in 1947 George Kennan, an American diplomat serving in the US embassy in Russia, put forward the strategy of containment for dealing with the Soviet Union. He envisioned that this strategy would employ the full tool box of US power. (He later asserted that his idea was misinterpreted and misapplied, saying that there was far too much emphasis on using military force to contain the Soviet Union.)

Tool box critics assert that President Donald Trump is the latest to embrace the military hammer with his call for increased military spending and cutbacks to the State Department budget. In May 2017 Secretary of State Rex Tillerson proposed cutting 2,300 jobs in the State Department. A few months earlier more than 120 retired generals and admirals sent a letter to key members of Congress opposing such cuts:

We know from our service in uniform that many of the crises our nation faces do not have military solutions alone—from confronting violent extremist groups like ISIS [the Islamic State in Iraq and Syria] in the Middle East and North Africa to preventing pandemics like Ebola and stabilizing weak and fragile states that can lead to greater instability…. The State Department, USAID, Millennium Challenge Corporation, Peace Corps and other development agencies are critical to preventing conflict and reducing the need to put our men and women in uniform in harm's way.[33]

According to some observers one way of expanding the size of the US foreign policy tool box is to make greater use of economics as an instrument of foreign policy. Robert Blackwell and Jennifer Harris note that historically the United States used economics often in conducting foreign policy, but this began to change with the Vietnam War. According to Blackwell and Harris, the United States has abandoned economic foreign policy tools, but other countries, most notably Russia and China, have embraced them.[34]

Georgia, which had been part of the Soviet Union, declared its independence in 1991. In the lead up to the 2008 Russo-Georgian War, Russia engaged in a number of economic moves designed to cripple the Georgian economy. First, it blocked the entry of all Georgian agricultural products into Russia, supposedly on health and safety grounds. Next, it blocked all air, sea, road, rail, and postal traffic to the Georgian capital. Later it placed an embargo on all Georgian wine, preventing its export to Russia. Similar tactics were later used against Moldova and the Ukraine, which had been part of the Soviet Union before its collapse, in response to their interest in signing trade agreements with the European Union (EU). Russia also struck back at the EU by banning EU dairy products from Russia and destroying large quantities of imported Dutch cheese.

What Is the Value of Grand Strategy?

grand strategy A plan that coordinates all of the power resources held by a state in order to achieve its fundamental foreign policy objectives and long-term goals.

In order to use power effectively, a state needs a plan. The language of strategic analysis identifies three types of plans: tactical plans, strategic plans and **grand strategy** plans. *Tactical plans* refer to the specific actions to be taken. Using armed drones against terrorists, for example, is a tactic and not a strategy.[35]

Strategic plans shift attention away from specific actions toward their results: ensuring that tactical successes will culminate in the realization of an overarching goal. In the case of drones, that goal is to defeat terrorism. A strategy plan involves creating a blueprint for how the tactics you have selected will work together for a common objective. In the drone example this would be the plan for how drone strikes contribute to larger foreign policy objectives such as regional stability or countering the influence of states supporting terrorism. *Grand strategy plans* go one step further. Where strategy plans seek to unify state action within a specific area of power, a grand strategy plan seeks to coordinate all of the power resources held by a state in order to ensure that achieving its strategic objectives will also result in the attainment of long-term goals. From the perspective of grand strategy, winning a war also requires winning the peace. In the example of drone strikes against terrorists grand strategy considerations direct attention to questions about what policy-makers envision what the politics of the Middle East will look like in ten years and what the role of the United States or outside forces will be.

With the end of the Cold War and breakup of the Soviet Union, the US strategy of containment became obsolete. While there was little consensus on what it should be, calls were routinely made for adopting a new grand strategy to guide US foreign policy. Proposals of this type continue to be put forward from both ends of the political spectrum as conservatives and liberals seek to advance their foreign policy agendas. Recently, a very different proposal has been put forward. Rather than formulate a new grand strategy for using US power (or, for that matter, for any state to use its power), Lawrence Freedman, Richard Betts and others have questioned the value of a grand strategy and even called for abandonment of the concept.[36] In its place policy-makers should formulate emergent strategies to guide foreign policy.[37] An *emergent strategy* is based on learning from events and the accumulated practice of responding to events. It requires the ability to change tactics and goals in a coherent fashion.

Why replace grand strategy with emergent strategy? Grand strategies are based on the often unstated assumption that international relations will remain stable, if not unchanged, well into the future. For example, containment served as the US grand strategy for nearly four decades. However, there is much uncertainty over the characterization of today's international system and the direction in which it is going. Under conditions of uncertainty, the foreign policy challenge is not how to design and implement a grand strategy but how to recognize emerging trends and patterns and adapt to new situations.

Drawing Red Lines in the Sand

Using power to prevent an adversary from engaging in unwanted actions is less costly than using it to try to reverse the behavior or undo an action already taken. The principal challenge of prevention is to convince the adversary of the commitment to follow through on warnings about dire consequences. A common tactic policy-makers use to signal their displeasure and commitment to act is to draw imaginary markers called "red lines in the sand." Both Presidents Obama and Trump used this tactic in seeking to stop Syria's use of chemical weapons. Obama put forward a red line but did nothing when it was crossed. Only days after stating that he wanted to withdraw US forces from Syria and let other countries deal with the problem Trump reacted angrily to reports of Syria's use of chemical weapons by threatening strong, quick retaliations. Retaliations did occur but almost a week later and were carefully reconstructed as part of a multinational effort that did little to weaken the power of Syria's government, leaving commentators unclear as to US goals in Syria.

Crossing these imaginary *red line* markers will result in an immediate and forceful counteraction that will severely harm the adversary. Drawing a red line involves a conscious commitment that gives up any freedom of action. Red lines are not easily created and often fail to deter an adversary. In 2012 President Barack Obama drew a red line when he tried to prevent Syria from using chemical weapons. In 1950, during the Korean War, China sought to deter the United States from crossing the 38th parallel into North

Korea by laying down a red line. Israel put down several red lines seeking to block Iran's development of nuclear weapons. All of these efforts failed.

There are many challenges in attempting to draw a successful red line. As one commentator noted, there are fifty shades of red.[38] Four problems stand out:

1. **Lack of clarity about consequences**. Obama's red line statement was far from exact in its wording. It said "a red line for us is we start seeing a whole bunch of chemical weapons moving or being utilized" and that "there would be enormous consequences." In 1950 China stated it would take a "grave view" of US forces crossing into North Korea. It did not say it would send troops into North Korea to counter the US action, which it did.

2. **An unconvincing threat**. In 1939 Great Britain and France signed a security agreement with Poland in an effort to signal to Nazi Germany that an invasion of Poland would have grave consequences. Having failed to block Hitler's takeover of part of Czechoslovakia the year before, the security pledge was not seen as credible.

3. **The gains outweigh the penalty**. Not only did Israeli's red lines fail to stop Iran's nuclear program, they failed to dissuade Iraq, Libya, or Syria from seeking nuclear weapons. The potential value of achieving nuclear weapons outweighed the damage inflicted by Israel's destruction of the Osirak nuclear reactor in Iraq or the threat of similar action in the future.

4. **Prompting the adversary to act**. One danger of putting down a red line is that it may actually encourage the adversary to come right up to the red line without fear of counteraction. This may have been the case in Russia's military involvement in the Ukraine. An outright Russian invasion of the Ukraine might easily have been viewed as crossing a NATO red line, but the policy pursued by Russia stopped just short of invasion and did not provoke a strong military counter move.

A number of responses to these challenges have been proposed to help policy-makers think more carefully about drawing red lines. The first and most obvious is to consciously balance clarity and flexibility. While some vagueness may be politically necessary, too much is dangerous. Second, drawing a red line is not a one-time act. As Bruno Tertrais notes, red lines need to be nurtured and often require "new coats of paint."[39] Periodic reminders may be needed and clarifications made as circumstances change. The danger to be avoided at all costs is to give the impression of having lost the will to undertake the threatened countermeasures. Finally, private communications or visits by key policy-makers may be as effective in blocking unwanted actions as publicly drawing red lines.

Summary

- A defining characteristic of states and other actors in international relations is power, the ability to influence and determine the actions of others.

- Giulio Douhet's path-breaking argument about the role of airpower illustrates the complex process by which new ideas are generated and the difficulty of accurately predicting the future.

- There are four aspects of power in international relations: (1) sources of power, (2) types of power, (3) the difficulty of measuring power, and (4) the challenge of using power. Being exact about the measurement of soft power is just as important as for hard power.

- Cyberpower, information used in order to inflict harm, persuade, or more generally gain an advantage over an adversary, is the newest source of power. A major question about cyberpower is identifying a strategic framework for its use. Commentators suggest that improved cybersecurity, international norms that define cyberattacks as illegal, and stricter prosecution of cybercrimes could be more effective than an approach modeled on nuclear strategy.

- A broad range of power instruments can be found in the foreign policy tool box, including the following: (1) the military, (2) economics, (3) diplomacy, and (4) covert action.

- US drone policy demonstrates the attraction that armed drones hold for policymakers as well as the controversy and disagreements about their effectiveness.

- Among the most significant future challenges to using power are (1) escaping from the tool box syndrome, (2) judging the continued value of grand strategy, (3) identifying when and how to draw red lines, and (4) understanding cyberpower.

Key Terms

Covert action *(151)*
Cyberpower *(143)*
Diplomacy *(148)*
Grand strategy *(158)*

Hard power *(138)*
Hybrid war *(147)*
Power *(129)*
Soft power *(138)*

Critical Thinking Questions

1. Who makes the stronger case: those in favor of strategic bombing or those opposed to it? Support your position using a conflict situation since the end of the Cold War.

2. Identify a conflict situation in the news and discuss how hard and soft power are used. Which is more effective?

3. Should the logic and language of nuclear strategy be used to think about cyberwar? Why or why not?

4. Which foreign policy-instrument provides the greatest challenges, risks, and benefits in using power? Explain your answer.

5. What are the major strengths and limitations in using armed drones?

6. Is grand strategy possible? Explain your answer.

Practice and Review Online
http://textbooks.rowman.com/hastedt-felice

▲ United Nations Security Council meeting in 2018 to discuss North Korea. *Source:* Jason DeCrow / AP Images

06

THE COOPERATION CHALLENGE:
WORKING TOGETHER

COOPERATION IN INTERNATIONAL POLITICS is not easy. **Cooperation** occurs when states and other international actors work together for their mutual benefit or to address shared problems. Issues in need of attention often go unaddressed. Stalemates drag on. Agreements are not implemented. There is widespread skepticism about the ability of political leaders to produce meaningful cooperation among states, international organizations, and nongovernmental actors. The 2016 Report Card by the Council of Councils, a survey of twenty-six foreign policy institutes from around the world, gave an overall grade of C- to international cooperation.[1] The highest grade (B) was given in two of ten policy areas: the promotion of global heath and mitigation of and adaptations to climate change. Expansion of global trade and prevention of and responses to internal violence received the lowest grades (D+). Just the year before, in 2015, global cooperation received an overall B grade.[2] Two A-level grades were given (mitigating and adapting to climate change and preventing nuclear proliferation), and the two lowest grades were C- (preventing and responding to internal violence and combating international terrorism). How could international cooperation decline so much in a single year?

cooperation When states and other international actors work together for their mutual benefit or to address shared problems.

In this chapter the challenges of cooperating to promote international health will be used as an example of the bigger challenge of international cooperation. Although improving global health has long been on the agenda in international politics, its priority and the reasons for concern have varied widely. The World Health Organization's 1946 constitution asserted that "health is a state of complete physical, mental and social well-being and not merely the absence of disease or infirmity." It continued "the health of all peoples is fundamental to the attainment of peace and security."[3] From the 1960s through the 1980s it was assumed that economic modernization in the developing world, sponsored by the International Monetary Fund and the World Bank, would lead to improved health. In 1978 the United Nations put forward a "Health for All, 2000" agreement that stressed the human rights dimension to global health issues. Members pledged to transform the health condition of all states by 2000. Despite all of this cooperation, significant health problems remain. A White House working group found that between 1973 and 1996 twenty-nine previously unknown diseases emerged and another twenty known diseases had reemerged. At that time, only three diseases—cholera, plague, and yellow fever—were subjected to international regulation.

The examination of international cooperation begins with a review of the 1976 and 2000 Ebola outbreaks. The chapter then introduces three key factors that must be taken into account in entering into negotiations involving international cooperation: preconditions, setting the table, and establishing the basis for cooperation. Five major forms of international cooperation are introduced next: alliances, summit diplomacy, Track II diplomacy, conference diplomacy, and international law. The discussion then turns to three health-related international cooperation challenges and proposed responses. The chapter concludes with a review of the most recent outbreak of Ebola in 2013 to demonstrate the continuing challenge of international cooperation in improving global health. Two Ebola outbreaks are examined for three reasons. First, international cooperation involves states and a variety of international organizations and non-state actors. Second, problems are not necessarily solved; they often reappear unexpectedly. And third, cooperation in one case is not necessarily exactly the same as cooperation in another.

LEARNING OBJECTIVES

Students will be able to:

- Identify the factors that made cooperation difficult in meeting the 1976 and 2000 Ebola crises and the extent to which they were overcome.

- Evaluate the different preconditions for cooperation and the foundations on which cooperation rests.

- Understand the costs and benefits of alliances from the perspective of weak and strong states.

- Distinguish among summit diplomacy, track II diplomacy, and conference diplomacy and identify what each contributes to international cooperation.

- Evaluate the merits of the different sources of international law and distinguish between hard and soft law.

- Judge the extent to which global cooperation on Ebola increased or decreased in 2013 compared to the earlier outbreaks.

- Compare and contrast the three responses to the challenges to international cooperation presented: track III diplomacy, house gifts and gift baskets, and delegated international regulation.

HISTORICAL PERSPECTIVE:
Ebola in 1976 and 2000

On August 26, 1976, the headmaster at a mission school in Yandongi Village in the northwestern part of the Democratic Republic of the Congo (then known as Zaire) went to the 120-bed Yambuku Mission Hospital, established in 1935 by Belgian Catholics, for care. He had developed chills and a fever after returning from a trip during which he purchased and ate smoked antelope. At the time the Yambuku Mission Hospital served as the primary care facility in the region, treating some 6,000–12,000 people each month. The headmaster was treated with medical injections and released. It was common practice at the hospital to administer medicine by injection and use needles multiple times before sterilizing them for further use. Days later the patient returned, complaining of nausea, severe headaches, muscle pain, and intestinal bleeding. Shortly after he died on September 6, dozens of patients who had received injections at the hospital became ill and then died about a week later. Many of those who came into contact with the patients outside of the hospital also died. A total of 318 cases occurred between September 1 and October 24, and 88% of those infected died.

News of this "mysterious disease" and the large numbers of deaths reached the capital city of Kinshasa

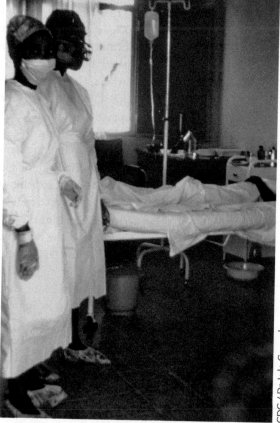

Medical personnel training to deal with the 1976 Ebola outbreak.

CDC / Dr. Lyle Conrad

on September 21. A medical team was dispatched and tentatively identified the malady as typhoid fever. As concern grew, representatives from the Belgian Fonds Médical Tropical (FOMETRO) and the French Medical Mission also arrived at the hospital. In early October an analysis of blood samples and organs by a Belgian hospital led to the conclusion that the cause of the outbreak in Zaire was not typhoid fever but a new type of viral hemorrhagic fever. It was named Ebola after the Ebola River (which is near Yambuku but not in the infected region).[4]

It is now known that Ebola is introduced into humans through contact with the blood, secretions, organs, or bodily fluid of infected animals such as fruit bats, monkeys, and the antelope the headmaster had eaten. Ebola can also be passed person to person through direct contact with the blood, secretions, organs, or bodily fluid of an infected individual, often through the provision of medical care, burial preparation, and burial ceremonies. No vaccine or treatment currently exists.

After it was notified of this discovery, the World Health Organization (WHO) instructed that all lab specimens be sent the Center for Disease Control in Atlanta and a research lab in Great Britain for further study. In mid-October, about eight weeks after the outbreak, the WHO formed an International Commission to aid in responding to the epidemic, determining where it began and how it spread.

By this time the Yambuku Mission Hospital had already been closed, and the 275,000 people living in the area were placed under a strict quarantine. Members of the WHO's International Commission were initially met with suspicion when they entered the quarantined zone to help stop the spread of the disease. Belgium, Canada, France, South Africa, Great Britain, and the United States also provided materials and logistical support. Within the United States Government, the US Agency for International Development took the lead in formulating the US response. Nongovernmental organizations played important roles within the impacted area in treating patients and curbing Ebola's spread. Numbered among them were FOMETRO, Mission Médicale Française, Fonds Médical Tropical (Belgium), Oxfam, the Catholic Church (Belgium), the Protestant Mission Aviation Fellowship (United States), and the Baptist Mission Hospitals (United States). The Ebola epidemic began to recede and was officially declared over on December 16; the International Commission was terminated on January 29, 1977.

This was not the only outbreak of Ebola in 1976, however. Almost simultaneously, an unrelated outbreak in Sudan infected 284 people and killed 151 (a 53% fatality rate). Nor was it the last major Ebola outbreak prior to the 2013–2016 epidemics in Guinea, Liberia, and Sierra Leone that are the subjects of the Contemporary Perspective section later in the chapter. In September 2000 an Ebola epidemic occurred in Uganda, afflicting 425 people and resulting in the same 53% fatality rate as the Sudan outbreak.

The Ugandan outbreak occurred in three different parts of the country.[5] It was most severe in Gulu, which was also the center of a thirteen-year-long insurgency led by the Lord's Resistance Army. Heath workers had to travel through Gulu in armored personnel carriers. Further complicating matters, many Ugandan soldiers were stationed in Gulu, and local residents believed that their families' relocation from the Congo caused the Ebola outbreak. The Ugandan government did not help matters, charging that the

Lord's Resistance Army was responsible for bringing Ebola to Gulu. The Ebola outbreak was quickly recognized, and Uganda contacted the WHO to coordinate the international response. More than twenty nongovernmental organizations and government agencies responded to help.

On day five of the outbreak neighboring Kenya began to screen people attempting to cross the border from Uganda. Representatives from the Centers for Disease Control (CDC) and Doctors Without Borders arrived in Uganda on day six of the epidemic. On day forty-four, Kenya implemented the Epidemic Control Act to expel 137 delegates from a meeting because half of them came from Uganda. Just as the Ebola epidemic was declining, Saudi Arabia instituted a ban preventing Ugandan pilgrims from travelling to Mecca during the March holy days; the ban remained in place even after the Ebola epidemic was declared over in February 2001. These actions by Kenya and Saudi Arabia were in violation of WHO guidelines, which specified that no special travel or trade restrictions were to be instituted during an epidemic outside of very specific areas of quarantine, as Ebola spreads though contact with body fluids and not by proximity to a patient.

The two Ebola crises document that cooperation is not easy. In both cases the outbreak of Ebola was unexpected. In both cases cooperation was difficult to achieve because the various actors involved judged the situation differently and had competing interests. In both cases the Ebola crisis ended with a false sense of confidence that the problem had been solved. This chapter will examine the challenges of cooperation and the variety of forms it takes so that the cooperation challenge in international politics is better understood.

THE DYNAMICS OF INTERNATIONAL COOPERATION

Cooperation is a risky undertaking and not all settings are equally conducive to successful risk taking. Failure is always a possibility and takes many forms. The failure to reach an agreement may have negative domestic political consequences. It may also make future efforts more difficult. Even a cooperative effort that results in an agreement may hold negative consequences if it is perceived that "too high a price" was paid in making the concessions that led to the agreement. The lengthy and uneven peace process that finally ended the Vietnam War is an example of the first risk. President Donald Trump's repeated campaign statements about the United States getting a "bad deal" in trade and defense agreements is an example of the second risk.

In making the decision to enter into a cooperative effort states need to address three questions:

- **Preconditions**. What conditions must exist for cooperation to be successful?
- **Setting the table**. Who should be invited to participate and under what terms?
- **Foundations for cooperation**. On what basis should a cooperative outcome be built?[6]

Preconditions

There are two preconditions for successful international cooperation. First, there must be shared interests accompanied by a conflict over one or more of those interests.[7] Without conflict over interests there is little or no need to enter into cooperative efforts, since mutually beneficial actions will come about naturally. Where few or no shared interests exist there is little reason to engage in cooperative efforts, since unconditional surrender by the opponent typically is the preferred option under these circumstances. This is the commonly held goal when states go to war. It is only when unconditional surrender cannot be achieved that negotiations begin, as was the case with both WWI and WWII, and the Korean War.

The second precondition relates to the global setting in which international cooperation takes place. Today considerable disagreement exists over whether the global setting is conducive to cooperation. One viewpoint characterizes the current situation as "a world adrift."[8] No one group of international actors has the authority or responsibility to create conditions conducive to global problem solving. Instead cooperative efforts take place under conditions in which power is widely diffused, global norms are contested, and nationalist perspectives challenge global ones. Another viewpoint holds that the crisis in global governance is overstated, arguing that global institutions and rules are effective and have successfully adapted to challenges in the past and will continue to do so in the future.[9] Falling between these two perspectives is one that believes that the challenges to effective management of the international system can be met through a reform of global institutions and rules. The question of preconditions for negotiation is an especially sensitive one when it involves starting negotiations with an enemy, the topic addressed in the Policy Spotlight feature.

Setting the Table

Common interests are not enough to overcome the inherent risks present in cooperative efforts. Those involved in the cooperative efforts may have different time lines on the need for action. Some may view an issue as a crisis that needs immediate attention, while others may take a longer view, seeing it as taking a long time to address or being only in its beginning stages. Disagreement may also exist over costs and who will pay them. Some may favor less expensive political, economic, or military solutions over more costly proposals. Yet another potential area of concern is prioritization. Some actors will consider the challenge a top priority; others may be cooperating primarily in response to international or domestic political pressure to participate.

The potential for disagreement over time line, cost concerns, and prioritization creates a need to look closely at who should be invited to participate in cooperative efforts and whether boundaries need to be set. Commonly used boundaries include limiting the duration of an agreement, identifying a point at which it is open to revision, creating an exit path from the agreement, establishing dispute resolution procedures, and phasing out specific obligations. Virtually all of these areas of disagreement and the strategies used to deal with them have arisen in international climate cooperative efforts. These will be reviewed in Chapter 10.

Today the question of who should be involved in cooperative efforts has taken on a new dimension with the growth of multi-stakeholder conferences.[11] *Stakeholders* are persons or organizations with a direct interest in the outcome of deliberations on an issue or with the ability to affect that outcome. In global multi-stakeholder conferences the most frequent stakeholders are states, international organizations, businesses, and nongovernmental organizations. Notable multi-stakeholder conferences have taken place to discuss such issues as placing limits on diamond mining in Africa, establishing the rights of garment workers in developing countries, and the terms of international aid. More generally multi-stakeholder conferences have become associated with environmental and development conferences such as the 1992 Rio Earth Summit and the 2000 Millennium Development Conference. Multi-stakeholder conferences also face the challenge of deciding whom to invite because not all stakeholders are equal. Some are essential to the success of a conference. Others are desirable participants given their knowledge, resources, or political leverage. Some might be considered for inclusion only if space permits.

Foundations for Cooperation

Five different conceptual foundations have been employed with great frequency in determining a reference point on which to build cooperative efforts.[12] The first is power. Not surprisingly, the winners of wars and the most powerful states in the international system have often sought to organize states to cope with the anarchic nature of world politics and preserve the status quo, which operates in their favor. For example, the states that lost WWI were stripped of their colonies. The victors kept theirs. The second foundation is international law. In this case, reciprocity is the basis for cooperation; states cooperate because the rights, privileges, and benefits they grant to other states would also be granted to them. Universally agreed-upon principles and rules, not power, regulate state behavior. Ideology has served as a third basis for the organization of cooperative efforts. The nature of the ideologies have changed, but over time have included communism, Nazism, fascism, liberal internationalism. To this list can be added nationalism and religion. While they vary considerably in their core principles, each promotes a distinct vision of a preferred world order that provides a basis for judging when to cooperate, for what purpose, and with whom. Science is a fourth foundation for international cooperative efforts. Empirical evidence and reproducible findings are seen as creating a "politics free zone" for cooperation. Debates over values, identity, and the national interest would be replaced by objective investigations into the nature of problems and their solution. A fifth foundation is the free market. Like science, it seeks to avoid using political criteria as the basis for cooperation. Supporters of free market solutions argue that they come about naturally as individuals join in cooperative ventures to achieve their goals. In their view, government intervention into policy areas distorts the potential for positive results and should be limited.

POLICY SPOTLIGHT

Negotiating with the Enemy

International talks in Moscow in 2018 on the future of Afghanistan, attended by both Afghan government officials and Taliban leaders.

It is one thing to negotiate with an ally. It is another to negotiate with an enemy. Compromises with allies are easily justified as being in the common interest. Compromises with an enemy are more likely seen as sellouts, giving in to evil, or treasonous acts. However, as Israeli Prime Minister Yitzhak Rabin once observed, "you negotiate peace with your enemies not with your friends." Still, success in negotiating with either is by no means ensured. Consider the following:

- When Ronald Reagan signed the 1987 Intermediate Range Nuclear Forces (INF) Treaty with the Soviet Union, conservative columnist George Will called it the day "the Cold War was lost" and William Buckley characterized it as "Reagan's suicide pact." Two years later the Berlin Wall fell. While the treaty was not even indirectly responsible for the end of communism, it was symptomatic of changes coming about in the Soviet Union.

- In 1994 Rabin, Israeli Defense Minister Shimon Peres, and Palestine Liberation Organization (PLO) Chairman Yasser Arafat received the Nobel Peace Prize for signing the Oslo Accords by which Israel accepted the PLO as the representative of the Palestinians and the PLO renounced terrorism and recognized Israel's right to exist in peace. The agreement produced strong disagreements among Israelis and Palestinians. In November 1995 Rabin was assassinated by an Israeli opposed to the agreement. A Middle East peace remains elusive today.

- From the time the communist government in China came into power, the United States refused to recognize it. Yet almost immediately the United States entered into talks with communist party officials. During the Korean War the United States and China entered into a series of talks in an effort to arrange a truce. From 1955 to 1970 the two sides held 136 ambassadorial-level talks. Secret contacts between the two sides, including a trip to China by Henry Kissinger, occurred in the early 1970s in the lead up to President Nixon's 1972 visit to China. Over twenty years of talks led to the establishment of formal diplomatic relations in 1994, but it has not brought an end to policy disagreements and competition for global influence.

- Contemporary negotiating dilemmas include questions about the value of the US-Iranian nuclear accord and the US–North Korean nuclear talks, negotiations about the future of the Ukraine, negotiating with the Taliban, and negotiating with terrorists. Let's take a closer look at attempts to negotiate peace in Afghanistan.

Studies of negotiating with the enemy provide some insights on how to proceed:

1. *Negotiations do not occur in a vacuum; the domestic and global settings must always be kept in mind.* A major factor driving the Trump administration's interest in peace negotiations is his desire to remove military forces from Afghanistan as quickly as possible. This has faced strong opposition from Congress and led Ryan Crocker to label the outlines of the agreement the Trump administration negotiated in 2019 as "surrender." Within Afghanistan there are concerns that a rapid exit of US forces would lead to a violent civil war similar to the one that followed the rapid Soviet exit in 1989.

2. *It is vital to make sure that negotiating demands can be met.* In January 2019 the United States and the Taliban reached an agreement in principle for the framework of peace. The Taliban agreed not to allow Afghanistan to be used by terrorists and to negotiate a cease-fire with the Afghan government. In return the United States would withdraw its troops. The Afghan government has refused to negotiate with the Taliban. It did not attend a 2019 Moscow conference between Afghan leaders and the Taliban, and it has offered to subsidize the continued presence of US troops. Concerns have also been raised that the Taliban, which has denounced the new Afghan constitution, is not strong enough or united enough to make good on its promise to end terrorism.

3. *Care must be taken in establishing preconditions for negotiating.* This often leads to excluding extremists or key actors from the cooperative process, a situation that can be self-defeating in the long run because those excluded have little reason to support any proposed agreement. It may be better to negotiate without preconditions even though those efforts may fail.[10] For a long time US insistence that the Taliban enter talks with the Afghan government stalled negotiations. For its part the Taliban have insisted that some of its key leaders who are under arrest be released so that they can join the negotiating team. Most recently the United States and the Taliban have talked without participation by the Afghan government, raising fears that whatever agreement is reached will fail to achieve its goals.

Think about It

1. How does one define an enemy?
2. Why do some states see themselves as having enemies and other states do not?

ALLIANCES

Alliances are formal agreements among states to cooperate and promote their common interest. The North Atlantic Treaty Organization (NATO) and the Warsaw Pact are two of the most prominent post-WWII alliances. NATO was formed in 1949 to strengthen the US commitment to defend its West European allies from a possible Soviet attack. The Warsaw Pact was created as a response in 1955 to create a protective shield for the Soviet Union along its European borders. In 2015 the United States had alliances with thirty-two different states. Alliances are different from *coalitions*, agreements considered temporary and focused on specific problems. Recent examples of coalitions include the Coalition of the Willing, constructed by the United States in 2003 to remove Saddam Hussein from power in Iraq, and the NATO-led coalition that removed Gadhafi from power in Libya in 2011.

As evidenced by the rationale for creating NATO and the Warsaw Pact, alliances are most commonly defensive in nature and formed to protect national security. Defensive alliances promote a country's security in two ways: (1) they add to its power and/or (2) serve as a means of controlling other states. Alliances can also be formed to better carry out offensive military actions or intimidate other states more effectively. A study of alliances from 1815 to 2003 found 263 defensive alliances, only 14 of which were organized strictly for offensive purposes. All of the offensive alliances operated in the nineteenth century, and only four of them existed for more than two years. In contrast defensive alliances lasted an average of just over thirteen years. Both types of alliances tended to have small memberships and generally consisted of just three states.[13]

Risks and Rewards for Powerful States

Forming an alliance is not a risk-free undertaking for powerful states. The ever-present danger is that they will become entrapped in an unwanted conflict provoked by a weaker ally, a situation called the *patron's dilemma*. Should this occur, the powerful state is faced with two options, each of which holds risks for its national security. If it supports the ally, it risks being dragged into a potentially unwinnable conflict that demands a considerable amount of military resources, and it may alienate other more valuable allies. If the powerful state does not come to the aid of its ally, its reputation and trustworthiness may be questioned by its other allies and by competing powerful states.

Recent evidence suggests that powerful states take two factors into account in seeking to escape the patron's dilemma:[14]

- To what extent does it share common interests with the weaker state and, most importantly, to what extent do they share a common adversary?
- To what extent can the weaker state deter or defeat its main adversary? Only when the stronger state shares a common enemy with a weaker state that cannot defend itself will the stronger state provide both a defense alliance and weapons through arms transfers. When the two states share a common interest but the weaker state can

defend itself, the stronger state will enter into a defense agreement but not provide it with weapons. When common interests are limited and the weaker state cannot protect itself, the stronger state will provide it with weapons but not with an unconditional defense agreement.

Another danger confronting powerful states in an alliance is the free rider problem, a concept originating in game theory. **Free riding** occurs when an alliance member does not contribute its fair share to the alliance's defense costs. Free riding allows these states to divert funds to pay for other goals such as building their economies or reducing the overall level of government expenditures. This situation places a greater financial burden on other alliance members and may result in a lower level of defense preparedness than desired.

free riding A situation in which an alliance member does not contribute its fair share to the alliance's defense costs.

   How big a problem free riding presents to alliances is unclear.[15] One complicating factor is that not all costs are financial. Some would argue that NATO members were often free riders, with the United States picking up a far greater share than it should have for defending Europe from a possible Soviet attack. In response many European leaders asserted they were paying a significant political cost by allowing US troops to be stationed on their territory. A second factor is that free riding may be agreed upon or negotiated into existence. One reason a dominant power might enter into such an agreement is to prevent other alliance members from becoming so powerful that they become potential challengers to its leadership. Some see this as having happened in NATO where the United States discouraged its European allies from developing nuclear capabilities. A third, more practical factor is that free riding by a weak ally does not seriously affect the overall military capabilities of an alliance and is not a problem.

Risks and Rewards for Less Powerful States

Joining an alliance also holds risks for less powerful states. **Bandwagoning**, or "jumping on the bandwagon" of a powerful state, is an attractive policy option for less powerful states because of the added national security protection it provides. But doing so comes at a cost. The less powerful state has given up some of its freedom to maneuver through international system crises and advance its own interests by being tied to a more powerful state. Should the powerful ally change the direction of its national security policy, the less powerful state could find itself in a vulnerable position. Such was the case for Taiwan. A Cold War ally of the United States, it found itself cut loose in 1979 when the United States officially recognized the People's Republic of China as the government of China and terminated formal diplomatic relations with Taiwan. Until then Taiwan had received military and economic aid from the United States through the Military Security Act; it had allowed US troops to be stationed there and had signed a Sino-American Mutual Defense Treaty.

bandwagoning A strategy in which secondary states join in alliances with the dominant state rather than try to unite together in opposition to powerful states.

   Given the potential dangers of bandwagoning, less powerful states may instead embrace a policy of *balancing*, in which they join a weaker opposition alliance in an effort to hold a powerful state and its allies in check. This option presents weaker states with a similar set of risks. Realist scholar Stephen Walt suggests that states will pay close attention to the overall condition of the international system in taking their position. His argument is that states will balance in peacetime or in the early stages of a conflict. They will bandwagon once it becomes clear who will win and then turn back to balancing once peace is restored.[16]

DIPLOMACY

The term "diplomacy" covers a wide variety of activities ranging from performing ceremonial duties to gathering information and conducting negotiations. The focus here is on diplomacy as a tool for conducting cooperative problem-solving efforts. Three very different forms of diplomacy will be introduced to demonstrate the range of ways in which diplomacy fosters cooperation: summit diplomacy, track II diplomacy, and conference diplomacy.

Summit Diplomacy

Face-to-face meetings between heads of government or high-ranking political figures have been occurring for nearly a hundred years, but the term currently used to refer to them—**summit**—is relatively new. It was coined by Winston Churchill in 1950 when describing meetings between the major powers. It is also only since the end of WWII that summit diplomacy came to play a prominent role in promoting global cooperation. Woodrow Wilson was the first US president to engage in direct meetings with other world leaders, in 1919 at Versailles when the peace treaty ending WWI was negotiated. It was only in the 1960s that American presidents began to actively participate in organized summit conferences on a regular basis. Once focused almost exclusively on military matters and involving only a small number of leaders, summit diplomacy is now employed in a variety of foreign policy settings, such as trade and finance, climate, and human rights, and brings together large numbers of heads of government. For example, the first US-Soviet summit meeting occurred in Tehran in 1943 and brought together Joseph Stalin, Winston Churchill, and Franklin Roosevelt. US-Soviet nuclear arms control summits during the Cold War were bilateral meetings. In contrast, thirty-eight heads of government attended the opening session of the first Nuclear Security Summit in 2010.

A number of developments at both the domestic and international system levels have contributed to the increased prominence of summit diplomacy.[17] Domestic interest in summits has risen as public opinion in democratic political systems have come to view them as a proper and necessary forum for solving global problems. Heads of governments in these countries turned to summits as they became more directly involved in conducting foreign policy and came to see media coverage of their attendance at summits as a valuable way to increase their political standing. At the international level summit diplomacy is driven by the increased number of states, the growth in the number of international organizations, and the increasing frequency of regional meetings.

summit A face-to-face meeting between heads of government or political figures of high rank.

The increased use of summit diplomacy as a way to advance cooperation has led to a closer examination of its place in building international cooperation as well as its advantages and disadvantages.[18] The most fundamental debate is whether summit conferences are best suited for negotiating political breakthroughs or exist simply as media events at which already agreed-upon policies or treaties are signed with great fanfare.

Advocates of summit diplomacy cite its potential for establishing good personal relationships among leaders. Summits also have the ability to energize bureaucratic decision-making. Related to this benefit is the notion that summits are just the "tip of the iceberg" and that they can stimulate government agencies, civil society groups, and others to focus on an issue and collaborate on generating policy proposals.[19]

Critics observe that there is a real potential for miscommunication among leaders. In addition, it is likely that leaders will come to summits with different expectations and negotiating styles. Some will see the event as a forum for problem solving while others will view it more as a symbolic statement of the parties' interest in cooperation and good will. This difference in perspectives and approaches can result in unrealistically high expectations from the public about what will be accomplished. Still others warn of the potential for *summit fatigue*; the increased number of summits places a strain on the ability of bureaucracies and leaders to prepare for them and implement agreements.

The historical record of summit diplomacy presents a mixed picture of its ability to advance cooperation. It also highlights potential risks. For example, consider the Ronald Reagan and Mikhail Gorbachev summits that began in Geneva in 1985. Their first meeting is credited with breaking the ice; the two leaders were able to establish a positive relationship, symbolized by an impromptu walk in the woods without the presence of aides. The good personal relations established in Geneva led to three more summit conferences and significant arms control agreements between the United States and the Soviet Union, but they did not prevent near disasters. At the second summit in Reykjavik, Reagan's insistence on the Strategic Defense Initiative—popularly known as Star Wars—prevented an agreement from being reached at the final summit in Moscow. In Moscow, Gorbachev appeared to have lost patience with Reagan and complained about missed opportunities for agreement due to US policies.

In the case of the Reagan-Gorbachev summits positive outcomes continued even as the personal relationship between the two leaders fluctuated. This was not the case with the June 1961 summit meeting between John Kennedy and Nikita Khrushchev. Advisors to Kennedy had urged him not to meet with Khrushchev so soon after taking office for fear that Kennedy would misjudge Khrushchev's intentions. The reverse happened. Khrushchev came away from the summit feeling that Kennedy was inexperienced and could be pushed around. This conclusion may have contributed to the Soviet decision to put missiles in Cuba, which led to the October 1962 Cuban Missile Crisis.

A study of 104 US-Soviet/Russian summit meetings that took place between 1943 and 2014 suggests that summits by themselves cannot change international events. While these summits were largely driven by changing global circumstances and foreign policy agendas rather than personalities, they neither reduced nor increased the intensity of conflict, and they did not represent turning points in history.[20]

Track II Diplomacy

In conventional thinking, diplomacy is carried out by professional diplomats. In the early 1980s a different view was put forward. Professional (Track I) diplomacy was still seen as central to the conduct of foreign policy, but some argued that there was also a need for "unofficial, informal interaction between members of adversarial groups or nations." These interactions came to be termed **Track II diplomacy**.[21] The purpose of Track II diplomacy is not to negotiate an end to a conflict but to help bring individuals together and open new channels of communication for the discussion of strategies and options that could help resolve the conflict or reduce tensions. Underlying the logic of Track II diplomacy is the belief that resolving conflicts involves more than government-to-government negotiations. It may also require developing new understandings of issues and the socio-psychological factors that lie behind a particular conflict situation. Nongovernmental officials are the core players in Track II diplomacy. Government officials may join the process but do so in an unofficial capacity, which allows governments to deny that they are engaged in talks with an adversary or that they are considering a particular policy.

One example of Track II diplomacy was the effort to mediate the conflict between the white South African government and the African National Congress (ANC) as a prelude to ending apartheid in South Africa. Three Track II initiatives were especially important for promoting a dialogue between these two sides. In 1985 a meeting of white journalists, business executives, and ANC leaders was arranged in Zambia. At that time many participants on both sides viewed the effort with suspicion and doubts. Two years later ANC officials met with dissident white Afrikaners in Senegal. Later that same year another meeting was held in Great Britain between ANC officials and white academics who had ties to the government. Apartheid ended in the early 1990s when a formal set of negotiations between black and white leaders took place.

A great deal of variety exists in the ways in which Track II diplomacy is carried out. One version involves a government reaching out to a private citizen to make contact with another government and open a dialogue in hopes of settling a dispute, such as when former President Jimmy Carter was approached in 1994 by Haitian military officials who hoped to avoid a US military intervention following a coup that removed President Jean-Bertrand Aristide from office. Carter informed the Clinton administration of the contact, which then asked him to help arrange for the military leaders involved in the coup to leave Haiti and return Aristide to power.

A second version of Track II diplomacy grows out of the initiative of private citizens who act as mediators. A frequently cited example is the lead up to the 1993 Oslo Accords, during which the Palestine Liberation Organization (PLO) recognized the state of Israel and Israel in turn recognized the PLO as the representative of the Palestinian people and accepted it as a negotiating partner for future agreements. The peace process began when a Norwegian researcher arranged for meetings between Israeli and Palestinian officials. Informal meetings followed, as did an offer by the Norwegian government to help facilitate communications between the two sides. After the two parties agreed upon a

Track II diplomacy
Unofficial and informal contacts between private sector groups and individuals to open lines of communication between adversaries and develop strategies for resolving a conflict.

draft document, formal Track I negotiations began. However, the progress made at Oslo in resolving the conflict between Israel and Palestine was short lived. By 2000 the Oslo peace process had broken down and violence resumed, and unrest continues today.

Track II diplomacy may also take a third form: problem-solving workshops led by trained conflict resolution specialists. These workshops bring together prominent individuals for the purpose of entering into a dialogue with the goal of developing a practical course of action to address the problem. One such workshop series was held over two years in the mid-1990s following the breakup of the Soviet Union. At issue was a two-year civil war between the newly independent Republic of Georgia and South Ossetia, a region within that republic that sought its own independence. The workshops succeeded in opening a new dialogue between the two sides that resulted in a cease-fire agreement in 1992 but did not resolve the conflict. New fighting erupted in 2008 involving Russian military forces. A cease-fire followed, but political tensions continued as Russia recognized South Ossetia as an independent country.

Track II diplomacy has become an established pathway of international cooperation efforts, yet it continues to be surrounded by disagreement, including how to position it within the context of diplomacy. One view is that Track II is best seen as a pre-negotiation stage leading toward Track I negotiations. According to a second view, Track II does not involve diplomacy at all and should be defined as a dialogue. Related to this definitional issue is a second area of disagreement. Track II diplomacy continues to encounter opposition from some members of the diplomatic corps and elected government officials who see citizen involvement in solving foreign policy and national security disputes as inherently dangerous. This concern is long standing. The 1799 Logan Act forbids unauthorized individuals from engaging in negotiations with a foreign government that had a dispute with the United States.

A third view focuses on the question of how to evaluate Track II activities. Evaluations of summitry and other forms of Track I negotiations are often politically charged and hinge on whether or not the observer supports the outcome. Still, these diplomatic efforts tend to have a clearly defined end point from which this judgment can be made. A treaty is signed or it is not. The conference ends with an agreement or it does not. Track II efforts take a variety of forms, occur under a wide range of conditions that often have unclear beginning and end points, and are undertaken for a variety of purposes. All of this complicates the evaluation of Track II undertakings and the ability to draw lessons from them.

Conference Diplomacy

Conference diplomacy is a category of diplomacy that is concerned with the process of negotiation and bargaining that takes place in large international gatherings of states. This section presents an overview of the pre-negotiation, negotiation, and implementation and evaluation phases of conference diplomacy. The following section provides descriptions of the key distinctions between the two major forms that exist today: multilateral and minilateral. Conference diplomacy is important both as an institution for

THEORY SPOTLIGHT

Regimes and Regime Complexes

States and other actors have multiple choices in pursuing cooperative efforts, but no one option fits all situations. Writing from a liberal theoretical perspective in the late 1970s, Robert Keohane and Joseph Nye advanced one largely unexplored option for fostering cooperation in an increasingly interdependent world.[22] They defined *interdependence* as a situation marked by reciprocal effects that does not imply equal benefit to or equal effects on all. The key feature of interdependence in their view was the emergence of *regimes*, governing arrangements that operate in an intermediate zone between the distribution of power among states and the political and economic bargaining strategies states follow to advance their national interests.

Regimes are constructed in specific policy areas such as human rights, arms control, trade, money, oceans, the environment, and cyberspace. They consist of a set of principles, rules, norms and procedures that establish expectations of proper behavior and desired outcomes. The existence of regimes reduces the level of uncertainty that states and other international actors face in cooperating and provides guidelines for developing policies. The sources of the ideas and viewpoints used to construct regimes are found in the forms of cooperation discussed in this chapter as well as in national laws and constitutions and the policies of private sector business and nongovernmental organizations.

Some thirty years after developing the concept of interdependence Keohane and David Victor along with others built on this foundation and put forward the concept of a regime complex.[23] Looking specifically at climate as a policy area, they asserted that some policy problems are too complex, are marked by too high levels of uncertainty, and have too wide a diversity of policy preferences to be placed in a single comprehensive regime; examples include the

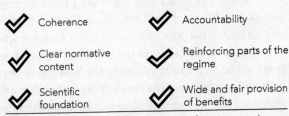

Figure 6.1 Six Dimensions for Success of Regimes and Regime Complexes.

Kyoto Protocol and the Paris Accord. Rather, it would be better to think of such policy areas as a loosely coupled groupings of more specific regimes, or a *regime complex*. Regime complexes would allow more efficient management of climate change and promote flexibility and innovation by reducing bargaining costs and encourage the creation of linkages between specific policy areas.

As with all efforts at international cooperation, success is not ensured. Once created, regime complexes are not frozen in place. They evolve over time as the power resources of participating members and the nature of the issues change. This evolution may result in both stronger and weaker complexes. One of the main conceptual challenges is to establish a basis for judging the degree of success of regimes and regime complexes. Keohane and Victor propose six dimensions for making such evaluations, shown in Figure 6.1.

Think about It

1. Can a regime complex succeed in promoting effective cooperation if no one state or international organization is in charge?

2. In what international policy areas are regime complexes most needed today? What would such a regime complex look like?

promoting cooperation and for creating broader networks of cooperation among states. One theoretical effort to highlight how networks of cooperation work is presented in the Theory Spotlight on Regimes and Regime Complexes.

PHASES OF CONFERENCE DIPLOMACY

The widespread attention given to international conferences obscures the fact that a great deal of behind-the-scenes diplomacy has already taken place in what is known as the *pre-negotiation phase*.[24] There are two different views of the pre-negotiation phase. From one perspective, the pre-negotiation phase is a filter during which time a definition of the problem is determined, boundaries for later negotiations are set, and options for resolution are sought. All three of these tasks require the development of "consensual knowledge" about the problem under discussion. Scientific and technological information often plays a significant role in developing a shared view of the problem and the options for solving it. Their impact is lessened considerably when great uncertainty and debate surround the validity of this information. In such cases political considerations and the influence of national bureaucracies are likely to be greater influences.

From a second perspective the pre-negotiation phase is a political risk management strategy employed by states.[25] This phase can provide states with international good will and domestic political benefits without requiring them to support or oppose a specific policy. Entering into pre-negotiation discussions allows states to gather in a low-key atmosphere where information can be acquired, competing views can be expressed, and the positions of other states identified. During this phase the political costs of stalemate are far less than at the negotiation phase, but they may on occasion be considerable. A case in point is the 1986 Stockholm Conference on Confidence and Security Building Measures. Attended by thirty-five countries, it provided a forum in which the United States and the Soviet Union could engage in a dialogue on increasing the openness and visibility of military actions in Europe that left many of the national security issues separating them off the table but did provide small steps for keeping the arms control process moving forward.

The historical record suggests that international crises often accelerate the pace of pre-negotiations. In these circumstances states that are reluctant to move on to the negotiation phase may find themselves pressured to do so. This was the case with the negotiations after WWII that led to the creation of the International Monetary Fund and the World Bank. The clear and present danger in everyone's mind was a repeat of the economic crises of the 1930s that contributed to the rise of Nazism and ultimately led to WWII.

Three factors are seen as particularly important to successful engagement in the *negotiation phase* of conference diplomacy.[26] One is the creation of blocks or *coalitions*, informal associations of states that seek to increase their power within organizations by acting as a group rather than individually. To a great extent, informal coalitions of like-minded states develop naturally. Prominent examples include the Group of 77 (G-77) and the nonaligned movement. The G-77 is a coalition of developing states that was created in 1964 to promote their common economic and political interests, which they felt were being ignored by international organizations. The nonaligned movement emerged during the Cold War as a group of states seeking neutrality in the US-Soviet global struggle. Coalitions are vital to the success of conference diplomacy for two reasons:

- They simplify the negotiating process by reducing the number of states that need to be actively involved in many aspects of the agreement. This adds an element of cohesion to the negotiating process that can get lost in large conferences.
- They accelerate the spread of information to participants in the negotiations and in the process help develop consensual knowledge.

Coalitions are not without their dangers. Over time they can become overly rigid and inflexible in their policy positions, making compromises harder to negotiate. To avoid such blocking coalitions from developing, many call for the creation of overlapping coalitions. In such an arrangement states are members of multiple coalitions. Overlapping coalitions lend themselves to finding solutions that many coalitions find acceptable.

A second key to successful conference diplomacy is the ability to translate a complex or highly technical agreement into one that has a clear focal point for consensus. Often a single concept such as fairness or efficiency is used to refer to either the procedures used in creating the agreement or the content of the agreement itself. In either case the core requirements are that the agreement brings together the competing interests of those involved in the discussion, speaks to their key demands, and is relatively simple. Two negotiations serve as contrasting examples of the importance of this aspect of conference diplomacy: (1) Bretton Woods, which created the International Monetary Fund and established a fixed rate for currencies, and (2) efforts to create an International Trade Organization.[27] The Bretton Woods agreement was sold on the basis of largely uncontested technical arguments over how to create a sound international financial system. The failure to establish an international trade system occurred in large part because there was no simple key concept around which agreement could be built. That debate centered on how to best guarantee full employment. This proved to be a highly charged political goal with little consensus on the best course of action. Similar problems have confronted environmental conferences, in which the main stalemate point has been "who pays?" rather than how to best protect the environment. These conferences will be discussed in detail in Chapter 10.

The third key to successful conference diplomacy is leadership. Building and maintaining overlapping coalitions is not easy, because they contain far more diverse interests than coalitions composed of states with narrowly defined policy preferences. There is also no one method for finding a clear focal point or selling an agreement. What works for one conference may not work for another, even if the subject under negotiation is the same. Creativity, political insight, and trust are needed. This combination of qualities can make it difficult for great powers to play leadership roles, as they can be perceived as having too great a stake in the outcome of the negotiations or as being fundamentally hostile to others' interests. It is not surprising that middle powers are often best positioned to play leadership roles in conference diplomacy. For example, Canada, Norway, New Zealand, Austria, and Switzerland have all played important roles in environmental negotiations.

One challenge faced in reaching an agreement via conference diplomacy is perception. As a former diplomat put it, in the age of mass media a conference needs a trademark that helps people identify with it, sympathize with its objectives, and build support over time. To this end, much of the time that could be spent negotiating an agreement is instead spent on public statements and speeches by delegates that are directed to domestic audiences.[28]

The final phase of conference diplomacy centers on the implementation of the agreement. Great variety exists in this *implementation and evaluation phase* for a number of reasons. First and foremost, disagreements involving both political and technical questions are likely to occur over what constitutes cheating on the agreement. On the political level, cooperative efforts are often couched in language that is deliberately vague in order to get all sides to agree, which makes determining whether cheating has occurred difficult. A complicating factor is that many agreements are self-policing, with no authority granted outside of the state to collect information or to make a judgment about whether cheating has occurred. On the technical level, self-policing can create problems due to a lack of data and/or a lack of transparency. Without good data and the ability to observe what other parties to a cooperative effort are doing, it is impossible to verify compliance. Concerns about the potential for cheating are highest where trust is lowest and the potential benefits from cheating are great. These conditions are frequently found in arms control negotiations, such as those between the United States and Soviet Union, and peace negotiations. An example of the latter is the peace talks between Colombia and the Revolutionary Armed Forces of Colombia (FARC) which engaged in military battles for over fifty years. Negotiations began in 2012. Early talks were held in secret, and the final round of talks were held in Havana and based on an agenda agreed to in advance. A peace agreement was signed in 2016.

An additional obstacle to implementation is the complex and uncertain nature of the problems addressed by conference diplomacy. No one conference or agreement can address the problems of international trade, human rights, environmental protection, nuclear weapons, or global health completely. Multiple conferences over long periods of time are required, each of which may address a different aspect of the problem. The domestic political climate of participants may change as the conferences progress; states that were once strong supporters of an agreement may become skeptics or withdraw completely. International conditions may also change, modifying the priority of the problem; if its impact on state security interests decreases, states may become less interested in contributing funds or expertise.

MULTILATERAL VERSUS MINILATERAL CONFERENCE DIPLOMACY

Underlying the increased prominence of conference diplomacy is the principle of democratizing global governance. No longer are the key agreements requiring international cooperation determined by a small group of powerful states. All states should now participate and all views must be heard if a true global consensus is to be established for solving global problems.

Multilateral, defined as many-sided, is the basis for a term that has become the dominant form of international conference diplomacy. *Multilateral conference diplomacy* is generally identified with the classical definition of conference diplomacy, one where large numbers of states are present. Multilateral conference diplomacy in practice has struggled to achieve the goals identified by those who support the democratization of international governance, producing few meaningful agreements. The last significant international trade agreement that used this approach was negotiated by 123 states in 1994. The last meaningful nuclear nonproliferation treaty using multilateral conference diplomacy was negotiated by 185 states in 1995. The Kyoto Protocol was negotiated by 184 countries in 1997. And the UN Millennium Declaration was completed in 2000 with the consent of 192 states.[29]

A number of factors have emerged that contribute to the repeated inability of multilateral conference diplomacy to achieve its goals. First, not all states are equally capable of fully participating in the negotiations due to such factors as a lack of funds and trained personnel. Second, the larger the number of states present and the greater the number of views articulated, the more difficult it is to negotiate an agreement that all parties can accept. The creation of coalitions or blocks does not necessarily solve this problem, since they will increase in number the larger the conference becomes. During the Law of the Sea III negotiations (1973–1981), land-locked states within the Group of 77 formed a separate negotiation group to promote their demands for open access to international waters, a demand that ran contrary to the bargaining position of most G-77 states. And during the 1986–1994 Uruguay Round of Trade Talks, blocks composed of rich and poor countries such as the Rio Group, the de la Pax Group, and the Cairns Group emerged, which succeeded in altering the agenda so that the interests of developing states were better represented.

In response to the perceived failings of multilateral conference diplomacy, some have begun to advocate negotiations by the few rather than by the many. This has come to be referred to as *minilateral conference diplomacy*.[30] Participation is limited to those committed to action and sharing a common set of values. In addition to speeding up the negotiation process, minilateral conference diplomacy is seen by its advocates as promoting experimentation and learning in problem solving. No consensus exists regarding the optimal number of participants; that number depends on such factors as the nature of the problem under discussion, the speed with which action is needed, and the extent to which a shared set of values exists.

In many cases groups of like-minded states that have come together in minilateral negotiations have come to be characterized as "clubs." In its most general sense, a *club* is defined as "a voluntary group deriving mutual benefits from sharing the costs of producing an activity that has public goods characteristics."[31] In essence, a club takes a public good, one that in theory is available to all states, and turns it into a quasi- or partial private good. Those not in the club can be penalized by club members for their actions or denied access to the public good. Because clubs are a much talked-about way to move forward on global climate policy, climate minilateral diplomacy will be examined in some detail in Chapter 10. Here it is important to note the underlying logic of climate clubs. Non-club members cannot be denied access to an improved global climate that results from club policies, but club members can penalize them through trade and financial sanctions for having policies such as high emissions that hurt the environment. Non-club members can be rewarded for improving their climate policies by preferential trade agreements with club members.

Minilateral clubs are not an entirely new dimension of conference diplomacy. What is new are calls for minilateral negotiations that stand alone and are not part of a larger multilateral conference.[32] One prominent example of a de facto minilateral club is the Bretton Woods conference that established the International Monetary Fund and the World Bank. Although forty-four states were represented at the conference, the agreements reached were largely the product of US and British negotiations that other states endorsed but had little voice in creating. The ability of these two great powers to control international economic policy gradually deteriorated as the number of new states grew and their desire for a meaningful voice increased. One result of this frustration was the creation in 1964 of the United Nations Conference on Trade and Development (UNCTAD) as a permanent setting for developing trade, investment, and development opportunities in developing states. A second product of this frustration was the demand to create a New International Economic Order (NIEO) in the 1970s. Taken as a group, the proposals contained in the NIEO would have transformed the governance of global trade relations. However, the movement to create a NIEO faltered and never achieved its goals. For more on the NIEO, see Chapter 8.

As these examples suggest, the ability of minilateral clubs to produce policy is not obvious.[33] Reducing the number of states participating in a club may simplify negotiations, but it may also exclude so many politically important states that its legitimacy as an instrument of global cooperation may be questioned. An additional fear raised by critics of minilateralism is that it may undermine the ability of large international organizations and conferences to carry out their responsibilities. Not all issues, it is argued, can be dealt with by clubs. Multilateral conference diplomacy is still essential to international cooperation, as is adherence to international law.

INTERNATIONAL LAW

International law is a broad term for the set of rules that govern relations among states. It promotes global cooperation by providing standards against which state behavior can be judged and increasing confidence that those standards will be followed. One area on which a great deal of activity in the international law field has focused in recent years is the Law of the Sea. The Regional Spotlight provides background information on international efforts to promote cooperation in the oceans.

international law
The laws, rules, and customs that define the legal responsibilities of states in their conduct with one another.

Two judicial bodies have global reach in the contemporary international system. The oldest, the International Court of Justice (also referred to as the World Court),

REGIONAL SPOTLIGHT

Oceans

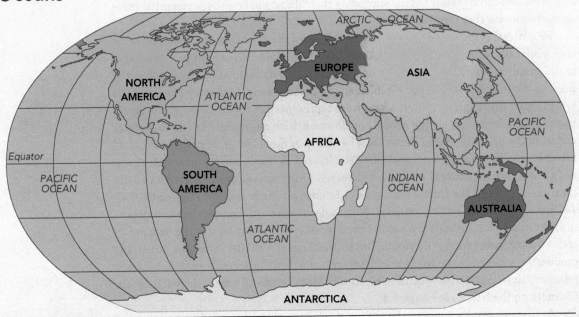

Map 6.1 A Global Map with Oceans as Its Core Feature.

Seventy percent of the earth's surface is covered by water. The sea is an avenue of transportation as well as a source of food and natural resources. It has also been the site of military conflict, as states have sought to control oceans for national security reasons. Dating back to the Middle Ages and continuing until the seventeenth century, states claimed national control over ocean waters leaving little room for international cooperation. Spain, Portugal, and Great Britain claimed various parts of the Atlantic Ocean, the Indian Ocean, the Pacific Ocean, and the Gulf of Mexico. Denmark, Sweden, and Norway claimed portions of the North Sea and the Baltic Sea.

In 1609 Hugo Grotius, a Dutch philosopher, put forward the idea of the freedom of the seas, which asserted the right to unobstructed navigation of the ocean waters because they were the common property of all people. Over time this principle became the foundation for thinking about the international law of oceans, but it did not end controversy over what should be done to those who violate this principle or what type of ships might be excluded from the right to the freedom of the seas. During the late eighteenth century naval powers sought to block trade between their enemies and other states. For example, Great Britain interfered with US shipping during the War of 1812 and set up a naval blockade against Napoleonic France. WWI saw both Great Britain and Germany, who were at war with one another, set up naval blockades and seek to intercept and destroy the other's ships. The United States vehemently opposed such actions as a

Vinoverde / Alamy Stock Photo

Japanese coastguard vessel approaching a Chinese fishing boat in disputed territorial waters.

violation of international law, only to actively engage in them once it entered WWI.

Today two general principles dominate thinking about how to govern the sea. The first holds that the oceans belong to no country. They are a public good, a global common, that all states are free to use as they wish. The second principle, enclosure, defines the ocean, or at least significant parts of it, as being private property. In other words, portions of the ocean belong to states, which determine how those portions can be used and what is permissible. In the post-WWII era advances in technology and changes in the climate of international politics focused attention on the tension between these competing principles. The result was a series of United Nations Law of the Seas (LOS) conferences.

LOS I met in from February to April 1958. The negotiations built largely on the work of the International Law Commission, which had been formulating proposals since 1949. The main point of disagreement was over the boundaries of the territorial sea. Four conventions emerged from LOS I, all of which became international law by 1964. These agreements were largely described as backward looking because they focused on defining jurisdictions and claims rather than addressing management questions. LOS II soon followed, meeting briefly in March and April 1960, but there were few changes from LOS I.

LOS III met for eighty-three weeks over seven years (1973–1981). Much had changed since LOS I. Some 90 states were represented at LOS I & II; 158 states attended LOS III. Until LOS III, the main division among states had been the East-West Cold War conflict. Now the principal division was between rich (North) and poor (South) states. In addition, where LOS I proceeded from a solid foundation laid by the International Law Commission, preparatory work for LOS III was uneven, leading to a large and unwieldy negotiating agenda. Much of the early debate in LOS III continued to be about defining territorial waters. The United States dropped its opposition to narrowly defined limits after Congress passed legislation establishing a 200-mile economic zone in response to domestic interest-group pressure. From that point forward, debate centered on issues related to deep seabed mining. LOS III produced a loosely worded agreement creating a 12-mile territorial sea, a 200-mile coastal-right zone, and an additional right to 200 miles attached to the continental shelf. Replacing the LOS I and LOS III agreements, LOS III came into effect in 1994. A total of 167 states plus the European Union have ratified the agreement. The United States has not, arguing that the International Seabed Authority created by LOS III is unfair to US economic interests. The United States does acknowledge LOS III as part of customary international law except for the International Seabed Authority.

Think about It

1. Should landlocked states or those with only small ocean borders be allowed to participate in decision-making about oceans? Explain your answer.

2. Can the Law of the Sea Treaty succeed if the United States does not join? Should it be replaced by a new treaty that the United States supports? Explain your answers.

was established in 1945 by the UN Charter and is the successor to the Permanent Court of International Justice that was created in 1922. Its structure and operation were introduced in Chapter 3. The second court system, the International Criminal Court (ICC), began operating in 2002 but has intellectual roots going back to the Paris Peace Conference that ended WWI. It is responsible for the operation of special military tribunals, such as those in Nuremberg and Tokyo that followed WWII, and special UN tribunals for genocide in Rwanda and Bosnia. The World Court presides over cases involving conflicts among states; in contrast, the ICC has jurisdiction over individuals charged with genocide, crimes against humanity, and war crimes. For more on the ICC see Chapter 9.

Sources of International Law

The World Court recognizes three major sources of international law: conventions or treaties, customs, and general principles. *International conventions* or *treaties* are formal written agreements between states that lay out the obligations and responsibilities of the participating states. The League of Nations Treaty Series lists a total of 408 treaties signed between 1920 and 1948. As of 2017 over 560 multilateral treaties were in force, covering topics as broad as human rights, disarmament, the peaceful settlement of disputes, and environmental protection, as well as narrowly focused agreements including a "Multilateral Agreement for the Establishment of an International Think Tank for Landlocked Developing Countries."

Unlike treaties, customs are not formally agreed to by states in a written document. *Customs* consist of norms, traditions, and best practices and emerge over time from what is considered to be the normal and proper way for states to interact. Diplomatic immunity, which provides diplomats with legal immunity and safe passage in carrying out their duties, is a well-known example of customary international law. Initially diplomatic immunity was granted on an ad hoc case-by-case basis. Over time it came to be viewed as a necessary foundation for diplomatic relations among states, especially between adversaries. In 1961 the concept of diplomatic immunity formally became part of international law when it was incorporated into the Vienna Convention on Diplomatic Relations during the height of the Cold War.

General principles exist at a deeper and more fundamental level than that of customs. The concept of sovereignty that emerged from the 1648 Treaty of Westphalia is a prime example of a long-standing guiding principle of state relations that has become incorporated into international law. Another is the concept of **just war**, which was developed by Plato, Cicero, Saint Augustine, Thomas Aquinas, and Hugo Grotius, among others. For a war to be considered just it must meet two general sets of conditions. First, there must be a proper justification for going to war. This includes the following: (1) the existence of a proper authority behind the decision to engage in violence, (2) a proper cause for which the war is being fought, (3) rightful intent, and (4) consistency of engagement and support for peace. The second set of conditions, how

just war A legal and philosophical concept that establishes the requirements for how and why war is started and how it is fought.

a war is fought, has two dimensions: proportionality and discrimination. The principle of proportionality requires that the amount of force used be proportional to the gravity of the issue being contested. The principle of discrimination requires a distinction to be made between combatants and noncombatants and acceptance that only the former may be the target of violence.

There are two long-standing schools of thought regarding whether conventions or treaties, customs, and general principles should be given priority. According to the *natural law* perspective, the foundations of international law are rooted in universal and unchanging general principles that were originally advanced by the Roman Catholic Church. In the seventeenth century the writings of Hugo Grotius on the nature of a just war and related topics shifted this perspective to one that emphasizes logic and reasoned inquiry. A second school of thought referred to as *positivism* emerged in the eighteenth century. In this view the basis of international law is not found in universal religious or secular principles but in the actions of states: international law is based on what states do and agree to by custom or signed conventions.

While treaties, customs, and principles may produce different interpretations of the proper content of international law, they are not inherently in conflict with one another. Just war theory is a case in point; it has its roots in general principles put forward by religious and secular philosophers, but it has also been included in international conventions:

- As originally written, the 1864 Geneva Convention focused on the proper treatment of those wounded on the battlefield; the fourth Geneva Convention, signed in 1949, was revised to include a provision to protect civilians during warfare because of the war crimes carried out during WWII which led to the Nuremburg trials.
- The 1899 Hague Conference produced three treaties that included provisions against the bombardment of undefended towns and against using certain weapons in war. A 1925 Geneva Protocol added a prohibition of the use of poisonous gases as a response to the use of these gases during WWI.

Although these efforts reflect progress, there is still significant disagreement over the content of international law. One challenge comes from the feminist theoretical perspective on international politics, which asserts that international law is gender based.[34] According to this perspective, the language of international law, the procedures it uses to establish truth, and the very definition of what is true are rooted in a masculine perspective on reality. Early international human rights statutes emphasized individual and civil rights over economic, cultural, and social ones. Since much of the oppression faced by women lies in these areas and occurs in the home or in the workplace, these laws offered women little justice. Similarly, the emphasis on protecting group and communal rights ignored the fact that in the developing world many groups adhere to practices that discriminate against women.

A second challenge comes from the developing world, where international law is not viewed as truly global in nature. Rather, it is seen as rooted in European law that spread globally through economic and military conquest and was imposed on conquered states through colonialism. As a former chair of the US Joint Chiefs of Staff observed about his discussions with China, "Whenever I would have a conversation with them about international standards or international rules of behavior, they would inevitably point out that those rules were made when they were absent from the world stage."[35]

This contemporary hostility and opposition to international law in much of the developing world centers on the workings of the ICC. Virtually all ICC investigations have centered on crimes committed in Africa, leading South Africa and Burundi to announce in 2016 that they planned to withdraw from the ICC. Philippine President Rodrigo Duarte made a similar announcement in 2018 and called upon other states to join in a "mass" exodus from the ICC. The ICC has also become the target of candidates seeking election in countries targeted by ICC investigations. For example, in the 2013 presidential election in Kenya the ICC was depicted as being a neo-imperialist tool under Western control.[36]

Hard Versus Soft Law

International law varies not only in sources but also in structure. Three different elements of international law have been identified: (1) precision in defining rules, (2) the level of obligation placed on states, and (3) the extent to which power is delegated to third parties such as courts. If all three of these elements are present and highly developed, international law is often referred to as *hard law*. In cases where one or more of these elements are missing, it is referred to as *soft law*.[37]

Disagreement exists over the relationship between hard and soft law. Critics of soft law tend to either deny that it is international law, reserving that designation for hard law, or see soft law as a half-way house on the way to hard law. Advocates of soft law assert that on occasion states find soft law preferable to hard law as a way to accomplish their foreign policy and security goals, because of the costs associated with precision, obligation, and delegation.

Hard law helps states reduce the transaction costs associated with adherence to international law by clearly specifying the type of behaviors permitted and reducing the likelihood of exploitation of loopholes. It increases the credibility of commitments and clarifies where decisions about international law will be made. Although soft law does not offer these benefits, it has benefits of its own. The negotiating costs are less; hard law agreements are difficult and time-consuming to pursue. Soft law can help overcome the roadblock of challenges to sovereignty. Sovereignty costs are less because states have not delegated decision-making and enforcement power to others; retaining a high degree of freedom to act may reduce the clarity of a state's commitment but may also be wise, given the complexity of international problems and uncertainty over evolving situations.

So which form of international law should a state pursue? According to one line of thought, states will pursue hard laws when they are certain of their national interest and have sufficient power to influence other states. When these conditions are absent, states are more likely to seek a soft law outcome. Consistent with this expectation is that the United States as a powerful economic power with clearly identified national interests pushed the World Trade Organization to a hard law position with clearly defined rules. In contrast, possessing neither clearly defined national interest and little economic power, developing states have advocated soft law positions to govern intellectual property rights.

Enforcing International Law

International law is seen as self-enforcing. It is in the self-interest of states to obey international law in order to avert the potentially chaotic consequences that might otherwise follow. When violations of international law do happen, states have three broad options at their disposal.

1. **Bring the case to the World Court**. States must voluntarily agree to have the World Court hear the case. Note that the World Court has no power of enforcement. It is up to the states that brought the case to implement its decision. A variation on this approach is for a state to bring a case to a regional court such as the Court of Justice of the European Union. It interprets European Union law to ensure it is implemented in the same way by all members and settles disputes between EU institutions and member states. Should the Court find that a member is in violation of an EU law, the member is expected to change its policy without delay. If it does not, the EU Commission may impose financial penalties.

2. **Bring the case to an international organization**. The principal organization involved in making judgments about state compliance with international law is the World Trade Organization (WTO). In joining the WTO states commit themselves to going before its Dispute Settlement Body if another state raises a complaint about its trade policy. If found to be in violation of WTO rules, the state must end its policy or offer financial compensation to the other state. Should it do neither the state that won the case may obtain permission from the WTO to impose retaliatory trade sanctions.

3. **Take unilateral action against the state perceived as violating international law**. Typical actions include cutting off economic or military aid or imposing trade and financial sanctions against the other state, its leaders, or key businesses. As this option makes clear, more powerful states are in a far better position than weak ones to disregard international law or act on their own against perceived violations.

Alliances, diplomacy, and international law contribute to the ability of states and other actors to cooperate. But challenges remain. Successful outcomes are not guaranteed. The Contemporary Focus section that follows highlights the continuing cooperation problems faced in dealing with Ebola.

CONTEMPORARY PERSPECTIVE:
Ebola in 2013 and Today

UNMEER / Alamy Stock Photo

A display of gloves and boots used by medical staff, drying in the sun at a center for victims of the Ebola virus in Guinea in 2014.

In December 2013 a two-year-old boy died of Ebola in the rainforest of Guinea. Health officials were slow to recognize the reemergence of the disease; earlier Ebola outbreaks had occurred in sub-Saharan Africa. Moreover, health care workers and facilities were in short supply; international health groups had left West Africa due to violent civil wars in the region. By the time the epidemic was declared over in December 2015, some 28,600 people were infected with Ebola and more than 11,300 died. In Guinea the fatality rate was 67%; in Sierra Leone it was 28%; and in Liberia it was 45%.[38]

The WHO did not identify Ebola as the cause of these deaths and issue health warnings until March 23, 2014. In mid-April it concluded that the outbreak was coming to a close. In contrast, Doctors Without Borders (Médecins San Frontières or MSF) asserted that the number of deaths only appeared to be down; local citizens were not reporting them due to distrust of the government.

The Ebola outbreak did *not* end. By mid-June MSF reported that the situation was out of control. Foreign health workers were being attacked by mobs who blamed them for bringing the Ebola virus into their country. In early September Liberian health workers went on strike. The sense of panic among the people was heightened by the initial wave of government health warnings which stressed that Ebola had no cure.

Other states shared this sense of panic. Neighboring states refused to warehouse gloves and surgical gowns, allow exhausted health workers to rest in their countries, or permit humanitarian relief planes to land. Canada and Australia denied all visa requests from West African states. Most African countries banned travel and trade with Guinea, Liberia, and Sierra Leone.

In May 2015 the annual meeting of the World Health Assembly, which has oversight over the WHO, did not address the Ebola outbreak. The WHO leadership continued to resist declaring a public health emergency, saying that this designation should only be used as a last resort; they feared that Guinea, Liberia, and Sierra Leone might view it as a hostile act and complicate cooperative efforts. Additionally, budget cuts had greatly reduced the WHO's epidemic response capabilities. From 2010 to 2014 the WHO's Africa response budget had fallen from $26 million to $11 million.

On August 6 Liberia declared a state of emergency. Two days later, some thirty-two weeks after the Ebola outbreak was identified, the WHO announced a "public health emergency of international concern" in West Africa, which led UN Secretary General Ban Ki-moon to appoint a special envoy on Ebola. Also in August, President Barack Obama hosted a US-African Leaders Summit in Washington during which economic—not health—issues dominated the agenda.

A more active global response only began to take shape in mid-September when an emergency meeting of the UN Security Council took up the Ebola crisis. Only the second meeting ever by the Security Council on a disease (the first was on HIV/AIDS), this led to the creation of the very first UN emergency health mission. In September President Obama stated that the Ebola outbreak was a potential threat to global security. He announced that the United States would send 4,000 military personnel to the region and provide $750 million to the relief effort. The World Bank estimated the cost of ending the Ebola epidemic at $1 billion. In February 2015, after the crisis had largely passed, less than 50% of the promised finances, personnel, or supplies had arrived.

Ebola did not disappear. 2018 saw outbreaks in the Democratic Republic of Congo. By the beginning of February 2019 the WHO judged the national and regional risk of Ebola spreading to be very high. It determined there had occurred over 700 confirmed cases of Ebola and almost 500 deaths resulting in a 62% fatality rate, making it the second largest Ebola outbreak. The first multidrug clinical trials of Ebola therapies began in November 2018.

Politics has made responding to this outbreak difficult. It takes place in an ongoing war zone in the eastern Congo where some 120 active guerrilla forces operate. Rebel attacks in November 2018 forced the suspension of efforts to contain the Ebola outbreak and killed eight UN Peacekeepers. Election protests by antigovernment groups prior to the December 30 Democratic Republic of Congo presidential election vandalized health care facilities and set on fire an Ebola care facility where patients were awaiting test results. Citing the Ebola threat, the government announced that it would not count the votes cast in areas affected by Ebola until March 2019, after the president took office. The repeated Ebola crises highlight the continuing problems of promoting international cooperation on global health issues. The following section introduces some cooperation challenges and responses that may play important roles in addressing these and other challenges in the future.

LOOKING TO THE FUTURE

This section applies the concepts of international cooperation presented in the chapter (alliances, diplomacy, and international law) to help formulate responses to three international political cooperation challenges. The first deals with efforts to incorporate a broader range of societal voices in the cooperation process. The second addresses the question of moving beyond lowest-common-denominator agreements to stricter, more specific, enforceable provisions. The third introduces private sector delegation as an alternate approach to promoting international cooperation.

Promoting and Expanding Track III Activities

Earlier in this chapter the concept of Track II diplomacy was introduced. Recall that Track II diplomacy involves unofficial dialogues, in contrast with Track I diplomacy, which involves official discussions among representatives from different states. Increasingly it is being argued that an even greater degree of outreach is needed to involve a broader range of societal voices in policy discussions for true peace to be realized in highly conflictual situations. This outreach effort is often referred to as Track III diplomacy.

The United States Institute of Peace defines *Track III diplomacy* as grassroots people-to-people diplomacy carried out by individuals and private sector groups for the purpose of promoting understanding among hostile communities. To foster positive interaction among such groups, common approaches include organized meetings, conferences, and workshops. Of particular importance to Track III diplomacy is involvement of marginalized groups that allows their voices to be heard in official policy-making circles. The focus of Track III diplomacy is thus as much on domestic politics as it is on politics in the international arena.[39]

The heart of Track III diplomacy is building a strong societal foundation on which international cooperative efforts can be built; this is also necessary for effective implementation of cooperative agreements of all types. A common lament of those who evaluate the execution of such agreements is how little societal support they have received. All too often implementation problems can be traced back to a lack of voice of, and investment in success by, key societal actors or a lack of accountability. For example, as a result of the 1998 Asian financial crisis the World Bank and the IMF pushed Indonesia to adopt international standards for its financial institutions. Having little choice, it did so. But Indonesian banks, which had been left out of these negotiations, fought a rearguard battle to delay, frustrate, and undermine implementation. As one observer put it, "for every two steps forward ... implementation took at least one step back."[40]

House Gifts and Gift Baskets

Another challenge facing international cooperation is that, all too often, multilateral agreements are lowest-common-denominator agreements organized around vaguely stated points on which all can agree. This occurs because most international conference diplomacy is based on a consensus acceptance of the outcome—it must be agreed to by all states.

In preparation for the 2010 Nuclear Security Summit attended by forty-seven countries, US officials developed a strategy referred to as "House Gifts" to move beyond a lowest-common-denominator agreement.[41] During the preparatory meetings for the summit, thirty states announced a total of sixty-seven "gifts," policy initiatives that they would unilaterally take to promote nuclear security. Among the gifts were individual pledges by Belgium, Kazakhstan, Mexico, New Zealand, Norway, and Great Britain to convert their highly enriched uranium (HEU) reactors to low enriched uranium (LEU) reactors. Norway promised an additional gift, a commitment of $3.3 million to the International Atomic Energy Association's nuclear security fund.

At the 2012 National Security Summit the logic behind house gifts was expanded to include the creation of "Gift Baskets" in which groups of countries agreed to jointly undertake policies to promote nuclear security. Among the gift baskets created was a pledge by twenty-three states to create and support International Network for Nuclear Security Training and Support Centers and a pledge by nineteen states to build national capacities and pass laws against nuclear smuggling in time for the 2014 summit meeting.

The presentation of house gifts and gift baskets continued at the 2014 and 2016 Nuclear Security Summits. In some cases these gifts were add-ons to previous gifts. For example, in 2014 twelve states announced the elimination of all HEU facilities. New gift baskets included a pledge by twenty-nine states to participate in cybersecurity workshops and a pledge by twenty-seven states to develop measures to reduce insider threats to nuclear security programs.

Critics of gift basket diplomacy correctly argue that many of these actions would have been taken by these states in the absence of a summit. Supporters counter by noting that gift baskets and house gifts move negotiations at a steady pace and create the basis for a "blame and shame" strategy that can be used against states refusing to participate.

Delegated International Regulation

The globalization of the world's economy has simultaneously created tremendous opportunities for growth of national economies and private sector firms and significant problems for national governments seeking economic control and regulation. The inadequacy of national controls and their variation from country to country are often cited as major contributing factors to the Asian financial crisis of 1997–98 and the global financial crisis of 2008–9. In both these cases national governments and international organizations struggled to address the problem.

Global conferences, the creation of regional and global trade agreements, and institutions such as the World Trade Organization are the most visible responses to these challenges. A less visible response is the delegation of international economic regulation to global private sector organizations that are considered to have the expertise and resources to bring about uniformity in state policies more quickly than governments. This is different from Track III diplomacy in that direct decision-making power is being given to private firms. Under track III diplomacy individuals and organizations support government cooperative efforts by creating a political environment favorable to these efforts. Notable examples include the International Accounting Standards Board, which sets the reporting rules used by multinational corporations in over a hundred countries and two regulatory organizations that together set international standards for 85% of products sold globally, ranging from freight containers, paints, radiation dosages for

X-ray machines, and battery sizes, to the establishment of electromagnetic thresholds so that one piece of electronic equipment does not interfere with the operation of another.[42]

A key argument for the delegation of regulation authority to private sector organizations is that their decisions advance the common good because they are based on technical, non-political criteria. Critics assert that, while the language of their decisions are technical, the process of setting standards is a political one. Experts often disagree and standards selected are those favored by the most powerful organizations and states. Organizations from smaller states tend to be ignored. One important policy area where small states have been ignored is the global standardization of financial reporting practices by companies.

Summary

- Cooperation in the context of international politics is not easy. Many obstacles must be overcome if states and other international actors are to work together for their mutual benefit and to address shared problems.

- Resolving the 1976 and 2000 Ebola crises required the cooperation of state and non-state actors, which was a challenge because the crises were unexpected, there were no procedures or institutions in place to promote cooperation, and those involved in resolving the crisis had different values and priorities.

- Cooperation efforts require identifying preconditions, setting the table, or determining who should attend, and establishing the basis for cooperation.

- The risks and rewards of alliances, as formal agreements among states to cooperate and promote their common interest, differ depending on whether a state is strong or weak.

- Diplomacy takes many different forms, each of which has its advantages and disadvantages. Summit diplomacy involves meetings of heads of government and senior officials. It has become increasingly popular.

- Track II diplomacy involves unofficial and informal interactions among adversaries. Conference diplomacy is best seen as progressing through a series of phases. It has two major forms: multilateral and minilateral.

- International law promotes global cooperation by providing standards against which state behavior can be judged and increasing confidence that those standards will be followed. It is based on treaties and conventions, customs, and principles; it can take different forms, including hard law and soft law; and it is not easily enforced.

- Global responses to the 2013 Ebola crisis highlighted the problems of promoting international cooperation on global health issues, which continue today.

- Looking to the future, significant cooperation challenges exist in (1) bringing a broader range of voices into the cooperation process using so-called Track III diplomacy, (2) moving beyond lowest-common-denominator solutions through the use of strategies such as "house gifts" and "gift baskets," and (3) developing additional ways of promoting cooperation.

Key Terms

Alliances *(172)*

Bandwagoning *(173)*

Cooperation *(163)*

Free riding *(173)*

International law *(183)*

Just war *(186)*

Summit *(174)*

Track II diplomacy *(176)*

Critical Thinking Questions

1. Which actors are most responsible for the lack of effective cooperation in the Ebola outbreaks in 1976 and 2000? Who should be the lead actor in global health crises?

2. How should the three factors that are important in promoting cooperation (preconditions, setting the table, and the foundations for cooperation) be ranked in order of importance?

3. Are alliances best seen as adding to a state's strength or weakening it by trapping it into coming to the help of another state? Explain your answer.

4. How compatible are the three forms of diplomacy (summits, Track II, and conference diplomacy)? Is there a form of diplomacy that needs to be added to this list?

5. Should soft law or hard law be given priority in international efforts at cooperation? Explain your answer.

6. Identify a current area in which efforts at international cooperation are taking place. Which of the three responses to the cooperation challenge (Track III, house gifts and gift baskets, and private delegated regulation) is most likely to be helpful in reaching an agreement, and why?

7. To what extent did policy-makers learn about cooperation from the earlier Ebola outbreaks in responding to the outbreaks in 2013 and today? What factors promoted and hindered learning?

Practice and Review Online
http://textbooks.rowman.com/hastedt-felice

▲ UN peacekeepers working with children in Africa. *Source:* Alberto Ramella / MARKA / Alamy Stock Photo

07

THE SECURITY CHALLENGE

NOT ALL SECURITY CHALLENGES INVOLVE the use of military force or escalate to the point of war. Many involve economic and environmental conditions. While their numbers have decreased, wars of various types continue to be the primary security challenge facing the world today.

In 2016 there were forty-nine active **state-based conflicts**,[1] conflicts in which at least one of the warring parties is a government. These include armed conflicts between two or more states, intrastate conflicts between a government and internal opposition groups, and internationalized intrastate conflicts in which a foreign state intervenes in an intrastate conflict. The 2016 number is down by three from 2015; that year and 1991 had the most state-based conflicts during the post-Cold War period. In 2017 there were 49 active state-cased conflicts, down from four from 2016. At the same time the number of active non state conflicts rose to 82, due largely to fighting in Africa.[2]

Only two of the 2016 conflicts were fought between states: Eritrea-Ethiopia and Pakistan-India. Since 2000 there have been seven years in which no conflicts involved two states; there have been only one or two in the others. Today's conflicts primarily are located within a state and take the form of civil wars, rebellions, and terrorism.

state-based conflict
A dispute between two actors, at least one of which involves the use of military force.

The primary location of state-based conflicts has also shifted. In the last decades of the twentieth century most conflicts occurred in Africa. During the 2000s this switched to Asia, most notably Afghanistan. In 2012 the Middle East became the primary location as a result of fighting within Syria, Afghanistan, and Iraq.

LEARNING OBJECTIVES

Students will be able to:

- Describe the evolution of the Arab-Israeli conflict.

- Identify the points of agreement and disagreement on the meaning of peace and war.

- Explain the various types of war and their causes.

- Describe the complex conditions under which peacekeeping operations and post-conflict reconstruction operate.

- Compare the reasons for stability and instability in the first and second nuclear ages.

- Identify the underlying dynamics of the Syrian civil war.

- Assess the merits of competing ideas for addressing national security challenges in the future.

HISTORICAL PERSPECTIVE:
The Arab-Israeli Conflict

Conflict is no stranger to the Middle East. It has experienced various types of war over thousands of years. However, the first official Arab-Israeli War, referred to by most observers as the Palestine War, did not take place until 1948. Many Israelis consider it "the war of independence," and many Arabs identify it as "the catastrophe." In 1917 the League of Nations had endorsed the creation of a Jewish state within Palestine. In February 1947, weary from WWII and its inability to stop growing tensions in the region, Great Britain announced that it was turning over governance of Palestine to the United Nations (UN). UN Resolution 181, passed in November 1947, divided Palestine into two states, one Arab and one Jewish, with Jerusalem becoming a neutral trustee area.

Neither side expected the partitioning of Palestine to be peaceful. On May 14, 1948, three hours before the British mandate was to expire, Israel declared its independence. The next day Israel was invaded from three sides by a coalition of Egyptian, Syrian, Lebanese, and Jordanian forces. After some ten months of fighting and periodic truces, the war ended in early 1949 with Israel signing separate agreements with all four of the invading nations. The war left Israel in control of almost 60% of the territory that was to have become part of the Arab state and resulted in some 700,000 Palestinian Arabs becoming refugees, fleeing from territory that was now part of Israel.

War next erupted in 1956 after Egyptian President Gamal Abdel Nasser nationalized the Suez Canal, a painful symbol of Egypt's colonial past. For Britain and France nationalization threatened business interests that owned the canal as well as their standing as colonial powers. Ending the free flow of goods through the Canal also threatened Israel's economic survival. Together, they created a plan to retake it. Israel's forces would cross into Egypt's Sinai Peninsula bordering the canal and take control, then France and Great Britain would issue an ultimatum. After Egypt rejected it, French and British forces would attack Egypt and take control of the Suez Canal.

Israel attacked on October 29 and within a week controlled most of the Sinai Peninsula. British and French forces began air attacks two days later. To their surprise, the United States supported a UN Resolution calling for an end to fighting and the withdrawal of foreign forces from Egypt. This left them with little choice but to comply because of the heavy military dependence of all three nations on the Unites States. A UN Emergency Force (UNEF) was created to replace the Israeli forces occupying the Sinai and act as a buffer between Egypt and Israel.

Just over a decade later, in June 1967, the next Arab-Israeli War, known as the Six-Day War, broke out. This conflict followed Nasser's demand for immediate withdrawal of the UNEF and closure of the Straits of Tiran, which again threatened Israel's economy by restricting free passage of Israeli ships. On the morning of June 5 Israel launched a surprise military offensive, taking control of the Sinai, the Gaza Strip, the West Bank of the Jordan River, and Jerusalem in a single week and soundly defeating Arab military forces.

Just six years later, on Yom Kippur in October 1973, Arab military forces struck Israel by surprise. Capitalizing on a combination of Israeli overconfidence and deception (the Egyptian attack was masked as a military training exercise), Syrian and Egyptian forces attacked the Golan Heights and Israel positions in the Sinai. Initially successful, inflicting heavy damage on Israeli forces, by the second week of intense fighting the tide turned. Israeli forces gained such a decisive advantage over Egyptian forces that Russia and the United States arranged a cease-fire, fearing that continued fighting would destabilize the entire region.

Arab-Israeli military conflicts have not reached the same level of violence between uniformed military forces since, but they did not end with the October 1973 War:

- **Israeli incursions into Lebanon**. On three occasions (1978, 1982, and 2006) Israeli forces entered Lebanon with the objective of making the Israel-Lebanon border more secure and forcing Palestine Liberation Organization (PLO) and Hezbollah fighters to withdraw from Lebanon and halt attacks on Israel.
- **Palestinian uprisings**. The first of two uprisings, known as Intifadas, began in December 1987 and continued until 1993. Growing out of Palestinian discontent

with the living and working conditions in Gaza and the West Bank, what started out as a spontaneous movement became increasingly organized over time; the Israeli military responded by making arrests, imposing curfews, imprisoning large numbers of protestors, and employing force. The second Intifada, which ran from 2000 to 2005, was ignited by the visit of future Prime Minister Ariel Sharon to the Temple Mount, considered to be the third most holy site in Islam. On September 29, 2000, the day following his visit, rioting broke out in Jerusalem and soon spread to Gaza and the West Bank; strikes and demonstrations occurred, along with suicide bombings and attacks against Israeli citizens. In response to one attack Israel launched Operation Defensive Shield (March–April, 2002).

- **Israeli military offensives into Gaza**. There were three of these, designed to end rocket and mortar attacks on Israeli cities and close tunnels being used for smuggling weapons from Gaza into Israel: Operation Cast Lead (December 2008–January 2009), Operation Pillar of Defense ((November 2012), and Operation Protective Edge (July–August, 2014). Hamas, a Palestinian terrorist group, had taken control of Gaza in 2007, leading Israel to declare the region a "hostile" territory and impose economic and political blockades.
- **Covert military action into Gaza**. In November 2018 a covert operation by Israeli Special Forces into Gaza was revealed and resulted in a military encounter killing Palestinian civilians and an Israeli soldier. Along with air attacks, the operation's mission was to kill a prominent Hamas military commander.

PEACE AND WAR / WAR AND PEACE

No two concepts are more closely linked in the study of international politics than peace and war. It is assumed that everyone knows and recognizes them, yet their meaning and the relationship between them has often gone undefined. Because both concepts mean different things to different people, this section identifies the most significant points of agreement and disagreement about the concepts of peace and war.

Peace

At the most elementary level peace is understood to be the absence of war. Peace defined as the absence of violence is referred to as *negative peace*. In international politics negative peace is often established through treaties, cease-fires, international conferences, balances of power, and peacekeeping forces. Efforts to create a negative peace occurred repeatedly during the Arab-Israeli Conflict. They ranged from separate cease-fire agreements with Egypt, Syria, and Jordan negotiated by Israel in 1948, to UN cease-fire resolutions in 1956 and 1967, to meetings between Arab and Israeli government leaders at Camp David (1978), Madrid (1991), and Oslo (1992). Figure 7.1 presents an overview of some of the major efforts to end the violence in the Middle East.

Figure 7.1 Peacebuilding Efforts in Response to Selected Arab-Israeli Conflicts.

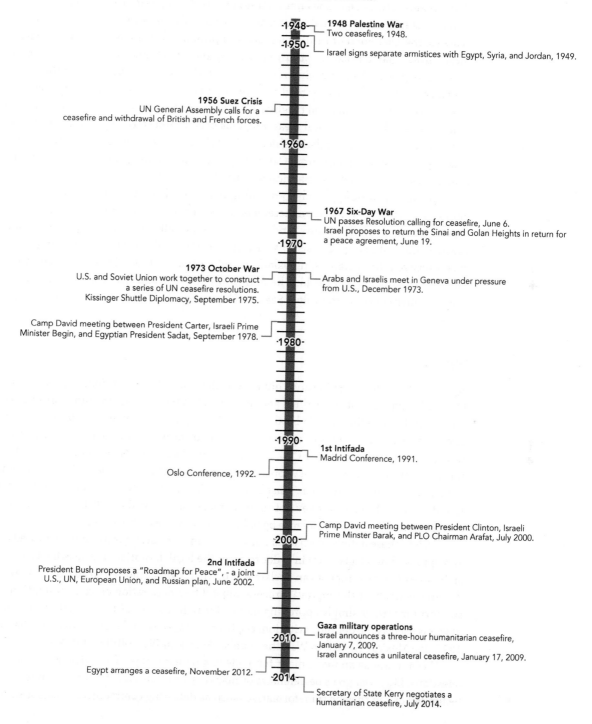

1948 Palestine War
Two ceasefires, 1948.

Israel signs separate armistices with Egypt, Syria, and Jordan, 1949.

1956 Suez Crisis
UN General Assembly calls for a ceasefire and withdrawal of British and French forces.

1967 Six-Day War
UN passes Resolution calling for ceasefire, June 6.
Israel proposes to return the Sinai and Golan Heights in return for a peace agreement, June 19.

1973 October War
U.S. and Soviet Union work together to construct a series of UN ceasefire resolutions.
Kissinger Shuttle Diplomacy, September 1975.

Arabs and Israelis meet in Geneva under pressure from U.S., December 1973.

Camp David meeting between President Carter, Israeli Prime Minister Begin, and Egyptian President Sadat, September 1978.

1st Intifada
Madrid Conference, 1991.

Oslo Conference, 1992.

Camp David meeting between President Clinton, Israeli Prime Minster Barak, and PLO Chairman Arafat, July 2000.

2nd Intifada
President Bush proposes a "Roadmap for Peace", - a joint U.S., UN, European Union, and Russian plan, June 2002.

Gaza military operations
Israel announces a three-hour humanitarian ceasefire, January 7, 2009.
Israel announces a unilateral ceasefire, January 17, 2009.

Egypt arranges a ceasefire, November 2012.

Secretary of State Kerry negotiates a humanitarian ceasefire, July 2014.

1948
1950
1960
1970
1980
1990
2000
2010
2014

Negative peace is an insufficient and incomplete conception of peace in international politics, because it does not address questions of justice that are central to the ability of states, international organizations, and individuals to create conditions that decrease the likelihood of future violence and promote human development. Peace in these terms, characterized as *positive peace*, expands our thinking about the nature of violence to include the human interest[3] as well as what John Galtung, one of the founding voices of peace studies, termed structural and cultural violence. *Structural violence* refers to laws, institutions, and the distribution of economic and political power. *Cultural violence* is found in the political ideas, religious beliefs, and stereotypes that perpetuate and reinforce the unequal relationships such as slavery, apartheid, and colonialism that make up structural violence. From Galtung's perspective, cultural and structural violence combined support systems of physical violence.[4]

Recently, a third approach to defining peace has been advanced. *Peace ecology*[5] emphasizes the global interconnectedness of issues. Peace can only be realized when "environmental, human rights, and economic issues all cohere to foster sustainable growth and well-being." Consistent with the notion of global justice, bringing about such unity requires establishing balanced and mutually supportive relations between humans and the natural world. The definition of peace and the related discipline of peace studies continue to evolve. See the Theory Spotlight feature for more on peace studies.

War

Agreement on how to define and think about the concept of war is just as problematic. Quincy Wright, one of the earliest and most widely cited scholars to study war in a systematic fashion, defines war in legal terms as "the legal condition which equally permits two or more hostile groups to carry on a conflict by armed force."[6] Others, dating back to Prussian military strategist Carl Von Clausewitz during the Napoleonic Wars, define war in political terms as military force used to accomplish political objectives.[7] Contemporary studies suggest that war must be defined independently of its objectives or legal foundations to focus on its key defining characteristic: armed conflict. From this perspective, war is "organized violence by political units against each other."[8]

Each of these definitions has its weaknesses. In some systems war must be voted on and approved by a legislature in order to meet the legal definition, but in others a monarch or head of government can declare war on their own authority. In addition, there is disagreement about the approval process. Must it be a declaration of war, a resolution of support for war, or simply approving money for fighting a war? If a formal declaration of war is used as the defining criterion, the United States has only fought five: the War of 1812, the Mexican American War, the Spanish American War, WWI and WWII.

Viewing war as an instrument for achieving political objectives raises a number of questions. Must war goals be defensive or may they be offensive? If offensive, must they be limited or can they be transformative (such as defeating communism or establishing

THEORY SPOTLIGHT

Peace Studies

Questions about how to define, create, and maintain peace are central to the theories about international politics you learned about in Chapter 2 and post-colonial theory, introduced in Chapter 11. This feature focuses on Peace Studies, an interdisciplinary space that draws on a wide range of theoretical perspectives to try to answer these questions.[9]

As scholar Istivan Kende observed, the meaning of peace has changed throughout history.[10] In the late Middle Ages peace was thought of largely in terms of Christianity. During the Renaissance and Reformation, this notion gave way to human peace, defined in terms of all humanity. During the Enlightenment two different definitions emerged. English thinkers defined peace in terms of economic benefits, and French writers defined it in terms of justice and human equality.

Peace studies became an organized area of inquiry in the 1950s with the 1957 publication of the *Journal of Conflict Resolution*. Two years later the Center for Research on Conflict Resolution at the University of Michigan and the International Peace Research Institute of Oslo in Norway were created. In 1964 the *Journal of Peace Studies* began publishing.

Many realist scholars equated peace studies with the idealist perspective of the interwar period and failed efforts by the League of Nations to promote disarmament. Early peace studies scholars took exception to this view. Some used quantitative analysis to advocate an objective and scientific perspective for creating peace. One example of this approach is the ongoing Correlates of War Project, which began in 1963.

The initial focus of most peace research was the causes and resolutions of interstate wars. Many came to argue that this focus was too narrow, arguing for expanding the focus to include civil wars and North-South conflicts between rich and poor states. Others

Dev Carr / Cultura Creative (RF) / Alamy Stock Photo

Students form a peace sign.

called for studying *one-side violence* (violence by governments against citizens) and *non-state violence* (violence by criminal groups, terrorists, and revolutionaries against citizens). Still others called for an even broader focus, noting that violence against women had largely been ignored and that the objective scientific mindset of the original studies paid insufficient attention to the subjective nature of peace and violence. From this perspective, peace studies should have an emancipatory focus and create justice. Supporters of the original focus countered that expansion of peace studies would cause it to lose focus and become something of an intellectual black hole.

Peace studies continues to evolve today. Recent overviews of the field and interest in democratic peace theory suggest that it is returning to its original focus on interstate war and violence.

Think about It

1. Should peace studies continue to focus heavily on international conflict resolution? Why or why not?

2. Propose a research agenda for peace studies for the next ten years.

democracy worldwide)? Must war goals advance the national interest or can they advance the interests of particular leaders or groups?

Defining war as armed combat raises its own questions. Is there a minimum number of deaths that must occur for a conflict to be termed a war? One of the most famous studies of war is the Correlates of War Project.[11] Begun in 1963, it has created a data set that measures the amount, locations, and causative factors of war in the international system. It defines wars as conflicts with a minimum of 1,000 battlefield deaths. Another data set created by the Uppsala Conflict Data Program expands its definition to include armed conflicts with at least twenty-five battle-related deaths (i.e., victims can be either soldiers or civilians).

TWENTY-FIRST-CENTURY WARS

Throughout history the most widely studied international wars have involved armed conflict between uniformed military forces. Distinctions have frequently been drawn among great power wars, *hegemonic wars* (between a dominant power and a rising challenger), *rivalry wars* (in which the same two states repeatedly engage in war), and *colonial wars* (in which an empire engages in armed conflict to prevent a colony from becoming independent). Today, the principal context in which war is waged and the nature of its adversaries have changed significantly. This section examines why states go to war in the context of the principal forms of contemporary warfare: terrorism, proxy wars, and hybrid wars.

Why War?

It should come as no surprise that there is no single explanation for why wars occur. The discussion in this overview of some of the major reasons is organized around the three levels of analysis introduced in Chapter 1: international system, state, and individual.

INTERNATIONAL SYSTEM CAUSES

Three frequently cited causes of war at the international system level of analysis include the security dilemma, power transitions, and war cycles.

- **Security dilemma**. States build up their power resources to protect themselves, but doing so often increases adversaries' sense of insecurity and threat, leading them to increase their power. This sets off a move/counter-move conflict spiral, which over time becomes uncontrollable. Security dilemmas begin with the existence of an anarchic international system in which international norms, laws, and rules are too weak to regulate competition among states. Anarchy makes the pursuit of power both necessary and self-defeating. Although it is one result, war is not inevitable. Economic and political exhaustion may lead to a period of negative peace.

- **Power transition**. For some analysts the problem is not the pursuit of power but changes in how it is distributed. The more rapidly that state power changes, the more difficult it becomes to predict the outcome of conflicts, leading to greater temptation to engage in war. Strong states may fear that waiting will allow challengers to become stronger, making victory less likely. Rising competitors may be tempted to act because of overconfidence about their increasing power.

- **War cycles**. War can be seen as an infectious disease rooted in the nature of the international system, recurring at predictable intervals. Like diseases, war may be hidden from view and disguised by a condition of nonthreatening calm but begin to strengthen over time and contaminate states, pushing them toward conflict. At the conclusion of war, calm returns and the cycle repeats.

STATE-LEVEL CAUSES

Three frequently cited causes of war are found at the state level of analysis: the type of government, nationalism, and natural resources.

- **Type of government**. Recall that, according to the concept of democratic peace, democracies do not go to war with other democracies; non-democracies are more prone to war (see Chapter 4 Policy Spotlight). The logical conclusion is that a world of democratic states will be a peaceful one. For some this idea has become a fundamental principle of international politics. Others consider it a highly debatable position that hinges on how democracies are defined.

- **Nationalism**. Often used interchangeably, the terms "nation" and "state" refer to different organizations. States are political organizations. Nations are groups of people who share an identity. Because the boundaries between the two concepts vary, the drive by nations to create more ethnically, religiously, or ideologically homogeneous states has become a frequent cause of war. Three war scenarios are rooted in nationalism. The first, *separatism*, involves efforts by one nation to take territory from an existing state to establish a new one. Examples include the creation of Israel, the secession of East Pakistan from Pakistan to form Bangladesh, and efforts by Chechnya to break away from Russia. The removal of territory from several states to create a homogeneous state is particularly problematic. For example, efforts to create Kurdistan involve bringing together Kurdish regions of Iran, Iraq, Turkey, and Syria. *Irredentism*, efforts by one state to take over territory of another in part or in whole, is a second type. Examples include Hitler's annexation of Austria and parts of Czechoslovakia, Russia's annexation of the Crimea in its conflict with the Ukraine, and Iraqi claims to Kuwait. The third type is *ethnic cleansing*, a form of genocide in which an ethnic majority forces a minority group to leave the state through repression and mass killings, like those that occurred in Rwanda and Bosnia.

- **Natural resources**. Many observers argue that international politics today is about economic growth. One of the most important forces driving economic growth is control of natural resources including oil and water and, to a lesser degree, timber and diamonds. There are two different approaches to studying the potential for resource wars. First, states adopting a strategic perspective make judgments about the value and need for control of a given resource; key issues include the level of global supply and demand, expectations about future resource shortages, and the level of dispute over resource ownership. Second, states may approach resource wars from the perspective of domestic policy and the onset of intrastate wars; contributing factors include the tendency of resource dependency to weaken the ability to rule, the potential for large-scale income inequality, and the use of natural resources to finance anti-government movements.

INDIVIDUAL-LEVEL CAUSES

Three important individual level causes of war include calculated choice, personality, and misperception.

- **Calculated choice**. The decision to go to war may be a deliberate policy choice to advance the national interest or a leader's personal interests, and is often made under one of two conditions. In the first, a window of opportunity, policy-makers have calculated that victory is likely under current conditions. In the second, a window of fear, policy-makers fear that, unless they act now, the situation will get worse and diminish the chances for victory.
- **Personality**. Not all policy-makers are equally prone to go to war. The impact of personality on war is implicitly assumed in many of the "great man" war histories such as those of Josef Stalin, Adolf Hitler, Winston Churchill, and Franklin Roosevelt in WWII. One of the major challenges is determining which aspects of personality are most relevant to war.
- **Misperception**. The decision to go to war may be based on leaders' inability to perceive their global context correctly. Four misperceptions by leaders are especially influential: self-image, view of the adversary's character, view of the adversary's intentions, and view of the adversary's capabilities and power. Leaders on the brink of war routinely expect a quick and relatively painless victory. This focus is relatively optimistic about the long-term potential for avoiding war. Little can be done to prevent war as the result of personality factors or calculated choice, but perceptions are learned.

The Changing Face of War

Once the hallmark of the security challenge, wars between states have become increasingly rare. In their place have arisen what some refer to as a fourth generation of warfare,[12] warfare that takes place both between states and within them. This concept is not entirely new; examples can be found throughout history. Terrorism, proxy wars, and hybrid wars are three of the most significant types of war now confronting policy-makers. One of the longest-lasting examples of fourth generation warfare took place in

Colombia. See the Regional Spotlight feature for an overview of the key participants in the Colombian civil war.

TERRORISM

Although al Qaeda and ISIS are less robust than in the past, the US State Department's 2016 annual terrorism report documents how great a challenge it remains. Terrorism is violence employed for purposes of political intimidation and the achievement of political goals. There are over sixty different terrorist organizations, the most recent of which, ISIS in Greater Sahara, was formed in 2018. Over 11,072 terrorist attacks caused more than 25,600 deaths in 2016, a 9% annual decrease in number of attacks and a 13% decrease in deaths. Although attacks took place in 104 countries, over half occurred in just five countries: Iraq, Afghanistan, India, Pakistan, and the Philippines.

A fundamental challenge in fighting a war against terrorism is not knowing what winning means.[13] Is the war won when the terrorist group is no longer a major security threat to the United States, or must the possibility of lone wolf terrorist attacks also be eliminated? Political scientist Audrey Kurth Cronin identifies four dimensions of this problem:

1. The means of fighting the war become the ends. Uncertain as to what defeating the enemy means, attention is directed to what can be measured: troop strength, budgets, technology.
2. Tactics become strategy. Winning battles and prevailing in encounters with terrorists become the measure of success, even though they may contribute little to the final outcome of the war on terrorism.
3. Political and ethical boundaries, which establish limits on use of military force, are blurred and trampled, resulting in growing domestic and global opposition to military efforts.
4. The search for a perfect peace replaces reality. The publicly stated goal is the equivalent of unconditional surrender and total military defeat, which are unlikely to take place given that terrorist wars are fought without clear battlefields and without uniformed personnel.

PROXY WARS

Proxy wars are conflicts in which an outside supporter (state or non-state actor) intervenes indirectly in order to influence the strategic outcome. Commonly used methods for intervention include funding, equipment, training, and military guidance.[15] President Dwight Eisenhower once referred to proxy wars as the cheapest insurance policy in the world.

A far-reaching proxy war involving Iran and Saudi Arabia is currently underway in the Middle East. During the Cold War, both states were important US allies. When the Shah of Iran was ousted and the Iran Revolution began, they became competitors for regional influence, with each providing military support to opposing sides in local

proxy war Conflict in which an outside supporter (state or non-state actor) intervenes indirectly in order to influence the strategic outcome.

REGIONAL SPOTLIGHT

The Colombian Civil War

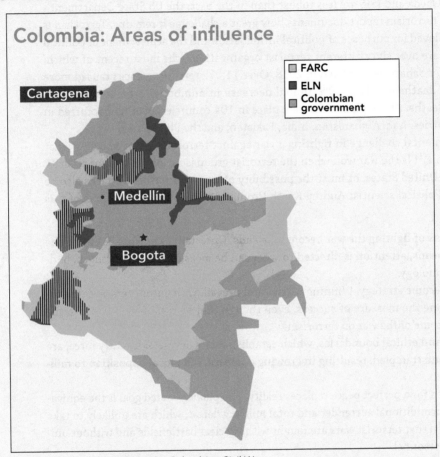

Colombia: Areas of influence

- ☐ FARC
- ■ ELN
- ▨ Colombian grovernment

Cartagena

Medellín

Bogota

Map 7.1 Areas of Influence in the Colombian Civil War.

On October 2, 2016, Colombians went to the polls to vote on a September 2016 peace agreement between the Colombian government and the Revolutionary Armed Forces of Colombia (FARC), opponents in a civil war that had lasted for over fifty years. Fifty-two percent of voters rejected the agreement. Just months before, 69% of Colombians had voiced support for ending the civil war through negotiations. After rejection of the 2016 agreement, a new agreement with FARC was negotiated. Rather than submitting it for a popular vote, it was sent it to Congress for approval.

Estimates place the number killed during the civil war at 220,000. In addition, some 50,000 disappeared,

Rodrigo Abd / AP Images

FARC recruits men and women into their military force.

and 3–6 million people were displaced from their homes. Colombia's prominent role in coca production and global drug trafficking contributed to the devastation. To complicate matters, the civil war became regional when conflict spilled over into Ecuador and Venezuela. The United States became involved through Plan Colombia, which provided the Colombian military and police with funding for counter narcotics and military campaigns.

Established in 1964 as a rural anti-government guerrilla movement with a Marxist ideology, FARC's roots can be traced back as far as 1948. Over time FARC became Colombia's largest guerrilla group, with twenty-seven battalions of fighters in the mid-1980s. Its numbers declined from 16,000 to about 8,000 members as a result of military defeats and amnesty programs. FARC relied on several different methods to fund its military operations, including "taxes" on small coca-growing farmers, larger landowners, and industrial firms in FARC-controlled areas and outright extortion and kidnappings for ransom. Its yearly drug-related income was once estimated to be $170 million.

A second major guerrilla movement, the National Liberation Army (ELN) was established at the same time as FARC. Originating on college campuses with an ideology that combined Cuban revolutionary thinking and Catholic liberation theology, the ELN had 3,000–4,000 members and was most active in Colombia's oil producing region. The ELN's main source of funds took the form of extortion from and kidnapping of those involved in the oil industry.

The third key participants, collectively referred to as paramilitary or self-defense forces, were described by one observer as consisting of "a dizzying array of ... warlords, military entrepreneurs, mafias, gangs, bandits, and so on."[14] The most notorious was the United Self-Defense Forces of Colombia (AUC), established in 1997 as an umbrella organization with as many as 20,000 members. The origins of the paramilitary forces can be traced back to 1959, when the US military recommended secret training of civilian and military personnel to form paramilitary civil defense groups. The AUC and other paramilitary groups gradually became engaged in protection rackets and money laundering. They also acted on behalf of the military to kill opposition leaders and intimidate the public. The Colombian National Police estimate that the AUC assassinated over 800 people in 2000 alone.

Colombian President Juan Manuel Santos was awarded the Nobel Peace Prize in 2016 for his persistent efforts to create peace, but problems remain. Implementation of the agreement was incomplete. Many promises such as health and education services for rebel areas did not materialize. Even more troubling, some 2,800 FARC fighters returned to fighting and in some cases have joined forces with a mafia group, Virgilio Peralta Arenas Bloc, that is linked to drug trafficking.

Think about It

1. Do you think that peace and justice can be realized in Colombia? Why or why not?
2. How could the Colombian civil war have been shortened?

conflicts throughout North Africa, the Middle East, and Central Asia. Efforts are particularly intense in Yemen, where a rebel group, the Houthi, is supported by Iranian weapons, including ballistic missiles. Forces loyal to the Yemeni government have received indirect support from both Saudi Arabia and the United States. In 2015 Saudi Arabia became more directly involved in the conflict, leading a coalition of nine African and Middle East states that sent troops to Yemen and conducted a coordinated bombing campaign and naval blockade.

Four major trends in the nature of warfare and international politics have brought increased attention to proxy wars:[16]

1. **"War on Terror Syndrome."** As with the "Vietnam Syndrome" in the 1960s, public support for sending troops abroad and engage in military conflicts with adversaries with unclear links to national security is declining.

2. **Increased reliance on private military companies (PMCs)**. Referred to by some as "coalitions of the billing," PMCs carry out military operations in proxy war settings. According to UN estimates, in 2007 there were nearly 20,000 Afghan and 6,000 western PMC personnel in Afghanistan. Because they are less visible than military forces and the use of PMCs gets around the public's reluctance to employ force abroad, there are fewer restrictions on their use than on that of troops subject to political oversight.

3. **Cyber warfare**. The difficulty of identifying who is conducting a cyberattack and the ability to conduct these attacks from great distances makes cyberwarfare an attractive option for outside forces intervening into a conflict.

4. **The rise of China**. China is now a power with global interests that uses proxies to spread its influence. This is most noticeable in Africa, where China seeks to protect Chinese oil workers from terrorist attacks and prop up African governments.

One danger is that proxy wars risk conflict escalation. The interests of the outside supporter and the proxy are unlikely to align perfectly. Differences in goals and strategies are common. With outside backing the proxy may become emboldened politically to reject compromises. If it fails to carry out key military tasks, the outside supporter is forced to become more involved. Another danger is diffusion, spreading the conflict to other areas. Weapons introduced into a conflict to aid a proxy may fall into the hands of groups hostile to the outside supporter, creating new security problems. This is what happened when the United States supplied weapons to the mujahedeen to fight the Russian army in Afghanistan. After the fighting ended, many weapons ended up in the hands of the Taliban, resurfacing in Bosnia, Iran, Kashmir, Tunisia, and Palestine.

HYBRID WARS

Hybrid warfare blends conventional, unconventional, and irregular approaches to warfare and may be carried out by governments or insurgent groups. Multiple approaches to warfare in a single conflict is not new. What makes it distinctive and particularly challenging is that, instead of having different approaches at different times and in different locations, hybrid warfare integrates them into a single integrated and synchronized strategy that operates simultaneously across the entire conflict. Significant ongoing examples of hybrid war are the Ukraine (see the Chapter 5 Contemporary Perspective section) and Syria (see the Contemporary Perspective section later in this chapter).

Key elements of the hybrid war tool kit include the following:[17]

- Information operations: targeted television programming, internet trolls, and fake news operations.
- Cyber activities: hacking to obtain data and attacks to compromise banking, information, and security systems.
- Proxies: insurgent military groups, political parties, and civil society organizations.
- Economic influence: shutting off access to energy sources and markets and using investments to gain influence.
- Clandestine measures: secretly infiltrating key government and societal organizations, fostering criminal activity, and providing military guidance and advice.
- Political influence: undermining the standing of opposition leaders, sowing discord within organizations, influencing elections.

Hybrid warfare is as much political as it is military. Its goal is to create political paralysis in the adversary and its supporters that reduces the necessary amount of military force and makes effective responses to military actions difficult.

Ending fourth-generation wars presents policy-makers with multiple challenges. Hybrid wars do not begin and end on the battlefield; they are long wars requiring long-term political and military commitments. Ending a proxy war may require either outright defeat of the proxy or agreement between the proxy and the outside party that ceasing hostilities is in both of their interests.[18] Defeating terrorism is perhaps the most difficult task; Cronin identifies seven different ways that terrorism has ended, including victory by the terrorists.[19] Complicating matters further is that ending a war does not end the security challenge. It is followed by another challenge: creating peace.

PEACE OPERATIONS

Building either negative or positive peace is not easily achieved and requires engagement in two forms of peace operations. The first, **peacekeeping**, is the deployment of military and civilian personnel to prevent a return to violent conflict by monitoring conflict situations and separating combatants. Peacekeeping is most closely associated with the UN.

peacekeeping
The deployment of military and civilian personnel to prevent a return to violent conflict by monitoring conflict situations and separating combatants.

UN Peacekeeping

This section provides a historical overview of the development of UN peacekeeping operations followed by a discussion of some of their principal operational and political challenges.

HISTORICAL OVERVIEW

The first UN peacekeeping operations, created in the late 1940s, consisted of observer missions to supervise a cease-fire between India and Pakistan over Kashmir, a territory claimed by India, Pakistan, and China.[20] Renewed fighting between India and Pakistan broke out in 1971, and a new cease-fire was agreed to in 1972. India asserted that the UN mandate to send observers to the region had lapsed, but Pakistan disagreed. The UN Secretary General took the position that only the Security Council could order observer withdrawal, and this mission continues today. The UN defends its continued presence, defining the India-Pakistan dispute as a "frozen conflict" that might erupt once the observers leave. Other long-standing UN observer missions to monitor frozen conflicts include the Middle East and Cyprus.

A second phase of UN peacekeeping operations came into existence with the creation of the United Nations Emergency Force (UNEF), which was sent to Suez as part of the agreement that ended the 1956 Suez Crisis. The UNEF was larger than the observer mission model of peace operations and functioned more as a paramilitary force. However, it was not to engage in combat activity, try to control territory, or enforce a political solution. At this time UN peacekeeping operations were viewed as an instrument of last resort. For example, in 1960 the UNEF was sent to the Congo after Belgium withdrew its troops and the newly independent state became embroiled in a civil war.

The end of the Cold War and the perception that the UN might play a more active role in resolving conflicts brought about a reexamination of UN peace operations. In Secretary General Boutros-Ghali's June 1992 *The Agenda for Peace,* he broke down UN peace operations into three categories: peacekeeping, peacemaking, and peacebuilding.[21] Boutros-Ghali's vision was quickly put to the test in the former Yugoslavia and Somalia.

In February 1992 the UN established a peacekeeping force, the United Nations Protection Force in the Former Yugoslavia (UNPROFOR). With the collapse of communism in 1991 Yugoslavia had begun to fracture into independent ethnic states with contested borders, leading to widespread violence. UNPROFOR's original mission limited use of force to self-defense or defense of its mandate. Expansion to include offensive force to protect UN-created safe areas was unable to prevent a Serbian campaign of genocide in 1995.

In April 1992, not long after UNPROFOR was formed, a United Nations Operation in Somalia (UNOSOM) began to assist with provision of humanitarian aid. UNOSOM was soon withdrawn because of the high level of fighting and replaced by a US-led operation in December 1992 and a second UN force (UNOSOM II) in March 1993. The casualties suffered by both efforts were so significant that their presence in Somalia ended.

The ineffectiveness of UN peacekeeping operations led to the Brahimi Report, a UN study issued in August 2000.[22] Recognizing that certain circumstances might require peacekeepers to use offensive military force, it called for reinventing peace operations. The report indicated that they needed to be "capable of defending themselves, other mission components, and the mission's mandate with robust rules of engagement." It also asserted that peacekeepers had an obligation to protect citizens and that peacekeeping forces be of a size and strength "to leave no doubt in the minds of would-be spoilers that peacekeeping was no longer 'non-threatening'."

In 2018 the UN operated fourteen peacekeeping missions employing some 90,000 troops and 13,000 police officers. The most recent peacekeeping mission was established in Haiti in 2014. The three largest peacekeeping missions operate in the Democratic Republic of the Congo, South Sudan, and Mali. Table 7.1 presents a listing of these operations. Read on to learn about the operational and political challenges facing these fourteen peacekeeping operations.

TABLE 7.1 United Nations Peacekeeping Missions, 2018	
Location & Total Personnel Size of Mission	**Mission (year initiated)**
The Americas	
Haiti (United Nations Mission for Justice Support in Haiti [MINUJUSTH]) 1,600	Strengthen rule of law institutions, develop the National Police, promote and protect human rights. (2017)
Europe	
Cyprus (United Nations Peacekeeping Force in Cyprus [UNFICYP]) 1,061	Contribute to a political settlement. (1964)
Kosovo (United Nations Mission in Kosovo [UNMIK]) 349	Promote security, stability, and respect for human rights. (1999)
Asia	
Kashmir (United Nations Military Observer Group in India and Pakistan [UNMOGIP]) 115	Observe the ceasefire in Jammu and Kashmir. (1949)
The Middle East	
Golan Heights (United Nations Disengagement Observer Force [UNDOF]) 1,100	Supervise cease-fire and disengagement agreement. (1974)
Lebanon (United Nations Interim Force in Lebanon [UNIFIL]) 11,282	Monitor cessation of hostilities and help ensure humanitarian access to civilian population. (1978)
Middle East (United Nations Truce Supervision Organization [UNTSO]) 373	Help bring stability to the Middle East. (1948)
Africa	
Western Sahara (United Nations Mission for the Referendum in Western Sahara [MINURSO]) 467	Ensure adherence to settlement plan approved by the UN Security Council for a transition period during which the people of Western Sahara would choose between independence and integration with Morocco. (1991)

(Continued)

TABLE 7.1 (Continued)	
Location & Total Personnel Size of Mission	Mission (year initiated)
Abyei (United Nations Interim Security Force for Abyei [UNISFA]) 4817	Demilitarize and monitor peace in the disputed Abyei area, which straddles Northern and Southern Sudan. (2011)
Central African Republic (United Nations Multidimensional Integrated Stabilization Mission in the Central African Republic [MINUSCA]) 14,870	Protect civilians and support transition processes. (2014)
Democratic Republic of Congo (United Nations Organization Stabilization Mission in the DR Congo [MONUSCO]) 19,074	Protect civilians and consolidate peace. (2010)
Darfur (United Nations–African Union Hybrid Operation in Darfur [UNAMID]) 13,980	Protect civilians, facilitate humanitarian aid, and help in the political process. (2007)
Mali (United Nations Multidimensional Integrated Stabilization Mission in Mali [MINUSMA]) 15,514	Support the political process and provide stability. (2013)
South Sudan (United Nations Mission in South Sudan [UNMISS]) 18,983	Protect civilians, monitor human rights, and support implementation of cessation of hostilities agreement. (2011)

Source: United Nations Peacekeeping, https://peacekeeping.un.org/en/where-we-operate. Personnel figures are from August 2018.

CURRENT OPERATIONAL AND POLITICAL CHALLENGES

Two interrelated challenges confront UN peacekeeping operations today.[23] The operational challenge involves relations between UN peacekeeping missions and host states. UN peacekeepers are deployed in volatile political environments where the government's ability to rule is limited both by internal weaknesses and external opposition. As a result, the peace that the UN operations are supposed to be protecting is often just a mirage. Compounding this problem is the frequent presence of spoilers.[24] Spoilers, which can be found both inside and outside the peace process, are leaders and groups that believe an end to conflict and the establishment of peace threaten their interests, so they use violence to undermine peace operations. Angola, Rwanda, Mozambique, and Cambodia are among the states in which spoilers have played major roles in undermining the peace process.

The political challenge centers on relations between peacekeeping operations and the UN system. The primary issue is burden sharing. Increasing tensions exist between the Security Council states, which authorize and finance peacekeeping mandates, and the developing states, which contribute the bulk of the military and police presence, run the highest risks, and carry the heaviest burden. Disagreement over mandate terms is a political challenge as well as an operational one. There is considerable debate between those who feel that peacekeeping mandates should include requirements to protect civilians and engage in the offensive use of military force and those who desire to go back to the original notions of neutrality and defensive force.

In 2009, largely in response to these continuing challenges, the UN initiated an effort called the New Partnership Agenda: Charting a New Horizon for United Nations Peacekeeping. Its central proposal was the development of new and stronger internal and external peacekeeping partnerships. Internal proposals included triangulated consultations among the Secretariat (the bureaucratic core of the UN), the Security Council, and those countries contributing troops and police. In order to meet external challenges, the report called for expanding the troop contributor base and strengthening cooperation with existing partners including regional organizations (such as the African Union) and security organizations (such as NATO).

Post-Conflict Reconstruction

A second area of peace operations falls under the broad heading of *peacebuilding*. It is concerned with creating conditions that reduce the recurrence of violence and enhance individual fulfillment. Within the field of peacebuilding is **post-conflict reconstruction**. It has the more limited objective of creating and strengthening governmental and economic institutions that will lay a foundation for peacebuilding. The challenges faced in post-conflict reconstruction efforts are many. Civil wars, periods of prolonged internal violence, and foreign military interventions eat away at the foundation on which states and societies are built. Creating a durable peace requires reconstruction or building new foundations. The following sections identify its operating conditions and the underlying tensions that accompany them.

> **post-conflict reconstruction**
> The creation and strengthening of governmental and economic institutions to lay a foundation for peacebuilding.

OPERATING CONDITIONS

Post-conflict reconstruction efforts face four fundamental truths. First, although it focuses on the situation inside a state, reconstruction has repercussions beyond its borders. These can serve as a stimulus for changes in other states but may be perceived as threatening rather than positive. In addition, groups within the state may undertake destabilizing actions elsewhere in hope of improving their positions at home. Second, no two states are alike. What worked in Germany must be modified before applying it to Japan, and neither blueprint might work in Afghanistan or Iraq. Third, post-conflict reconstruction efforts are not neutral. They can place great stress on societies because the changes in government, the legal system, and the economic operations they propose will create opportunities for some but not others and may also produce frustration and anxiety. Finally, the tool kit of post-conflict reconstruction is limited. Military and police personnel may be available in relatively large numbers, but the same is not likely to be true for doctors, engineers, economists, or accountants.

Given these realities, advanced planning and priority setting efforts are essential to success. James Dobbins and colleagues at the RAND Institute have proposed the following hierarchy of priorities:[25]

- **Security**. First-order efforts are directed at peacekeeping, the rule of law, law enforcement and security agency reforms to ensure effective functioning of the military and police. One crucial task is to establish a balance between retribution (war crimes trials) and reconciliation (truth commissions). A second important task is disarming combatants and reintegrating them into society.
- **Humanitarian relief**. Manage the return of refugees, avoid health epidemics and hunger, and provide housing; this is often begun prior to post-conflict reconstruction.
- **Governance**. Resume public services and reduce corruption and inefficiency to establish public support for the government.
- **Economic stabilization**. Stabilize the currency and establish an economic system that encourages domestic and international trade and investment.
- **Democratization**. Build political parties, hold elections, create a free press, and encourage the development of civil society groups.
- **Development**. Reduce poverty, build up infrastructure (roads, ports, electric power plants, sanitation systems) and promote economic growth.

None of these complex tasks are easily accomplished. Just as no war plan remains intact following initial contact with the enemy, the RAND Report stresses that no plan for post-conflict reconstruction can survive its first contact with the state to be rebuilt without modifications. The following section highlights some factors that are particularly likely to require modifications to those plans.

UNDERLYING TENSIONS

Two fundamental tensions are present in every post-conflict reconstruction effort.[26] The first is the *footprint dilemma*: how big an international presence should be created, what tasks should external interveners take on, and how aggressively should these tasks be pursued? If the footprint is too light, needed reforms may not occur. Old policies may reappear, or widespread civil unrest may arise. Too heavy a footprint may provoke domestic opposition and rob reforms of legitimacy.

Second is the *duration dilemma*: how long should external interveners stay? Holding elections or writing a new constitution too soon and without the proper foundation is likely to open old wounds and undermine peace-building. Putting in place political or economic reforms may continue to privilege individuals and groups who were in positions of power before the conflict and work against underprivileged groups. Staying too long or having an open-ended mission risks passivity and a lack of ownership of the reforms by the local population. It also creates the risk that the forces involved in post-conflict reconstruction lose sight of their mission with over involvement in local conflicts and disputes. The financial and political sources of support may lose interest in an extended effort, undermining its ability to succeed.

NUCLEAR STABILITY

Shortly before the United States and Soviet Union found themselves locked in the October 1962 Cuban Missile Crisis, researchers Thomas Schelling and Morton Halperin defined *strategic stability* as a situation in which the risks of war are low.[27] Neither side has an incentive to strike first. Just as important, both sides are so confident of their assessment of the situation that unexpected shocks or alarms would not alter their thinking. The Cuban Missile Crisis centered on the secret attempt by the Soviet Union to place nuclear armed missiles in Cuba and the US response, a demand backed by threatened military action that they be removed. During the crisis President John Kennedy estimated the likelihood of nuclear war between 33% and 50%.

As shown by Kennedy's calculation, strategic stability could not be taken for granted during the Cold War. The central role of nuclear weapons in international politics began to fade with the breakup of the Soviet Union and end of communist rule in 1991 Strategic stability concerns remain today, but they have taken on a different character. This section provides an overview of how thinking about nuclear weapons and strategic stability have evolved over time by dividing the discussion into the first and second nuclear eras.

The First Nuclear Era

The first nuclear era spans the period from development of the atomic bomb through the end of the Cold War. The strategic logic and language about how to use and control nuclear weapons that came into existence during this time continue to shape our approach to these questions today.

USING NUCLEAR WEAPONS IN THE FIRST NUCLEAR ERA

The uniqueness of nuclear weapons was not immediately recognized when they were first developed in the 1940s. They were simply treated as the largest explosive devices yet created. It was expected that the next war would be fought along the same lines as WWII, with long-range bombers delivering nuclear weapons against Soviet cities, industries, and military targets. The first nuclear war plan that was developed, entitled *Broiler*, called for dropping thirty-seven bombs on twenty-four cities in the USSR.

During the Eisenhower administration thinking shifted from war, fighting, to **deterrence**, using nuclear weapons to prevent an adversary from undertaking an unwanted action. The first deterrence strategy was "massive retaliation" in which the United States promised to respond to unwanted aggressive Soviet behavior instantly, by means and places of our own choosing. Concerns were soon raised about credibility (would the United States really do this?) and feasibility (the size of the Soviet nuclear arsenal had grown along with the potential for response). Deterrence required flexible and limited retaliatory strategies that focused on military rather than civilian targets and took into account increasingly significant Soviet nuclear capabilities.

deterrence Use of nuclear weapons to prevent an adversary from undertaking an unwanted action.

CONTROLLING NUCLEAR WEAPONS IN THE FIRST NUCLEAR ERA

Stopping the proliferation or spread of nuclear weapons can have a vertical or horizontal focus. *Vertical nonproliferation* focuses on the size of existing stockpiles. *Horizontal nonproliferation* seeks to prevent the spread of nuclear weapons capability to more and more countries. Two different strategic options were used: *disarmament* (elimination of all weapons) and *arms control* (reduction in numbers and placement of restrictions on their use). Negotiations on a treaty to stop the spread of nuclear weapons began in 1965, and the Nonproliferation Treaty (NPT) came into force in 1970. According to the terms of the NPT, non-nuclear states agreed not to acquire nuclear weapons, and nuclear states agreed to work with them on the peaceful uses of nuclear power and to pursue disarmament negotiations "in good faith."

Only since 1970 has there existed a rough balance, or parity, among US and Soviet nuclear forces. When the Soviet Union exploded its first nuclear device in 1949, the US inventory stood at 100–200 weapons. When the Soviet Union successfully tested its first intercontinental ballistic missile (ICBM) in 1957, demonstrating that it could easily attack the United States, estimates placed the US inventory at about 2,000 nuclear bombs and the Soviet inventory at a few hundred. In 1972, when the Strategic Arms Limitation Treaty (SALT) was signed, there was rough parity. The United States had 2,140 nuclear warheads and the Soviet Union had 2,142. The composition of their nuclear forces was not identical, however. The largest percentage of Soviet nuclear warheads (68%) were ICBMs. In contrast, US warheads were distributed relatively equally across all three delivery systems (ballistic missiles, manned aircraft, and submarines). This last point was significant because of differences in accuracy, payload speed, and vulnerability. Land-based ICBMs are a highly accurate delivery system, but as fixed targets they are also highly vulnerable. Submarine-launched ballistic missiles are far less accurate and have limited range, but because of submarine mobility they are highly invulnerable targets.

Given these numbers and the lack of trust between the United States and the Soviet Union, it is not surprising that the primary emphasis was initially on vertical reductions. A wide range of arms control agreements were enacted in response to the Cuban Missile Crisis, including the following:

- **The Hot Line Agreement, 1963**. Established direct radio, wire-telegraph, and satellite communication links between Moscow and Washington.
- **The Limited Test Ban Treaty, 1963**. Banned the testing of nuclear weapons in the atmosphere, outer space, and underwater, and placed limits on underground testing.
- **The SALT I Agreements, 1972**. Each state was limited to two anti-ballistic missile (ABM) defense systems, and limits were placed on the size of their nuclear forces.
- **The Prevention of Nuclear War Agreement, 1973**. Required that the United States and Soviet Union enter into consultations if there is a danger of nuclear war.
- **The SALT II Agreements, 1979**. Placed limits on the number of launchers each side could possess and set up restrictions on efforts to improve nuclear weapons.

Cold War arms control efforts faced two major hurdles. The first involved domestic politics. Not everyone in the United States agreed with these controversial agreements. SALT I had two parts: a formal treaty requiring Senate approval, and an executive agreement that did not require approval. SALT II also had two parts: a treaty and a *protocol* (set of agreed upon rules). Because the treaty portion, dealing with the limit on launchers, was never ratified by the Senate, it did not go into force. The second hurdle was verification. There was no agreed-upon standard to judge cheating back then or even today. This question was sidestepped in favor of a focus on methods to detect cheating, including cooperative measures and technical surveillance by satellites, radars, communication, and other instruments.

This combination of large nuclear forces, a reliance on deterrence strategies, and an emphasis on vertical arms control efforts provided the foundation of strategic stability on which the second nuclear age began.

The Second Nuclear Era

The foundation of nuclear security established during the first nuclear era is wearing thin. The nuclear world has changed.[28] States possessing nuclear weapons often find themselves in conflicts with two or more potential adversaries, complicating questions of deterrence, war fighting, and arms control. In some cases conventional weapons now can offset the advantages of nuclear weapons as instruments of foreign policy. Perhaps most significantly, in February 2019 first the United States and then Russia suspended the Intermediate Nuclear Force (INF) Treaty setting off fears of a new nuclear arms race. For years the United States had accused Russia of violating the agreement by testing new land-based missiles. Russia had long argued that the United States had violated the agreement, most notably in creating a NATO Missile Defense System in Europe.

USING NUCLEAR WEAPONS IN THE SECOND NUCLEAR ERA

In the first nuclear era the United States and Soviet Union were the only parties that seemed to matter when it came to policy debates over nuclear weapons. This is not the case in the second nuclear era,[29] in which attention is now focused on how emerging nuclear powers, including China, India, Pakistan, Israel, North Korea, and Iran, might use their nuclear weapons. Many strategists are moving away from superpower nuclear strategies to think in terms of strategic options more suited to these situations.

Based on the historical record, political scientist Vipin Narang suggests that three nuclear strategies exist for emerging nuclear powers:[30]

- **Catalytic strategy**. A state employs nuclear weapons to force or blackmail an ally to come to its defense militarily or diplomatically. This might be accomplished through threats to increase inventory or to use a limited supply of nuclear weapons in a crisis situation. Israel, Pakistan, and South Africa (which gave up its nuclear capability in 1989) employed a catalytic strategy directed at the United States during the first nuclear age.

- **Assured retaliation**. This strategy requires a large or protected nuclear force capable of surviving a nuclear attack. The emerging nuclear state seeks to deter a nuclear attack by threatening an adversary with nuclear retaliation. China and India have adopted this strategy.
- **Asymmetric retaliation**. The goal of this strategy is to deter a large-scale conventional ground attack through the threat of the first use of nuclear weapons against military and civilian targets. Pakistan has adopted this strategy.

Narang's analysis leads him to conclude that North Korea has embraced a catalytic strategy with its ally China. He speculates that, should Iran develop a nuclear force, it would likely adopt an asymmetric retaliation strategy.

CONTROLLING NUCLEAR WEAPONS IN THE SECOND NUCLEAR ERA

Today nine states possess nuclear weapons: the United States (1,800 deployed warheads; 4,000 stockpiled warheads), Russia (1,600 deployed; 4,350 stockpiled), China (270 warheads), Great Britain (120 deployed; 95 stockpiled), France (280 deployed; 10 stockpiled), Pakistan (130–140 warheads), India (120–130 warheads), Israel (80–85 warheads), and North Korea (said to possess material needed to make 20 warheads). These stockpiles continue to grow. The United States and Russia are committed to modernization and expansion of their nuclear forces through the addition of low-yield nuclear weapons. China has reportedly begun deployment of an intermediate range ballistic missile and nuclear-capable air-launched ballistic missiles. In addition, fifteen states possess weapons-grade nuclear material, and nearly thirty have sought nuclear weapons in some way or another. Following President Trump's decision to terminate the Iran nuclear deal, Saudi Arabia announced that it does not want to acquire nuclear weapons but should Iran do so it is prepared to obtain them as well.

With the United States and Russia still possessing over 90% of the world's nuclear warheads, concerns over vertical proliferation continue during the second nuclear era, but progress has been slow, with many setbacks. Beginning in 1991, the United States and Russia negotiated a series of Strategic Arms Reduction Treaties (STARTs). START 1, which reduced the number of deployed nuclear weapons, was enacted in 1994 and expired in 2009. The 1993 START II provided for further reductions, but Russia withdrew before it was enacted in response to the 2002 US withdrawal from SALT I, which banned ABMs. START III talks also failed. A New START treaty was signed in 2010, went into force in 2011, and will expire in 2021. Its future is uncertain. At the outset of the Trump administration Russian President Vladimir Putin expressed interest in extending the treaty, but Trump identified it as one of the "bad deals" of the Obama administration.

Global concerns with horizontal proliferation continue in the second nuclear age. At an NPT Review Conference in 1995 the treaty was extended indefinitely. The NPT has been signed by 191 states, but India, Pakistan, Israel, and South Sudan have not signed it. North Korea signed it in 1985 but withdrew in 2003.

A significant horizontal nonproliferation agreement, the Comprehensive Test Ban Treaty (CTBT), was signed in 1996. Technically the CTBT is not yet operational, since eight of the forty-four states with nuclear capabilities have yet to sign it. Still, the CTBT has been credited with strengthening the global norm against nuclear testing. Only North Korea has engaged in nuclear testing since the treaty was signed.

Global horizontal nonproliferation efforts face several challenges. They are viewed by some non-nuclear states as efforts by nuclear states to maintain their superiority, dividing the world into have and have-not states. This feeling is reflected by the limited success of vertical disarmament talks. A second challenge is that non-nuclear states seek nuclear weapons for a variety of purposes, not all of which have to do with national security. The drive to acquire nuclear weapons may be the product of domestic political factors such as demands by interest groups or the military and/or enhancement of a leader's political standing.[31]

A third challenge to the nonproliferation of nuclear weapons is operational. States seeking nuclear weapons have gone down several different paths.[32] They may pursue a *hedging* strategy, in which they delay acquisition but seek to preserve a future break-out option. States may also *sprint*, or move quickly to acquire nuclear weapons, the strategy followed by the United States and the Soviet Union during the Cold War. A third strategy, *hiding*, is secret acquisition of nuclear weapons. This is a high-risk/high-reward strategy because of the potential military, political, and economic costs if the effort is discovered before the weapons are developed. In a final strategy, *sheltered pursuit*, the nuclear program is carried out with the protection of a major power. Israel, North Korea, and Pakistan all followed this strategy, sheltered by China, the United States, and China, respectively. States may also alter their strategies over time. India initially pursued a hedging strategy but later began sprinting. China first followed a sheltered pursuit strategy under Russia's wing and then began sprinting. Iran has moved from a hedging strategy to a hiding strategy and back to a hedging strategy.

Beyond diplomacy, a combination of carrots and sticks have been employed to stop nuclear proliferation. Libya's decision to abandon its pursuit of nuclear weapons was reported to be influenced heavily by US economic sanctions, the US invasion of Iraq, and a communication from President George Bush threatening to destroy those weapons. Global efforts to limit Iran's pursuit of nuclear weapons were based on the benefits Iran would receive from agreeing to the plan negotiated in 2015 by the P5+1 (the five permanent members of the UN Security Council plus Germany and the European Union). Iran agreed to limit key portions of its enrichment capacity and stockpiles for ten to fifteen years and to a series of monitoring procedures. In return, nuclear-related economic sanctions by the EU and the United States would end, and the United States would end financial sanctions against companies doing business with Iran. From the outset this agreement met with strong political opposition in the United States and became a major issue in the 2016 presidential campaign. President Donald Trump unilaterally withdrew the United States from the agreement in May, 2018 over the objections of its European allies. The split between the US and its European allies grew in the following months as the US moved forward with economic sanctions and European allies sought ways to continue providing Iran with access to international financial markets. Relations between the US and Iran worsened. Iran's Revolutionary Guard was next identified as a terrorist group setting off military moves and countermoves raising fears of regional war.

A variety of carrots and sticks have been employed by US presidents to end North Korea's nuclear weapons program. George W. Bush and Obama employed diplomacy, Clinton considered—but rejected—military action, and Trump has used an ever-changing combination of approaches that have included highly charged rhetoric and the on-again–off-again summit, which resulted in a promise to suspend "provocative" US-South Korean war games. Trump has swung between saying that he "loathed" North Korean leader Kim Jong-un and promising to unleash "fire and fury" and "destroy North Korea" and praising Kim, saying that the two had "developed a very special bond" and that he was "a very talented man." Following the June 2018 summit Trump claimed that Kim agreed to denuclearize North Korea, but it quickly became clear that there was no shared understanding of this pledge.

Three additional developments influence thinking about nuclear proliferation and establish strategic stability. The first, the blurring of the line between nuclear and non-nuclear weapons that is beginning to occur, is the focus of the Policy Spotlight feature. The other two are ongoing problems: terrorism and weapons of mass destruction.

Terrorism and Weapons of Mass Destruction

Neither terrorism nor weapons of mass destruction (WMDs) are new to international politics. They are long-standing, persistent problems. As noted in Chapter 3, commentators often characterize today's terrorist attacks as the fourth wave of terrorism. WMDs include nuclear, chemical, and biological weapons. International controls regulating chemical and biological warfare date back to 1925 when the Geneva Convention forbid the use of asphyxiating and poisonous gases and bacteriological weapons of war in response to the extensive use of mustard gas during WWI. A 1972 Biological Weapons Convention banned the development, production, and stockpiling of biological and toxic weapons.

Terrorism presents two horizontal proliferation challenges. One is stopping terrorists from acquiring the technology and ingredients needed to make nuclear weapons. Diplomacy has taken the lead here. In 2010 a National Security Summit (NSS) was held in Washington to strengthen national and international security systems designed to stop nuclear proliferation and end nuclear smuggling. Three follow-up conferences were held in 2012, 2014, and 2016, but Russia did not attend in 2016.

The second challenge is how to influence the behavior of states that sponsor and support terrorism in order to reduce terrorist access to nuclear weapons.[33] Existing deterrence strategies may be inadequate. To be successful, deterrence must have a clearly defined target, but the starting point for state sponsors of terrorism is deniability. Open state support for terrorism is rare. Uncertainty is deliberately created over the existence and extent of support to maximize the freedom to maneuver and escape punishment.

Chemical and biological weapons present a very different challenge to nuclear non-proliferation efforts. Few would deny that the use of these weapons is morally wrong

POLICY SPOTLIGHT

A New Arms Race?

During the Cold War US-Soviet nuclear relations took on the form of an arms race, an action-reaction cycle that produced increasing numbers of deadly weapons and raised fears of catastrophic war between the two superpowers. Over the last decade a new arms race has developed with equally ominous implications for international politics. The development of a prompt global strike (PGS) capability by the United States will allow it to launch precision-guided conventional weapons from the United States at targets anywhere in the world in one hour or less.[34]

Development of PGS began during the George W. Bush administration. Its 2001 Nuclear Posture Review called for creation of a new class of offensive strike weapons by integrating precision conventional weapons with strategic nuclear weapons.[35] One factor leading to this proposal was the long-standing desire of presidents for additional nuclear options in confronting aggression; being boxed into a corner and forced to choose between largely doing nothing or going nuclear in an all-out war was a persistent fear. A second factor was the changing nature of international conflicts. During the Cold War strategists anticipated that military confrontations would take place in a relatively small number of predictable areas, allowing the United States to station troops abroad in strategic locations both to deter and counter Soviet aggression. Today potentially serious conflicts may arise suddenly in unexpected locations and involve a variety of adversaries. This greatly increases the range of military resources the United States might need. PGS would be able to strike not only stationary targets such as missile sites but also "fleeting targets" such as leadership locations and mobile weapons systems. Overall, advocates argue that PGS would enhance global stability by reducing reliance on nuclear weapons.

Critics assert that it is unclear whether PGS can replace nuclear weapons as an effective deterrent, since they lack the psychological effects associated with nuclear weapons. A possibly even greater danger

Everett Collection Historical / Alamy Stock Photo

A navy submarine launching a Tomahawk land attack missile.

lies in the inability of an adversary to determine whether the missiles that were just launched contain nuclear or conventional warheads. The specific target might also be unclear. Was it a command and control site, a conventional military base, or the site of nuclear forces? Such uncertainties might lead the adversary to escalate the conflict and perhaps use nuclear weapons.

One visible result of the US program is the beginnings of a possible arms race. Vladimir Putin has characterized PGS as a threat to Russian security. Other Russian officials have cited the program as complicating nonproliferation discussions, including the ban of nuclear weapons from space. In 2013 Russia announced plans to modernize its rail-mounted ICBM missile system in response to the US PGS system, and it has been reported that China began testing its version of the PGS missiles the following year.

Think about It

1. Should PGS missile development be considered the start of an arms race? Why or why not?

2. Develop a strategy for stopping the PGS arms race.

and needs to be banned, but many also question their military value and ability to create mass casualties on the scale of nuclear weapons. This raises the question of whether nuclear, chemical, and biological weapons should be grouped in the same category. Some would argue that doing so decreases attention to the nuclear proliferation problem. Others disagree but concede that they are fundamentally different. The focus of nuclear weapons strategy is interstate war, and the proliferation challenge is to stop their *spread*. Chemical and biological weapons have been used for this purpose in the past in Vietnam, the Soviet invasion of Afghanistan, and the Iran-Iraq War, but they have also been employed in civil wars and intrastate conflicts in North Yemen, Angola, and Syria. The proliferation challenge for chemical and biological weapons is to stop their *use*. The following section describes how the situation in Syria led to the use of chemical weapons.

CONTEMPORARY PERSPECTIVE:
Syria

Syria erupted into civil war in 2011 as the impact of the pro-democracy Arab Spring movement, which first emerged in Tunisia, began to be felt across the Middle East. The catalyst in Syria was the March arrest of a boy for creating graffiti saying that "the people want the fall of the regime." Protests calling for political reforms and the release of political prisoners began in Damascus and spread quickly throughout Syria. The protests soon transformed into organized military challenges to the government.

Diaa Hadid / AP Images

Anti-Assad graffito on a school wall in Daara that provoked retaliation by the government.

The first major rebel force to organize within Syria against the government of Bashir al-Assad was the Free Syrian Army (FSA), which emerged in July and was composed largely of defectors from the Syrian army. The FSA's military effectiveness was severely limited by political infighting among its many largely independent units and a lack of discipline among its forces. Defined as a moderate opposition force, the FSA received military air support for its units, funding, equipment, and training from states including the United States, Turkey, and Saudi Arabia. Foreign troops and mercenaries or volunteers from Libya, Croatia, and Kuwait also fought with the FSA.

The more significant military threat to Assad came from jihadist military forces. Initially the most effective among them, al-Nusra, was created in August 2011 when Al Qaeda and the Islamic State of Iraq (which became known as ISIS) created it to defeat Assad and establish an Islamic state in Syria. In 2013 a formal split occurred, and al-Nusra and ISIS became separate jihadist forces. Where al-Nusra sought to remove Assad from power, ISIS was more interested in carving out territory within Syria to establish an Islamic caliphate (religious state). An important source of strength for the jihadist forces was the estimated 2,000–5,000 foreign fighters who came to Syria to join their cause. Originally the United States incorrectly viewed ISIS as a minor problem in the region.

Assad relied on a twofold strategy to defeat his opponents. First, a strategy of military escalation was carefully orchestrated to prevent calls for foreign military intervention. When his use of heavy artillery against rebels in Homs in 2012 did not produce significant international response, Assad escalated the use of force to include helicopter attacks, Scud missiles, and rockets. It was only when Assad began to use napalm, cluster bombs, and chemical weapons that the international community responded strongly, but even then military intervention was not forthcoming. President Obama threatened to use military force if chemical weapons were used but failed to take action. Assad defused the intervention threat by agreeing to a US-Russian framework for eliminating Syrian chemical weapons.

Assad's second strategy was obtaining foreign military support. Iran, Hezbollah, and Russia were the principal supporters. Russia's support was vital for turning the tide of battle in favor of Assad. At one point, ISIS controlled significant portions of Eastern Syria and Western Iraq, with a population of up to eight million people. In September 2015 Vladimir Putin announced that Russia would begin carrying out air strikes in order to stabilize legitimate power in Syria and lay the foundation for a compromise solution. This foundation included keeping Assad in power, which the United States opposed. Russia claimed its air strikes were directed against ISIS targets, but evidence suggested that the FSA and other rebel forces secretly supported by the United States were the main targets. Russia also sent military advisors and special operations forces to Syria. In December 2017, one month after China's announcement that it would send troops to support Assad, Putin announced that Russian troops would be stationed in Syria permanently.

Assad's military campaigns were aided by deep divisions between and within the pro–United States rebel groups and the jihadist forces. Conflicts also ran deep between US-backed Kurdish fighters and Turkey, which saw them as a potential threat because of their desire to carve out a Kurdistan state from Turkey. In 2016 Turkey sent troops into Syria to fight with pro-Turkish Syrian rebels against both ISIS and Kurdish forces, defining both groups as terrorists.

Diplomatic efforts to create a cease-fire inside Syria and negotiations to end the fighting outside the state made little headway. The first international conference to end the Syrian civil war took place in Geneva in 2012. In 2017 Geneva Peace Talks IV, V, VI, VII, and VIII took place, but the central point of disagreement about whether Assad would remain in power remained throughout. The US position was that Assad must be removed, but Russia insisted that he remain in power. Russian military intervention led to a series of ISIS military defeats, tipping the scales in favor of Assad.

By the end of 2018 the military and political situation in Syria had stabilized, but fundamental issues had not been resolved. Assad remained in power. While it was estimated that ISIS retained control of only 2% of its territory, observers were far from convinced that ISIS was defeated. Russia had firmly established a presence in Syria. And in 2019, after announcing that the United States would leave Syria since ISIS had been defeated, President Trump changed direction, committing the United States to remain in Syria to counter Iranian influence.

LOOKING TO THE FUTURE

The question of whether Syria is a model for future conflicts or a unique case remains open. What is certain is that future security challenges will emerge. This section introduces three possible security challenges and proposed responses: arms control and the humanitarian pledge, just war norms for proxy warfare, and reverse engineering of peace operations.

Arms Control and the Humanitarian Pledge

From the very beginning of the nuclear age, an ongoing debate has existed over the proper framework for thinking about nuclear weapons. The dominant perspective places nuclear weapons within a strategic framework, evaluating their use or nonuse within the context of national security. Will the proposed use of nuclear weapons in response to a specific threat advance the national interest? The minority perspective emphasizes the impact of nuclear weapons on the human interest, evaluating the personal consequences of using nuclear weapons. With the bombing of Hiroshima and Nagasaki as a reference point, this perspective documents the existence of both short-term and long-term consequences. Short-term consequences include shock waves, falling buildings, and radiation. Long-term consequences include birth defects, increased cases of cancer, and crop damage.

This second, humanitarian framework has received increased attention and support over the past decade. In 2010 the final document of the Nonproliferation Treaty (NPT) Review Conference held every five years described "the catastrophic humanitarian consequences that would result from the use of nuclear weapons." It called upon all states "to at all times comply with applicable international law, including humanitarian law."

This declaration led to the organization of three Humanitarian Impact of Nuclear Weapons Conferences, attended by both states and nongovernmental organizations such as the International Red Cross. The initial meeting in Oslo in 2013 drew 127 states. The second in Nayarit, Mexico, in 2014 included 147 states. The third, held in Vienna in 2015, was the first attended by the United States and Great Britain, and China sent an unofficial observer. At the conclusion of the Vienna Conference, Austria forwarded a statement that became known as the Austrian Pledge. Now referred to as the Humanitarian Pledge, it pledged Austria to "all relevant stakeholders ... in efforts to stigmatize, prohibit, and eliminate nuclear weapons in light of their unacceptable humanitarian consequences and associated risks."[36] The pledge was endorsed by 107 states.

Support for the Humanitarian Pledge continues to grow. At the 2015 NPT Review Conference, its advocates had pushed for the adoption of a legally binding agreement to ban nuclear weapons, which was rejected by nuclear-weapons states. However, there has been speculation that it could have succeeded in being adopted if it had been put forward as a non-binding statement.[37] The Humanitarian Pledge was also incorporated into the 2017 Treaty on the Prohibition of Nuclear Weapons negotiated in the UN. It requires the ratification by fifty states to come into force. As of July 2019 twenty-two states had ratified the treaty.

Just War Norms for Proxy Warfare

Changes in the location and nature of warfare have raised questions about the rules by which wars should be fought. Scholars and practitioners have agonized over this question for thousands of years. In its most modern form **just war theory** addresses two sets of questions: the proper criteria or right way to go to war (*jus ad bellum*), and the proper criteria or right way to fight a war (*jus in bello*). One of the main challenges today and in the future is how to think about new forms of warfare in terms of just war theory.

Proxy wars present a special challenge to just war theory. As you have already learned, proxy wars are more attractive than direct military confrontations because they are seen as an inexpensive way for an outside power to advance its national interest. Judging the justness of a proxy war is complicated. Where does the responsibility for going to war reside, and who is responsible for fighting a proxy war? A case in point is the US support for the Contras, a right-wing rebel force that opposed the socialist Sandinista government of Nicaragua for over a decade beginning in 1979. The Central Intelligence Agency secretly helped organize and finance the Contras. The United States would only later support them publicly. In one decision the International Court of Justice ruled that although the United States had "financed, organized, trained, supplied equipment, and armed" the Contras, it was not ultimately responsible for their human rights violations. In another decision the Court ruled that the United States had violated international law by supporting the Contras and mining Nicaragua's harbors.

In reviewing the literature on proxy wars, C. Anthony Pfaff, a retired Army colonel and professor of the military profession and ethics, found that little attention had been

just war theory
A theory that addresses two sets of questions: the proper criteria or right way to go to war (*jus ad bellum*), and the proper criteria or right way to fight a war (*jus in bello*).

paid to the application of just war theory to proxy wars. He has proposed a set of just war norms that should guide proxy-outside supporter or proxy-benefactor relations:[38]

- Outside benefactors bear the greater moral burden to ensure conformity to *jus ad bellum* and *jus in bello* norms. Benefactors should make good faith efforts to seek nonviolent solutions first and ensure they are always available.
- When the proxy's just resort to war depends on benefactor intervention, the benefactor's cause must be also be just as well as necessary. It must serve some overriding good.
- Benefactors should account for all costs to those affected by the war.
- When the proxy wins, the proxy relationship should end and transform into something that contributes to order rather than create future chaos.

Reverse Engineering Peace Operations

Winning the war and losing the peace is an all-too-frequent occurrence in international politics.

This truth has long been recognized by civilian strategists and military planners. British military historian and strategist Sir Basil Liddell Hart observed that is vital to conduct war with constant attention to the peace you want to establish. Standard military operations planning does not end with victory on the battlefield. It is divided into four phases. Phase I is deterrence and engagement; Phase II is initial combat operations; Phase III is major combat missions; and Phase IV is post-combat stabilization and transition to civilian governance. In the terminology employed in this chapter, Phase IV is very much about post-conflict reconstruction.

Along with the political and bureaucratic problems inherent in determining the desired outcome, the very nature of the planning process also contributes to the difficulty of linking military and political victory. As just described, planning moves in linear fashion from Phase I to Phase IV. Decision-making studies suggest that in evaluating options, people tend to deal with immediate issues in terms of their feasibility and issues that will confront them down the road in terms of their desirability. Pessimism or realistic appraisals of situations dominate the present, but overconfidence, simplistic thinking, and best-case scenarios characterize discussions of the future. As one participant in the planning for post-war Afghanistan said, it was assumed by the White House that "military victory would produce its own rewards magically, out of the clouds."[39]

One corrective to this planning problem is reverse engineering:[40] Start with Phase IV issues and work back to Phase I. Ask first where you want to end up, then begin moving backward to create a military path or to come to the realization that no such path exists. Reverse engineering of post-conflict reconstruction is no guarantee of success, because of the uncertainty about the outcome of military operations and changing political goals. The desired outcome at the start of the conflict may not be the same as what is desired near its end. However, reverse engineering would require policy-makers to constantly ask themselves whether the proposed strategy and tactics will in fact contribute to creating the desired outcome.

Summary

- Arab-Israeli wars have evolved over time to include multiple forms of warfare.
- War and peace are multidimensional concepts that are difficult to define.
- The causes of war can be found at the international system, state, and individual levels of analysis. Three important contemporary forms of warfare include terrorism, proxy wars, and hybrid wars.
- Peacekeeping and post-conflict reconstruction are two important forms of peace operations. One seeks to end conflict and the other builds a foundation for positive peace.
- The central role played by nuclear weapons in the first nuclear era (how to use them and how to control them) has diminished in the second nuclear era, but concerns and the problem of strategic stability remain.
- The Syrian civil war illustrates the evolving character of modern warfare.
- Three possible future responses to the challenges faced by states in pursuing national security include development of norms for proxy wars, addition of a humanitarian dimension to arms control thinking, and use of reverse engineering to better link military and political warfare objectives.

Key Terms

Deterrence *(217)*

Just war theory *(227)*

Peacekeeping *(211)*

Post-conflict reconstruction *(215)*

Proxy wars *(207)*

State-based conflict *(197)*

Critical Thinking Questions

1. Are the Arabs and Israelis locked into a conflict spiral that makes another military conflict inevitable? Explain your answer.
2. What is the dividing line between war and peace?
3. How is the type of war fought related to its underlying causes?
4. Can a successful peacekeeping operation result in a failed post-conflict reconstruction? Explain your answer.
5. Does the spread of nuclear weapons make nuclear stability more or less likely? Explain your answer.
6. Is the Syrian conflict a model for future wars or a unique case? Explain your answer.
7. Write three additional just wars norms for proxy warfare and explain why they are necessary.

Practice and Review Online
http://textbooks.rowman.com/hastedt-felice

▲ The globalization of trade has created economic vulnerabilities for rich and poor nations alike. *Source:* Wissanu01 / iStock

08

ECONOMIC CHALLENGES:
WHO IS IN CHARGE OF THE GLOBAL ECONOMY?

IN THE INTERCONNECTED WORLD of the twenty-first century, national "borders" are very permeable. Information, ideas, capital, investments, goods, services, and technology freely cross national lines. **Economic globalization**—the increased flows of trade, investment, technology, and capital among states—goes beyond economics; economics, politics, and culture must be viewed together through a world lens. The power of nations and national leaders is today impacted, and often constrained, by these global forces. A government leader must focus on global as well as national policy in order to protect citizens' economic livelihood and personal security. This chapter explores the challenges involved in economic globalization.

economic globalization The increased interdependence of the world's economies as a result of the growing flows of trade, investment, technology, and capital among states.

In their landmark 1977 work *Power and Interdependence* Robert Keohane and Joseph Nye describe how global economic and environmental forces impact both rich and poor nations in the world system. These scholars refer to an era of *complex interdependence* in which individual nations find themselves sensitive and vulnerable to world dynamics outside of their individual control.[1] Statesmen and academics in the 1970s and 1980s struggled to understand the impact of this new interconnected world on sovereignty, as state power seemed more and more constrained in this interdependent era. How can a national leader protect the safety and well-being of citizens in a period of complex interdependence? How can a nation promote national economic growth and the human development of its citizens when economic institutions, multinational corporations (MNCs), and markets operate globally with their own priorities and interests?

The answers to these questions remain controversial. In the twenty-first century profound disagreement persists about the impact of economic globalization on the world's peoples and environment. Some argue that economic globalization has brought the highest levels of human development in history, with improved health, sanitation, and living standards around the world. Others argue that the globalization of trade and finance is responsible for high unemployment, increased inequality, greater poverty, and environmental degradation. This chapter explores these debates about the economic challenges that globalization presents to the world's nations and peoples.

The chapter opens with a review of the 1994 North American Free Trade Agreement (NAFTA), which captures the fundamental controversies surrounding free trade and economic globalization. The chapter then presents the benefits and weaknesses of economic globalization today. Next is a discussion of the three central theories of international political economy (IPE)—economic liberalism, economic nationalism, and economic structuralism—including their application to a complex interdependent world. The chapter concludes by revisiting NAFTA in 2019 and provides a look at possible future attempts to control the movements of speculative capital and excessive military spending.

LEARNING OBJECTIVES

Students will be able to:

- Articulate the arguments for and against the 1994 North American Free Trade Agreement (NAFTA).

- Discuss the impact of economic globalization on a nation's economic growth and on the human development of its citizens.

- Compare and contrast the three central theories of international political economy: economic liberalism, economic nationalism, and economic structuralism.

- Evaluate the merits of the United Nations Sustainable Development Goals for 2030.

- Assess the impact of NAFTA on Canada, Mexico and the United States after twenty-five years in operation.

- Identify possible future public policy to better control the movement of speculative capital across borders.

- Evaluate the impact of excessive military spending on economic development.

HISTORICAL PERSPECTIVE: The North American Free Trade Agreement, 1994

On November 10, 1993, over sixteen million television viewers watched Vice President Al Gore debate with billionaire businessman Ross Perot on the proposed **North American Free Trade Agreement (NAFTA)**. The platform of the 1992 Clinton/Gore campaign had emphasized the benefits of free trade and economic globalization to the US economy, and a prominent, well-publicized slogan at campaign headquarters was: "It's the economy, stupid." After the election the new administration made NAFTA a central component of their effort to have the United States lead the world in the promotion of economic integration and the advancement of trade and investments across borders.

> North American Free Trade Agreement (NAFTA) Agreement established in 1994 that eliminated most tariff and nontariff barriers to trade and investment among Canada, Mexico, and the United States.

In contrast, Ross Perot believed that NAFTA would greatly harm the US economy and cause American companies to move their operations to Mexico to take advantage of lower wages and weaker environmental laws. As a candidate for President in 1992, Perot famously described a "giant sucking sound" as companies packed up and moved south:

> We have got to stop sending jobs overseas....[It's] pretty simple: If you're paying $12, $13, $14 an hour for factory workers and you can move your factory South of the border, pay a dollar an hour for labor...have no health care—that's the most expensive single element in making a car—have no environmental controls, no pollution controls and no retirement, and you don't care about anything but making money, there will be a *giant sucking sound going south*.[2]

In the middle of his televised debate with Perot, Gore brought out a 1930s-era black and white photo of Senator Reed Smoot and Representative Willis C. Hawley, whose protectionist trade policies were widely blamed for deepening the Great Depression. The Smoot-Hawley Act of 1930 raised US tariffs on over 20,000 imported goods. America's trading partners retaliated, resulting in a 50% reduction in US exports and imports. A strong consensus among historians and economists is that these protectionist measures exacerbated the Great Depression and contributed to the suffering experienced by millions of American families.[3]

By holding up the photo during the debate, Gore implied that a rejection of NAFTA would bring similar results of high unemployment and economic hardship. He argued that joining NAFTA would open up markets abroad for US products and revive well-paying jobs for the American working class. To most observers the Vice President clearly won the debate. Beforehand, national support for the Clinton Administration's attempt to finalize NAFTA was at only 34%. After the debate it rose to approximately 57%, convincing wavering Congressional Democrats to get on board and approve the trade legislation. The NAFTA trade agreement, setting the rules of trade among Canada, the United States, and Mexico, went into effect on January 1, 1994.[4]

Televised debate on NAFTA between Al Gore and Ross Perot on CNN.

The Gore-Perot debate captured one of the fundamental divisions in international political economy: globalist economic liberals versus economic nationalists (also referred to as mercantilists). This divide will be explored in detail later in this chapter.

NAFTA created one of the world's largest free trade zones by working to eliminate most tariff and nontariff barriers to trade and investment among the three participating countries. When it was implemented in 1994, the combined economies of the three nations measured $6 trillion and impacted more than 365 million people. Once it was ratified, tariffs on the majority of goods produced by the NAFTA signatories were lifted immediately, followed by a fifteen-year phased elimination of further barriers to investments, increasing the movement of goods and services among the three countries.

NAFTA was an ambitious attempt to unleash a globalist liberal economic framework throughout North America. In addition to eliminating tariff barriers in agriculture, manufacturing, and services, it sought to remove investment restrictions, protect intellectual property rights, and address environmental and labor concerns through specific side-agreements. The Clinton/Gore administration, and other proponents of the accord, believed that these actions would result in a win-win-win for small businesses and working people in all three countries. Economic globalization was viewed not as a zero-sum game of winners and losers but as a world in which rich and poor states could move forward together.

The NAFTA countries agreed to increase health, safety, and industrial requirements to meet the highest existing standards (almost always those of the United States and Canada). A labor side-agreement established a commission to ease the concerns of trade unionists who believed that lower wages would cause US companies to move their production to Mexico (Perot's "great sucking sound"). An environmental side-agreement established a commission to handle environmental issues to ease the concerns of environmentalists who believed that Mexico's lax environmental laws would lead to rampant pollution. These commissions were given powers to impose penalties, including steep fines, against any of the three governments that did not enforce its laws consistently.[5]

In 1989 the Canada-US Free Trade Agreement (CUSFTA) went into effect. This opening of the Canadian economy to the US market thus predated NAFTA and led to a huge increase in trade. Prior to NAFTA Canadian exports to the United States totaled $110 billion; post-NAFTA this rose to $346 billion. In addition, since 1993, US and Mexican investments in Canada have tripled.[6]

The Contemporary Perspective, near the end of this chapter, examines the positive and negative impacts of NAFTA after twenty-five years in effect. NAFTA demonstrates how three nations—Canada, Mexico, and the United States—have approached the challenges of economic globalization. This next section looks at how these challenges have manifested among nations globally.

THE CHALLENGE OF ECONOMIC GLOBALIZATION

In many respects economic globalization has been a tremendous success. Interstate agreements and domestic politics have enhanced the ability of the private and public sectors to operate globally. In addition, technological advances—internet, computers, satellite communications—have made location less important for governments and non-state actors, including multinational corporations (MNCs). According to the United Nations Development Program (UNDP), this interconnected world has brought significant progress in human development. The following trends occurred over the twenty-five-year period between 1990 and 2015:[7]

- As the global population grew by 2 billion—from 5.3 billion in 1990 to 7.3 billion in 2015—more than 1 billion people escaped extreme poverty.
- 2.1 billion people gained access to improved sanitation.
- More than 2.6 billion people gained access to improved sources of drinking water.
- The global under-five mortality rate decreased by more than 50%.
- The incidence of HIV, malaria, and tuberculosis declined.
- Women's representation in parliaments world-wide rose to 23%—up 6 percentage points over the preceding decade.
- Forest loss declined from 7.3 million hectares per year in the 1990s to 3.3 million in 2015.

Economic globalization has another, darker side. Inequality, environmental damage, poverty and hunger remain central features of the global economy. Consider the following UNDP global statistics for 2015:[8]

- One person in nine is hungry.
- One person in three is malnourished.
- Air pollution causes 18,000 deaths each day.
- HIV infects 2 million people each year.
- On average, twenty-four people are displaced from their homes every minute.
- Approximately 15 million girls under age 18 marry each year, one every two seconds.
- Over 370 million indigenous peoples in 70 countries face discrimination and exclusion from the legal system and are denied access to land, water, and intellectual property rights.

purchasing power parity (PPP) The conversion of the currency of one country to the amount needed to purchase the same basket of goods and services available in other countries; in practice the conversion is often to purchasing the same basket that a US dollar would purchase in the United States.

The World Bank has defined acute poverty as the inability to attain a minimum standard of living; it has established an extreme poverty line of $1.90 a day based on **purchasing power parity (PPP)**. PPP refers to the conversion of the currency of one country to be able to purchase the same basket of goods and services in other countries; in practice, the conversion is often to purchasing the same basket that a US dollar would purchase in the United States. After adjusting for cost of living differences, $1.90 a day was the average minimum consumption required for subsistence in the developing world. The World Bank reports that 10% of the world's population, 735.9 million poverty-stricken people, lived on less than $1.90 a day in 2015. Many just above that level are still very poor and often in debt. In the same report, the World Bank notes that 26.3% of the world's population, 1.9 billion, live on less than $3.20 a day, and 46% of the world's population, 3.4 billion, on less than $5.50 a day.[9]

Keep in mind that this $1.90 a day figure did not mean what that $1.90 would buy when converted into a local currency. Rather, it was the equivalent of what $1.90 would buy in the United States—a quart of milk, a local bus ride, and so on. The World Bank claims that this $1.90 figure captures the minimum subsistence levels across developing countries. In fact, $3.20 and $5.50 a day are not much better.[10]

The economic globalization of the last few decades has increased levels of inequality significantly. Oxfam, the British humanitarian and development organization, reported that 82% of all global wealth generated in 2017 went to the world's richest 1%. Tragically, those living among the bottom 50% saw no increase in wealth at all and instead performed often dangerous and poorly paid work to support the extreme wealth of the few.[11]

These startling global trends hold true in the United States as well. For example, in 1980 the top 1% of adults in both Europe and the United States earned around 10% of national income. By 2018 the 1%'s share rose to 12% in Europe and 20% in the United States. During this same period the annual income earnings for the top 1% in the United States rose by 205%; for the top 0.001% the figure is an astounding 636%. In contrast, the average annual wage of the bottom 50% has stagnated since 1980.[12]

Economic globalization is not solely responsible for creating the inequities between the rich and the poor around the world, but political leaders have capitalized on public fear and economic insecurity to create a populist backlash against free trade and economic integration. This was exemplified dramatically by the Brexit vote in Britain (discussed in Chapter 3) and the election of Donald Trump to the US Presidency, but it extends much further. Workers around the world express concern about losing their jobs or receiving lower wages as a result of global agreements, legal and illegal immigration, and foreign competition. Populists want to strengthen national borders and back away from global agreements such as the Trans-Pacific Partnership and the Paris Agreement on global climate change. The elites are seen as the "winners" of economic globalization at the expense of the poor, the working class, and the middle class.

Entire developing countries are also moving away from integration into the global economy. One protectionist method is called **nontariff barriers to trade**. According to the World Trade Organization (WTO), nontariff barriers to trade are bureaucratic acts designed to restrict imports or exports of goods or services, such as import licensing, rules for the valuation of goods at customs, pre-shipment inspection of imports, rules of origin, and investment measures.[13] The UN Conference on Trade and Development reports that nontariff barriers in place among the ten members of the Association of Southeast Asian Nations (ASEAN) ballooned from 1,634 in 2000 to 5,975 in 2015.[14]

nontariff barriers to trade Restrictions of imports or exports other than tariffs, such as import licensing, quotas, rules for valuing goods at customs, and inspections of imports.

In addition, an anti-globalization movement has emerged among nongovernmental organizations (NGOs), trade unions, and activist organizations and individuals. Some of the first demonstrations against economic globalization took place in **developing countries**—often referred to as *less-developed countries (LDCs)*—to protest the structural adjustment programs (SAPs) of the International Monetary Fund (IMF) (as discussed in Chapter 3). IMF-designed SAPs required developing countries to implement certain policies in order to receive loans. SAP policies, intended to push the developing country to become more market oriented, have included reduction of barriers to trade, privatization and deregulation of the economy, and openness to foreign investment. SAPs were criticized for applying a "cookie cutter" formula to diverse nations, which in many cases failed to either help the country develop or eliminate poverty. Since many of these policies pushed governments to eliminate food subsidies and welfare policies, the poor, particularly poor women, were hurt the most. Dozens of riots against these IMF policies broke out in numerous developing countries in the 1980s and 1990s.

developing countries Some of the poorest nations in the world; also referred to as less-developed countries (LDCs), underdeveloped countries, and undeveloped countries.

Other key anti-globalization protests included a grassroots rebellion launched on January 1, 1994, led by an indigenous organization called the Zapatistas in the Mexican state of Chiapas. The Zapatistas protested specifically against economic liberalism and the NAFTA agreement, which they saw as damaging to both the indigenous peoples and the agrarian economy in Chiapas. An energetic protest of 60,000 to 80,000 demonstrators, led by a coalition of environmentalists, trade unionists, and human rights activists, disrupted the WTO's meeting in Seattle in 1999. Further demonstrations by tens of thousands of protestors against the WTO and economic globalization took place in

Prague (2000), Genoa (2001), and Cancún (2004). Protests continued at the G8 summit in Gleneagles, Scotland, (2005) and the G20 London Summit (2009). The Occupy Wall Street movement that began in 2011 focused on the extreme inequality between the rich 1% and the remaining 99% resulting from global economic integration.

These efforts have sometimes been referred to collectively as a global justice movement, as they all call attention to the negative externalities of the global free market, including job loss, environmental destruction, human rights abuse, and worker exploitation. Critics charge that the economic interest of the few has been put ahead of the protection of public goods for all, victimizing the poor and the vulnerable.

The debates for and against economic globalization can be examined using three key theories of international political economy—economic liberalism, economic nationalism, and economic structuralism. All three theories agree that economic globalization is taking place, but they disagree on its implications for economic policy.

THEORIES OF INTERNATIONAL POLITICAL ECONOMY AND ECONOMIC GLOBALIZATION

International political economy (IPE) The study of the interaction and tension between (1) the market and the state and (2) the market and international economic entities— including MNCs, international organizations such as the IMF and the World Bank, and global and regional trade organizations such as the WTO.

International political economy (IPE) is the study of the interaction and tension between (1) the market and the state and (2) the market and international economic entities including MNCs, international organizations such as the IMF and the World Bank, and global and regional trade organizations such as the WTO. (These international organizations were described in Chapter 3.) Economic policy-making is concerned with protecting a free market while also preventing exploitation and negative externalities through government regulation.

Economic policy-making involves four central principles: efficiency, autonomy, equity, and order. States work to create economic efficiency, protect their sovereign autonomy, respond to demands for the equitable distribution of goods and services, and follow the rules of international finance and trade organizations in order to create order in international economic relations.[15]

In the real world these four principles often conflict, and states are forced to make trade-offs among them. A state may enact laws to regulate the market and sacrifice efficiency to ensure state autonomy and the protection of key economic sectors. For example, Japan views self-sufficiency in rice production as central to its culture and food security. To protect its rice farmers, Japan imposed a whopping 778% tariff on imported rice in 2015.[16] Such state intervention harms efficient production; Japanese farmers do not have to compete with agricultural producers from abroad that may have integrated modern technology and increased the efficiency of rice production. Japan is obviously willing to sacrifice efficiency in order to protect its autonomy. This is just one example of how a state's interests may collide with the other principles.

However, state interventions in the market intended to protect autonomy or equity (fairness) are controversial and can produce unforeseen side effects. One key issue is the protection of the most vulnerable members of society (such as the poor, minorities, and women). For example, should the state subsidize food distribution to the poor? Or does such state intervention undermine the efficiency of the agricultural market sector? What is the proper balance between the state and the market to guarantee human rights protections for the most vulnerable? How far should regulations and controls on the actions of MNCs, trade organizations, and international economic organizations go to create fair and just opportunities for all members of society?

The following sections outline three key IPE theories: economic liberalism, economic nationalism, and economic structuralism. Table 8.1 provides a summary of some of the key differences among these three theories, which are subsequently described in detail.

Economic Liberalism

The theory of **economic liberalism**, reflecting a globalist perspective, is based on efficiency. The central idea is that open and free global trade and investments across borders

economic liberalism
Theory that open and free trade and investments across borders with minimal state intervention will create a world in which all nations and individuals will be better off.

TABLE 8.1	Comparing Theories of International Political Economy		
	Economic Liberalism	Economic Nationalism	Economic Structuralism
Key IPE Principle	Efficiency	Autonomy	Equity
Perspective	Globalist	Statist	Radical
Economic Relations	"Win-Win"	"Win-Lose"	"Win-Lose"
	Harmonious	Conflictual	Conflictual
	Positive-Sum Game	Zero-Sum Game	Exploitation
Main Actors/Unit of Analysis	Individuals/Consumers Private Firms/MNCs	States	States and Economic Classes
Economic Goals	Maximize Global Production and Consumption	Maximize State Power and the National Interest	Maximize State and Class Interests
Relationship between Economics and Politics	Economics Should Be Autonomous and Free from Politics	Politics Is Decisive and Should Determine Economics	Economics Is Decisive and Strongly Influences Politics
Policy Recommendation	Relative Laissez-faire	State Intervention and Protectionism	State Action and Global Action to Help the Developing Countries and Poorer Classes within Countries
Examples of Advocates	President Bill Clinton	President Donald Trump	Developing Countries

Updated and expanded version of a chart prepared by Professor Ken Rodman at New York University in 1990.

with minimal state intervention will create a world in which all nations and individuals will be better off. In such a globalized market economy, economic growth and world production will be maximized, benefitting rich and poor states alike. This creates a win-win situation for all states. For example, from this perspective economic growth in Argentina would not hurt economic growth in Brazil: both nations can prosper.

Economic liberals argue that the elimination of political barriers to free trade, investment, and currency movements among countries will maximize world production. This is accomplished through the logic of the market, which is guided by the "invisible hand." This phrase, coined by Adam Smith in *The Wealth of Nations* (1776), identifies how a free market can create the most goods and services for the most numbers of people through the simple laws of supply and demand. Each individual actor in the market pursuing his or her own self interest will unintentionally produce the interests of the community by maximizing production and consumption. Open and free competition breeds efficiency by driving inefficient producers out of business. Government interference in this free market process—such as subsidizing or protecting failing businesses—can impede economic growth.

In addition, economic liberals believe that human beings—as aggressive and calculating individuals—need positive material incentives (such as wage raises) and negative ones (such as threats of unemployment) to be productive. A competitive, free market economy allows each individual to achieve maximum personal liberty and material well-being. If decision-making units (individuals, households, or firms) are allowed to act freely and rationally through the market, society as a whole will flourish.[17]

Box 8.1 clarifies how economic liberalism differs from political liberalism and other uses of the word *liberal*.

comparative advantage Theory that each nation should produce those goods and services that it can produce most efficiently, then export them and use the revenues gained to import those goods that it produces less efficiently.

The application of liberal economic principles to the global economy revolves around the concept of **comparative advantage**. This theory argues that each nation should produce those goods and services that it can produce most efficiently, then export them and use the revenues gained to import those goods that it produces less efficiently. A nation's comparative advantage can be determined through an examination of its key factor endowments, including labor, capital, energy, technology, and land. For example, a poor country, in which capital, technology, and energy are scarce but labor and land are bountiful, might want to focus on labor-intensive manufacturing or agricultural production. A developed country most likely has a comparative advantage in capital-intensive or technology-intensive goods and should focus production in these areas. Focusing on comparative advantage gives each nation the opportunity to grow its economy, which will eventually allow for diversification. For example, a country with rich agricultural land and the appropriate climate may begin as an exporter of bananas or coffee but, using the proceeds gained through trade, could eventually diversify and develop production in light manufacturing. If this is successful, further diversification into heavy manufacturing and even high-tech goods becomes possible. Recognition of comparative advantage can allow a nation to move up the ladder of development.

Box 8.1 / What Does "Liberal" Mean in IPE?

The word *liberalism* has different meanings in diverse contexts. The word *liberal* comes from the Latin word *liber* meaning "free" and is rooted in ideas of liberty and freedom. As you learned in Chapter 2, liberal political theory in international relations focuses on democracy and free trade as bases on which to build cooperation in the international system.

Liberalism in the US political system refers to an ideology promoting an activist state committed to policies to protect and provide for public goods, environmental sustainability, and helping the poor. However, liberalism in IPE means almost exactly the opposite. Economic liberals fear an activist state and the "heavy hand" of too much governmental regulation. Instead, they ask the state to pursue a more *laissez-faire* ("let be" or "hands off") approach toward the market.

Both political liberals and political conservatives in the United States support a market economy and the fundamentals of economic liberalism. Where they differ is in the types and degrees of government intervention in the market that they favor. Political conservatives often promote high levels of military spending and "law and order" policies to protect the state's autonomy. Political liberals, on the other hand, often promote social welfare policies to address issues of fairness and equity in relation to market outcomes.

Think about It

1. In what ways would a political conservative in the United States be considered an economic liberal?

2. How does the issue of health care in the United States demonstrate the differences between political liberals and political conservatives in regards to a laissez-faire market (economic liberal) approach to public goods?

Economic liberals further argue that integration into the global economy can actually help a nation exploit its comparative advantage. Integrating diverse and separate economies can result in an overall gain of output from which everyone could potentially benefit over time. Joel Cohen gives the following hypothetical example to demonstrate the benefits of economic integration and international trade: Countries A and B each have 1,000 acres of land. Country A has 1,000 workers and 100 mules. Country B has 100 workers and 1,000 mules. Neither a worker alone nor a mule alone can cultivate any land. However, one worker plus one mule can cultivate one acre per year. The advantages of integration are clear. Only 100 acres can be cultivated in Countries A and B if neither workers nor mules can move between them. If, however, Country B could ship 900 mules to Country A, then the two countries combined could cultivate 1,100 acres. Alternatively, the migration of 900 workers from Country A to Country B would equally increase the total cultivated land.[18]

The economic globalization of the twentieth and twenty-first centuries has been based on these fundamental principles of economic liberalism—open borders to trade and investments, comparative advantage, and minimal governmental regulation. Economic liberals believe that such a global market economy is morally desirable because it will create efficiency and increase global production, enabling poor countries to gain as much as wealthy states. An individual or a MNC selfishly interested in private gain and personal wealth may seek to obtain the largest return possible on their investments. This should lead to more investments in the poor countries of the underdeveloped world, where maximal gains can be made. According to the globalist perspective, economic globalization can create a harmonious global market place based on the free movement of capital and goods in which order can only be achieved through competition and the "invisible hand."

From this perspective, economics should never be subject to politics because markets can only satisfy human needs when governments do not intervene. IPE scholar Robert Gilpin defines liberal economics as "a doctrine and a set of principles for organizing and managing economic growth, and individual welfare."[19] Free trade allows each country to specialize and develop its particular niche in the global economy.

However, the economic liberal laissez-faire approach was considerably discredited by the Great Depression of the 1930s. In response to that economic catastrophe John Maynard Keynes argued that the capitalist market economy would not maintain full employment without government intervention. He felt strongly that the government had the responsibility to borrow and spend money to prevent economic depressions and recessions. So-called Keynes correctives, which are now commonly accepted practice, were meant to stimulate the market, not overregulate or overthrow it. The economy in general was free to respond to the profit-maximizing producers and the welfare-maximizing consumers.[20]

Although laissez-faire liberal economists argue that markets inherently tend toward a socially beneficial equilibrium, or *Pareto optimum*, Keynes convincingly demonstrated that this is not the case. Instead, production and consumption cannot be balanced when unemployment is high. In this situation the state must intervene to stimulate both employment and investment. Keynes successfully challenged the basic argument of laissez-faire by contending that government intervention was necessary to achieve full employment and stimulate consumption.[21]

The economist Milton Friedman coined the celebrated phrase, "We are all Keynesians now." In 1971 former US President Richard Nixon declared, "I am now a Keynesian in economics" after taking the United States off the gold standard. These two hard-core laissez-faire economic liberals recognized the truth of Keynes's analysis of market failure. In times of economic stagnation and depression, a "hands-off" approach to the economy will be counterproductive and a more interventionist policy is needed. Such actions do not undermine market principles but instead support market fundamentals.

The international economic institutions created at Bretton Woods, New Hampshire, in 1944 described in Chapter 3—the IMF, the World Bank, and the GATT/WTO—were charged with building a system of economic governance committed to the principles of economic liberalism.

Economic Nationalism

Because of its dedication to protecting a state's autonomy, there is a strong overlap between economic nationalism and political realism (which was discussed in Chapter 2). Both perspectives are primarily concerned with building and protecting the power of the state. According to **economic nationalism**, reflecting a statist perspective, economic activity should be involved primarily with promoting and shielding national industries and the local economy from the vulnerabilities that emerge with global economic interdependence. In the eyes of an economic nationalist, economics is a tool of politics: economic policy should be organized around state priorities. The global economy is viewed as highly conflictual, with each nation pursuing national strategies to maximize wealth and power. From this perspective the global economy is viewed as a "zero-sum" game in which one state's gain is another's loss. Nations must be concerned about their relative power positions vis-à-vis other states. In contrast to economic liberalists, who envision cooperation and the development of mutual gains, economic nationalists see a world of competition and struggle with winners and losers. According to this view, economic wealth can be translated into military power and used for political advantage. In such a dog-eat-dog atmosphere it is imperative for a state to focus on its own economy and power position in order to survive and thrive. Economic growth and success in other states has the potential to harm your own national interest.

Modern-day economic nationalism draws from the historical principles of mercantilism, a perspective developed during the rise of the nation-state system in Europe in the seventeenth century. Mercantilism arose at a time when states were interested in acquiring wealth and power, not only to protect themselves from other states but also to participate in the colonization of newly discovered regions of the world. Trade surpluses increased national wealth and could be used for national security and military purposes. One strategy was to generate trade surpluses by promoting exports and limiting imports. Mercantilists promoted economic policies of support and protection to national industries and their investments allowing them to out-compete foreign firms.

In contrast to economic liberalism, which is organized around the logic of the market, mercantilism and economic nationalism are organized around the logic of the state to control the process of economic growth and accumulation of capital.[22] (This division is clearly seen in the earlier discussion of NAFTA.)

To an economic nationalist, global economic interdependence built around free trade and investment threatens national autonomy. Although a country may benefit overall from aggregate wealth, certain sectors within the global economy may lose. National leaders often feel they can't politically afford to jeopardize disrupting "key sectors" or "infant industries" by subjecting them to global competition. For example, the US auto industry has been disrupted by the economic interdependence of the global economy. Free trade agreements and increased imports of foreign cars have led to a loss of approximately 350,000 jobs since 1994—representing one-third of the industry.[23] Economic

economic nationalism
Theory that economic activity should be involved primarily with promoting and shielding national industries and the local economy from the vulnerabilities that emerge with global economic interdependence.

nationalists, such as President Trump, argue that these key economic sectors must be supported and protected from aggressive foreign firms and countries.

A second way in which economic interdependence can harm a nation is by exposing it to extreme external vulnerability. Allowing a global market based on efficiency and comparative advantage to operate freely may expose a country to negative forces beyond its control, creating dependence on other states and a weak position in the global economy. For example, many developing countries found their comparative advantage in the production of one or two primary products produced for export. Unfortunately, in many cases this created conditions of extreme vulnerability. For example, Zambia today depends on copper exports for 70% of its export earnings.[24] Jamaica depends on sugar and bauxite for 60–80% of its export earnings.[25] Because the prices of these primary products fluctuate widely on the international commodities markets, these countries are at the mercy of global economic forces over which they have no control.

Some economic nationalists in developing countries thus assert that in today's globalized economy comparative advantage may hurt, rather than help, a nation's economy. Since some goods have more power in the global economy than others, a government may need to protect its "infant industries" from foreign competition. These countries don't want to lose power to the economically strong states. A country's leader, for example, may argue that the government needs to insulate its industrial sector and/or its high-tech computer industries from foreign competition, independent of the efficiency principles underlying comparative advantage. National power (and security) requires an autonomous and strong industrial sector and computer industry. Even if foreign goods in these sectors are cheaper, the high cost of protecting these domestic sectors may seem worthwhile in order to guard a nation's security and long-term viability.

Japan, South Korea, Taiwan, and China are often used as examples of successful implementation of economic nationalist policies. (See the Regional Spotlight feature on China's Belt and Road Initiative.) Each of these governments has intervened in the market to direct economic growth and lead development efforts, subsidized key sectors, protected infant industries, and identified strategic industries and shielded them from outside competition. Economic nationalists consider these countries shining examples of the type of state-guided economic development needed in a world of economic interdependence.

Gilpin argues that economic nationalism can be either "benign" or "malevolent." Benign actions are defensive, and attempt to "protect the economy against untoward economic and political forces." Such actions, designed to protect a country's security, do not necessarily harm other states. Malevolent actions, on the other hand, are aggressive and seek to increase the country's geopolitical power through expansionary economic policies. Malevolent economic nationalism is, more or less, economic warfare designed to expand a country's political and economic influence regionally and globally.[26]

In response to increased competition from imported goods, domestic firms may shift production abroad to cut costs or fire workers, leading to higher unemployment. Levying tariffs on imported goods makes them more expensive, which should increase the demand for domestically produced goods. Tariffs have also been employed to insure the health and safety of a country's citizens. Tariffs and barriers have also been imposed to protect national security. Certain industries, such as defense companies, have been deemed strategically important and subsidized and protected by the state.

For all of these reasons, economic nationalists view free trade arrangements as problematic and not beneficial to all parties. For example, Donald Trump's presidential campaign in 2016 was to a large degree focused on an anti-trade platform. In 2018 President Trump followed through and imposed billions in tariffs on products from Canada, China, the European Union, Japan, Mexico, Canada, and other countries. The affected countries immediately vowed retaliatory actions. Mexico quickly imposed tariffs on around $3 billion worth of American pork, steel, cheese, and other goods.[27] China's response was equally swift, announcing tariffs on $50 billion worth of American goods including beef, poultry, tobacco, and cars. China also threatened to back away from an agreement to buy $70 billion worth of American agricultural and energy products since this deal was conditioned on the United States lifting its threat of tariffs.[28]

Following negotiations at the Group of 20 summit in Buenos Aires in November 2018, trade friction between the United States and China eased a bit. Trump and President Xi Jinping of China agreed to a "temporary truce" in the trade dispute. While the United States will continue to impose a 10% tariff on up to $250 billion of Chinese goods, it will hold off on its threats to raise that duty to 25% in the near future. And China was reported to be willing to lower some tariffs on American-made autos and resume buying soybeans and other US agricultural produces. However, tensions between the two countries remain high, and it is unclear how this trade war will end.[29]

Economic Structuralism

The theoretical and political dimensions of economic structuralism were introduced in Chapter 2. Recall that *economic structuralism*, reflecting a radical perspective, draws extensively from Marxist theory and emphasizes the pursuit of wealth in international politics and the exploitive relations it creates. Economic structuralists argue that class exploitation and inequality are dominating features of capitalist development both historically and in the current global system. This section explores the economic dimensions of this approach in a world of complex economic interdependence.

The economic structuralist perspective of IPE is based on equity or fairness. Structuralist are concerned with fair distribution and identifying whether market outcomes are just, impartial, and evenhanded. Liberal economic theory and economic nationalism both focus on accumulating maximum national and global wealth and say almost nothing about distribution. Economic structuralists challenge these other perspectives, arguing that the global free market system of economic interdependence is historically and structurally biased against the poor and weak. According to this view, unless radical changes are implemented, the current economic system will perpetuate the economic power of the dominating states and work against the interests of the developing nations.

REGIONAL SPOTLIGHT

One Road, One Belt

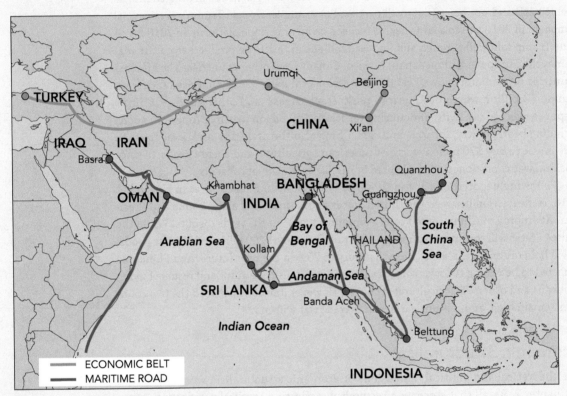

Map 8.1 China's Belt and Road Initiative.

In 2013 China unveiled a new development strategy to create a large integrated market focusing on physical and digital infrastructure investments, including railways, highways, real estate, power grids, iron and steel. The Belt and Road Initiative (BRI) is designed to become one of the largest infrastructure investment projects in history; it will reach more than sixty-eight countries with over 65% of the world's population.

colonialism Period from the late fifteenth to the twentieth century when the European powers brutally conquered, settled and exploited large areas of the world.

Economic structuralists base their analysis on the impact of their histories on the positions of the less-developed countries in the global economy of the twenty-first century. This history is so important that this perspective is sometimes referred to as *historical structuralism*. The structure of today's world economy is a product of approximately 500 years of **colonialism**. From the late 1400s to the outbreak of WWI in 1914 the European states brutally conquered nations and peoples all over the world. By 1914 it

Blaine Harrington III / Alamy Stock Photo

China's Belt and Road Initiative hopes to transform infrastructure and development in up to sixty-eight countries.

China today is spending around $150 billion a year in participating countries. To many observers this program represents China's claim on global leadership. If successful, the BRI will allow China to dominate Eurasia, creating an economic and trading area to rival the US-dominated transatlantic alliance.[30]

Depending on how the program evolves, the estimated overall costs for BRI range from a low of $1 trillion to a high of $8 trillion.[31] From 2014 to 2017 estimates put China's investments in BRI projects at more than $340 billion. Geographically, infrastructure projects will pass through countries in Asia, the Middle East, Europe, Oceania, and East Africa.

BRI allows China to gain access to markets, influence and power by implementing its economic policy globally. Some view China's actions as a clear economic nationalist (mercantilist), "China First" approach to development. The countries participating in BRI need assistance to build infrastructure, including roads, railways, and telecommunications networks.

Many of them have no alternative but to accept help from China. To date China has favored loans over grants, which unfortunately may result in growing unsustainable debt for some developing countries, creating dependency and political weakness. Recipients may find their foreign policy options constrained and influenced by Beijing's preferences.[32]

BRI is not limited to infrastructure. China's "new digital Silk Road" promotes information technology connectivity across the Indian Ocean rim and Eurasia with new fiber optic lines, undersea cables, cloud computing capacity, and artificial intelligence research centers. In addition to railroads, highways, and dams, the BRI plan in Pakistan includes development of a system of video and Internet surveillance "similar to that in Beijing and a partnership with a Pakistani television channel to disseminate Chinese media content." Chinese military objectives are also advanced through BRI. "Chinese state-owned enterprises now run at least 76 ports and terminals out of 34 countries, and in Greece, Pakistan, and Sri Lanka, Chinese investment in ports has been followed by high-profile visits from Chinese naval vessels." Beijing also plans to establish special arbitration courts for BRI projects, which will promote a legal system with Chinese rules.[33]

Think about It

1. Do China's BRI investments represent globalist economic liberalism or an economic nationalist approach to development? Explain your answer.

2. How similar is China's BRI program to the US Marshall Plan in the 1950s to rebuild Europe after WWII? Explain your answer.

is estimated that the Europeans had gained control of 84% of the globe.[34] The European powers, including Belgium, Britain, France, Germany, Italy, the Netherlands, Portugal, Spain, and Sweden established colonies to create markets for their goods and to gain access to raw materials for their industries. Colonialism was designed to benefit the economies of the conquering nations, not those of the indigenous peoples under occupation.

For example, examine Africa under colonial rule in 1914 (see Map 8.2).

Map 8.2 European Colonial Rule in Africa, 1914.

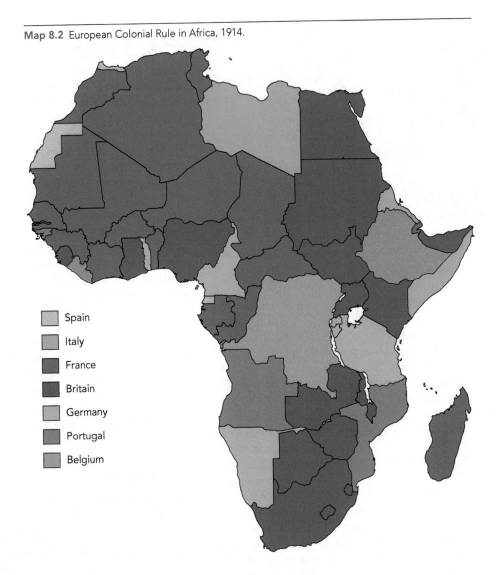

Spain

Italy

France

Britain

Germany

Portugal

Belgium

After colonialism ended, the world system evolved quickly into a period of *neocolonialism*, which entailed the control of the less-developed countries through less direct means. Colonial-style exploitation continued even after the end of direct foreign rule. The former colonial powers, the United States, and other leading states used their diplomatic, economic, and military power to maintain access to inexpensive raw materials and low-priced labor in these less-developed countries. American and European multinational corporations (MNCs) pursued global strategies to expand their operations. International organizations including the World Bank and the International Monetary Fund (IMF) asserted a global reach. Structuralists argue that these financial and trade policies, based on unequal power relationships between rich and poor states, perpetuated the exploitation of the former colonies. As you have learned in previous chapters, the United States and other countries intervened legally and illegally—diplomatically and with force—to ensure continued access to markets and investment opportunities in Latin America and elsewhere.

Economic structuralists argue that the current global interdependent economy is a product of this history. According to Andre Gunder Frank, the exploitation of many of the countries of the Southern Hemisphere created the "development of underdevelopment."[35] As noted in Chapter 2, this led to stark economic divisions between the core rich countries, a poor periphery, and a partially developed semi-periphery. In addition, the former colonies found themselves dependent on technology and capital from the countries in the developed core, so it was very difficult for countries victimized by colonialism and neocolonialism to grow their economies and create true human development.

At least in part, this history explains the vast differences in poverty between and within nations in the twenty-first century. For example, forty of the fifty countries at the bottom of the United Nations Human Development index, with the worst rates of life expectancy, literacy, and economic development overall, are former colonies. Approximately 85% of the fifty-seven nations with per capita gross national income (GNI) below $4,500 are former colonies that didn't gain independence until after WWII.[36] (In fact, only a very few former colonies are wealthy states with high human development today, including the United States, Canada, Australia, and New Zealand.)

Correlation does not necessarily equal causation. Each country's specific history would need to be fully researched to identify its multiple causes of poverty and wealth. However, some basic facts about and economic outcomes of the colonial and neocolonial periods can be identified.

It is clear that colonialism weakened the indigenous economies of the conquered nations, often resulting in the inability of these peoples to provide for their own material needs. Country after country was relegated to providing raw materials to the European manufacturing core. Instead of being produced locally, everyday products consumed in the colonies were now produced in the industrialized core countries.

Indigenous landholdings and agricultural practices were either distorted or obliterated, helping create a situation of dependency. Agriculture, mining, transportation, and communication in the colonies were dependent on modern machinery and technology only available in the industrialized countries. To obtain these inputs the less-developed countries often had to export increasing amounts of raw materials and/or borrow heavily from international banks and lending institutions. Such actions deepened the reliance of these nations on the developed northern states. (In addition to the impact on indigenous peoples, colonialism and modern economic globalization has also disproportionately affected women, as discussed in Theory Spotlight: Feminist International Political Economy.)

The distortion of the global economy by colonialism and neocolonialism continues to plague the world today. Unsurprisingly, the global free market continues to benefit developed nations while less-developed states have difficulty advancing. Free markets have always gravitated towards those with wealth and worked against those with competitive disadvantages. Because of these conditions, structuralists argue that there is a legitimate need for state intervention to rectify existing structural inequalities.

THEORY SPOTLIGHT

Feminist International Political Economy

Women are too often the first to experience the negative effects of economic globalization. For example, the overwhelming majority of workers in export-processing zones (EPZs), set up around the world to promote a manufacturing and industrial export economy, are women. According to the International Labor Organization (ILO), these zones are "industrial zones with special incentives set up to attract foreign investors, in which imported materials undergo some degree of processing before being exported again." To attract foreign companies, governments often lower labor, health, and environmental regulations, so working conditions in these zones often do not meet ILO standards. By 2014 there were EPZs in at least 130 countries employing over 66 million people.[37]

Women dominate the garment and electronics sectors, in some cases making up 70–90% of the workforce. According to the ILO, employers prefer female employees in the EPZs because "they are cheaper in terms of labor costs, show great endurance in the monotonous production work, and are less prone to organize in trade unions."[38] According to the Women's Environment and Development Organization (WEDO): "This feminization of employment, often interpreted as a positive outcome of structural adjustment, is in fact a result of international and local demand for cheap and docile labor that can be used in low-skill, repetitive jobs in unsafe and insecure conditions without minimum guarantees."[39] Women workers in EPZs often face poor transportation services to and from work, inadequate childcare, sexual harassment, and illnesses due to insufficient health services and poor and hazardous working conditions.

Since the 1970s feminist scholars and women's NGOs have worked to highlight the particular impact of economic globalization on women. Modern

Since WWII the less-developed countries have used different strategies to bring about structural reform. In the 1970s the Group of 77 at the United Nations (composed of the seventy-seven poorest countries) proposed a New International Economic Order (NIEO) to replace the liberal economic order and produce a more equitable sharing of the world's wealth and power. The NIEO called for an increased flow of wealth to less-developed countries through the following reforms:

1. International commodity agreements that would stabilize the prices of raw materials and agricultural goods.
2. Trade preferences benefiting products from developing nations.
3. Increased aid with fewer strings attached.

In addition, the NIEO called for technology transfer from MNCs, arguing that technology ought to be part of the common heritage of humankind. Finally, the program asserted the principle of permanent sovereignty over natural resources, which implied the right to nationalize foreign investments, allowing nations to determine for themselves whether compensation was due.

However, as economic globalization continued to expand in the 1980s and 1990s, the NIEO reform measures lost political support. Many developing countries instead

Shafiqul Alam / Alamy Stock Photo

Women working in the garment industry in Bangladesh.

as gender neutral, implying that it is possible to understand the interactions between the market and the state without reference to gender distinctions. Feminists assert, however, that ignoring gender distinctions hides the social and economic inequalities of men and women. According to this view, all three IPE theories have a bias toward male representation and often do not reflect the motivations and needs of women.[40]

development and economic integration have affected women differently than men, causing them to lose access to land and resources and be channeled into the lowest and most exploitative sectors of the new global economy.

Feminists contend that all three central IPE theories—economic liberalism, economic nationalism, and economic structuralism—present themselves

Think about It

1. Are feminists correct in their assertion that the three main IPE theories—economic liberalism, economic nationalism, and economic structuralism—reflect a male perspective and thus ignore gender bias and women's oppression and needs? Explain your answer.

2. How does the social construction of gender manifest itself in economic development planning at the national and global levels?

hoped to emulate the successes of Japan, South Korea, Singapore, and Taiwan through further integration into the global trading system. The NIEO structural reforms were sidelined.

Today many developing countries have put their faith in the UN's program for human development and sustainability for the twenty-first century. Yet the question remains: do the UN proposals really address the underlying structural issues raised by the structuralist perspective?

FROM THE UN'S MILLENNIUM DEVELOPMENT GOALS TO THE SUSTAINABLE DEVELOPMENT GOALS

In the UN's *Millennium Declaration* of September 2000 UN member states declared that they would "spare no effort to free our fellow men, women and children from the abject and dehumanizing conditions of extreme poverty, to which more than a billion of them are currently subjected." To realize this, these states adopted ambitious **Millennium Development Goals (MDGs)**, pledging by 2015 to cut income poverty and hunger in half; achieve universal primary education; eliminate gender disparity in primary and secondary schools; reduce child mortality by two-thirds; reduce maternal mortality by three-quarters; halt and reverse the spread of HIV/AIDS and malaria; halve the proportion of people without consistent access to safe drinking water; integrate principles of sustainable development; and open up a new global partnership for development that would include debt relief and increased aid. On September 25, 2008, world leaders again came together in New York to renew their commitments to achieve these MDGs by 2015.[41]

In addition, the UN launched the Millennium Project, a large network of policymakers, practitioners, and experts led by Professor Jeffrey Sachs of Columbia University, to monitor and promote these goals. A Millennium Campaign was initiated to mobilize civil society, and efforts were made to produce national MDG reports in developing countries. Every major development agency and international organization focused on the MDGs, as did the developed nations with a renewed commitment to increase aid to and lower the debt of developing nations.

By 2015 the MDG campaign had met many of its goals and was considered by many to be an enormous success. UN Secretary-General Ban Ki-moon stated: "The global mobilization behind the Millennium Development Goals has produced the most successful anti-poverty movement in history." Ban Ki-moon continued:

> The MDGs helped to lift more than one billion people out of extreme poverty, to make inroads against hunger, to enable more girls to attend school than ever before and to protect our planet. They generated new and innovative partnerships, galvanized public opinion and showed the immense value of setting ambitious goals. By putting people and their immediate needs at the forefront, the MDGs reshaped decision-making in developed and developing countries alike.[42]

The final progress report on the MDGs, *United Nations Millennium Development Report 2015,* highlighted the successes in the campaign, including the following:

- Globally, the number of people living in extreme poverty declined by more than half, with the most progress occurring since 2000.
- The proportion of undernourished people in the developing regions fell by almost half since 1990, from 23.3% in 1990–1992 to 12.9% in 2014–2016.
- The net primary school enrollment rate in the developing regions reached 91% in 2015, up from 83% in 2000.
- Many more girls are now in school compared to fifteen years ago. The developing regions as a whole have achieved the target to eliminate gender disparity in primary, secondary, and tertiary education.
- The global under-five mortality rate declined by more than half, dropping from 90 to 43 deaths per 1,000 live births between 1990 and 2015.

- The maternal mortality rate declined by 45% worldwide since 1990; most of the reduction occurred since 2000.[43]

This MDG record of success is noteworthy. Brazil and Mexico, in particular, have developed innovative poverty alleviation programs (see Policy Spotlight: Eliminating Poverty in Mexico and Brazil).

However, the United Nations report also acknowledged the failures and limitations of the MDG campaign, indicating that development occurred unevenly around the world with millions of the poorest and disadvantaged left behind. Areas of continuing concern include:

- Gender inequality. Women are still more likely to live in poverty than men. In Latin America and the Caribbean the ratio of women to men in poor households increased from 108 women for every 100 men in 1997 to 117 women for every 100 men in 2012, despite declining poverty rates for the whole region.
- Economic inequality. Big gaps exist between the poorest and richest households and between rural and urban areas. In developing regions children from the poorest 20% of households are more than twice as likely to be stunted as those from the wealthiest 20%.
- Environmental concerns. Climate change and environmental degradation undermine progress achieved, and poor people suffer the most. Global emissions of carbon dioxide have increased by over 50% since 1990.
- Conflict. Conflicts remain the biggest threat to human development. By the end of 2014 conflicts had forced almost 60 million people to abandon their homes—the highest level recorded since WWII. If these people were a nation, they would make up the twenty-fourth largest country in the world.
- Poverty. Despite enormous progress, about 800 million people continue to live in extreme poverty and suffer from hunger and a lack of access to basic services.[44]

THE UNITED NATIONS 2030 AGENDA FOR SUSTAINABLE DEVELOPMENT

To address these remaining challenges, the 193 member states of the UN developed a new set of development goals. On Sept 25, 2015, these nations adopted the ambitious 2030 Agenda for Sustainable Development, with seventeen **Sustainable Development Goals (SDGs)** at its center. The SDGs are based on three pillars of sustainable development: economic development, social inclusion, and environmental sustainability. The SDGs differ from the MDGs in two important ways. First, the SDGs are universal and apply to all countries, rich and poor alike. Second, the SDGs are more comprehensive than MDGs and include 169 specific targets. However, this is not a "one-size-fits-all" approach; each nation is to choose its own national targets based

sustainable development goals (SDGs) adopted by the UN in 2015, are based on three pillars of sustainable development: economic development, social inclusion, and environmental sustainability.

POLICY SPOTLIGHT

Eliminating Poverty in Mexico and Brazil

The plight of the poor and vulnerable often seems overwhelming. As previously reviewed, the World Bank reports that around 735.9 million people live below the absolute poverty line of $1.90 a day, one person in nine is hungry, and one person in three is malnourished. These discouraging facts can lead to paralysis and a sense that nothing can be done to alleviate suffering at the global level. The good news is that some policies have proven effective in reducing poverty and extreme inequality.

In 2014 in Mexico, a national conditional cash transfer program titled Prospera (established as Oportunidades in the 1990s) benefited 5.8 million families, representing 25% of the country's total population. Designed to improve the school enrollments and nutrition rates of Mexican children, Prospera provides cash to mothers if their children attend school and receive health care.

The achievements of Prospera in nutrition, education and health have been well documented. According to a World Bank report:

Young male beneficiaries of the program have 0.85 years or nearly ten additional months of schooling, on average, whereas young women participating have 0.65 years or nearly eight additional months

of schooling, on average. Moreover, the program has led to a decline of 11.8 percentage points in the incidence of anemia among children under age of two.[45]

School enrollment rates increased, even among nonparticipating families because of increased social pressure to enroll. In addition, children participating in the health program for two years were 40% less likely to be reported ill and grew about one centimeter taller than children not in the program.[46]

Prospera is based on three basic social rights—health, education, and nutrition. Because of its success, fifty-two countries have replicated the model. Similar programs in Bangladesh, Colombia, Pakistan, Nicaragua, Kenya, Honduras, and Cambodia have been successful. In the Cambodia program, which focused on girls in the lower secondary school system, participating families were awarded a scholarship of $45 per year for three years if their girls stayed in school and maintained passing grades. The impact was remarkable and equalized the probability of enrollment and attendance of girls from both poor and rich families.[47]

Brazil has one of the most successful conditional cash transfer programs to the poor. Entitled Bolsa Família (Family Grant), the program was innovative in both size

on its unique history and circumstances. Countries report to the UN on their progress toward meeting the nationally agreed upon goals and targets. The seventeen SDGs[48] are outlined in Box 8.2.

As a whole, the UN's SDGs are intended to provide a clear, goals-based agenda and push all nations to make a difference. The UN has called on the world's governments to embrace this challenge and develop national plans to achieve all seventeen SDGs by the end of 2030. Such goals are useful for mobilizing both state and non-state actors (such as NGOs). Although the pace of change was too slow, the response to the Millennium Development Goals demonstrated that the international community can make

VANDERLEI ALMEIDA / AFP / Getty Images

Bolsa Família: Fighting poverty in Brazil.

economists have labeled this approach "a pro-market approach to combating poverty." The results have been spectacular: the income of Brazil's poorest, most destitute families doubled; after three years Bolsa Família cut extreme poverty by 15%; thirty-six million people were lifted out of general poverty; and, the income of the poorest 20% of Brazilians rose by 6.2% between 2002 and 2013.[50]

In addition, Bolsa Família children graduate at a rate double that of poor Brazilian children outside the program. Malnutrition rates in Brazil's poorest regions decreased by 16%; vaccination rates rose to 99% of the population; and infant mortality rates dropped by 40%. The program is also credited with empowering Brazilian women by giving them more authority over their families' bank accounts. All of this has made the program very popular in Brazil and abroad. At least sixty-three countries have sent experts to Brazil to learn from its model.[51]

and scope. All families living in extreme poverty are eligible for payments. Recipients must guarantee the following: all children between six and fifteen years old attend school at least 85% of the time; all children under seven get immunized; and both mothers and children get regular medical checkups. In addition, pregnant women receiving the cash transfer must get prenatal care and commit to breast-feeding their infants.[49]

Bolsa Família remains very inexpensive compared to other social welfare programs. In 2016 it cost Brazilian taxpayers less than 0.5% of the country's $2.2 trillion GDP and benefitted all Brazilians, not just the poor. As former Brazilian President Lula da Silva explained, "When millions can go to the supermarket to buy milk, to buy bread, the economy will work better. The miserable will become consumers." Some

Think about It

1. Why did Prospera and Bolsa Família succeed? What elements of these poverty alleviation programs could be applied in other countries?

2. How do these conditional cash transfer programs differ from traditional welfare-state policies? Do these approaches represent a "pro-market" approach to combatting poverty and inequality?

progress when united behind specific goals, such as major reductions in child mortality and maternal mortality. The UN plans to build on these successes in order to achieve the SDGs by 2030.

Critics maintain that the SDG approach is problematic because it remains within an orthodox economic liberal framework. While its intentions are admirable, the program does not address the relationship between liberal economic development and the maldistribution of wealth or the link between economic and political power and the perpetuation of class divisions, exploitation, and poverty. For example, the specifics of SDG 8 set a target economic growth rate of 7% for all nations, including the developing countries,

Box 8.2 / The United Nations Sustainable Development Goals

SDG 1: End poverty in all its forms everywhere.

SDG 2: End hunger, achieve food security and improved nutrition, and promote sustainable agriculture.

SDG 3: Ensure healthy lives and promote well-being for all at all ages.

SDG 4: Ensure inclusive and equitable quality education and promote lifelong learning opportunities for all.

SDG 5: Achieve gender equality and empower all women and girls.

SDG 6: Ensure availability and sustainable management of water and sanitation for all.

SDG 7: Ensure access to affordable, reliable, sustainable modern energy for all.

SDG 8: Promote sustained, inclusive, and sustainable economic growth, full and productive employment and decent work for all.

SDG 9: Build resilient infrastructure, promote inclusive and sustainable industrialization, and foster innovation.

SDG 10: Reduce inequality within and among countries.

SDG 11: Make cities and human settlements inclusive, safe, resilient, and sustainable.

SDG 12: Ensure sustainable consumption and production patterns.

SDG 13: Take urgent action to combat climate change and its impacts.

Randy Duchaine / Alamy Stock Photo

UN Sustainable Development Goals.

SDG 14: Conserve and sustainably use the oceans, seas, and marine resources for sustainable development.

SDG 15: Protect, restore, and promote sustainable use of terrestrial ecosystems, sustainably manage forests, combat desertification, and halt and reverse land degradation and halt biodiversity loss.

SDG 16: Promote peaceful and inclusive societies for sustainable development, provide access to justice for all, and build effective, accountable, and inclusive institutions at all levels.

SDG 17: Strengthen the means of implementation and revitalize the Global Partnership for Sustainable Development.

which is to be realized through international financial and trade institutions such as the IMF and the WTO. Structuralists maintain that the current liberal model of economic globalization sustains global poverty and inequality, so it is a highly unlikely means to an end for developing nations. The global market of free trade and investment may create needed economic growth, but it has proven unable to tackle the deeper issues of wealth redistribution and the protection of global public goods. From a radical perspective, the SDG framework lacks adequate focus on the ways in which globalization perpetuates inequality and adversely effects vulnerable segments in societies around the world.

In sum, advocates can point to evidence to support the MDG/SDG approach, while critics can point to counterevidence demonstrating its ineffectiveness. Perhaps this is a good time to quote F. Scott Fitzgerald: "The test of a first-rate intelligence is the ability to hold two opposed ideas in mind at the same time and still retain the ability to function."

Opinions on the NAFTA agreement in our contemporary world also remain divided, with critics and supporters marshaling competing evidence to support their views.

CONTEMPORARY PERSPECTIVE:
NAFTA 2019

Today the NAFTA agreement links 450 million people, and the economies of Mexico, Canada, and the United States generate around $20.8 trillion in gross domestic product. Despite this record growth, the NAFTA accord remains controversial. During his campaign for President in 2016 Donald Trump declared NAFTA to be "the worst trade deal ever signed anywhere" and pledged to either rewrite the agreement or scrap it altogether. In addition, he blamed NAFTA for the loss of US manufacturing jobs and a trade deficit. His promise: "A Trump administration will renegotiate NAFTA and if we don't get the deal we want, we will terminate NAFTA and get a much better deal for our workers and our companies. 100 percent."[52]

Although it has now been in place for close to twenty-five years, opinions about NAFTA remain divided. The agreement has produced both advantages and disadvantages for Canada, Mexico, and the United States. On the positive side, trade among the three countries has quadrupled, reaching $1.1 trillion in 2016. Economists estimate

Martin Mejia / AP Images

President Donald Trump, center, sits between Canada's Prime Minister Justin Trudeau, right, and Mexico's President Enrique Peña Nieto after they signed a new US-Mexico-Canada agreement that could replace the NAFTA Trade Deal (November 30, 2018).

that NAFTA boosted US economic output by as much as 0.05% each year, representing several billion dollars of added growth. NAFTA supporters also point to the approximately fourteen million American jobs that rely on trade with Canada and Mexico, as well as the nearly two hundred thousand export-related jobs created annually, which pay 10% to 15% more on average than the jobs that were lost. In addition, US foreign direct investment (FDI) in Mexico increased from $15 billion in 1993 to over $100 billion in 2016.[53]

Yet critics of NAFTA, including the Trump administration, can point to another set of statistics. US wage stagnation, job loss, and a trade deficit have occurred due to companies moving to Mexico to take advantage of lower wages. According to the Office of the United States Trade Representative (USTR), between 1994 and 2016 the US bilateral goods trade balance with Mexico went from a $1.3 billion surplus to a $64 billion deficit.[54] Although some of this surge in imports would have happened without NAFTA, some economists argue that it caused a loss of up to 600,000 US jobs over those two decades. The US auto sector was particularly hard hit; the loss of 350,000 jobs since 1994 represents one-third of the industry.[55]

The deficit claim is based on trade in goods, but trade balances are generally measured in both goods and services. The USTR acknowledges that, rather than a trade deficit with Canada, the overall trade balance in goods and services in 2017 gave the United States a substantial trade surplus of $8.4 billion. Supporters of NAFTA argue that the Canadian and American economies both benefit from this relationship. Because of Canadians' substantial purchases of American products, nearly nine million jobs in the United States are dependent on trade with Canada. Despite negative impacts on sectors such as the auto industry, the increased trade from NAFTA is beneficial to the US economy overall. Some jobs were lost, but others were created. Consumers in both countries benefit from the falling prices and improved quality created by competition with imports.[56]

NAFTA's impact on Mexico is also contentious. Supporters point to the hundreds of thousands of manufacturing jobs created in the auto industry, and studies found a positive correlation between NAFTA and Mexican productivity and consumer prices. Yet the pact did not bring rapid economic growth to Mexico. Its economy grew only 1.3% each year between 1993 and 2013, and the level of poverty remained unchanged. In addition, so-called "wage convergence" between the two countries didn't happen. Mexican agriculture couldn't compete with heavily subsidized US farms. Economist Mark Weisbrot estimates that NAFTA put almost two million small-scale Mexican farmers out of work, contributing to illegal migration to the United States.[57]

On November 30, 2018, President Trump, President Enrique Peña Nieto of Mexico, and Prime Minister Justin Trudeau of Canada signed a new trade agreement among the three economies. Trump described it as a "modernized NAFTA" and relabeled it the United States-Mexico-Canada Agreement (USMCA). Many analysts saw the new agreement as less than transformative and instead as simply a rewriting of some of the rules governing commerce among the countries. For example, the deal updates riders on the digital economy, agriculture, and labor unions. In addition, more cars will be manufactured in North America where wages must average $16 an hour to be exempted from tariffs. The future of the USMCA is now in the hands of the US Congress, which will approve or reject the measure.[58] However, Trump announced that no matter what action Congress takes, he intends to quickly terminate and withdraw the United States from the original NAFTA.[59]

LOOKING TO THE FUTURE:
Controlling Speculative Capital and Excessive Military Spending

A nation's ability to determine economic policy and provide public goods for its citizens is often hindered by speculative capital movements from abroad and enormous military budgets from within. This has prompted national and global attempts to regulate the movement of speculative capital around the world and increased attention to the economic impact of excessive military spending. Both of these areas will continue to have a significant impact on the world economy of the future.

Controlling Speculative Capital

Capitalism is built on capital. Enterprises must gain access to investments in order to grow. All investments are speculative to a degree because of market fluctuations and changing consumer preferences. When investments are linked to real jobs and businesses, a banker or investor can calculate the actual risk and invest accordingly, anticipating significant rewards to investors, business owners, employees, and the community overall.

However, when an investment is solely speculative, that is, when it is far removed from the actual assets of the company, the economic damage can be severe. For example, complex financial transactions known as *derivatives* gamble on the value of underlying assets including stocks, bonds, commodities, currencies, and interest rates. Investors basically place very short-term bets on the success or failure of a business, economic sector, or national currency. Focused on fast returns, these investments have little to do with building businesses and jobs and are incredibly risky. This type of speculative capital investment contributed to both the stock market crash of 1929 and the 2008 financial crisis.

To stabilize global finance and investment, James Tobin, winner of the Nobel Prize for Economics in 1981, first suggested a small tax on the international movement of speculative capital. In his Janeway Lectures at Princeton in 1972 Tobin viewed this tax as a way to enhance the efficacy of macroeconomic policy. Tobin estimated that 80% of foreign exchange transactions involve "round trips of seven days or less" and that most occur within a single day.[60] Tobin went on to explain:

> Speculators invest their money in foreign exchange on a very short-term basis. If this money is suddenly withdrawn, countries have to drastically increase interest rates for their currency to still be attractive. But high interest is often disastrous for a national economy.[61]

Developing countries are particularly vulnerable to the harmful economic impact of short-term speculation by global investors. Successful economic planning and policy is dependent upon the stability created by long-term capital investments. On the other hand, a rapid withdrawal of capital, often called capital flight, can cripple national economic policy and growth and contribute to human suffering. A very small tax of 0.05% or 0.10% would force investors to focus on the long-run, rather than short-run expectations and risks, serving as a strong disincentive for irresponsible speculative capital investments.

Tobin's idea has gained political momentum over the last decade, with supporters from the left to the right. According to 2015 estimates by the nonpartisan Tax Policy Center, an "itty-bitty" transaction tax of 0.01% would raise $185 billion over ten years. This is enough money to restore college assistance funding for low-income students and expand pre-kindergarten programs in the United States.[62] In addition, according to Jared Bernstein, a senior fellow at the Center on Budget and Policy Priorities,

> a financial transaction tax could significantly reduce the amount of high-frequency trading. This trading, most of it automated, is used to make windfall profits through arbitrage (taking advantage of small differences in price) in milliseconds. It does nothing to help ordinary investors and can destabilize financial markets.[63]

A transaction tax would be most effective if adopted globally, and that may actually be happening. Eleven countries in the European Union have agreed to implement such a tax, and Britain, Hong Kong, and Singapore have implemented a variety of transaction taxes that affect high-volume traders rather than long-term investors, helping to solidify financial markets.

Back in the 1960s the Organization of Economic Cooperation and Development (OECD) made a distinction between speculative money and long-term investments, encouraging the enactment of policies that discouraged and punished short-term cross-border speculation.[64] Looking to the future, a key issue is whether international organizations will implement such regulatory policies. Will the world's nations enact a small tax on speculative capital investments in order to stabilize the global financial system?

Reducing Excessive Military Spending

Critics of excessive military spending point to two trade-offs, often characterized as "guns versus butter" and "guns versus investment." According to the "guns versus butter" argument, high military spending is harmful when it is financed by reducing public expenditures on health, education, food stamps, Medicare, and other such programs. The consequences of dramatic reductions in vital social services can be devastating to millions and harmful to the economy overall. As President Dwight Eisenhower famously stated:

> Every gun that is made, every warship launched, every rocket fired signifies, in the final sense, a theft from those who hunger and are not fed, those who are cold and are not clothed....The cost of one heavy bomber is this: a modern brick school in more than 30 cities. It is two electric power plants, each serving a town of 60,000 population. It is two fine fully equipped hospitals. It is some 50 miles of concrete pavement.[65]

The "guns versus investment" argument focuses on the negative consequences of financing military spending through debt and borrowing. Military spending financed through an increase in the budget deficit (borrowing) can lead to an increase in interest rates, which discourages private investment. An alternate approach, printing new money to finance military spending, can create inflationary pressures in the economy, which reduces incentives to invest or save.[66]

The US military budget for 2019 rose to approximately $716 billion, spending more on defense than the next seven countries combined. Economists estimate that US defense spending accounts for approximately 15% of all federal spending and half of all discretionary spending.

Although some of the poorest countries in the world spend more on the military than on education and health today, according to UN calculations, the chances of dying from social neglect (malnutrition and preventable diseases) in developing countries were around thirty-three times greater than the chances of dying in a war. The human cost of excessive military spending in developing countries is enormous. Just 12% of military spending in developing countries could provide funds for primary health care for all, including immunization of all children, elimination of severe malnutrition, reduction of moderate malnutrition by half, and provision of safe drinking water for all. Four percent could reduce adult illiteracy by half by providing universal primary education and educating women to the same level as men. Eight percent could provide basic family planning to all and stabilize the world population.[67]

On the other hand, military spending can generate jobs and income, and military research and development can potentially create positive spin-offs to society overall. In developing countries, the military can also provide critical vocational and technical training that creates skilled workers who can boost the economy.

Looking to the future, a key issue is whether the global community will develop effective mechanisms of "positive peace" like those described in Chapter 7 to allow nations to reduce excessive military spending without fear of jeopardizing their national security.

Summary

- The 1994 NAFTA agreement produced clear benefits and losses for Canada, Mexico, and the United States.
- Economic globalization has brought significant progress in human development; however, inequality, environmental damage, poverty and hunger remain central features of the global economy.
- Economic liberalism, based on efficiency, operates globally through the principle of comparative advantage and promotes free trade and investments across borders to maximize world production.
- Economic nationalism, based on autonomy, focuses on protecting the economic power of the state and views global economic interdependence as potentially threatening to national wealth and national autonomy.
- Economic structuralism, based on equity, argues that class exploitation and inequality are defining features of modern economic globalization.
- The UN's 2030 Agenda for Sustainable Development outlines an ambitious program of seventeen goals applied to all countries, rich and poor alike.
- After twenty-five years NAFTA remains controversial, with efforts to revise and/or eliminate this trade agreement.
- In the future, efforts to control the movement of speculative capital abroad and limit excessive military spending will have a significant impact on the world economy.

Key Terms

Colonialism (246)
Comparative advantage (240)
Developing countries (237)
Economic globalization (231)
Economic liberalism (239)
Economic nationalism (243)
Economic structuralism (245)

International political economy (IPE) (238)
Millennium Development Goals (MDGs) (252)
Nontariff barriers to trade (237)
North American Free Trade Agreement (NAFTA) (233)
Purchasing power parity (PPP) (236)
Sustainable development goals (SDGs) (253)

Critical Thinking Questions

1. Why was the 1994 NAFTA agreement controversial in both Mexico and the United States? How are these controversies related to the "logic of the market" and the "logic of the state"?

2. What is the definition of international political economy?

3. What are the fundamental principles of economic liberalism? Economic nationalism? Economic structuralism?

4. Do comparative advantage and economic liberalism benefit all countries equally or only those states with key

factor endowments? Explain your answer.

5. What is the economic logic for protecting key strategic sectors and infant industries from foreign competition?

6. How does a poor less-developed country compete in an unequal world? What economic strategy for development might best serve its interests?

7. In what ways were MDGs successful? Where did they fail?

8. Is the UN's ambitious 2030 Agenda for Sustainable Development a workable program? Do you think that the SDGs will be achieved by 2030? Explain your answers.

9. After over twenty-five years in operation, do the benefits of NAFTA on balance outweigh the agreement's problems and deficits or vice versa? Explain your answer.

10. How would a small transaction tax on the movement of speculative capital abroad potentially benefit the economies of the developing nations?

11. Is it possible to create a UN-coordinated program to facilitate global arms reductions to rein in excessive military spending in rich and poor countries alike? Why or why not?

Practice and Review Online
http://textbooks.rowman.com/hastedt-felice

▲ Eleanor Roosevelt holding the Universal Declaration of Human Rights, 1948. *Source:* National Archives Identifier 6120927

09

HUMAN RIGHTS CHALLENGES: PROTECTING HUMAN DIGNITY

Where, after all, do universal human rights begin? In small places, close to home—so close and so small they cannot be seen on any maps of the world. Yet they *are* the world of the individual persons; the neighborhood... the school or college...the factory, farm or office.... Such are the places where every man, woman and child seeks equal justice, equal opportunity, equal dignity without discrimination. Unless these rights have meaning there, they have little meaning anywhere. Without concerned citizen action to uphold them close to home, we shall look in vain for progress in the larger world.[1]

Eleanor Roosevelt, 1958

US PRESIDENT FRANKLIN DELANO ROOSEVELT (FDR) and First Lady Eleanor Roosevelt were instrumental in creating the vision of human rights adopted by the nations of the world following WWII. In 1941 FDR dictated his famous declaration for "a world founded upon four essential human freedoms": freedom of speech and expression; freedom of religion; freedom from want; and freedom from fear. FDR called for a "new moral order" based on the "supremacy of human rights everywhere." FDR's vision became the moral cornerstone of the United Nations. The Preamble to its **Universal Declaration of Human Rights (UDHR)** states: "[T]he advent of a world in which human beings shall enjoy freedom of speech and belief and freedom from fear and want has been proclaimed as the highest aspiration of the common people."

After her husband's death Eleanor Roosevelt served as the US Representative to the United Nations in the late 1940s, the chair of the first UN Human Rights Commission, and a key player in the drafting of the UDHR in the face of deep ideological, religious and philosophical divisions in the US and around the world. To a large degree the UDHR, eventually adopted by the UN, was a result of her personal diplomacy, hard work, and vision.

Today human rights are essential to modern diplomacy and represent a worldwide vision of human dignity for all regardless of sex, race, nationality, or economic class. This chapter outlines the long struggle to create an effective international human rights system. The chapter begins with an historical overview of the Nuremberg War Crimes Tribunal (1945–1946), a key event in the development of new human rights categories in international law. Next is a discussion of the global roots of human rights and clarification of how they are defined. The evolution from the Westphalian system based on absolute state sovereignty to the current UN Human Rights system is explored, along with an analysis of the latter's strengths and weaknesses. The chapter then turns to the efforts of the International Criminal Court (ICC) to further the cause of international justice. The chapter concludes with a look into the future by probing critical human rights issues facing two leading, powerful states in the world today, the United States and China.

LEARNING OBJECTIVES

Students will be able to:

- Explain the historical importance of the Nuremberg War Crimes Tribunal to human rights norm creation.

- Understand the global roots of human rights.

- Identify the evolution of international human rights from the Westphalian state system to the norms, institutions, and enforcement included in the UN human rights system.

- Evaluate the work of the International Criminal Court from 1998 to 2019.

- Assess the future role the United States and China will uphold in the UN human rights system.

HISTORICAL PERSPECTIVE:
The Nuremberg War Crimes Tribunal, 1945–1946

On November 20, 1945, an international tribunal was charged with trying the highest-ranking survivors of Hitler's Third Reich. The Nuremberg War Crimes Tribunal was tasked with enshrining the principle of "justice before vengeance" and offering legal norms as a deterrent to war. US Justice Robert H. Jackson's opening statement addressed the justifications for these legal norms, including treatment of aggressive war as a crime, the personal liability of government officials, the inapplicability of a defense of superior orders, and the purpose of indicting the principal Nazi agencies and the General Staff–High Command as a criminal organization. Jackson's eloquent and moving statement concluded:

Holocaust survivors liberated from a Nazi concentration camp at the end of WWII.

> The real complaining party at your bar is Civilization.... [I]t points to the dreadful sequence of aggressions and crimes I have recited, it points to the weariness of flesh, the exhaustion of resources, and the destruction of all that was beautiful or useful in this world, and to greater potentialities in the days to come.
>
> ...
>
> Civilization asks whether law is so laggard as to be utterly helpless to deal with crimes of this magnitude by criminals of this order or importance. It does not expect that you [the Tribunal] can make war impossible. It does expect that your juridical action will put the forms of international law, its precepts, its prohibitions and, most of all, its sanctions, on the side of peace, so that men and women of good will, in all countries, may have "leave to live by no man's leave, underneath the law."[2]

The idea of trying defeated leaders for launching an aggressive war and extending international criminal law to include domestic atrocities against religious and racial groups, which had both been raised unsuccessfully at Versailles following WWI, resurfaced after WWII and formed the core principles of the Nuremberg War Crimes Tribunal. The initiative hoped to establish penalties not only for war crimes but also for the act of war itself, except in self-defense.

The United States, Great Britain, and the USSR jointly declared the legal principles that would guide the Nuremberg Tribunal. The major war criminals of the European Axis countries were to be held individually responsible for crimes against peace, war crimes, and crimes against humanity:

a. Crimes against peace: planning, preparation, initiation or waging of a war of aggression, or a war in violation of international treaties, agreements or assurances, or participation in a Common Plan or Conspiracy for the accomplishment of any of the foregoing;

b. War crimes: violations of the laws or customs of war. Such violations shall include, but not be limited to, murder, ill-treatment or deportation to slave labor or for any other purpose of civilian population of or in occupied territory, murder or ill-treatment of prisoners of war or persons on the seas, killing of hostages, plunder of public or private property, wanton destruction of cities, towns, or villages, or devastation not justified by military necessity;

c. Crimes against humanity: murder, extermination, enslavement, deportation, and other inhumane acts committed against any civilian population, before or during the war, or persecutions on political, racial, or religious grounds in execution of or in connection with any crime within the jurisdiction of the Tribunal, whether or not in violation of domestic law of the country where perpetrated.[3]

The full horror of the acts committed by Hitler, Goebbels, Himmler, Goering, Hess, Kaltenbrunner, Ribbentrop, Speer, and their Nazi co-conspirators was revealed during the Tribunal, establishing a historical record now impossible for anyone to honestly deny. The German invasions of Poland, Denmark, Norway, Luxembourg, the Netherlands, Belgium, Yugoslavia, Greece, and France were clearly aggressive wars, making them crimes against peace. The German war crimes were hideous and many; they included elimination of intellectuals, landowners, and clergy from the leadership of invaded countries, the barest of living conditions for their people, and the roundup and resettlement of Jews in ghettos and camps.

Germany's most heinous actions involved its crimes against humanity, a new category introduced at the Nuremberg proceedings by Hersch Lauterpacht, considered to be one of the finest legal minds of the twentieth century and a founder of the modern human rights movement. The "final solution to the Jewish problem," later called the **Holocaust**, involved the mass extermination of Jews from all occupied countries at Auschwitz, Treblinka, and other death camps. In the end, six million Jews and five million socialists, communists, homosexuals, and others were murdered by the Nazis. Hermann Friedrich Graebe submitted testimony as evidence of these atrocities on January 2, 1946:

> Armed Ukrainian militia drove the people off the trucks under the supervision of an SS man.... All these people had the regulation yellow patches on the front and back of their clothes, and thus could be recognized as Jews.... Now I heard rifle shots in quick succession, from behind one of the earth mounds.... Without screaming or weeping these people undressed, stood around in family groups, kissed each other, said farewells, and waited for a sign from another SS man, who stood near the pit, also with a whip in his hands.... I walked around the mound, and found myself confronted by a tremendous grave. People were closely wedged together and lying on top of each other so that only their heads were visible...the pit was already 2/3 full. I estimated that it already contained 1,000 people.[4]

Holocaust The planned genocide of approximately six million European Jews by Nazi Germany and its collaborators between 1941 and 1945.

The central idea at Nuremberg was to hold individuals, including state leaders, generals, soldiers, business executives, and others, responsible for their participation in aggressive wars and for violating the laws and customs of war and international law. No one could plead not guilty by saying they were merely following orders.

The Nuremberg Tribunal ended in October 1946 with the following verdicts: twelve death sentences, three life imprisonments, four prison terms ranging from ten to twenty years, and three acquittals. Hitler, Goebbels, and Himmler had already committed suicide and Goering avoided his death sentence by swallowing cyanide.

Crimes against humanity represented a new category of crimes under international law to address atrocities against civilians. It is significant that leaders were to be held accountable for acts occurring both *before* and *during* the war. Up until this time, the laws of war only included the protection of civilians during a war. The inclusion of acts committed before the war was in essence a declaration of the existence of fundamental human rights. The Nuremberg Tribunal declared that no leader could hide behind sovereignty and commit inhumane acts against their civilian populations on religious, ethnic, or political grounds.

Following the Nuremberg Tribunal, thousands of individuals throughout Europe were convicted of war crimes. The norms developed at Nuremberg—crimes against peace, war crimes, crimes against humanity—have now been incorporated into the legal systems of modern states around the world. These norms and the UN's *Universal Declaration of Human Rights* form the two pillars of the modern conception of human rights.

At the end of the twentieth century these norms informed the work of international tribunals on former Yugoslavia and Rwanda and in 1998 led to the creation of the International Criminal Court (ICC), which will be described in the Contemporary Perspective section later in the chapter.

THE GLOBAL ROOTS OF HUMAN RIGHTS

Even before humanity was divided into separate nation-states, and well in advance of human rights being drafted into international law, through both religious and secular endeavors individuals and groups strove to create a world that protected individuals from abuse, helped the needy, protected freedom, enhanced dignity, and prevented suffering.

For example, scholar Paul Gordon Lauren documents how "all of the great religious traditions share a universal dissatisfaction with the world as it *is* and a determination to make it *as it ought to be*. They do this by addressing the value and the dignity of human life, and, consequently, the duties toward those who suffer."[5] The modern understanding of human rights evolved in part from faith-based attempts to define individual duties and obligations to one another. In other words, these religious traditions tried to articulate the ways in which we are our "brothers' and sisters' keeper."

Early notions of human rights are found in all major world religions. For example, the Ten Commandments of the Hebrew Bible, embraced by both Judaism and Christianity, stress the importance of protecting contracts and the right to property with the injunctions, "you shall not steal" and "you shall not covet ... anything that belongs to your neighbor" (Exodus 20:15–17). In addition, individual actions should not come at the expense of the poor: "[W]hen you knock down the fruit of your olive tree, you shall not go over the branches a second time: it shall be for the stranger, for the fatherless and for the widow" (Deuteronomy 24:20). Christianity upholds the importance of basic equality in human dignity and condemns greed in the New Testament with Jesus' famous statement that "it is easier for a camel to pass through the eye of a needle, than for a rich man to enter the kingdom of God" (Mark 10:25). Papal encyclicals in the Catholic Church have consistently promoted equal human dignity and rights to subsistence for all. The Quran recognizes basic economic and social rights, including protection against poverty (Surah 107:1-3 and 17:26-27), rights to a place of residence (Surah 2:85 includes a condemnation of "evicting a party of your people from their homes...although their eviction was forbidden to you."), and rights to sustenance (Surah 17:70). In addition, an integral part of Islamic teaching is the doctrine of social service defined in terms of alleviating suffering and helping the needy.[6]

Believers in Hinduism, the world's oldest religion, are adjured to practice selfless concern for the pain of others, particularly for the hungry, the sick, the homeless, and the unfortunate. Buddhist principles focus on awareness of human suffering (*dukkha*) and emphasize the duty to overcome selfish desires by practicing charity (*dana*), loving-kindness (*metta*), and compassion (*karuna*) toward those in need. A practitioner of Buddhism, which is an outgrowth of Hinduism, the Dalai Lama has stated that the world's problems can only be solved if people show kindness, love, and respect for all and "understand each other's fundamental humanity, respect each others' rights, share each other's problems and sufferings."[7]

In the secular world, over thousands of years, philosophers, leaders, and scholars as diverse as King Hammurabi (1728–1686 BCE), Plato (360 BCE), Thomas Paine (1792), Immanuel Kant (1793), and John Rawls (1971) have emphasized different visions and norms that overlap with modern conceptions of human rights. For example, King Hammurabi established Babylonian laws securing both creditors' and employees' rights and regulated work relationships. The issue of property rights divided Socrates and Aristotle and remain contentious today. In *The Republic* (360 BCE), Socrates warns that property rights could fragment the polity, undermine the common end, and tear "the city in pieces by differing about 'mine' and 'not mine.'" Aristotle, on the other hand, supported property rights, stating, "When everyone has his own separate sphere of interest, there will not be the same ground for quarrels."[8]

Modern conceptions of human rights did not originate exclusively in the West or with any particular economic or political system of governance. Philosophers in the Middle East, Africa, and pre-Columbian civilizations in the Americas all addressed the dignity of the person and the importance of social justice. Writing in the tenth century, the Islamic philosopher Abu Al-Farabi advocated a moral society in which individuals endowed with rights live in charity with their neighbors.[9]

Indian philosopher Amartya Sen asserts that "pluralism, diversity, and basic liberties can be found in the history of many societies." He goes on to document how democratic ideas and public debates on political, social, and cultural matters took place historically in India, China, Japan, Korea, Iran, Turkey, the Arab world, and many parts of Africa.[10]

In many traditional African societies, kings and chiefs ruled to a degree by consent. Accountability and participation were part of their political heritage. In his autobiography Nelson Mandela describes the democratic nature of local meetings in his childhood village:

> Everyone who wanted to speak did so. It was democracy in its purest form. There may have been a hierarchy of importance among the speakers, but everyone was heard, chief and subject, warrior and medicine man, shopkeeper and farmer, landowner and laborer.... The foundation of self-government was that all men were free to voice their opinions and equal in their value as citizens.[11]

Although the roots of human rights are global, Western "natural rights" theorists in the seventeenth century and eighteenth centuries, the "Enlightenment" philosophers, did play pivotal roles in the development of modern conceptions of rights and duties. Leading philosophers, including Hugo Grotius, John Locke, Jean-Jacques Rousseau, and Immanuel Kant, challenged traditional authority and raised questions that resonate today regarding the proper relationship between the state and the people. Human rights language first emerged in this period. In earlier periods those experiencing injustice rarely put their claims in terms of rights. Prior to the Enlightenment the moral order was based in "natural law" associated with duties to one another and to God. Modern secular rights replaced this divinely sanctioned order with new rights claims, the "rights of man," based on individual freedom and liberty.

These ideas included a vision based on liberty, equality, and fraternity and inspired revolutionaries in America and France. Human dignity and human rights served as the backbone of these eighteenth-century revolutions. In 1774 the American colonists enacted their "Bill of Rights," declaring entitlement to "life, liberty, and property" for all men. At the First Continental Congress Thomas Jefferson declared that Americans were a free people "claiming their rights as derived from the laws of nature and not as a gift of the Chief Magistrate,"[12] and expressed this philosophy in the Declaration of Independence on the 4th of July, 1776: "We hold these truths to be self-evident, that all men are created equal, that they are endowed by their Creator with certain unalienable rights, that among these are life, liberty and the pursuit of happiness." It is important to note that these newly declared rights in the United States were for white males only and definitely not for women and slaves.

These ideas also inspired the French Revolution. The National Assembly proclaimed in their Declaration of the Rights of Man and Citizen in 1789 that all men "are born and remain free and equal in rights" which are universal and "natural and imprescriptible" and include "liberty, property, security, and resistance to oppression."[13]

Following this revolutionary period, the task facing America, France, and other nations was to transform these visions and ideas into national laws and workable public policy, demonstrating the power of ideas and the strength of religious and secular visions of human dignity. However, the vision remained at the community and national levels. International recognition and protection of human rights for peoples across national borders had yet to emerge.

Human rights today are commonly understood to embrace key moral principles regarding human behavior that everyone is entitled to simply because she or he is a human being. Individuals can claim certain inalienable entitlements based on these moral principles, such as the right to life, liberty, freedom from slavery and torture, freedom of opinion, the right to work, education, and so on. Human rights have been defined as claims on others to a certain type of treatment fundamentally linked to the prevention and alleviation of suffering.[14] Human rights are considered "a special class of rights, the rights that one has simply because one is a human being ... moral rights of the highest order."[15] Human rights claims arise from a shared moral conception of the nature of the human person and the conditions necessary for a life of dignity. Because such claims are essential to protecting human life and enhancing human dignity, they should receive full social and political approval. Everyone is entitled to these rights regardless of race, sex, nationality, ethnicity, religion, sexuality, or any other status.[16]

Modern human rights are social constructions, that is, ideas that over time have been created and accepted by a society or the global community. Human rights are claims or entitlements that derive from evolved legal and moral rules that are seen as essential to protecting human life, eliminating avoidable suffering, and enhancing human dignity across cultures, political boundaries, and ideological divides. The global community over time has collectively constructed a shared social understanding of the content of these human rights claims. International human rights norms and laws are designed to give individuals and groups effective tools and means of protection from the actions of predatory state and non-state actors, including multinational corporations and individuals. Human rights claims have also been designed to provide relief and protection from *structural violence*, the denial of economic and social rights to the most vulnerable sectors as a by-product of economic globalization. As you learned in Chapter 8, vast impoverization and suffering has accompanied expansive economic globalization. This has led to the emergence of human rights claims to promote economic justice for the poor. Human rights are not written in stone like the Ten Commandments but evolve to address modern sources of human suffering.[17]

Prior to WWII, the international community of nation-states was unwilling to endorse or codify universal human rights. It has been a long journey from Westphalian norms of absolute state sovereignty to the current United Nations human rights system.

human rights
Fundamental entitlements for all human beings designed to prevent and alleviate human suffering; based on moral principles including liberty, equality, and fraternity.

FROM WESTPHALIA TO THE UN HUMAN RIGHTS SYSTEM

As you learned in Chapter 3, the principle of nation-state *sovereignty*, the principle that no authority exists above the state and that states decide what goals to pursue and how to pursue them, arose out of the Treaty of Westphalia in 1648, which ended the Thirty Years War in Central Europe. The Thirty Years War, an international battle between Protestants and Catholics with each side promoting their own beliefs and values, was a bloodbath; around eight million people were killed. To avoid such bloodshed in the future, the nations of Europe agreed that the principle of state sovereignty was central to international relations. Each nation-state was now considered legally equal and sovereign with the power and right to manage its own internal and external affairs, including religious matters, and no state had the right to intervene in another state's sovereign territory. Nonintervention, the legal equality of states, and state sovereignty became the three principles undergirding the international system.

The Westphalian State System

In the **Westphalian state system**, each state would judge for itself what rights its citizens would enjoy. Because there were no international norms or global human rights for nations and peoples to follow, human rights were not a part of traditional international diplomacy. Individuals had no standing in international law, which only provided tools to govern relations between equal sovereign states. National leaders and global institutions did not concern themselves with the rights of individuals or groups in other states. Even if a government exploited, tortured, and abused its citizens, the international community was forbidden to intervene. What went on within the domestic jurisdiction of a state was not a subject of international regulation. In fact, state action in support of oppressed individuals in a foreign state was viewed as a violation under this system.

While this approach may seem cold-hearted, it is important to recognize the ethics underlying the principle of **nonintervention**. The leaders of Europe asserted the importance of separating diplomacy from morality, citing the disastrous outcome of the Thirty Years War as a key historical lesson. A leader might despise the immoral actions of a foreign country against its people, but intervention could create even more suffering and pain. The peaceful coexistence of nations, requiring some toleration of abuses, was seen as the only path forward.

These Westphalian principles were clearly on display at the beginning of the twentieth century. The Turkish government accused the Armenians of aiding the Russian enemy and proceeded with a massive slaughter. Reliable studies place the number of Armenians killed at around one million. This genocide, or "race murder," began in 1915 with the execution of Armenian leaders and intellectuals. The Ottoman armies then rounded up Armenian citizens and forced them to march across deserts and mountains,

Westphalian state system System based on principles of national sovereignty, the legal equality of states, and nonintervention in the domestic affairs of foreign states.

nonintervention The principle that states should not intervene in the affairs of foreign countries; based on the idea of separating morality and ethics from foreign policy.

leading to the starvation, disease, and death of hundreds of thousands more. Because of its massive scale, this genocide became widely known and led to protests around the world. Global citizens argued that the Turkish government could not hide behind sovereignty to avoid accountability for "crimes against humanity," a new term that emerged during this period.[18]

The Armenian community and the Christian community abroad appealed to the American Ambassador to Turkey, Henry Morgenthau, for US action. After receiving firsthand reports and documentation of the genocide, Morgenthau urged his country and the international community to act:

> I earnestly beg the Department to give this matter urgent and exhaustive consideration with a view to reaching a conclusion which may possibly have the effect of checking [Turkey's] Government and certainly provide opportunity for efficient relief which now is not permitted. It is difficult for me to restrain myself from doing something to stop this attempt to exterminate a race, but I realize that I am here as Ambassador and must abide by the principles of noninterference with the internal affairs of another country.[19]

Morgenthau's dilemma captures the ethical limitations of an international system focused solely on protecting state sovereignty. In a time of extremity and obscene violence, it is problematic for nations to continue to cleave to these norms. Instead of preventing a larger conflagration, the nonaction and nonintervention of outside powers validated the despotic behavior. The Turks seemed to get away with their brutality, and the world moved on. On August 22, 1939, Adolf Hitler urged his generals to show no mercy towards women and children when invading Poland, fearing no retribution from the international community. As he said, "who, after all, speaks today of the annihilation of the Armenians?"[20]

The UN Human Rights System

The revelations of the genocide and crimes against humanity committed by the German Nazis, including the murders of six million Jews and five million socialists, communists, homosexuals, and others, shocked people around the world, causing leaders and citizens to fundamentally question the Westphalian state system. In the 1930s Hitler's murders and repression of Jews within the boundaries of Germany was technically not a violation of international law. After Hitler's defeat and the end of WWII, a strong movement emerged to establish some minimum standards of dignity and obligations to the persons inside all sovereign nation-states, developing a new norm—that states do have obligations beyond their borders.

To a certain extent, the events of WWII defied the logic and reversed the conclusions drawn from the experience of the Thirty Years War. Many concluded that the practice of "nonintervention," which in this case meant ignoring Hitler's actions and human rights abuses, contributed to the violence becoming a world war. Intervening across borders was now seen as a possible way to prevent war and protect international peace and security.

Working through the UN, in the late 1940s the international community began work on establishing a global system of human rights. This resulted in the **UN Human Rights System**, which includes three components: (1) norm creation and standard setting, (2) permanent institutions, and (3) compliance procedures.[21] As you will see, the UN has been most successful in creating norms and least effective in ensuring compliance with them.

NORM CREATION

The codification of international human rights law surged after WWII. Beginning with the United Nations (UN) Charter, which included the respect for and promotion of human rights as a key purpose of the organization, the members of the UN drafted a series of core human rights resolutions and treaties. The first UN document to provide a clear list of human rights, the Universal Declaration of Human Rights (UDHR), was adopted nearly unanimously by the UN General Assembly in 1948. The UDHR includes both civil and political rights (e.g., freedom of speech and religion) as well as economic, social, and cultural rights (e.g., rights to work and social security). The members of the UN adopted two additional key treaties in 1966: the International Covenant on Civil and Political Rights (ICCPR) and the International Covenant on Economic, Social and Cultural Rights (ICESCR). The UDHR, ICCPR, and ICESCR are often referred to collectively as the **International Bill of Human Rights**.

The human rights codified in these legal instruments include freedom from racial and equivalent forms of discrimination; the right to life, liberty, and the security of person; freedom from slavery or involuntary servitude; freedom from torture and cruel, inhuman, or degrading treatment or punishment; freedom from arbitrary arrest, detention, or exile; the right to a fair and public trial; freedom from interference in privacy and correspondence; freedom of movement and residence; the right to asylum from persecution; freedom of thought, conscience, and religion; freedom of opinion and expression; freedom of peaceful assembly and association; and the right to participate in government, directly or through free elections.[22]

Human rights law also endorses norms of "equality" through the promotion of economic, social, and cultural rights, including the right to social security; the right to work and protection against unemployment; the right to rest and leisure; the right to a standard of living adequate for the health and well-being of self and family; the right to education; and the right to the protection of scientific, literary, and artistic production.[23]

In response to the phenomenon of global interdependence, a new category of rights has emerged, reflecting the norm of fraternity. Individual states acting alone can no longer satisfy their human rights obligations. The need for international cooperation to solve contemporary problems has led to the establishment of solidarity rights, including the right to peace; the right to a healthy and balanced environment; the right to humanitarian disaster relief; the right to political, economic, social, and cultural self-determination; and the right to participate in and benefit from "the common heritage of mankind" (including earth-space resources). These solidarity rights are often seen as collective human rights because they benefit both individuals and groups.[24]

UN Human Rights System System composed of norms, institutions, and compliance procedures, which establish a framework for the global community to discuss and create policies to protect human dignity around the world.

International Bill of Human Rights Collective name for three core human rights documents: the Universal Declaration of Human Rights, the International Covenant on Civil and Political Rights, and the International Covenant on Economic, Social and Cultural Rights.

Figure 9.1 The UDHR and the Core International Human Rights Conventions.

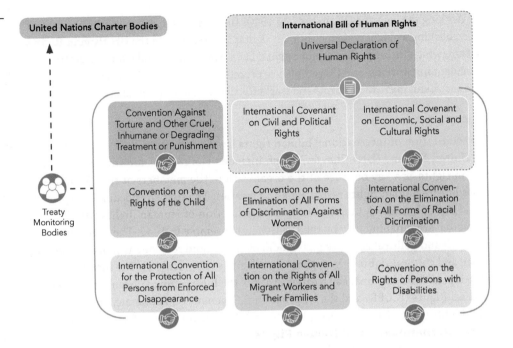

Work on norm creation and standard setting continued through the end of the twentieth century. Today, international human rights law includes legally binding protections for women, racial minorities, migrants, children, and refugees, and prohibitions against apartheid, torture, and genocide (see Figure 9.1). Upon ratification, states are required to incorporate human rights protections into their domestic legal systems.

The United Nations provides an institutional forum for discussion and resolution of internationally affirmed human rights claims. Through UN agencies and councils, states pass resolutions, declarations, charters of rights and duties, and final acts from international conferences on human rights principles and practices. These instruments are often referred to as *soft laws* because they do not involve treaties or customary laws. As discussed in Chapter 5, *soft power*, the power of persuasion using information, culture, values, and ideas to accomplish foreign policy goals, can significantly impact state behavior by creating an environment of strong expectations of conduct that meets the requirements of internationally approved resolutions or declarations. When hard law fails, soft law can articulate new human rights guidelines and establish standards of accountability that governments often find difficult to ignore.

Human Rights Council (HRC) Established in 2006, the leading human rights body at the UN responsible for evaluating and monitoring member states' compliance with universal human rights.

PERMANENT INSTITUTIONS

Figure 9.2 identifies the permanent human rights institutions and mechanisms established by the United Nations. These include UN Charter–based bodies such as the **Human Rights Council (HRC)**, special procedures, and mandates on minority issues, racism, torture, violence against women, and other issues. The UN also has treaty-based

Figure 9.2 UN Human Rights Institutions and Mechanisms.

Structure of the UN Human Rights Bodies and Mechanisms

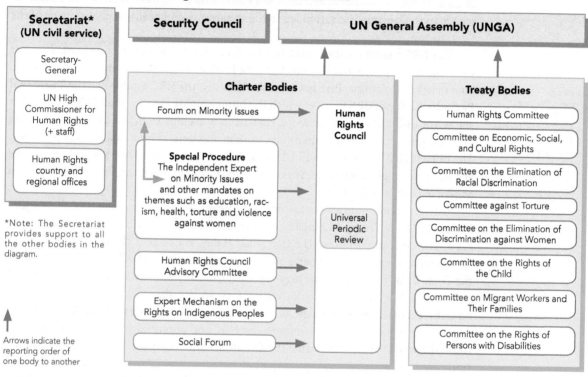

bodies, including the committees established to monitor state compliance with specific human rights treaties. Upon ratification of a human rights treaty, states are under a legal obligation to follow through on their word. Perhaps most importantly, the ratifying state is obligated to incorporate these norms into its domestic legal system. For example, countries that have ratified the Convention on the Rights of the Child are monitored by the Committee on the Rights of the Child to ensure compliance with rules designed to protect and improve the status of children. Through these human rights bodies and mechanisms, the member states of the UN engage in constructive dialogue, pushing one another for full compliance with all human rights obligations.

Established in 2006, the HRC replaced the largely discredited UN Commission on Human Rights. From the date of its founding in 1946 to its end in 2006, the Commission was plagued by member states that used it to advance political agendas. As a result, when serious human rights abuses were taking place in Burundi, South Korea, Argentina, Guatemala, the Sudan, and elsewhere, these regimes were more or less exempt from scrutiny. They were protected by the great powers because of Cold War politics. The Soviets and Americans overlooked the human rights violations of their allies in order to consolidate their positions in the global balance of power. As a result, the actions of some of the most brutal governments of the late twentieth century, such as Pol Pot's reign of terror in Cambodia and Idi Amin's atrocities in Uganda, received only minimal reprimands. Overt politicization led to the irrelevance and eventual abolishment of the Commission.

The HRC has established procedures to limit the politicization of its work. It meets year-round in Geneva and has mechanisms in place to recall any member involved in human rights violations. Perhaps most significantly, the HRC established the **Universal Periodic Review (UPR)**, under which the human rights records of all 193 UN member states are analyzed every four years. No nation is exempt from the UPR, including the great powers. Every UN member must explain and defend its human rights practices. The hope is that this review will allow the HRC to act as the world's moral conscience and bring new legitimacy to human rights work at the UN and to apply global pressure to adhere to human rights law.

Universal Periodic Review (UPR) Examination by the HRC of the human rights records of all member states of the UN.

Unfortunately, politics has recently intervened in the work of the HRC once again. In June 2018 the Trump administration accused the HRC of bias against Israel and withdrew. The US Ambassador to the UN, Nikki Haley, stated that the HRC had become a "protector of human rights abusers and a cesspool of political bias." The decision to leave the Council was part of a US strategy to retreat from any international organizations and agreements that the Trump administration feels are not aligned with American interests on trade, defense, climate change, and human rights. Critics note that the US withdrawal deprives Israel of its chief defender in the HRC and potentially allows US adversaries to fill the void. The decision came the day after harsh criticism of the Trump administration policy of separating migrant parents from their children at the Mexican border. UN High Commissioner Zeid Ra'ad Al Hussein called the US policy "unconscionable" and akin to child abuse.[25]

Office of the High Commissioner for Human Rights (OHCHR) Body that spearheads the UN's human rights efforts by supporting, administering, and monitoring human rights compliance and enforcement mechanisms.

UN Treaty Bodies are serviced by the **Office of the High Commissioner for Human Rights (OHCHR)** in Geneva, Switzerland. The composition, powers and functions of each committee are outlined in the relevant treaty. For example, the Committee on the Elimination of Racial Discrimination (CERD) consists of 18 "experts of high moral standing and acknowledged impartiality elected by States Parties from among their nationals." Members of the Committee are not state representatives but experts in the field of racial discrimination who serve in a personal capacity. Each is elected by secret ballots submitted by the parties to the convention. The hope is that these individuals can be more objective in their assessments of human rights practices than political appointees.

CERD and the other treaty body committees conduct two types of compliance reviews: self-reports, and analysis of human rights data collected from nongovernmental organizations (NGOs) and outside experts. After a public session dedicated to reviewing all of this information, the Committee then issues public Concluding Observations in which they acknowledge good practices, areas of concern, and noncompliance. Although the treaty body committees have no power to issue sanctions, public exposure can make a difference. NGOs and individuals in civil society have used these reports to focus public attention on egregious violations. Governments are concerned about their reputations and seek to be viewed in a positive light. As a result, this constructive dialogue between the treaty body committees and states-parties to the Convention has been surprisingly effective in many cases.

Most treaty body committees have also incorporated individual complaint procedures. After exhausting all domestic remedies, individuals may submit complaints directly to the relevant treaty body. Once admissibility is determined, a special investigator is often appointed to investigate the merits of the case. If a violation has been committed, the Committee will call on the violating state to provide compensation or even change national legislation. Although these judgments are not legally binding, states have responded. For example, many states have released political prisoners, awarded compensation, reinstated individuals in the civil service, and amended legislation that was incompatible with the International Covenant on Civil and Political Rights (ICCPR).[26]

ENFORCEMENT: GLOBAL

The UN institutions and mechanisms focused on human rights are often viewed as weak and ineffective due to the lack of enforcement power. It is one thing to "monitor" state behavior and make "recommendations" for change, and quite another to have the ability to sanction and force abhorrent behavior to cease. UN failures are often well publicized and recognized. From Bosnia and Rwanda in the 1990s to Yemen and Myanmar in 2018, the international community has been unable to either prevent or stop crimes against humanity, including ethnic cleansing and genocide. (See the Regional Spotlight feature on the events in Myanmar.)

Critics also charge that UN human rights reports are too mild. In fact, many states use their participation in UN human rights bodies to present a false image to the world about their human rights practices. For example, Saudi Arabia has used its ratification of the Convention on the Elimination of All Forms of Discrimination Against Women (CEDAW) to publicly proclaim a commitment to the human rights and dignity of Saudi women. Yet at the same time elite male Saudi rulers implement public policies that undermine women's civil, political, economic, and social human rights. Saudi hypocrisy makes a mockery of their CEDAW ratification. As activist Upendra Baxi writes: "The near-universality of ratification of [CEDAW]... betokens no human liberation of women. Rather, it endows the state with the power to tell more Nietzschean lies.... 'State' is the name of the coldest of all cold monsters. Coldly, it tells lies, too; and this lie grows out of its mouth: 'I, the state, am the people.'"[32] UN human rights institutions have no power to force the Saudi government to honor its treaty obligations. The primary tool at the UN's disposal is deterrence through exposure.

Genocide or Ethnic Cleansing in Myanmar? Is There a Difference and Does It Matter?

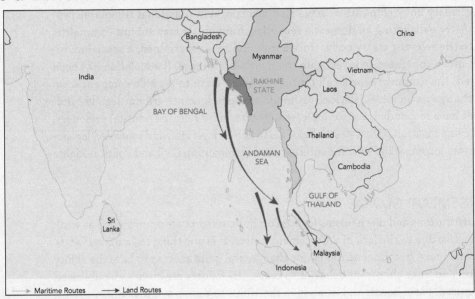

Map 9.1 Hundreds of Thousands of Rohingya Muslims Have Fled the Massive Brutality Occurring in Myanmar by Land and Sea.

In August 2017 hundreds of thousands of Rohingya Muslims began fleeing to southern Bangladesh from a military-led crackdown in Myanmar, also known as Burma. Around 1.1 million Rohingya were living in Myanmar at that time, many in the Rakhine state. More than 680,000 have now fled into Bangladesh by land and by boat. This exodus began on August 25, 2017, when a Rohingya insurgent group killed a dozen members of Myanmar's security forces. The government military responded with massive brutality, which included burning villages, raping women, and murdering anyone who got in the way. Thousands of Rohingya were killed, but the total number remains unknown because of restricted access to the conflict zones.

Human Rights Watch and Amnesty International both described these acts as crimes against humanity and as ethnic cleansing. Human Rights Watch provided the following report:

> Military units, assisted by ethnic Rakhine militias, attacked Rohingya villages and committed massacres, widespread rape, arbitrary detention, and mass arson. Some Rohingya who fled were killed or maimed by landmines laid by soldiers on paths near the Bangladesh-Burma border. Satellite imagery showed that more than 340 primarily Rohingya villages were either substantially or completed destroyed.[27]

Although Rohingya Muslims had long faced severe discrimination from the Buddhist majority in Myanmar, who viewed them as illegal migrants who should be removed, they had never before been confronted with this extreme level of violence.[28]

Protesters against Myanmar's treatment of Rohingya Muslims.

The term *ethnic cleansing* refers to the removal, expulsion, imprisonment, or killing of an ethnic minority by a dominant majority in an attempt to achieve ethnic homogeneity. In July 2018 UN Secretary-General Antonio Guterres wrote: "These victims of what has been rightly called ethnic cleansing are suffering an anguish that can only stir a visitor's heartbreak and anger. Their horrific experiences defy comprehension, yet they are the reality for nearly 1 million Rohingya refugees." According to Guterres, the Rohingya people are left with two dreadful options: stay on in fear of death or leave everything simply to survive.[29]

After spending eight months analyzing the abuses in Myanmar through examination of testimony, UN documents, Myanmar government statements and documents, and other reports, scholars from the International Human Rights Clinic at Yale Law School concluded that this situation meets the criteria for genocide.

In July 2018 the rights advocacy group Fortify Rights also charged Myanmar's military with systematically planning a genocidal campaign to rid the country of Rohingya Muslims, presenting detailed evidence of meticulous planning by security forces, including arming and training ethnic Rakhine Buddhists, destroying fences around Rohingya homes, and cutting off international aid to the Rohingya community.[30]

In testimony to the UN Human Rights Council in March 2018 Yanghee Lee, the UN Special Rapporteur on human rights in Myanmar stated: "I am becoming more convinced that the crimes committed … bear the hallmarks of genocide and call in the strongest terms for accountability." Myanmar denies these charges, claiming that its military only targets terrorists.

Does it make a difference whether to label the actions against the Rohingya as "ethnic cleansing" as opposed to "genocide"? For the victims these distinctions may seem academic and meaningless. However, there is a legal difference. Ethnic cleansing is not recognized as an independent crime in international law, and there is no precise definition of the concept or the acts that qualify. Genocide, on the other hand, is clearly defined as "acts committed with intent to destroy, in whole or in part, a national, ethnical, racial or religious group."[31] The 149 states that have ratified the Genocide Convention are legally obligated to punish offenders. The International Court of Justice has stated that the Genocide Convention embodies principles of customary international law, so all states, whether they have ratified the Genocide Convention or not, are bound to its prohibition under international law. All states thus have a legal obligation to prevent and punish the crime of genocide.

Think about It

1. As you learned in Chapter 4, the member states of the United Nations have adopted the responsibility to protect (R2P), which means that they must protect their populations from genocide, war crimes, ethnic cleansing, and crimes against humanity. When a state fails to protect its population, as in Myanmar, the international community must take decisive and timely action. What actions can the international community take to stop the crimes being conducted against the Rohingya people?

2. How significant is the difference between genocide and ethnic cleansing in relation to events in Myanmar? Does the legal distinction between the terms alter policy options and moral obligations to end the massive human rights violations? Explain your answer.

When constructive dialogue and soft pressure fail, the UN has attempted to force change by bringing economic sanctions against human rights violators. The imposition of substantial economic sanctions forces the target state to either comply with international human rights law or prolong economic hardships on its people. Some sanctions have been successful, including those imposed against the former apartheid regimes in South Africa and Rhodesia (now Zimbabwe). However, sanctions can create unintended consequences in the target society and may hurt children, the poor, and other vulnerable members.

There are few policy options for states and International Organizations (IOs) to pursue when a nation actively ignores diplomatic and economic pressures to correct internal practices and local policies. In fact, UN member states are protected from outside interference by Article 2, Section 7, of the UN Charter, which denies the right of the United Nations to intervene in the internal affairs of sovereign states, creating a difficult challenge for the international community.

Finally, a lack of agreement about priorities exists among member states. It has been difficult for UN members to simply agree on human rights priorities, never mind the path toward fulfilling them. Northern, developed nations primarily prioritize civil and political rights, together with capitalist notions of private property and the free market, and consider economic, social, and cultural rights secondary, as seen by the US refusal so far to ratify the International Covenant on Economic, Social and Cultural Rights (ICESCR). For the poor developing countries these economic, social, and cultural rights are the clear priority, as millions of their citizens lack basic needs, including food, water, education, and health care. To these countries, civil and political rights are only truly meaningful if economic and social rights are also met. In the oft-quoted words of Leopold Senghor, the former president of Senegal: "[H]uman rights begin with breakfast."[33] The right to vote becomes meaningful only if the right to food and water has been protected.

ENFORCEMENT: NATIONAL

As you have already learned, international human rights law is primarily enforced through national legal systems and juridical structures. The state retains primary responsibility for implementing human rights laws. Governments have legal and moral obligations to respect, protect, and fulfill internationally ratified human rights. This three-part approach to human rights implementation, first formulated by scholar Henry Shue[34] in 1980, is widely utilized today in evaluating state human rights practices. Legal experts articulate the obligations to respect, protect, and fulfill economic and social human rights as follows:

> The obligation to respect requires States to refrain from interfering with the enjoyment of economic, social and cultural rights. Thus, the right to housing is violated if the State engages in arbitrary forced evictions. The obligation to protect requires States to prevent violations of such rights by third parties. Thus, the failure to ensure that private

employers comply with basic labor standards may amount to a violation of the right to work or the right to just and favorable conditions of work. The obligation to fulfill requires States to take appropriate legislative, administrative, budgetary, judicial and other measures toward the full realization of such rights. Thus, the failure of States to provide essential primary health care to those in need may amount to a violation.[35]

This three-part approach to the implementation of all human rights forms the basis of the "constructive dialogue" between the UN human rights institutions and the member states. Given the worldwide scope of human rights violations, it is difficult to discern progress, but there have been successes. For example, in 1998 the CERD committee received an individual complaint from Anna Koptova against Slovakia. Koptova, a Slovak citizen of Romany ethnicity, was represented by the independent European Roma Rights Center based in Budapest. In her complaint Koptova asserted that Slovakia engaged in acts of racial discrimination against her and other Roma and failed to protect them from acts or practices of racial discrimination by public authorities and institutions, basing her claim on articles 2–3 of the CERD. Anti-Roma hostility forced Romany families to flee the country, leading to unemployment and homelessness. The CERD committee determined that local municipal ordinances prohibiting Roma from settling in Rokytovce and Nagov were clear violations of the CERD and decided in 2000 in Koptova's favor. The committee recommended that the Slovak government "take the necessary measures to ensure that practices restricting the freedom of movement and residence of Romas under its jurisdiction are fully and promptly eliminated."[36]

Feeling pressure from the CERD as well as a variety of individuals and organizations both domestic and international, Slovakia finally rescinded the discriminatory municipal ordinances and guaranteed freedom of movement for all. The actions of a single woman working with NGOs in civil society to bring her case to Geneva brought international attention to the plight of the Roma in Slovakia. The reputation and international standing of the Slovak government became a topic of debate in the global human rights community, supporting the efforts of other Slovak citizens to bolster their laws on nondiscrimination and freedom of movement. Their work with individuals and groups has allowed the UN to help nations enforce human rights within their borders.

Since the founding of the UN many areas of human rights have improved dramatically. There have been declines in genocide, the number of battle deaths, the number of civilians killed in war, and the use of the death penalty. In addition, there have been dramatic improvements in equality for women, recognition of LGBT rights, and recognition of the rights of people with disabilities. Democracy has grown, as has criminal accountability for individual human rights violations. Overall, both violence and human rights violations in the world have declined significantly, but there is still work to be done.[37] (See the Policy Spotlight feature for more on the global struggle for LGBT rights.)

POLICY SPOTLIGHT

The Global Struggle for LGBT Rights

As you have learned in this chapter, international human rights law references race and sex and has attempted to provide protections to specific groups including refugees, children, women, ethnic minorities, indigenous peoples, migrant workers, and the disabled. However, the major human rights treaties make no mention of sexual orientation or gender identity. The human rights of LGBT individuals have been intentionally left out of this body of law because of efforts by a coalition of powerful states and major religions to block efforts to prioritize LGBT rights.[38]

Instead, the general provisions in human rights law have been interpreted to include the protection of the LGBT community. Broad commitments to equal rights and nondiscrimination are seen as prohibiting discrimination against LGBT individuals. As the former UN High Commissioner for Human Rights Navi Pillay stated: "The case for extending the same rights to lesbian, gay, bisexual and transgender (LGBT) persons as those enjoyed by everyone else is neither radical nor complicated. It rests on two fundamental principles that underpin international human rights law: equality and nondiscrimination."[39]

Unfortunately, high levels of discrimination and brutal violence toward LGBT individuals, and the LGBT community overall, continues unabated around the world. Approximately 70 countries criminalize same-sex activity, and about a dozen can invoke the death penalty against people who engage in same-sex sexual relations. Violence against the LGBT community is often severe. In 2017 in Azerbaijan, for example, police conducted a brutal campaign, arresting and torturing transgender women and about 80 men identified as gay, bisexual, or transgender. Also in 2017 police in Jakarta, Indonesia, arrested 50 people at a sauna "on the basis of their perceived sexual orientation"; while transgender women were stripped, beaten, and had their heads shaved.[40]

According to Amnesty International, thirty-three out of fifty-four African countries, about 70% of the continent, criminalize "consensual same-sex conduct." Gay men have been arrested in Cameroon, Kenya, Malawi, Nigeria, Senegal, Sierra Leone and Zambia. Mauritania, Sudan, Northern Nigeria, and Southern Somalia can all administer the death penalty as punishment for same-sex conduct.[41]

Citizens are now holding their leaders to human rights standards. According to a database of justice mechanisms throughout the world developed by Kathryn Sikkink and her colleagues, over 500 cases of domestic human rights prosecutions involving over 1,100 accused individuals, have been recorded since the end of the Cold War. Many of these prosecutions ended in guilty verdicts. It is thus not rare for states to prosecute their own officials for human rights violations. Sikkink describes the results of her study as a "justice cascade" or dramatic increase in human rights prosecutions around the world. Sikkink argues that this increase is "evidence of a new legitimacy for the norm that state officials should be held accountable for past crimes."[45]

These improvements indicate that governments around the world have taken actions to incorporate internationally affirmed human rights into their national legal

Gay rights are human rights.

essence of liberty. This freedom can only be fulfilled when each of us realizes that the LGBT community possesses equal rights."[43]

A remarkable political divide has thus emerged in the global community over homosexuality and LGBT rights, which has blocked progress in this area. At the global level the institutional framework to support and protect LGBT people from persecution and abuse is very weak.[44]

Yet, in other parts of the world there is a growing acceptance and support for the rights of the LGBT community. In the first decades of the twenty-first century LGBT individuals in the United States experienced enormous progress toward equality in civil society, in marriage, and in the military. In 2015 Ireland became the first country in the world to legalize gay marriage by popular vote with a large margin, 62% to 38%. Twenty-six countries throughout the world have now legalized gay marriage.[42] In 2018 the Supreme Court in India unanimously struck down a 157-year-old law criminalizing gay sex. India's chief justice, Dipak Misra, stated to an overflowing courtroom: "Respect for individual choice is the

Think about It

1. Rightly or wrongly, many nations see homosexuality as incompatible with traditional cultural and religious values. How can the international community engage in a cross-cultural dialogue on the fundamental issues of respect and equality for LGBT individuals?

2. The Convention on the Elimination of All Forms of Discrimination Against Women (CEDAW) clearly articulates the obligations and duties that states must uphold to guarantee the human rights of women. Should a similar international treaty be drafted to guarantee the human rights of LGBT individuals? Why or why not?

systems. Individual countries are leading by example and advancing specific areas of rights protection globally:[46]

- Brazil and South Africa assumed leadership on LGBT rights in the UN Human Rights Council.
- The Constitutional Court of South Africa has issued decisions affirming the rights to health and housing.
- India's Supreme Court has reaffirmed a constitutional right to food and ordered the government to invest heavily in school lunch programs.
- Brazil has been on the forefront of efforts to establish global standards to rein in mass electronic surveillance.

In the first decades of the twenty-first century, there continue to be tremendous human rights violations leading to grotesque levels of suffering. These include the violence of war and terrorism, growing inequality and poverty, the lack of health care and education, and discrimination against racial minorities, women, and the LGBT community. Yet the global human rights movement has made significant progress. Human rights remain globally recognized as a critical defense against injustice today, as evidenced by the activity of the International Criminal Court.

genocide Acts intended to destroy, in whole or in part, a national, ethnic, racial or religious group.

International Criminal Court (ICC) An international tribunal charged with prosecuting individuals for the international crimes of genocide, crimes against humanity, and war crimes.

CONTEMPORARY PERSPECTIVE:
The International Criminal Court, 1998–2018

As you learned in the Historical Perspective section at the beginning of this chapter, lawyer and judge Hersch Lauterpacht was key to the development of crimes against humanity as a new category of crimes that were included in the Charter of the Nuremberg Tribunal in 1945. Another central figure in the development of

BAS CZERWINSKI / AP Images

Fatsuo Bensouda, Chief Prosecutor at the ICC.

modern human rights, lawyer and activist Rafael Lemkin, first articulated the definition of **genocide**, which refers to "acts committed with intent to destroy, in whole or in part, a national, ethnical, racial or religious group."[47] Lemkin's writings, lobbying, and persistence were critical to the adoption of the Genocide Convention by the UN General Assembly in 1948. While crimes against humanity centers on the killing of large numbers of individuals, genocide focuses on the destruction of particular groups. The two concepts are complementary, developed side by side, and connect the individual and the group.

In 1998 120 nations gathered in Rome voted in support of the creation of a new **International Criminal Court (ICC)** with jurisdiction to try cases of genocide, crimes against humanity, and war crimes. The rules for the new ICC were hammered out by hundreds of international lawyers, scholars, and diplomats over a five-year period. After receiving ratifications from 60 nations, the court formally came into existence[48] in 2002. The ICC is located in The Hague, The Netherlands, with ratifications from 123 State Parties. The preamble to the treaty states that it is "the duty of every State to exercise its criminal jurisdiction over those responsible for international crimes."

Following the 1998 Rome Conference, the world witnessed a series of prosecutions of state leaders and other individuals for crimes against humanity, war crimes, and genocide. Consider the following events:[49]

- In September 1998 Jean-Paul Akayesu, a Rwandan political leader who oversaw the massacre of Tutsis, became the first person ever convicted for the crime of genocide. His trial took place at the International Criminal Tribunal for Rwanda.
- In November 1998 former Chilean president Augusto Pinochet was imprisoned in London for crimes against humanity, held responsible for the torture that took place during his dictatorial rule.
- In May 1999 Serbian president Slobodan Milošević became the first sitting head of state to be indicted for crimes against humanity during the wars in Bosnia, Croatia, and Kosovo following the breakup of Yugoslavia; in 2001, after he left office, he was indicted for genocide in relation to atrocities committed in Bosnia. Milošević died before the completion of his trial.
- In September 2007 the International Court of Justice at The Hague determined that Serbia had failed to prevent genocide in Srebrenica, Bosnia, the first time a state had been condemned by an international court for violating the Genocide Convention.
- In May 2012 former Liberian President Charles Taylor was convicted of crimes against humanity, including terror, murder, and rape, for his involvement in the Sierra Leone civil war and sentenced to 50 years in prison, the first head of state to be convicted of these crimes.

Since beginning its work, ICC's record has been controversial. In 2010 the Court indicted President Omar al-Bashir of Sudan for genocide, the first sitting head of state charged at this level. Successful prosecutions included those against Thomas Lubanga Dyllo and Germain Katanga of the Democratic Republic of the Congo. In March 2012 Lubanga, the first person arrested under a warrant issued by the ICC, was found guilty of enlisting and conscripting children under the age of fifteen years and using them as child soldiers. In March 2014 Katanga was found guilty on one count of a crime against humanity and four counts of war crimes (murder, attacking a civilian population, destruction of property and pillaging) during an attack on a village.

Because the United States, China, and Russia have refused to ratify the Rome Statute, these great powers have exempted themselves from its legal norms, creating a double standard in which only less powerful countries are prosecuted for war crimes, crimes against humanity, and genocide. Critics point to examples of individuals from these leading states committing war crimes and escaping any accountability. The work of the ICC to create universal norms of accountability is thus clearly undermined by this unfortunate double standard.

As discussed in Chapter 6, nearly all of the ICC investigations have focused on crimes committed in Africa but have ignored those committed by Russia, the United States, China, and Israel, which has led many critics to conclude that the organization is deeply flawed. The widespread perception is that Africa is being unfairly targeted for prosecution; however, it is important to remember that five of the eight African countries under investigation by the ICC were the ones who had invited the Court to look at the cases. Since the United States, Russia, China, and Israel have not ratified the Rome Statute and the ICC is based on state consent, there is little the Court can do about the actions of those countries. Those individual states who thwart the efforts of the international community to create legal systems of international justice may be the problem to be solved as the ICC looks to the future of international justice.[50]

LOOKING TO THE FUTURE:
The United States, China, and the UN Human Rights System

Powerful states, particularly the United States and China, will likely impact the future viability of the UN human rights system and the actions of the ICC. This section first describes the reasons behind US hesitation to ratify international human rights treaties and fully join in the UN efforts to universalize rights claims. Then China's abysmal human rights record is examined, along with the reluctance of the international community to hold this formidable state to global standards.

The United States and International Human Rights

As shown in Map 9.2, the United States and China have the dubious distinction of being among the leading world's laggards in the ratification of international human rights treaties. As of 2019 the United States had only ratified five of the eighteen central human rights treaties: the International Covenant on Civil and Political Rights (ICCPR), the International Convention on the Elimination of All Forms of Racial Discrimination (ICERD), the Convention against Torture (CAT), and two Optional Protocols to the Convention on the Rights of the Child (CRC). The United States continues to refuse to ratify the overall treaties protecting children, women, migrant workers, people with disabilities, and people victimized by enforced disappearances, and it has not ratified the International Covenant on Economic, Social and Cultural Rights (ICESCR). This poor ratification record makes the United States appear hypocritical when its government lectures other states on human rights issues.

Despite the ratification failure, the United States has led by example in many of these areas. US domestic legislation related to women's rights and the rights of

Map 9.2 Ratification of International Human Rights Treaties.

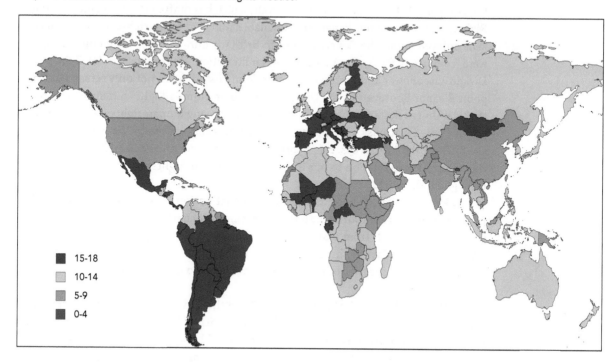

persons with disabilities has been in the progressive forefront, and US practices in these areas indicate more compliance with treaty norms than many of the countries that have ratified them. Scholar Harold Koh calls this practice "compliance without ratification."[51]

If the United States is in compliance, why not ratify the treaties? Immediately after the formation of the UN and the adoption of the UDHR in the 1940s, politics interfered. With the outbreak of the Cold War following WWII, neither the United States nor the USSR was interested in "binding obligations" that might challenge their sovereign power. It was one thing to sign onto the UDHR, a "declaration" with few obligations and no enforcement abilities. It was quite another to ratify an international treaty with compliance and enforcement mechanisms.

Then in the 1950s, the United States experienced the rise of McCarthyism, a zealous anti-Communist, xenophobic movement. Segregationists and racists opposed UN efforts to fight racial discrimination, fearing challenges to existing Jim Crow and racial immigration laws. Hysteria against the UN and human rights reached a high point when Republican Senator John Bricker introduced legislation demanding that the United States withdraw from all human rights treaties "to bury the so-called covenant on human rights so deep that no one holding office will ever dare to attempt its resurrection."

Bricker went on to say: "I do not want any of the international groups, and especially the group headed by Mrs. Eleanor Roosevelt, which has drafted the covenant of Human Rights, to betray the fundamental, inalienable, and God-given rights of American citizens enjoyed under the Constitution." In Bricker's mind, international human rights were "completely foreign to American law and tradition." In response, in 1953 President Dwight Eisenhower and Secretary of State John Foster Dulles not only refused to reappoint Eleanor Roosevelt to the UN Commission on Human Rights but also announced that the United States would not become a party to any human rights treaty approved by the United Nations. In response, Eleanor Roosevelt declared: "We have sold out to the Brickers and McCarthys. It is a sorry day for the honor and good faith of the present Administration in relation to our interest in the human rights and freedoms of people throughout the world."[52]

The United States showed other nations that national sovereignty and Cold War politics were more important than protecting international human rights, effectively removing itself from a constructive leadership role. Except for limited efforts by President Jimmy Carter, throughout the Cold War no administration fundamentally challenged this perspective or exerted political capital to push the United States toward ratification.

With the fall of the Berlin Wall in 1989 and the end of the Cold War shortly after, the human rights community hoped that this political dynamic might change. However, the horror of the terrorist attacks at the World Trade Center, the Pentagon, and in Pennsylvania on Sept 11, 2001, focused US efforts on security and the prevention of terrorism. Unfortunately, a false dichotomy emerged: fighting effectively against terrorists meant that human rights had to be suspended. International human rights treaties were sidelined once again.

The second decade of the twenty-first century has witnessed a rise in nationalism, a backlash against economic globalization (as discussed in Chapter 8), and an attempt by the major powers to sideline the UN. The Trump administration, and in particular Trump's National Security Adviser John Bolton, have consistently expressed contempt for the UN and international law overall. Human rights were barely mentioned in the 2016 presidential election and are clearly not a priority in the current administration.

In the short term it does not seem likely that the United States will act to either ratify new human rights treaties or play a leading role in the UN human rights system, but perhaps this will change in the long term. The human rights movement continues to evolve in dynamic, ever-changing, and unanticipated ways. Human rights are now central to modern diplomacy, represent a global vision of ethics and morality, and play a critical role in the world's political, legal, and moral topography. Nelson Mandela declared: "human rights have become the focal point of international relations."[53] It remains to be seen whether the United States of the future will embrace this vision and become a leader in the world struggle for international human rights.

China and International Human Rights

In 2010 Chinese dissident and intellectual Liu Xiaobo was awarded the Nobel Peace Prize for his actions in Tiananmen Square in 1989 to protect protesters from oncoming soldiers and for his advocacy for democracy and human rights, but he was unable to accept the prize in Oslo due to his imprisonment. In 2008 Mr. Liu had been arrested and later convicted on charges of inciting subversion after he helped launch Charter 08, a petition calling for democracy, the rule of law, and an end to censorship. At his trial Mr. Liu stated to the court and his country: "Hatred can rot a person's wisdom and conscience. An Enemy mentality will poison the spirit of a nation and inflame brutal life and death struggles, destroy a society's tolerance and humanity, and hinder a country's advance toward freedom and democracy."[54]

In July 2017 Mr. Liu died of liver cancer in a hospital while under guard, surrounded by state security. With his death, he became the first Nobel Peace Prize laureate to die in state custody since 1938 when Carl von Ossietzky, the German pacifist and foe of Nazism, died after years of mistreatment. (China's resistance to universal human rights reflects a position of cultural relativism, as discussed in Theory Spotlight: Cultural Relativism versus Universality.)

2010 Nobel Laureate Liu Xiaobo died in Chinese state custody in 2017.

BJ Warnick / Newscom / Alamy Stock Photo

Unfortunately, Mr. Liu's warnings went unheeded. Today China continues to fail to uphold international human rights standards and engages in abusive practices towards its citizens. Its human rights violations are well documented by states, IOs and NGOs. According to the US State Department human rights report for 2017:

> The most significant human rights issues for which the [Chinese] government was responsible included: arbitrary or unlawful deprivation of life and executions without due process; extralegal measures such as forced disappearances, including extraterritorial ones; torture and coerced confessions of prisoners; arbitrary detention, including strict house arrest and administrative detention, and illegal detentions at unofficial holding facilities known as "black jails"; significant restrictions on freedom of speech, press, assembly, association, religion, and movement (for travel within the country and overseas), including detention and harassment of journalists, lawyers, writers, bloggers, dissidents, petitioners, and others as well as their family members; censorship and tight control of public discourse on the internet, in print, and in other media ...[59]

The report goes on to criticize the lack of democracy, severe repression of human rights advocates, coercive birth-limitation policy, human trafficking, and severe labor rights restrictions. Amnesty International estimates that 500,000 people are currently enduring punitive detention in China without charge or trial and millions more are unable to

THEORY SPOTLIGHT

Cultural Relativism Versus Universality

In 1947 the Executive Board of the American Anthropological Association (AAA) submitted a passionate statement endorsing cultural relativism to the UN Commission on Human Rights:

> If we begin, as we must, with the individual, we find that from the moment of his birth not only his behavior, but his very thought, his hopes, aspirations, the moral values which direct his action and justify and give meaning to his life in his own eyes and those of his fellows, are shaped by the body of custom of the group of which he becomes a member.
>
> Ideas of right and wrong, good and evil, are found in all societies, though they differ in their expression among different peoples. What is held to be a human right in one society may be regarded as anti-social by another people, or by the same people in a different period of their history. ... [We] must embrace and recognize the validity of many different ways of life.[55]

Cultural relativism is the position that values and norms of conduct are determined by local communities, and thus moral and ethical systems vary from culture to culture. In this view, rights and duties are not universal but flow from the political, religious, and institutional structures of a people's society and local culture. No

cultural relativism The view that ethics differ from culture to culture and that judgments of right and wrong behavior are a product of particular societies.

universality In ethics this refers to the idea that there are certain truths that can be considered universal and applicable to all everywhere.

one ethical vision or system of justice is better than any other. In the modern world, this perspective has made it possible to justify a multitude of conflicting norms and morals.

Relativists correctly point out that humans are a diverse species composed of multiple cultures, languages, religions, and political systems. However, a fervent cultural relativist will assert that the attempt to create global human rights standards is arrogant and shows a lack of respect for local autonomy. From this perspective, the UDHR is not a universal framework of fundamental human rights but instead reflects the values of the powerful states that were central to the creation of the UN system after WWII and can be seen as a form of cultural imperialism. Such actions can harm cultural diversity and damage local cultures.[56]

As documented in this chapter, international human rights law rejects cultural relativism and instead embraces **universality**, an approach stating that cultural exceptions to the rights to

access the legal system for redress. In addition, Amnesty documents the growing repression of minority groups, including Tibetans, Uighurs, Mongolians, Falun Gong practitioners, and Christians.[60]

Despite this horrific record of abuse, the response from the international community has been muted at best. IOs and governments issue periodic statements of concern but rarely exert pressure or political capital to bring about change. In fact, a normalization of China and acceptance of its authoritarian rule by the key actors in the international system is taking place. Governments and businesses continue engagement and investments. For example, executives from American technology companies, including Tim Cook the CEO of Apple, attend global information technology summits and meetings on

The NGO Amnesty International strongly promotes the universality of human rights with chapters around the world.

are only too anxious to benefit from perceived universal standards. … Individuals everywhere want the same essential things: to have sufficient food and shelter; to be able to speak freely; to practice their own religion or to abstain from religious belief; to feel that their person is not threatened by the state; to know that they will not be tortured, or detained without charge, and that, if charged, they will have a fair trial. … They are as keenly felt by the African tribesman as by the European city-dweller, by the inhabitant of a Latin American shanty-town as by the resident of a Manhattan apartment.[57]

Internal cultural discourse and cross-cultural dialogue can be used to enhance the universal legitimacy of human rights and strengthen existing international standards.[58]

liberty, equal protection, an adequate standard of living, protection from torture, and so on are not allowed.

The universalist position on international human rights was eloquently stated by Rosalyn C. Higgins, the former president of the International Court of Justice (ICJ):

It is sometimes suggested that there can be no fully universal concept of human rights, for it is necessary to take into account the diverse cultures and political systems of the world. In my view this is a point advanced mostly by states, and by liberal scholars anxious not to impose the Western view of things on others. It is rarely advanced by the oppressed, who

Think about It

1. Where do you stand in the debate between cultural relativism and universalism? Does respect for local traditions and culture override international human rights, or do norms of human dignity override local traditions and cultures?

2. What would a cross-cultural dialogue on human rights look like? How could it be used to strengthen international human rights law?

connectivity in China, express support for Beijing's plans for a "common future in cyberspace," and overlook China's widespread censorship and electronic surveillance. In May 2017 China hosted the largest gathering to date for its "Belt and Road Initiative" (BRI) (see Chapter 8), which will span sixty-five countries with potential investments of over $1 trillion. Participating states set aside human rights concerns and jumped at this opportunity. According to Human Rights Watch, the Asian Development Bank, the World Bank and the Asian Infrastructure Investment Bank, they "have not taken adequate steps to ensure that they place strong human rights conditions on OBOR-related projects."[61]

In the 1990s the Clinton administration argued that China's integration into the global economy could push the country to embrace and respect the rules and norms of the international system. China's admission to the World Trade Organization (WTO) in 2001 was to a large degree based on the hope that trade and engagement would prove to be effective means of promoting human rights and democracy. Unfortunately, the opposite seems to have occurred. China has more or less declared itself off limits to criticism by outsiders and uses its economic power to pressure governments and businesses, silencing their efforts to raise human rights concerns. As a result of individual, business, and government failures to defend human rights in China, the communist government has been whitewashed. Engagement, investments, and profits have taken priority over the protection of human dignity. China continues to move away from democracy, a free press, and an independent legal system.

If China continues to view human rights as an internal matter and to consider individual, organization, and state interference inappropriate, what can outsiders do? Practical steps for the international community—including states, IOs, NGOs, businesses, and individuals—to take to help China acknowledge and respect international human rights remain to be determined.

Summary

- The Nuremberg War Crimes Tribunal defined and clarified the following concepts in international law: crimes against peace, war crimes, and crimes against humanity.

- The roots of the ideas of human rights can be found in the works of philosophers, scholars, and religious leaders of all regions of the world over hundreds of years.

- Modern human rights are social constructions outlining claims on others to a certain type of treatment linked to the prevention and alleviation of suffering.

- The Westphalian state system was based on state sovereignty, nonintervention, and the legal equality of states. The three parts to the UN Human Rights System are norms, institutions, and enforcement mechanisms. Its global human rights enforcement mechanisms remain limited, but national enforcement is much more robust and effective.

- The ICC continues to struggle to develop effective means to prosecute individuals for genocide, war crimes, and crimes against humanity, and the major powers have yet to fully commit to this new international legal system.

- The United States refuses to ratify many major human rights treaties. China's abysmal human rights record has not stopped governments and businesses from pushing forward with full engagement with the dictatorial communist regime.

Key Terms

Cultural relativism *(292)*

Genocide *(286)*

Holocaust *(268)*

Human rights *(272)*

Human Rights Council *(276)*

International Bill of Human Rights *(275)*

International Criminal Court (ICC) *(286)*

Nonintervention *(273)*

Critical Thinking Questions

1. What was the role of the Nuremberg Tribunal in the development of human rights law after WWII?

2. What was the role of the world's religious traditions in the creation of our modern understanding of human rights?

3. Do you as an individual feel bound by international human rights law? Do you personally feel that you have human rights obligations that extend beyond your family and nation to include the alleviation of suffering abroad? Explain your answers.

4. If a conflict emerges between a local cultural practice and an international human right codified in international law, which should prevail, and why?

5. How do human rights claims challenge the legitimacy of state sovereignty and the basis of the Westphalian state system?

6. Are there fundamental strategies that the United Nations can pursue to stop human rights abuse inside a sovereign member state?

7. How can the UN Human Rights Council act proactively? Does the Universal Periodic Review provide a vehicle for the UN to move early to prevent human rights violations in member states?

8. Can the International Criminal Court create a legal regime to hold the leaders of all nations accountable for genocide, war crimes, and crimes against humanity? How can ICC decisions be enforced?

9. Will the United States and China use their extensive economic, political, and military power to promote human rights in the twenty-first century? Will these powerful nations work to strengthen the UN human rights system? Why or why not?

Practice and Review Online
http://textbooks.rowman.com/hastedt-felice

▲ Smoke rises above the skyline of Beijing on a moderately polluted day in 2017. *Source:* Mark Schiefelbein / AP Images

10

GLOBAL ENVIRONMENTAL CHALLENGES: THE GLOBAL COMMONS

It really boils down to this: that all life is interrelated. We are all caught in an inescapable network of mutuality, tied into a single garment of destiny. Whatever affects one directly, affects all indirectly. We are made to live together because of the interrelated structure of reality.[1]

Martin Luther King Jr., 1967

THE SECOND DECADE OF THE TWENTY-FIRST century has been filled with environmental crises, some of which are identified in this chapter. The interdependent and fragile structure of our global ecosystem is threatened and under siege. United Nations member states grapple with mechanisms to contain and control the impact of human activity on the natural environment, unfortunately with limited success thus far.

The nations of the world suffered a seemingly unending series of environmental emergencies throughout 2018 and the first months of 2019. California experienced the largest wildfire in the state's history. Countries as varied as Sweden and El Salvador suffered sharp drops in harvests of staple grains. Nuclear power plants in Europe had to close down because the river water needed to cool the reactors was too warm. Four continents experienced heat waves that shut down their electricity grids, and Japan experienced dozens of heat-related deaths. Seventeen of the eighteen warmest years ever recorded have occurred since 2001. Scientists predict that heat waves in the near future will become even more intense, with potentially cascading system failures threatening basic needs such as food and electricity.[2]

This chapter begins with an historical overview of the evolution of international environmental governance, leading up to the significant Conference on the Environment and Development in Rio de Janeiro in 1992, and introduces the idea of the global commons. Specific global policies intended to preserve the planet's atmosphere, oceans, and biodiversity are reviewed. The chapter then turns to contemporary developments in global environmental governance, leading up to the UN Conference on Sustainable Development in Rio in 2012. The chapter concludes with a look to the future, examining the intersection of trade and the environment and whether the precautionary principle provides a framework for effective environmental policy making in the twenty-first century.

LEARNING OBJECTIVES

Students will be able to:

- Outline the evolution of global environmental governance in the nineteenth and twentieth centuries.

- Identify three major global environmental challenges impacting the atmosphere, oceans, and species survival.

- Explain how global environmental governance has changed since the UN Conference on Environment and Development in 1992.

- Assess the future ability of the international community to reconcile conflicting trade and environmental priorities and make use of the precautionary principle as a policy framework for sustainable development.

HISTORICAL PERSPECTIVE:
Global Environmental Governance, 1870–1992

The ecological fragility of Planet Earth is widely recognized by governments and individuals throughout the world today. Environmental challenges that can only be addressed through international cooperation include climate change, acid rain, ozone depletion, air pollution, loss of biodiversity, hazardous wastes, pollution of rivers and freshwater resources, overfishing in the world's seas and oceans, soil degradation, and natural habitat destruction. These challenges do not respect national sovereignty or a state's national borders but can entangle whole regions, and sometimes the whole world, and cannot be solved by individual nations. Effective environmental policy relies on regional action and global cooperation among nations.

1992 Earth Summit at Rio de Janeiro, Brazil.

International efforts to protect the natural environment date as far back as the late nineteenth century. For example, in the 1870s Switzerland tried to establish a regional agreement to protect the nesting sites of migratory birds. During this same period nations began to recognize the transboundary consequences of shared rivers and destruction of wildlife. The Treaty for the Preservation and Protection of Fur Seals was ratified and affirmed by Russia, the United Kingdom, Japan and the United States in 1911 to curb the slaughter of northern fur seals. In the early twentieth century air pollution floating from one nation's atmosphere to another became an international concern. Often located near national borders, factories and industrial plants significantly increased transboundary air pollution. The first and most well-known adjudication of transboundary air pollution was the 1941 *Trail Smelter Arbitration* between British Columbia and the United States. The arbitration tribunal concluded, "under the principles of international law...no State has the right to use or permit the use of its territory in such a manner as to cause injury by fumes in or to the territory of another." British Columbia was held responsible for emitting sulfur dioxide (SO_2) emissions from its smelter across the border into the United States.[3]

A major breakthrough in international environmental cooperation took place in 1972 at the **UN Conference on the Human Environment in Stockholm**, during which the international community enacted multiple measures designed to protect the environment. The *Stockholm Declaration* contained twenty-six key principles regulating the environment and development. Many of these principles have endured and now reflect *customary international law*, a concept binding on all states that was introduced in Chapter 6. Embracing the Trail Smelter decision, Principle 21 of the *Declaration* stated:

UN Conference on the Human Environment in Stockholm The UN's first major conference on the environment, held in 1972, represented a major turning point in the development of global environmental law and policy.

Global Commons The areas and resources beyond the sovereignty of any state, including the oceans and seas, the atmosphere, biological diversity, and outer space.

Common Heritage of Humankind A principle in international environmental law that areas of the global commons should benefit all of humanity and not be unilaterally exploited by individual states; also known as the *Common Heritage of Mankind*.

United Nations Environment Program (UNEP), The leading UN environmental organization, established at the Stockholm Conference, which sets the global environmental agenda and coordinates implementation of environmental agreements and sustainable development practices.

UN Conference on Environment and Development (UNCED) A conference held in Rio in 1992 that brought together the largest gathering of world leaders to date to reconcile economic development with protection of the environment.

"States have…the sovereign right to exploit their own resources pursuant to their own environmental policies, and the responsibility to ensure that the activities within their jurisdiction or control do not cause damage to the environment of other States or of areas beyond the limits of national jurisdiction."[4]

Other key principles involved limits on the use and abuse of the **global commons**, which include the atmosphere, oceans and seas, biological diversity, and outer space. In addition, resources identified as part of the **Common Heritage of Humankind** should be collectively managed and used for the benefits of all peoples.

The conference further recognized differing levels of environmental responsibility among developed and underdeveloped nations. Participating nations also laid the foundation for the creation of the **United Nations Environment Program (UNEP)** as the chief global coordinating body tasked with encouraging environmental cooperation among UN member states.

Following the Stockholm Conference, there was an explosion of environmental treaties negotiated and ratified in the 1970s and 1980s. Working with UNEP within the UN system, the international community developed an impressive list of international environmental laws during this period, including the following: Convention on Wetlands of International Importance (1971), the Convention on the International Trade in Endangered Species (1973), the Convention on Long-Range Transboundary Air Pollution (1979) and subsequent protocols in the 1980s to curb acid rain, the UN Convention on the Law of the Seas (1982), the Vienna Convention on the Protection of the Ozone Layer (1985), and the Basel Convention on Control of Transboundary Movements of Hazardous Wastes and their Disposal (1989).[5]

By the late 1980s ecological issues had become a central feature of diplomacy and international relations. Climate change emerged as a pressing international priority. In his 1984 State of the Union Address US President Ronald Reagan declared: "Preservation of our environment is not a liberal or conservative challenge, it's common sense."[6] At the 1989 G-7 summit meeting environmental questions dominated the discussions, and the leaders of the world's most powerful states, including Gro Harlem Brundtland (Norway), Mikhail Gorbachev (USSR), and Margaret Thatcher (UK), appeared to be competing to be the "greenest" actors. Also in 1989 the UN General Assembly voted to convene an Earth Summit in Rio de Janeiro, Brazil, in 1992 to foster further instruments of international environmental law and develop a consensus on *sustainable development*, defined as "development that meets the needs of the present without compromising the ability of future generations to meet their own needs."[7]

The **UN Conference on Environment and Development (UNCED)** convened in Rio in 1992 with around 7,000 delegates from 178 nations, over 1,400 nongovernmental organizations (NGOs) from around the world, and approximately 9,000 world journalists. Major divisions emerged between countries from the North and those from the South. The South wanted to discuss curbing consumption, but the North wanted to focus on population control. There were also major disputes over the establishment of financial mechanisms to help poorer countries in the South meet the ambitious environmental goals. Despite these divisions, UNCED delegates agreed to the following:

- two binding conventions, the Biodiversity Convention and the Climate Change Convention;
- the Rio Declaration on the Environment and Development;
- *Agenda 21*, an 800-page "blueprint" for sustainable development;
- a set of nonbinding forestry principles;
- agreements to develop subsequent legal instruments on desertification, straddling fish stocks, and land-based sources of marine pollution;
- an agreement to create the UN Commission on Sustainable Development to monitor and implement the Rio Agreements and *Agenda 21*.[8]

The implementation and impact of these measures will be analyzed later in this chapter as they relate to specific environmental issues.

Rio's 1992 Earth Summit was the first attempt following the end of the Cold War to build a new global architecture to guide development planning and economic relations between rich and poor nations. State and nongovernmental organization leaders sought to define the concept of sustainable development by creating workable laws and policies. While it was just a beginning, the Earth Summit did expand existing international environmental law and launch new initiatives successfully. Environmental conventions, protocols, and agreements soon emerged on climate change, biodiversity, desertification, fisheries, mercury, persistent organic pollutants, biosafety, access to genetic resources, forests, and ozone depletion. For a brief moment in history, it seemed that the "environmental regimes...[had] moved to the center of international affairs."[9]

GLOBAL ENVIRONMENTAL CHALLENGES:
Climate Change, Overfishing, Species Extinction

The famous ecologist and philosopher Garrett Hardin coined the phrase **Tragedy of the Commons** to demonstrate the challenge of using common resources. Hardin made an analogy to "a pasture open to all" where, with open access, it is in the interest of each herdsman to graze as many of his own cattle as possible. Such actions by all herdsmen would lead to overgrazing the pasture and environmental destruction rendered by the cattle's consumption, but the individual herdsman, driven by short-term economic gain, knows that if he doesn't take advantage of this opportunity to increase his use of the resource, others will do so. Because individual conservation efforts would be overwhelmed by the actions of others, it is "rational" for each herdsman to graze as many of his cattle as possible. Hardin wrote:

Tragedy of the Commons A theory that describes how individuals may exploit natural resources for their advantage without considering potential resource depletion and the need for long-term sustainability; highlights the conflict between individual and collective rationality.

Planet Earth.

NASA / NOAA / GOES Project

this is the conclusion reached by each and every rational herdsman sharing a commons. Therein is the tragedy. Each man is locked into a system that compels him to increase his herd without limit—in a world that is limited. Ruin is the destination toward which all men rush, each pursuing his own best interest in a society that believes in the freedom of the commons.[10]

The planet's global commons are often utilized like Hardin's open pasture without regard to the full social costs. No individual, business, or state is excluded from utilizing the global commons and its natural resources. Although regulatory progress has been made in international environmental law and by international organizations, the global commons remains threatened and endangered.

The following sections examine responses by the international community to three global environmental challenges—climate change, overfishing, and biodiversity loss—in hopes of answering the following questions. What instruments of international environmental law are operative? Has global environmental governance helped to halt and reverse destructive environmental policies and actions or been proven impotent in confronting the desire for economic growth of governments and businesses?

The Atmosphere: Climate Change and Global Warming

climate change
Changes in weather patterns and global warming caused by human activity combined with the earth's natural processes.

In 1988 National Aeronautics and Space Administration (NASA) scientist James Hansen testified to Congress that the era of global warming leading to **climate change** had arrived and would become the defining ecological issue of our time. Hansen presented evidence from NASA indicating how the greenhouse gases (GHGs) emitted in modern societies—notably carbon dioxide from the burning of fossil fuels—trap heat from the earth's surface that normally would be radiated out to space, just as the glass over a greenhouse traps the sun's heat. The so-called greenhouse effect leads directly to *global warming*, an increase in global average temperatures in the earth's climate patterns.

Climate Change Convention A convention created at the Rio Conference in 1992 that established a general framework for nations to work together to mitigate and limit global warming; the objective is stabilizing atmospheric greenhouse gas concentrations at a level that would prevent dangerous human interference with the climate.

Politicians responded vigorously to Hansen's testimony. In the midst of his presidential campaign George H. W. Bush stated: "Those who think we are powerless to do anything about the greenhouse effect forget about the 'White House effect'; as President, I intend to do something about it.... We will talk about global warming and we will act."[11] Yet, as president, his actions did not match his rhetoric. At the end of his term he did briefly attend the 1992 Rio Earth Summit, during which the United States became a founding member of the United Nations Framework Convention on Climate Change (the **Climate Change Convention**). Although this treaty continues to direct global climate action today, it was clearly inadequate. When Hansen delivered his speech in 1988 fossil fuels provided around 79% of the world's energy needs. Thirty years later, in 2018, its actually worse—81%. In fact, since 1988 global carbon dioxide emissions have risen 68%.[12]

Also in 1988 the UN created the **Intergovernmental Panel on Climate Change (IPCC),** which brings together hundreds of the world's leading scientists to assess the scientific evidence for global warming. Since its creation the IPCC has produced a series of scientific reports on human-induced global climate change.

In 2001 the IPCC reported that fossil fuel combustion was estimated to have raised atmospheric concentrations of carbon dioxide to their highest levels on record and stated that societies' release of carbon dioxide and other greenhouse gases (GHGs) "contributed substantially to the observed warming over the last 50 years." The warming in the twentieth century was likely the greatest of any century in the Northern Hemisphere over the last thousand years. The 1990s was its warmest decade: snow cover decreased by 10% from the 1960s to the turn of the twenty-first century and sea levels rose at a rate ten times faster than the average over the last three thousand years. The IPCC concluded that by the end of the twenty-first century temperatures would likely be approximately eleven degrees higher than in 1990, greater than the change in temperature between the last Ice Age and today.[13]

The 2007 IPCC Synthesis Report was even more alarming. "Warming of the climate system is unequivocal, as is now evident from observations of increases in global average air and ocean temperatures, widespread melting of snow and ice and rising global average sea level. Eleven of the last twelve years (1995–2006) rank among the twelve warmest years in the instrumental record of global surface temperature (since 1850)." The report concluded that, "anthropogenic warming could lead to some impacts that are abrupt or irreversible, depending upon the rate and magnitude of the climate change.... Climate change is *likely* to lead to some irreversible impacts" (emphasis in original).[14]

The Nobel Peace Prize in 2007 was awarded jointly to the IPCC and former Vice President Al Gore for "their efforts to build up and disseminate greater knowledge about man-made climate change, and to lay the foundations for the measures that are needed to counteract such change."[15]

Experts from more than eighty countries contributed to the IPCC's most recent assessment released in 2014, which stated the following:

> Human influence on the climate system is clear, and recent anthropogenic emissions of greenhouse gases are the highest in history. Recent climate changes have had widespread impacts on human and natural systems....

> The atmosphere and ocean have warmed, the amounts of snow and ice have diminished, and sea level has risen.... The period from 1983 to 2012 was *likely* the warmest 30-year period of the last 1400 years in the Northern Hemisphere....[16]

Environmental scientists note that the world has already warmed more than one degree Celsius since the Industrial Revolution. Unfortunately, the planet is well on its way to a two-degree warming, a more likely three-degree warming, and possibly a four-degree warming. A two-degree warming will lead to the extinction of the world's tropical reefs and a sea-level rise of several meters, possibly leading to the abandonment of the Persian Gulf. A three-degree rise could lead to the growth of forests in the Arctic and the loss of

Intergovernmental Panel on Climate Change (IPCC) An international organization established in 1988 that is charged with assessing the science related to climate change.

most coastal cities. A four-degree rise could produce permanent drought in Europe and emergence of deserts in vast areas of China, India, and Bangladesh and could make the American Southwest largely uninhabitable. Some of the world's leading scientists warn that a five-degree warming could bring "the end human civilization."[17]

Upon launching UN Climate Change's first-ever annual report in April 2018, the international organization's Executive Secretary Patricia Espinosa stated: "Climate Change is the single biggest threat to life, security and prosperity on Earth."[18]

The 2014 IPCC report also authenticated human activity as a source of GHG emissions:

[G]reenhouse gas emissions...driven largely by economic and population growth, are now higher than ever. This has led to atmospheric concentrations of carbon dioxide, methane and nitrous oxide that are unprecedented in at least the last 800,000 years. Their effects...have been detected throughout the climate system and are *extremely likely* to have been the dominant cause of the observed warming since the mid-20th century.[19]

The skyrocketing increase in global CO_2 emissions is shown in Figure 10.1.

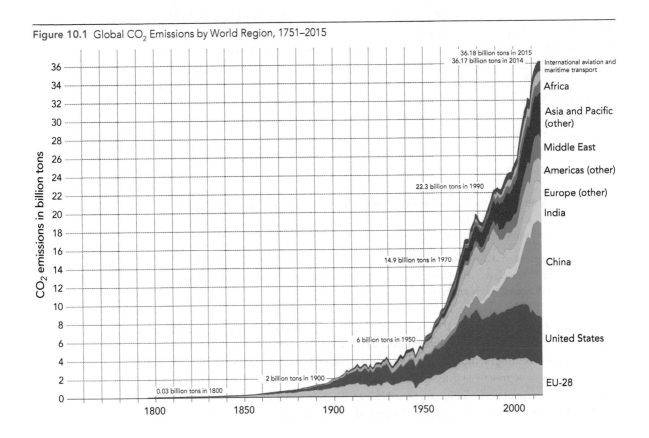

Figure 10.1 Global CO_2 Emissions by World Region, 1751–2015

Despite all of this scientific evidence, until recently the international community has been unable to agree on a binding treaty to limit the production of GHGs or an effective process to address the crisis. The 1992 Climate Change Convention signed in Rio established a general framework but included few specifics or substantive obligations to mitigate or limit climate change. The 1997 Kyoto Protocol to the Climate Change Convention would have required countries to reduce greenhouse gas emissions, primarily coal and oil, to 7% below 1990 levels and was supported by many European states, but the United States resisted and instead attempted voluntary measures, which failed. According to the US Energy Department, Americans produced 12% more carbon dioxide each year during the last decade of the twentieth century than they did when President Bill Clinton took office in 1992. Adoption of the Kyoto Protocol would have at least forced participating countries to slow these harmful trends.[20]

In 2014 the Obama administration negotiated a joint plan with China to curb carbon emissions. The United States pledged to emit 26–28% less carbon in 2025 than it did in 2005, double the reduction targeted for the period from 2005 to 2020. China pledged to stop its emissions from growing by 2030 by increasing use of clean energy sources, such as solar power and windmills, to 20% of China's total energy production.[21]

This agreement between the world's No. 1 and No. 2 carbon polluters (China and the United States, respectively) was remarkable and notable. China and other developing countries had previously maintained that they could continue to claim a moral right to develop since the developed world's consumption of resources and creation of pollutants on a per capita basis was still much higher. However, because of internal public pressure to contain high levels of toxic smog and some of the worst air pollution levels in the world, the Chinese government changed its position and worked with the Obama administration on this joint agreement.[22]

Cooperation between China and the United States helped stimulate international progress. In December 2014 developing countries met in Lima, Peru, and for the first time agreed to limit their own emissions.

In December 2015 195 nations met in Paris and committed to lowering emissions of GHGs in an attempt to prevent a further damage. The goal of the **Paris Climate Change Agreement** was to limit the rise in the world's temperature to 1.5 degrees Celsius (2.7 degrees Fahrenheit). Each signatory nation agreed to establish a national plan identifying reductions in GHG emissions. In the first year after the Paris pact was signed 186 nations put forward individual plans on cutting carbon emissions through 2025 or 2030. However, because these plans alone are not enough to prevent the worst effects of global warming, the pact also includes a series of legally binding requirements for countries to ratchet up their policies every five years to increase emissions cuts and monitor and report on emissions levels using a universal accounting system. While this system is voluntary, the hope is that by publicly monitoring and verifying compliance, peer pressure, or "naming and shaming," will produce results.[23]

The Paris agreement supports a principle of international environmental law of "common but differentiated responsibilities." Since developed countries have historically

Paris Climate Change Agreement A 2015 agreement that builds on the Climate Change Convention and aims to limit the rise of the world's temperature to 1.5 degrees Celsius.

emitted the most GHGs, they are obligated to help finance developing nations' climate transition programs. The Paris pact estimates that $100 billion must be raised each year to help poor countries mitigate and adapt to climate change.[24]

While the Paris agreement was a healthy start, it quickly became clear that it was still not enough. National domestic politics will determine the content of individual plans, so the science of climate change is likely to again be secondary to local politics.

The politics of global warming changed dramatically in the United States with the transition from the Obama administration to the Trump administration. Once in office Trump moved quickly to limit US participation in multilateral policies and in 2017 pulled the United States out of the Paris accord, describing the pact as "an agreement that disadvantages the United States to the exclusive benefit of other countries." During his presidential campaign Trump had repeatedly called climate change a "hoax" in speeches, tweets, and media appearances and stated that action on climate change "is

POLICY SPOTLIGHT

Is a Carbon Tax a Viable Policy Option?

In 2018 Young College Republicans at twenty-two schools around the country, including Yale, Clemson, North Carolina State, and Texas Christian, organized a campaign promoting a **carbon tax**. The "Students for Carbon Dividends" picked up an idea initially proposed by two former Secretaries of State and Republican heavyweights: James A. Baker III and George P. Shultz. The idea is two-fold: (1) Tax the carbon pollution produced by the burning of fossil fuels; then (2) return the money to consumers as dividends in the form of monthly cash payments. Their conservative plan involves an initial tax of $40 per ton of carbon, levied at the point where fossil fuels enter the economy such as a mine or port. The Climate Leadership Council, created by Mr. Baker and Mr. Shultz, estimated that the dividend would amount to about $2,000 a year for a family of four.[28]

As proposed by the Climate Leadership Council, the carbon tax has received support from key oil companies, including Exxon Mobil, BP, Royal Dutch Shell, and Total SA. The central logic is that, by making the energy obtained from fossil fuels more expensive, the market will move more quickly toward renewable energy, including solar and wind, and away from the burning of carbon. This market-driven approach is appealing to some oil companies as it avoids heavy government regulation and they are able to pass the extra tax onto consumers. Yet, since the proceeds from the new tax are eventually returned to consumers, the hope is that this proposal could gain public support.[29]

Some key environmental organizations and individuals have also endorsed the plan, including the Nature Conservancy, the World Resources Institute, the late theoretical physicist Stephen Hawking, former secretary of energy Steven Chu, and former New York City mayor Michael Bloomberg.

Some environmentalists are highly skeptical of oil company support for the proposal. Jamie Henn, a co-founder of 350.org, stated: "Exxon is signing on to this carbon tax proposal because they know it's

> **carbon tax** A fee on fossil fuels designed as a market mechanism to reduce the emissions of carbon dioxide into the atmosphere.

done for the benefit of China."[25] The fossil fuel industry had heavily influenced his campaign and transition into the presidency,[26] and the 2016 Republican Party Platform had stated categorically: "We reject the agendas of both the Kyoto Protocol and the Paris Agreement."[27]

Because there is no way for the United States—or any signatory country—to withdraw from the Paris accord until four years after it is in effect, Trump's announcement didn't actually lead to immediate US withdrawal. The United States can only begin to withdraw the day after the 2020 US presidential election. However, US actions have undermined the global unity forged over many years to confront climate change. Once Syria signed the agreement, the United States became the only country in the world to reject it. With the United States now taking a back seat, China and the EU are about to emerge as the new global leaders on multilateral environmental policy.

Angel_nt / iStock

Could a carbon tax limit pollution and GHG emissions?

a tax might damage America's overall economic competitiveness, as higher energy costs will increase the cost of US goods in comparison to those of our economic competitors.

Short-term enactment by Congress of a carbon tax thus may be difficult to envision, but it could conceivably receive bipartisan support in the long term. Polls of millennials indicate that 60% of young Republicans and 88% of young Democrats accept that human-induced climate change is real.[31] Perhaps this new generation can help push the United States to take the necessary steps to slow climate change.

dead on arrival [in Congress]." He also noted that the proposal gives Exxon protection from liability at a time when the firm is under investigation for past statements and actions on climate change.[30]

In addition, opposition to any type of carbon tax remains strong. Those opposed argue that higher energy prices would be passed onto consumers, creating more expensive goods throughout the economy. Furthermore, a carbon tax could potentially harm low-income communities and seniors the most, since energy costs are a larger portion of their overall budgets. And finally, such

Think about It

1. Is there a "market" solution to climate change? Will a carbon tax raising the price of fossil fuels change consumer behavior and create a new market for renewable energy? Explain your answer.

2. In terms of environmental awareness and action, are millennials and postmillennials really that much different from earlier generations? Explain your answer.

With politics limiting the effectiveness of international environmental law, conservative and liberal environmentalists have developed market-based proposals to address climate change, including a carbon tax (see the Policy Spotlight feature).

Despite recent US actions, US scientists, particularly those at NASA, continue to raise the alarm and thoroughly document the dangers of global warming. According to NASA:

> Global climate change has already had observable effects on the environment. Glaciers have shrunk, ice on rivers and lakes is breaking up earlier, plant and animal ranges have shifted and trees are flowering sooner. Effects that scientists had predicted in the past would result from global climate change are now occurring: loss of sea ice, accelerated sea level rise and longer, more intense heat waves.[32]

The Oceans and Seas: Overfishing

Law of the Sea (LOS) Treaty An international convention finalized in 1982 that established the rights and responsibilities of nations on the world's oceans, including the protection and management of the environment and marine natural resources.

In Chapter 6 you learned that two conflicting general principles undergird global governance on the oceans and seas. According to the first position, the seas are a global commons that all are free to utilize and exploit. The second position maintains that areas of the oceans are the sovereign property of different states. The **Law of the Sea (LOS) Treaty**, established in 1982, attempts to resolve these positions by establishing certain sovereign rights of coastal states: It identifies a twelve-mile *territorial sea*, a twenty-four-mile *contiguous zone*, a two-hundred-mile *exclusive economic zone (EEZ)*, and potential rights to an area two hundred miles beyond the EEZ, as shown in Figure 10.2.

Figure 10.2 Ocean Zones Established in the Law of the Sea Treaty

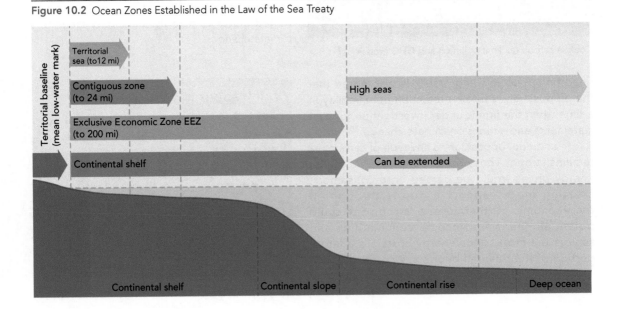

With regard to fishing, the LOS Treaty gave coastal states sovereign rights over all economic resources of the sea, seabed, and subsoil in its EEZ, allowing them exclusive rights not only to fish but also to mine the minerals beneath the seabed.

Ocean fishing is the perfect setting for Hardin's tragedy of the commons. Freedom of the seas can lead to a situation in which the "rational" behavior of the individual fisherman is to exploit this common resource for short-term gain. Since others are free to fish in this global common area, there is little incentive to limit fishing and conserve the resource to ensure long-term sustainability. Even though it is clearly in the common interest of all nations to conserve fish stocks, each state's immediate interest is best served by catching as many fish as possible. If every nation fishes unimpeded, effective sustainability management is limited.

In its most recent report on *the State of World Fisheries and Aquaculture,* the UN Food and Agricultural Organization (FAO) reported that total fish production reached an all-time high in 2016 of 171 million tons, of which 88% was utilized for human consumption. Since 1961 the overall growth in fish consumption has been twice as high as population growth and is not sustainable. The FAO reports that biologically sustainable levels of fish stocks decreased dramatically from 90.0% in 1974 to 66.9% in 2015. An abundant fish stock is biologically sustainable when it can produce a maximum sustainable yield (MSY). When the abundance level falls below this MSY, it is considered biologically unsustainable. So the percentage of biologically unsustainable levels has increased from 10% to 33.1% in just forty years.[33]

In an earlier report the FAO estimated that 57.4% of major marine fish stocks had been fully exploited and 29.9% were overexploited. So there is literally no room for further catch expansion, and the "risk of decline if not properly managed." The FAO identified the Atlantic Ocean, Mediterranean Sea, and Black Sea stocks as those with the greatest need for recovery. Tuna, swordfish, Atlantic salmon, and cod are all making their way toward the endangered list. Contributing to these problems is *by-catch*, the unintentional catching of fish, seabirds, sea turtles, marine mammals, and other ocean life, which totals approximately twenty million tons each year.[34]

Marine fish harvesting beyond sustainable levels can have devastating consequences for both rich and poor countries. Developing countries depend heavily on fishing trade with an estimated fishery trade surplus of approximately $16.8 billion a year, exceeding their income from coffee, tea, and rubber. Because more than one hundred million of the world's poorest people work in this industry, there is clearly a vital need for international cooperation to address sustainability, conservation and survival.[35]

Areas close to the shore of coastal states are particularly rich in fish. Modern technologies, improvements in trawling techniques, and state-of-the-art refrigeration and freezing methods make long-distance fishing possible. Prior to the LOS Treaty fishing vessels from one nation could catch huge quantities of fish near the coasts of distant countries and ship them home safely. This approached favored rich states with large and technologically advanced fishing fleets, such as the United Kingdom, the United States, and Japan. Poor coastal states that could not afford large trawlers or expensive refrigeration equipment were dependent on local fisheries. Historically, poorer coastal states sought to extend territorial seas to exclude foreign fishing vessels. At the time of the LOS Treaty negotiations, geographical claims to territorial sea ranged from three miles to two hundred miles. The establishment of the two-hundred-mile EEZ by the LOS Treaty was an attempt to adjudicate this dispute.[36]

Beyond the EEZs, ships of all nations, including land-locked states, are free to navigate and fish the high seas. A ship on the high seas is subject to international law and the laws of the flag-state (i.e., the nationality of the ship). Coastal states generally negotiate agreements to give land-locked states the rights to use their ports and travel through their territories.

Because national EEZs cover over 30% of the world's seas and approximately 90% of commercial fisheries, creation of the EEZs dramatically weakened the traditional freedom of the seas doctrine and brought an important portion of the ocean's resources under national jurisdiction. In addition to rights to exploit and explore, the LOS Treaty charged coastal states with efforts to conserve and manage their EEZ's mineral and living natural resources. Coastal states have the right to enforce their environmental laws and fishing restrictions and to board, inspect, and arrest crews in the EEZ that violate these laws.[37]

In establishing a two-hundred-mile EEZ, supporters of the LOS Treaty hoped to resolve the tragedy of the commons dilemma. The allocation of property rights significantly enhanced coastal states' ability to manage fisheries. The Treaty also attempted to impose environmental responsibility. Articles 192 and 193 indicated the following: "States have the obligation to protect and preserve the marine environment.... States have the sovereign right to exploit their natural resources pursuant to their environmental policies in accordance with their duty to protect and preserve the marine environment."[38]

In theory, with approximately 90% of the world's fish catch within national jurisdiction, national oversight should lead to better conservation of domestic fish stocks. Unfortunately, the opposite has occurred. Coastal states sought to maximize their new access to these resources by subsidizing large fishing fleets, doubling the global fishing fleet from 585,000 to 1.2 million commercial boats between 1970 and 1990. As a result the FAO now estimates that fishing fleets have double the capacity to catch the "maximum sustainable catch," and scholars estimate that, from 1950 to 2004, 36–53% of fish stocks in more than half of the world's EEZs were overfished.[39] When EEZ resources become depleted, vessels move on to fish in the high seas or in foreign seas. Poor developing states are increasingly willing to sell fishing permits to foreign vessels. For example, Senegal has been paid by EU fleets to allow intensive fishing of its waters. The creation of EEZs has not resulted in sustainable ocean fishing. Much overfishing is clearly due to the actions of those coastal states charged with conserving fish stocks and managing their recovery.[40]

To complicate matters, states have begun to assert sovereign rights in disputed ocean areas. As you learned in Chapter 2, Russia, the United States, and other states are all claiming rights to access new fish stocks in the now melting, shrinking Arctic. The entire South China Sea, home to a tenth of the global fish catch, has been claimed by China, causing tremendous friction and conflict with its coastal neighbors.

One approach to containing this unbounded growth of the fisheries industry is efforts by the World Trade Organization (WTO) to limit fishing subsidies, which total $30 billion per year. The WTO estimates that 60% of coastal states subsidize their own fishing industries, with the vast majority (seven of every ten dollars) handed out by rich developed states. Pascal Lamy, the former director-general of the WTO, argues that these subsidies contribute to harmful fishing practices and that enforceable trade rules limiting such practices could significantly contribute to sustainability. Another proposed course of action is to establish more protected areas within EEZs and on the high seas. These include some "no-take" zones in which fishing would be banned completely to create "breeding spaces" allowing stocks to recover. A permanent ban has been successful in the Antarctic (see Regional Spotlight feature), but fishing nations may be more open to temporary bans or "rolling closures."[41]

New technology can help identify violators of maritime fishing rules. For example, the International Maritime Organization (IMO) requires ships over three hundred tons to have an Automatic Identification System (AIS), which identifies the boat's position, speed, and identity. Global Fishing Watch, an online platform created by Google in conjunction with other companies and NGOs, uses AIS transmissions to determine what the ships are doing. For example, boats long-lining for tuna have a distinctive zigzag path. According to Google's Brian Sullivan, Global Fishing Watch now follows 60,000 vessels responsible for 50–60% of the world's catch. Such information can be especially helpful to poor countries without a strong coastguard or navy to monitor suspicious foreign vessels.[44]

As of December 2018 168 states had ratified the LOS Treaty.[45] Although the United States, Peru, Turkey, and other major fishing powers have not yet ratified it, many provisions have now become part of customary international law and are mandatory for all states. The establishment of EEZs resulted in greater benefit to large developed states with long coastlines than small developing coastal states, and exploitation of the coastal waters of smaller states continues. Although the convention provided a good starting point, the problems of overfishing remain and have gotten worse. If the United States and the other major fishing nations not only sign the Treaty but work to strengthen it, there may be a chance for its conservation and sustainability provisions to succeed so that the oceans can provide the world's peoples with food for generations to come.

Biodiversity: Species Extinction

The broad concept of **biodiversity** (short for *biological diversity*) is grounded in the variety and variability of life. Biodiversity includes genetic diversity (the building blocks of life), species diversity (different life forms), and ecosystem diversity (interrelationships of species). These distinctions are critical to the development of multiple conservation strategies. For example, development of a strategy to protect *keystone species* critical to maintaining the stability of an entire ecosystem, such as the sea otter, would be a clear ecological priority. A different strategy might be needed to protect *umbrella species*,

biodiversity The total variety of life found on Earth, including the genetic variety within each species and the ecosystems that species create.

REGIONAL SPOTLIGHT

The Antarctic Treaty Regime

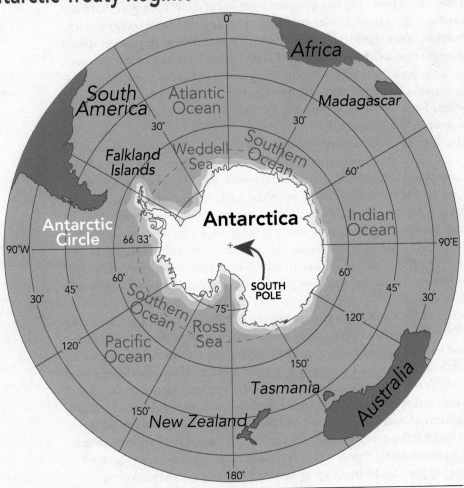

Map 10.1 Antarctica.

Global environmental regimes with strong common policies and expectations have emerged in a variety of areas, including the Antarctic. The **Antarctic Treaty Regime** is a useful model for development of international environmental law and regulation. Participating nations have adopted innovative and far-reaching rules for the protection of the Antarctic and its ecosystem. The Antarctic is now subject to a large body of international environmental regulations with clear norms establishing environmental standards.

The Antarctic continent is larger than the United States and Mexico combined. Extending over fourteen million square kilometers, it represents 26% of the world's wilderness area, 90% of terrestrial ice, and 70% of the world's fresh water. With 98% of the continent covered by ice and snow and six months of darkness

The Antarctic Treaty Regime has substantive provisions to protect Antarctic living resources, including these aquatic flightless birds.

KeithSzafranski / iStock

Antarctic Treaty Regime A set of international agreements that regulate relations among states in the region to ensure that the area will be used exclusively for peaceful purposes.

and subfreezing temperatures, it is the only continent that has not supported significant human habitation, but it is of critical ecological importance. It supports an abundance of wildlife, composed of plants, marine mammals, fish, birds, and krill, central to the marine food chain, and it plays a critical role in regulating the earth's climate and sea levels.[42]

The Antarctic Treaty Regime consists of five central treaties, which establish substantive environmental standards and institutional and procedural techniques to monitor compliance:[43]

- The 1959 Antarctic Treaty jettisons national claims to sovereignty on the continent, declaring that "Antarctica shall continue forever to be used exclusively for peaceful purposes." Military activities, nuclear explosions, and disposal of radioactive waste are all prohibited. Preservation and conservation measures and scientific investigations are encouraged.
- The 1972 Antarctic Seals Convention limits the number of seals that can be killed or captured by state parties, regulates hunting, and establishes scientific and breeding reserves.
- The 1980 Convention on the Conservation of Antarctic Marine Living Resources (CCAMLR) establishes an innovative ecosystem approach that was modeled in subsequent agreements on ozone depletion, climate change, and

biodiversity. It was the first multilateral environmental treaty to include an environmental impact assessment.
- The 1988 Convention on the Regulation of Antarctic Mineral Resource Activities (CRAMRA) attempts to establish a framework to govern Antarctic mineral-resource prospecting, exploration, and development, with extensive environmental protection measures. Although nineteen states have signed the treaty, none has ratified it.
- Article 7 of the 1991 Protocol on Environmental Protection to the Antarctic Treaty states that "[a]ny activity relating to mineral resources, other than scientific research shall be prohibited." It adopts a fifty-year moratorium on any mineral resource activities and establishes Antarctica as a "natural reserve, devoted to peace and science."

These innovative treaties have been successful in protecting the Antarctic natural environment and resolving claims of national sovereignty and evoking aspirations to protect a global commons. It is of particular historical significance that the 1959 treaty was the first arms control agreement established during the Cold War, banning military activities on the continent completely.

Think about It

1. How do you explain the contrast between the extreme national rivalry and struggle to exploit the natural resources in the Arctic compared to the agreement to preserve the ecosystem of Antarctica?

2. Is the Antarctic Treaty Regime, which impressively incorporates progressive elements of international environmental law including the precautionary principle, sustainable development, and environmental impact assessments, a model for other regions and/or issue areas? Can this successful approach be replicated? Explain your answers.

such as large carnivores, that ensure adequate amounts of habitat for other species. Yet another approach might be needed for sensitive *sentinel species*, such as frogs and other amphibians, which are important indicators of the health of an entire ecosystem.[46]

Since 1964 the International Union for the Conservation of Nature and Natural Resources (IUCN) has published a "Red List of Threatened Species," one of the world's most comprehensive sources of information on the health of the world's biodiversity. Unfortunately, biodiversity is declining. There are more than 91,520 species on the current Red List, "and more than 25,820 of them are threatened with extinction." To be clear: this means that from their current total populations 41% of amphibians, 34% of conifers, 33% of reef building corals, 25% of mammals, and 13% of birds face looming destruction.[47]

Scientists state that we are undergoing a sixth wave of mass extinctions, "the worst spate of species die-offs since the loss of the dinosaurs 65 million years ago." In the history of life on earth, scientists are aware of only five mass extinctions, caused by diseases, natural disasters, and predators and competitors that overhunt or co-opt food sources. The fifth mass extinction sixty-five million years ago was most likely caused by a meteor striking the earth. What's different this time is that the Earth is losing species at 1,000 to 10,000 times all historical extinction rates. Some estimates predict that by the middle of the twenty-first century 30–50% of all species on earth could be headed toward extinction.[48]

This is occurring because of human consumption and the daily patterns of the world's 7.6 billion human beings, sharing the planet with over 14 million other species. The human impact on the natural environment harms and sometimes even destroys complex ecological webs and ecosystems through activities such as unsustainable logging, urbanization, slash and burn agriculture, damming rivers, draining wetlands, contaminating the air and water, and overexploiting species for food and clothing. Climate change and ozone depletion have also contributed.[49]

The ecological consequences of severe habitat and species loss can threaten the interdependent ecological system that encompasses all life on earth. There is no technological substitute for the ecosystem services created by natural processes and species interactions.[50]

These critical services include the purification of air and water, mitigation of floods, droughts, erosion, detoxifying and decomposing wastes, renewal of soil fertility, pollination of crops and natural vegetation, dispersal of seeds, and protection from the sun's harmful ultraviolet rays. They are created by the interactions of living organisms with the environment and are considered public goods benefiting all people. The alarming levels of species extinctions threaten to undermine these complex ecosystem services. Governments and international organizations have a duty to act to protect the world's biodiversity.[51]

In 2001 over 1,350 scientists and environmental experts from around the world came together to examine the impact of ecosystem change on human well-being and survival. Four years later they published the Millennium Ecosystem Assessment (MEA), perhaps the most important global study to date on the world's major ecosystems. In identifying the links between biodiversity and ecosystem services, the report argues that "healthy ecosystems are central to the aspirations of humankind." Unfortunately, the report also notes that "[n]early two-thirds of the services provided by nature to human-kind are found to be in decline worldwide. In effect, the benefits reaped from our engineering of the planet have been achieved by running down natural capital assets."[52] The relationship between ecosystem services and human well-being identified by the MEA is shown in Figure 10.3.

Figure 10.3 includes four categories of ecosystem services: provisioning, regulating, supporting, and cultural. Provisioning refers to the ways in which ecosystems directly meet human needs for food, fresh water, wood and fiber, and fuel. Regulating denotes its management and control of cycles including climate, flooding, diseases, and water purification. Supporting services include nutrient cycling and the formation of soils, crucial underpinnings to agricultural productivity. Cultural services are enhancements to aesthetic, spiritual, educational, and recreational well-being. The links between these critical ecosystem services and human well-being are identified clearly in Figure 10.3. The protection of biodiversity is a key aspect of the UN's linking of environmental and human rights protection (see Theory Spotlight feature).

Figure 10.3 Biodiversity, Ecosystem Services, and Human Well-being.

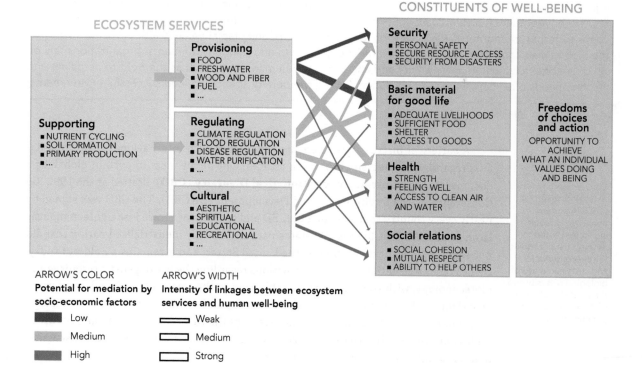

THEORY SPOTLIGHT

Human Rights and the Environment

Both human rights law and environmental law seek to establish norms to modify human behavior. Despite growing awareness of the links between the two, tensions have emerged between human rights activists and environmental activists.

Some environmentalists contend that the anthropocentric focus on human rights can lead to ecological ruin. Economic development intended to increase consumption and improve the general standard of living for the world's 7.6 billion people could lead to a rapid depletion of natural resources and have devastating environmental repercussions.

Human rights activists fear that prioritizing long-term ecological balance can displace the urgency of ending human suffering today. From this perspective, the environmental movement privileges the rights of other species while neglecting the economic human rights of the sick and the hungry.

Yet environmental and human rights concerns come together in countless ways. One of these is the high human costs of environmental degradation, which are often distributed unfairly. Poor and minority neighborhoods often bear the brunt of pollution. Such

environmental racism The disparate impact of environmental degradation and hazards on disadvantaged groups, including the disproportionate exposure to pollutants and the lack of access to clean air, water, and natural resources.

harsh outcomes, often referred to as **environmental racism** or *environmental injustice*, raise fundamental human rights issues of equality and discrimination. For example, a 2018 report from the US Environmental Protection Agency reports that people of color are much more likely to live near polluters and breathe polluted air as contaminating industries are often located in the middle of their communities. As a result, people in poverty are exposed to more fine particulate matter and "results at national, state, and country scales all indicate that non-Whites tend to be burdened disproportionately to Whites." Such heavy exposure to fine particulate matter leads to serious health problems, including lung and heart disease, asthma, and premature deaths.[53]

In addition, environmental organizations rely on key human rights, such as the right to associate and freedom of speech, to lead successful environmental

---

Convention on Biological Diversity (CBD) An international treaty requiring states-parties to develop national plans for the conservation and sustainable use of biological diversity and the equitable sharing of the benefits from genetic resources.

A variety of instruments to ensure compliance with international environmental laws regarding biodiversity have been created. One of the most important global legal documents is the **Convention on Biological Diversity (CBD)**, drafted at the 1992 Rio Conference on the Environment and Development (UNCED). The CBD was signed by nearly every country that attended UNCED and entered into force just eighteen months later. As of 2018 the CBD has 196 states-parties. The only industrialized nation that did not sign the Convention at Rio was the United States, and it remains a hold-out today. US hesitancy was initially based on provisions regarding the use of genetic resources and biotechnology, with the United States objecting to the treatment of intellectual property rights and the requirement to share benefits and technology gained from biological resources.[56] Non-ratification is also a result of the United States' general mistrust of multilateralism and international organizations, which was described in the discussion of international human rights in Chapter 9.

Nathan King / Alamy Stock Photo

"The destruction of the earth's environment is the human rights challenge of our time."
—Archbishop Desmond Tutu, Nobel Peace Prize Laureate

movements. Countries such as Russia, where civil and political rights are weak, often experience high levels of ecological damage but lack the political space for organizing environmental efforts.

Environmental protection can also be seen as a vehicle for the fulfillment of human rights that cannot be actualized in a degraded physical environment. Deforestation, oil spills, and toxic dumps are clear violations of recognized human rights and can literally deprive a local population of the ability to survive. Environmental law is critically important not only to future generations but to those alive today, including indigenous groups, who depend on natural resources for their survival.[54]

In 1994 Fatma Zohra Ksentini, the UN's special rapporteur on human rights and the environment, released her final report titled "Human Rights and the Environment," which argues that there has been "a shift from environmental law to the right to a healthy and decent environment." Part one of the report declares: "Human rights, an ecologically sound environment, sustainable development and peace are interdependent and indivisible."[55]

The UN sees both environmental and human rights protections as key to basic human survival. A "human right to a healthy environment" pertains to both biological necessities such as access to food and water and the management of ecosystems to ensure environmental sustainability.

Think about It

1. Where do you stand in the debate between human rights and environmental organizers?

2. Can a claim to a "human right to a healthy environment" bridge the perceived gap between economic development and ecological balance? Explain your answer.

The CBD has three central aims: the conservation of biological diversity, the sustainable use of its components, and the fair and equitable sharing of benefits from the use of genetic resources. States-parties are legally required to inventory and monitor biodiversity, incorporate conservation strategies based on sustainable development into their economic development plans, and preserve indigenous conservation practices.

To achieve a compromise between those states interested in conservation (primarily developed nations) and others interested in benefitting from biological resources (primarily developing nations), CBD negotiators described conservation of biological diversity as a **Common Concern of Humankind**. This new principle of international environmental law is weaker than the common heritage of humankind described earlier in the chapter. Some viewed the common heritage principle as too great an infringement on state sovereignty and the ability to benefit from biological resources within national borders. The common concern principle implies less infringement on sovereignty and

Common Concern of Humankind A principle in international environmental law that signifies the need for collective action to protect areas of critical importance to all of humanity, even if those areas fall solely within a nation's jurisdiction.

retains a state's ability to direct its own plans for sustainable use of biological resources. Yet it still makes clear that vulnerable environmental assets of critical importance are a common concern of the global community, regardless of where they are located, and it leaves the door open to the possibility of collective action to protect them.[57]

Each state-party to the CBD is required to create a national strategy for conserving biodiversity based on accurate and comprehensive information regarding the threats to ecosystems, including clear objectives and priorities. Since the passage of the CBD, dozens of countries have developed plans for both *in situ* and *ex situ* conservation. *In situ* conservation involves actions to protect and retain biological components in their natural habitats. *Ex situ* conservation refers to zoos, gene banks, and other efforts outside of natural habitats to conserve species and ecosystems.[58]

Some nations have begun to set up implementation plans, but there is no mechanism to monitor implementation at the national level and no process for systematic review of national reports. These weaknesses of the treaty were clearly demonstrated by the failure of the international community to meet the 2010 global targets. These goals, first established in 2002 and later incorporated into the Millennium Development Goals, were to decrease the rates of biodiversity reduction. To apply "soft" pressure to its member states the UN had even established 2010 as the "International Year of Biodiversity." As documented in the 2010 Global Biodiversity Outlook, trend lines continued to move in dangerous directions.[59] The report noted the following:

- Species already assessed for extinction risk are moving closer to extinction. Amphibians face the greatest risk, and coral species are deteriorating most rapidly. Nearly 25% of plant species are threatened with extinction.
- Based on assessed populations, the abundance of vertebrate species fell by nearly 33% between 1970 and 2006 and continues to fall globally, with especially severe declines in the tropics and among freshwater species.
- Natural habitats in most parts of the world continue to decline in extent and integrity.
- Extensive fragmentation and degradation of forests, rivers, and other ecosystems have contributed to loss of biodiversity and ecosystem services.
- Crop and livestock genetic diversity continues to decline.
- The five principal pressures directly driving biodiversity loss (habitat change, overexploitation, pollution, invasive alien species, and climate change) are either constant or increasing in intensity.[60]

It seems only too clear that international cooperation and action to protect the atmosphere, oceans, and biodiversity remain tragically inadequate. While significant progress has been made since the 1972 Stockholm Conference in codifying a large body of international environmental laws, they are often ineffective. The agreements lack monitoring compliance provisions, and there are few sanctions or punishments for states that violate them.

Global institutions are needed to help all nations fulfill their duties under international environmental law and avoid harmful environmental practices, but their success depends on nations agreeing on environmental norms, rules, procedures, and mechanisms of compliance. The construction of neutral global environmental organizations, based on a true understanding of ecological interdependence and dedicated to scientific objectivity in the formulation of public policy, is essential for the survival of the planet.

CONTEMPORARY PERSPECTIVE:
Global Environmental Governance, 2002–2019

Ten years after the Rio Conference the UN held a World Summit on Sustainable Development (WSSD) in 2002 in Johannesburg, South Africa. The Millennium Development Goals (MDGs; see Chapter 8) heavily influenced the Johannesburg conference as leaders tried to integrate poverty alleviation efforts with sustainability objectives. The international atmosphere in 2002 differed significantly from the hopeful climate of the Rio conference. In 2002 the United States was still reeling from the terrorist attacks of Sept 11, 2001, and was focused on national security and planning the wars in Afghanistan and Iraq. Because the United States had only been on the sidelines during the environmental

Bubaone / iStock

Global environmental governance is essential for sustainable and equitable development for all.

negotiations leading up to the event, it was highly criticized for its role at the conference itself. Over a hundred world leaders, including Nelson Mandela (South Africa), Tony Blair (UK), and Vladimir Putin (Russia), were present, but US President George W. Bush refused to attend. In addition, the US delegation fought hard to remove targets and timetables from the implementation agenda and sought to shift the focus away from climate change. In the end the United States remained indifferent to the outcome of the WSSD Johannesburg conference.[61]

In addition, less-developed countries (LDCs) were frustrated by the lack of implementation of many of the promises and commitments made at the Rio conference, particularly the failure to provide funding mechanisms and financial resources to help LDCs transition to sustainable practices. In the ten years following the Rio Summit there had been a noticeable lack of progress on fulfilling either the *Rio Declaration* or *Agenda 21*. Most troubling of all, according to key scientific indicators, the environment had continued to deteriorate during that time.

Yet the WSSD ultimately adopted the *Johannesburg Declaration,* a *Plan of Implementation,* and nearly three hundred partnership agreements. The *Johannesburg Declaration* differed significantly from the *Rio Declaration.* While the Rio document focused on developing legal principles to strengthen international environmental law, the Johannesburg text was merely a general political statement in support of sustainable development. The meekness of the document is shown in article 26:

> We recognize that sustainable development requires a long-term perspective and broad-based participation in policy formulation, decision-making and implementation at all levels. As social partners, we will continue to work for stable partnerships with all major groups, respecting the independent, important roles of each of them.[62]

The *Johannesburg Plan of Implementation* outlined a set of action items necessary for achieving sustainable development. Instead of working on new instruments of international law, the plan focused on implementation of the existing legal framework. Goals focused on water and sanitation, energy, health, agriculture, and biodiversity, and these were intended to complement the MDGs.[63]

The next major assessment of global environmental governance took place ten years later. In 2012 the **UN Conference on Sustainable Development (UNCSD)**, also known as Rio+20, was held in Rio de Janeiro. Rio+20 was again attended by thousands of delegates from states and civil society, but the optimism of the initial environmental conferences continued to fade, and pessimism and frustration grew. The environmental goals agreed to by the nations of the world at previous conferences had again not been met and, most significantly, ecological problems continued to get worse. Global forums and meetings since the first Rio conference had too often degenerated into implementation battles and political arguments between rich and poor states over finances, technology transfer, and ultimate responsibility. The economic costs of reversing ecological degradation had increased with each passing year. Although the stakes were never

UN Conference on Sustainable Development (UNCSD) A 2012 conference in Rio that launched international working groups to define and develop the UN's Sustainable Development Goals.

higher, the world's leaders fumbled and seemed stymied about how to move forward. Ultimately, the delegates at Rio+20 failed to agree to establish a stronger framework for global environmental governance. As a result, the institutional framework for sustainable development remains weak to this day.[64] Many critics labeled Rio+20 a failure and began to question the overall effectiveness of the UN's multilateral approach to sustainable development.[65]

Perhaps the biggest accomplishment of Rio+20 was establishment of a defining set of Sustainable Development Goals (SDGs; see Chapter 8). Working groups were launched following the conference to develop the SDGs with targets designed to enhance and guide public policy for sustainable development. The governments at Rio+20 stated: "[The] sustainable development goals should be action oriented, concise and easy to communicate, limited in number, aspirational, global in nature and universally applicable to all countries while taking into account different national realities, capacities and levels of development and respecting national policies and priorities."[66] As you learned in Chapter 8, these guidelines were followed and the SDG agenda is now the principal framework guiding global environmental governance.

LOOKING TO THE FUTURE:
Trade and the Environment and the Precautionary Principle

In the coming decades the international community faces daunting collective challenges; the rules, norms, procedures, and laws designed to protect the global environment must all be strengthened. This section describes the intersection between trade and the environment and the difficulties of achieving the right balance between these too often conflicting priorities. Then it turns to an evolving norm in international environmental law called the Precautionary Principle and examines its utility in resolving conflicts between economic development and environmental protection.

Trade and the Environment

International trade law developed as a self-contained field focused on the principles and ideology of free trade. International environmental law came later and raised new norms and rules governing sustainability and environmental protection. As environmental and trade policies have become more intertwined, clashes of ideas and rules regarding competition, trade, and the environment are occurring in international relations. One example is the adoption by one or more states of unilateral environmental protection measures, which may limit international trade.

In 1998 former US President Bill Clinton argued that sovereign unilateral state action to protect the environment has priority over trade law. Clinton declared:

We must do more to harmonize our goal of increasing trade with our goal of improving the environment and working conditions.... International trade rules must permit sovereign nations to exercise their right to set protective standards for health, safety, and the environment and biodiversity. Nations have a right to pursue those protections—even when they are stronger than international norms.[67]

The World Trade Organization (WTO) disagrees with this position, and in a multitude of decisions it has prioritized trade rules.

Conflict came to a head in the late 1990s when rulings by a WTO Appellate Body struck down US legal protections for sea turtles, an internationally protected species endangered around the world by the loss of their habitat. This became an international trade issue with the development of mechanized shrimp trawling, which by 1990 had caused some 100,000 adult turtles to drown each year, a loss that is easily preventable. An inexpensive, easy to install turtle excluder device has proven effective in keeping turtles out of shrimp nets. The United States not only required its domestic shrimp industry to use turtle excluders but applied identical standards to countries selling shrimp in US markets. In response, Malaysia, Thailand, India, and Pakistan filed a complaint with the WTO, claiming that the requirement deprived them of market access guaranteed under most-favored-nation (MFN) status, an obligation that prohibits discrimination between products of different member states. For all WTO members, "every time a country lowers a trade barrier or opens up a market, it has to do so for the same goods or services from all its trading partners." The WTO Appellate Body decided in favor of the four Asian countries, expressing concern over the coercive effect of the US measure on the policies of other governments.[68] The United States lost this case because the WTO determined that the United States applied its rules regarding shrimp fishing arbitrarily, which discriminated against the nations filing the complaint. The decision was not based on environmental criteria but on the perceived unfair application of trade rules.

Another key WTO core principle that impacts trade and the environment is *National Treatment*. According to this principle, WTO member states are required to give foreign goods the same treatment as their own national goods.[69]

Key to understanding both MFN and National Treatment is the meaning of "like products" such as shrimp. WTO members cannot discriminate between "like products." Shrimp harvested in Malaysia or in the United States or in Thailand should be treated equally in the market.

Environmentalists argue that it is sometimes important to distinguish between similar products on the basis of environmental impacts. Attention must be paid to how the product is being produced. If a WTO member's shrimp trawling methods endanger sea turtles, environmentalists believe that discrimination against that country's shrimp harvest should be allowed. Environmentalists and human rights advocates contend that governments should be entitled to discriminate on the basis of how products are produced in the exporting country. The process or production methods (PPMs) of physically similar products should be taken into account. In their view, if a production method is environmentally destructive, that product should not be considered a "like product."

The WTO is hesitant to incorporate PPM into its definition of "like products" because this type of discrimination could open the door for nations to erect inappropriate protectionist barriers and interfere in the sovereignty of exporting countries. WTO panels have historically adopted a restrictive reading of "like products" based on physical characteristics and not PPMs. However, recent WTO Appellate Bodies have pursued a more nuanced approach and seem to indicate the need to consider non-trade concerns, including environmental impact.

Nearly all WTO disputes have been resolved in favor of trade rules over environmental concerns. A key issue is whether the international community will modify the existing free trade regime organized through the WTO to take environmental considerations more fully into account. This seems possible, given WTO rules that state "nothing... shall be construed to prevent the adoption or enforcement by any contracting party of measures...necessary to protect human, animal or plant life or health." Perhaps going forward the global trade regime will pursue a more balanced approach between international trade and environmental law.

The Precautionary Principle: An Environmental Paradigm for the Twenty-First Century?

In the mid-1980s the **precautionary principle** emerged in international environmental law to provide a framework for action when there is scientific uncertainty about the ecological impact of economic development. As stated in Principle 15 of the Rio Declaration: "In order to protect the environment, the precautionary approach shall be widely applied by states according to their capabilities. Where there are threats of serious or irreversible damage, lack of full scientific certainty shall not be used as a reason for postponing cost-effective measures to prevent environmental degradation."[70] The precautionary principle has been widely adopted in many international environmental treaties since Rio.

To a certain extent, the precautionary principle reverses the more traditional approach to science and development. Established approaches called on states to adapt decisions based on scientific findings and knowledge, taking preventive actions only when there was scientific evidence that significant ecological damage was occurring. No action was required in the absence of firm evidence.[71]

The precautionary principle takes anticipatory actions to avoid ecological damage before it occurs, shifting the burden of proof to the institution or individual engaged in a potentially dangerous activity. Such activity could not be undertaken unless the public was guaranteed that it was harmless. For example, if a company wanted to use a particular chemical, they would have to prove that it was not harmful to the environment. The burden of proof is on the company. According to this principle, polluting industries and states would have to establish that their activities and discharges would not negatively impact the environment before they were granted the right to carry on the proposed activity.[72]

The central idea is that states cannot wait for proof of harmful effects before taking action. Modernization, economic globalization, and industrialization can lead to

precautionary principle A framework for action stipulating that when an action may cause serious environmental threats and potentially irreversible damage, the lack of full scientific certainty should not be used to prevent implementation of measures to avert environmental degradation.

irreversible damage to the atmosphere, oceans, and biodiversity. Measures to prevent environmental degradation cannot wait for full scientific certainty. The precautionary principle calls for prudent and precautionary actions now to prevent future ecological destruction.

The precautionary principle could provide an overall paradigm for environmental policy-makers. Advantages include the focus on prevention, which would not allow the lack of complete scientific unanimity to sideline needed environmental protectionist policies. In addition, shifting the burden of proof to those who engage in an activity or development project would greatly strengthen environmental protection policy. Such a precautionary approach has the potential to provide a viable framework for effective environmental policy-making in the twenty-first century.[73]

Summary

- The UN Conference on the Human Environment in Stockholm (1972) and the UN Conference on Environment and Development (UNCED) in Rio (1992) significantly enhanced global norms, rules, and procedures in international environmental law to protect the world's ecosystem.

- The 1992 Climate Change Convention established a general framework to mitigate and limit climate change due to global warming. Under the 2015 Paris Climate Change Agreement 195 nations committed to national plans to lower greenhouse gas (GHG) emissions to prevent a further dangerous rise in the world's temperature. The 1994 Law of the Seas Treaty granted coastal states sovereign rights over a two-hundred-mile exclusive economic zone with responsibility to prevent overfishing and conserve ocean resources for long-term sustainability. The 1992 Convention on Biological Diversity has three central aims: the conservation of biological diversity, the sustainable use of its components, and the fair and equitable sharing of the benefits arising from the use of genetic resources.

- The 2012 UN Conference on Sustainable Development (UNCSD) played a key role in the development of sustainable development goals (SDGs) designed to guide public policy.

- Resolutions of current conflicts between international trade law and environmental law are critical to the preservation of the natural environment. The precautionary principle may provide a framework for mediating the dilemmas between economic development and environmental protection.

Key Terms

Antarctic Treaty Regime *(313)*

Biodiversity *(311)*

Carbon Tax *(306)*

Climate Change *(302)*

Climate Change Convention *(302)*

Common Concern of Humankind *(317)*

Critical Thinking Questions

1. Did the UN environmental conferences from Stockholm (1972) to Rio (1992) succeed in creating a new global framework for addressing the key ecological crisis confronting humanity? Explain your answer.

2. What is the "tragedy of the commons?" What are the "commons?" What is the tragedy?

3. In what ways have environmental problems become increasingly global in nature?

4. How did the 2015 Paris Climate Change Agreement modify and potentially strengthen the Climate Change Convention? Will the Paris agreement be effective without the participation of the United States? Why or why not?

5. The "exclusive economic zones" established in the Law of the Seas Treaty unfortunately did not curb overfishing by coastal states. What additional measures by the international community might help to create sustainable fishing on the oceans?

6. Why is biodiversity considered a "common concern of humankind" in international law? What does this concept imply about state sovereignty over biological resources?

7. A proposal was made in 2012 for the creation of a new and more powerful "United Nations Environmental Organization" (UNEO) to replace the existing, weak UN Environment Program (UNEP). Is a strong, centralized UNEO needed to monitor and coordinate compliance with international environmental law? Explain your answer.

8. Is it possible to reconcile the conflicting priorities between international trade law and global environmental law? Why or why not?

9. Should individual nations implement and enforce the "precautionary principle" or should it be monitored and implemented by the UN? Explain your answer.

Practice and Review Online
http://textbooks.rowman.com/hastedt-felice

...ns clamber onto overcrowded pickup trucks that are ready for a journey across a deserted ...scape. *Source:* Jerome Delay / AP Images

11

LOOKING FORWARD:
NEW POLICY CHALLENGES AND RESPONSES

CHAPTER 1 BEGAN BY RAISING THE FOLLOWING QUESTION: how do you make sense out of international politics? Given the complex and wide range of global problems that exist, as well as great inconsistencies in the ability of people and states to cooperate, we return to this question in this concluding chapter but place it in a different context: how do we make sense of the future directions that international politics might take?

The point in asking this question is not to make predictions about the future or engage in fortune telling. Because too much uncertainty and disagreement exist about how and why events unfold as they do, surprises cannot be eliminated. Instead, the purpose is to clarify and provide insight into the thought process involved. As one former intelligence analyst observed, "having a picture is not the same as knowing the significance of what you see."

So it is with looking to the future. To say that nuclear proliferation will continue, environmental problems will multiply, democracy will flourish, or economic prosperity will spread does not explain the significance of these events or their implications for the national, global, or human interest. Along these same lines, investigations into the future are important because they challenge our thinking. As author Peter Schwartz observed in *The Art of the Long View*, all too often "we pay attention only to what we think we need to know."[1] We may be wrong. Thinking about the future is also important from a policy perspective. The key concept here is **risk management**, the procedure for identifying, assessing, and controlling potential threats. Management of the risk of war, famine, or a natural disaster is a function of two distinct factors: (1) the likelihood of an event; and (2) its consequences. The risk of a global nuclear war is low, but the consequences are great. Conversely, the risks of a terrorist attack in a fragile state are much higher, but the global consequences are not as great. Effective risk management requires not only making judgments about likelihood and consequences but also developing strategies for anticipating them.

A continuing challenge in anticipating the future is identifying the pattern of economic relations among states and their impact on international politics. On the eve of World War I British journalist and future Nobel Peace Prize winner Norman Angell authored a book titled *The Great Illusion*.[2] In it he argued that the increased economic interdependence of states had made war unprofitable to such a degree that it would be disastrous, transforming war into "the great illusion." Although WWI proved him wrong, elements of his argument continue to influence thinking about international politics.

LEARNING OBJECTIVES

Students will be able to:

- Explain the significance of trade wars for international politics.

- Outline the steps followed in creating global images of the future.

- Compare the fundamental dynamics of the three alternative futures identified in the Global 2035 report.

- Distinguish between conservative internationalism and postcolonialism as frameworks for studying international politics.

- Explain the significance of cities and private military armies as independent global actors.

- Define the concepts of risk cascades and trauma states.

- Identify the key issues for international politics in promoting green growth and responding to mass human migrations.

TRADE WARS

A recurring fear is the onset of **trade wars**, conflicts in which one state imposes economic restrictions on another, which then retaliates.[3] In the early years of the twentieth century US international economic policy was built around high tariffs and protectionism. In 1913 a Democratic Congress reversed this policy orientation and lowered tariffs. After WWI Republicans regained control of Congress and once again began to pass protectionist trade legislation. Its most notable legislation was the 1930 Smoot-Hawley Tariff which raised tariffs on over twenty thousand foreign-made goods imported into the United States. Other nations soon retaliated, leading to a dramatic reduction in the level of international trade. US imports from Europe fell from $1,334 million in 1929 to $390 million in 1932, and US exports to Europe fell from $2,341 million to $784 million over the same period.

Just prior to the passage of the Smoot-Hawley Tariff Act, 1,082 economists wrote a letter to Congress urging then to reject it. In this letter they warned that:

> A higher level of protection would raise the cost of living and injure the great majority of our citizens ... since they produce no products which could be protected by tariff barriers. The vast majority of farmers, also, would lose. ... Our export trade, in general, would suffer. Countries cannot permanently buy from us unless they are permitted to sell to us ...[4]

Diametrically opposed to this analysis of the future, in the summer of 1929 Yale economist Irving Fisher wrote that "stock markets have reached what looks like a permanently high plateau."[5] Less than two months later the stock market crashed. The Great Depression followed as did a global trade war in which states created protectionist trade restrictions in hopes of keeping jobs at home.

trade war A conflict in which one state imposes economic restrictions on another, which then retaliates.

Idealink Photography / Alamy Stock Photo

Tracking daily activity at China's stock market.

The post-WWII era began with a major international effort to prevent a reoccurrence of these "beggar-thy-neighbor" international trade wars, which became known as the Bretton Woods System (see Chapter 1). This system expanded greatly over time but also began to tire. Meaningful global trade and financial agreements became more difficult to negotiate. Attention began to shift to regional and bilateral agreements. Most recently, international economic relations have begun to revert back to the protectionist rhetoric and practice of the 1930s.

In the leadoff to this most recent period, the Trump administration has imposed economic sanctions on a number of states, most notably North Korea and Iran, and has engaged in competitive tariff-raising policies with the European Union, Mexico, Canada, and China. This has created what is commonly regarded as a trade war between the United States and China. Between January and September 2018 the United States imposed tariffs of 10–25% on $250 billion worth of Chinese goods coming into the United States. China retaliated following each announcement. In April it placed tariffs on 128 products imported from the United States including aluminum, airplanes, cars, and soybeans. In July when the United States imposed tariffs on $34 billion of Chinese goods, China responded by placing increased tariffs on a similar amount of US goods. At that point both sides pulled back and entered into trade talks designed to lessen tensions. Expectations of an agreement were high, but expectations of a major breakthrough were limited. China was expected to continue running a large trade surpluses with the United States and would not accept major trade and industry reforms.

The Trump administration defended its global trade policy, stating that it was simply seeking to level the playing field and establish fair and reciprocal trade relations with other states, and promised that economic success would follow. However, over 1,100 economists signed an open letter warning of the dangers of this approach. Their letter quoted directly from the 1930 letter to Congress opposing the Smoot-Hawley Tariff policy. How can we determine who is correct?

CREATING IMAGES OF THE FUTURE

No single strategy exists for creating future images of international politics. This section introduces some of the common models that are used to construct such visions.

The first step in thinking about the future is to compose a *plot*, a storyline that lays out the relationships among key characters and their consequences. Any number of different plots can be identified and used to construct alternative visions of the future. According to theorist Peter Schwartz, those frequently used include challenges and responses; winners and losers; cycles, revolution, evolution, and generational change.

Once one or more plots are identified, the next step is to establish a set of anchoring assumptions that drive it. The focus here is on the social, economic, political, and technological contexts within which individuals act, rather than on the specific actions

Figure 11.1
Anticipating Wild
Cards and Black
Swans Is Key
to Anticipating
the Direction of
Future Events in
International Politics.

they take. One starting point for establishing future drivers of international politics is an examination of the theories of international politics introduced in Chapter 2 as well as the commentaries included in the Theory Spotlight features throughout the text. A second starting point is an understanding of the four underlying dynamics of international cooperation discussed throughout *Introduction to International Politics: Challenges and Responses*: war, economics, human rights, and environmental change. Do not assume that only one of these will drive changes in the future or that they will operate in silos independent of one another.

It is also necessary to anticipate **wild cards**, unexpected developments that hold the potential for invalidating or contradicting the influence of plot drivers and altering plot outcomes. Wild cards (see Figure 11.1) may create barriers to expected changes or send change in a different direction than anticipated. Because wild cards are not necessarily total surprises or events that cannot be imagined, they are often referred to as *Black Swans*. We know that black swans exist—they breed mainly in Australia—yet historically the dominant shared perception of swans is that they are white. When a black swan appears it catches people by surprise and is treated as a rare and even abnormal occurrence.

wild cards
Unexpected developments that hold the potential for invalidating or contradicting expected outcomes; also referred to as *Black Swans*.

The last step in thinking about the future is to clarify the time frame. Is this future ten years out, twenty years from now, or even longer? The further into the future that you look, the greater the uncertainty, imprecision, and fuzziness will become in visions of future international politics. Conversely, the shorter the time frame, the greater the amount of detail that can be provided and the more well defined the implications and consequences of the plot will be. Regardless of the selected time frame, avoid the danger of falling victim to *assumption drag*, an over-reliance on assumptions that are currently in vogue or have guided thinking in the past.

GLOBAL TRENDS 2035

Beginning in 1997, every four years the National Intelligence Council has published an unclassified assessment of key trends, uncertainties, and alternative images of how international politics might look twenty years into the future. Government officials, academics, and individuals from the private sector work together in constructing the *Global Trends* report. Issued just prior to the presidential inauguration, its stated goal is to spark policy discussions about foreign policy key assumptions, priorities, and choices.

Global Trends 2035, released in January 2017, identifies seven key global trends.[6] Listed in Table 11.1, they cover domestic and international affairs; economic relations and military conflicts; and global hazards such as the health, the environment, and climate change. These trends will converge at an unprecedented pace to make governing and cooperation harder and to change the nature of power—fundamentally altering the global landscape. Economic, technological, and security trends, especially, will expand the number of states, organizations, and individuals able to act in consequential ways.

According to the report, the bottom line is that the unipolar moment that came with the end of the Cold War has passed and the post-WWII world order may be fading away as well. In its place an international system is emerging, in which governing and cooperation are more difficult and the nature of power has changed. As a result of these changes tensions will remain high, but opportunities for creating a more secure future will also be present.

Three sets of uncertainties guided the construction of scenarios for the international politics of 2035:

- The nature of domestic political dynamics, particularly how governments and public created new political orders in an era of change.
- The patterns of cooperation and conflict among countries, individuals, and groups.
- The long-term and short-term tradeoffs states and others were willing to make in addressing complex global issues.

Based on the interaction of these three factors, three visions of the international system in 2035 and how it will have got there can be constructed: islands, orbits, and communities.

| TABLE 11.1 | Global Trends and Key Implications Through 2035 |

The rich are aging, the poor are not. Working-age populations are shrinking in wealthy countries, China, and Russia, but they are growing in developing, poorer countries, particularly in Africa and South Asia, increasing economic, employment, urbanization, and welfare pressures and spurring migration. Training and continuing education will be crucial in developed and developing countries alike.

The global economy is shifting. Weak economic growth will persist in the near term. Major economies will confront shrinking workforces and diminishing productivity gains while recovering from the 2008–09 financial crisis with high debt, weak demand, and doubts about globalization. China will attempt to shift to a consumer-driven economy from its long-standing export and investment focus. Lower growth will threaten poverty reduction in developing countries.

Technology is accelerating progress but causing discontinuities. Rapid technological advancements will increase the pace of change and create new opportunities but will aggravate divisions between winners and losers. Automation and artificial intelligence threaten to change industries faster than economies can adjust, potentially displacing workers and limiting the usual route for poor countries to develop. Biotechnologies such as genome editing will revolutionize medicine and other fields, while sharpening moral differences.

Ideas and identities are driving a wave of exclusion. Growing global connectivity amid weak growth will increase tensions within and between societies. Populism will increase on the right and the left, threatening liberalism. Some leaders will use nationalism to shore up control. Religious influence will be increasingly consequential and more authoritative than many governments. Nearly all countries will see economic forces boost women's status and leadership roles, but backlash also will occur.

Governing is getting harder. Publics will demand that governments deliver security and prosperity, but flat revenues, distrust, polarization, and a growing list of emerging issues will hamper government performance. Technology will expand the range of players who can block or circumvent political action. Managing global issues will become harder as actors multiply—to include NGOs, corporations, and empowered individuals—resulting in more ad hoc and fewer encompassing efforts.

The nature of conflict is changing. The risk of conflict will increase due to diverging interests among major powers, an expanding terror threat, continued instability in weak states, and the spread of lethal, disruptive technologies. Disrupting societies will become more common, with long-range precision weapons, cyber and robotic systems to target infrastructure from afar, and more accessible technology to create weapons of mass destruction.

Climate change, environment, and health issues will demand attention. A range of global hazards pose imminent and longer-term threats that will require collective action to address—even as cooperation becomes harder. More extreme weather, water and soil stress, and food insecurity will disrupt societies. Sea-level rise, ocean acidification, glacial melt, and pollution will change living patterns. Tensions over climate change will grow. Increased travel and poor health infrastructure will make infectious diseases harder to manage.

Source: National Intelligence Council, *Global Trends 2035* (Washington, DC, January, 2017), 6.
https://www.dni.gov/files/documents/nic/GT-Full-Report.pdf.

The *islands pathway* takes as its starting point the difficulties of restructuring the global economy in a way that produces economic prosperity and expands globalization. One attractive response, out of choice or necessity, will be to adopt a defensive posture in which states seek to wall themselves off from the perceived costs, unpredictability, and challenges of globalization and international cooperation. States become islands.

The *orbits pathway* to the future focuses on the tensions created by competition for establishing spheres of influence by the major powers as they seek to maintain domestic stability. The combination of rising nationalism, new patterns of conflict, new disruptive technologies, and decreasing global cooperation are seen as sowing the seeds for increased interstate conflict and the decay of a rule-based international order.

The *community pathway* directs attention to the changing nature of power and who wields it. In this model states will continue to dominate the area of military power. However, individuals, nongovernmental organizations, religious and advocacy groups, and private businesses will become increasingly powerful actors in economic policy through their control and direction of the global flow of capital assets and their ability to control and manipulate information. In some cases this will result in the collapse of fragile states. In other cases it will lead to a trial-and error-approach to creating a new style of global governance in which non-state actors are empowered through the establishment of multi-stakeholder coalitions. The remainder of this chapter presents a series of changes and developments that might arise in the four different themes of this text: war, economics, human rights, and environmental change.

FUTURE FOUNDATIONS OF INTERNATIONAL POLITICS

conservative internationalism
A framework for studying international politics that occupies a middle ground between liberal internationalism and isolationism; emphasizes states as the central actors in international politics, protecting the national interest, practicing armed diplomacy, and prioritizing foreign policy goals.

Throughout *International Politics: Challenges and Responses* we have stressed that no single conceptual lens is used to study international politics. There is no reason to assume that future studies of international politics will continue to use the same conceptual frameworks of realism, liberalism, economic structuralism, constructivism, and feminism. Two possible new conceptual frameworks are conservative internationalism and postcolonialism.

Conservative Internationalism

Conservative internationalism, a framework for studying international politics that occupies a middle ground between liberal internationalism and isolationism, is not new. In various forms it has existed for centuries in European and American perspectives on international politics. In Europe it has been associated with the diplomacy of Metternich and Bismarck. The US foreign policies of James Polk, Teddy Roosevelt, and Ronald Reagan are often characterized as conservative internationalism.[7] What has been lacking is an agreed-upon definition like those that exist for liberal internationalism and realism. Recently this has begun to change, and the foundation for such a definition has begun to emerge. However, variations in how to conceptualize this idea still exist.

One of those who has advanced the concept of conservative internationalism is political scientist Henry Nau,[8] who defines it in terms of four key dimensions:

- **Actions of sovereign states**. International politics centers on the actions of sovereign states, not international organizations, collective security, or globalization.
- **Political and ideological composition of states**. International politics is about more than the defense of territorial borders and balances of power. A democratic world is a safer world within which to conduct foreign policy and protect national interests.
- **Armed diplomacy**. The key component of foreign policy in a world of ideological competition is armed diplomacy. Traditional diplomacy is insufficient to curb the aggressive actions of authoritarian states. It must be accompanied by the use of force outside of and during negotiations if these negotiations are to succeed in weakening authoritarian states and curbing their behavior.
- **Prioritization**. Foreign policy must be built around priorities, especially the promotion of freedom and democracy. These goals must be pursued selectively. For the United States this means actively promoting democracy in key areas such as Europe and Asia. Elsewhere it should take a *long-haul perspective*, in which the immediate pursuit of democracy takes second place to security considerations.

In sum, Nau defines conservative internationalism as "embracing the goals of liberal internationalism (reforming the international system, not settling for the status quo), the means of realism (the use of force during negotiations, not as a last resort), and the purpose of nationalism (a world of sovereign but free states, not global international institutions)."

Postcolonialism

At first glance **postcolonialism** theory would seem to be easy to define, as *postcolonialism* refers to the period following the end of colonialism. In practice it is anything but easy to define. It is home to a wide variety of approaches and involves a wide range of topics. One point on which postcolonialism theorists agree is that it is not a time-bound perspective and not what is "leftover" from the colonial period.[9]

Postcolonialism is about the politics of knowledge. Its goal is to challenge conventional and widely accepted cultural, social, and political images of the relationship between colonizers and those they colonized. It is commonly accepted that colonialism transformed the world politically and economically. Less recognized is that it transformed the self-identities of those involved in colonialism at home and abroad, as well as

postcolonialism
Theory that critically examines the ongoing legacy of imperialism and colonialism on both the colonizers and the colonized in order to highlight how ideas are created, defined, and evaluated.

Idealized depiction of the oriental world in western art.

The Reception of the Venetian Ambassadors in Damascus by Giovanni di Niccolò Mansueti, c. 1511, Musée du Louvre

their perceptions of others. From the perspective of postcolonialism theory, the normative legacy of colonialism is very much with us today, and the images of the world it has created continue to be a source of power.

Central to the power dynamics inherent in colonialism was the division of the world into two homogeneous but conflicting parts. Theorist Edward Said, perhaps the most influential founding voice in postcolonialism, observes that the colonial powers created the now-dated image of the peoples of Asia, the Middle East, and the Indian subcontinent (collectively identified as "the Orient") as inferior, backward, irrational, and wild.[10] The colonization of Africa produced a similar artificial and uniform image of Africa as the "Dark Continent." Said goes on to note that this portrayal facilitated the adoption of a positive homogeneous cultural European identity. These two sets of characterizations legitimized colonialism, transforming it from an exploitive act into one carried out in service to civilization.

Postcolonial theory first emerged within the humanities where scholars examined the writings and art work of the colonized and colonizers for evidence of the continued influence of colonialism and efforts to challenge these roles. More recently, postcolonialism has become a voice within the study of international politics.[11] The following points are central to its argument:

- The conceptual approaches dominating the study of international politics, including liberalism, realism, and Marxism, are all Eurocentric, so they place limits on its conceptualizations and the nature of alternative solutions to problems.
- The prominence of globalization and the spread of democracy reinforce the Eurocentric bias. Democratization, good government, strong civil societies, and a vibrant private economic sector are portrayed as universally desirable qualities

because the world is moving toward a uniform global culture based on these values. Postcolonialism argues instead that the diversity of historical and cultural experiences of those involved in colonialism, which are different in different settings, must be recognized.

- Struggles against supposedly universal values and those who spread them are depicted as dangerous. They are treated as the product of local failures rather than rooted in how the colonial experience transformed those societies and how it continues to influence global identities.

NEW ACTORS IN THE FUTURE INTERNATIONAL SYSTEM

Dating back to the Treaty of Westphalia in 1648 (see Chapter 3), states have been identified as the dominant actors in international politics. They are not the only important actors, however. Depending on the issue, international organizations, nongovernmental groups, multinational organizations, and terrorists can also play important roles. Two actors noticeably absent from this list are cities and private armies, which could gain in importance in the future.

Two key questions surrounding the increased importance of cities and private armies as global actors are "why this is happening?" and "will it continue?" For some the reason lies with the breakdown of the international order. A competing perspective sees the growing influence of non-state actors such as cities and private armies as a natural result of changing global agenda and the importance of local issues in international politics.[12]

Cities

Cities occupy only 2% of the global landscape but hold over 50% of the world's population. In 1950 only seventy-five cities around the world had populations of over one million. By 2011 this number had increased to 447, and by 2050 it is estimated that over 66% of the world's population will live in cities. It is increasingly recognized that cities are positioned to play a significant role in international politics. In its *2015 Quadrennial Diplomacy and Development Review* the US State Department went so far as to recommend building stronger relationships with cities as part of US foreign policy.[13] Table 11.2 presents a list of cities and the areas in which they hold important global positions in such diverse areas as business activity, human capital, information exchange, cultural experience, and political engagement.[14]

Cities around the globe have already begun to organize to promote and protect their own interests as well as those of their states and the international community.[15] Acting individually, cities such as New York, Washington, DC, and Miami have engaged

TABLE 11.2	2018 Global Cities Index

OVERALL GLOBAL CITY INDEX LEADERS

Business Activity: New York

Human Capital: New York

Information Exchange: Paris

Culture Experience: London

Political Engagement: Washington, DC

LEADING GLOBAL CITY LEADERS BY METRIC

Category	City	Measure
Business Activity	Beijing	Fortune 500
	Hong Kong	Global services
	New York	Capital markets
	Hong Kong	Air freight
	Shanghai	Sea freight
	Paris	ICCA conferences
Human Capital	New York	Foreign-born population
	Boston	Top universities
	Tokyo	Populations with tertiary degrees
	Melbourne	International student population
	Hong Kong	Number of international schools
Information Exchange	Geneva, Brussels	Access to TV news
	London	News agency bureaus
	Geneva, Zurich	Broadband subscribers
	Brussels, Stockholm, Amsterdam	Freedom of expression
	Singapore	Online presence
Cultural Experience	Moscow	Museums
	New York	Visual and performing arts
	London	Sporting events
	London	International travelers
	New York	Culinary offerings
	St. Petersburg	Sister cities
Political Engagement	Brussels	Embassies and consulates
	Washington, DC	Think tanks
	Geneva	International organizations
	Brussels	Political conferences
	New York	Local institutions with global reach

Source: A. T. Kearney, "Learning from the East—Insights from China's Urban Successes," *2018 Global Cities Report*, https://www.atkearney.com/2018-global-cities-report.

in cooperative counterterrorism efforts with foreign police and intelligence officials. New York, Toronto, Beijing, and Rotterdam have set up their own biosafety labs so that they do not need to rely on national labs to take effective action in the face of a disease pandemic.

Cities are also forming organizations in order to promote their interests. Notable examples include the following:

- **Mayors for Peace**. Proposed in 1982 by the mayor of Hiroshima at a UN Special Session on Disarmament, its initial objective was to raise citizen support across the globe for abolishing nuclear weapons. Over time the Mayors for Peace agenda has grown to include questions of poverty reduction, refugee assistance, human rights, and environmental protection. In 2018 members included 7,668 cities from 163 countries and regions.
- **Strong Cities Network**. Founded in 2015 at a meeting of the UN, the Strong Cities Network is an organization of mayors and other local political actors and activists to counter violent extremism (racial, political, religious, and ideological) through building social cohesion and community resilience. It does so through such activities as the sharing of best practices and practitioner training. To help cities realize their goals, the Strong Cities Network holds annual global summit conferences.
- **C40**. Created in 2005 by the mayor of London, C40 is a network of global cities dedicated to reducing greenhouse gas emissions and addressing climate change. With ninety-six members in over fifty countries, one in twelve people worldwide live within its boundaries. Their cooperative efforts have resulted in creation of a platform on which cities can showcase their efforts, work with technical experts, and influence national and international policy decisions by organizing their collective voice. C40 estimates that about 70% of its member cities have implemented improved climate action plans. Specific policy areas C40 addresses include modernizing food, waste, and water systems; enhancing transportation systems; building energy efficiencies; and improving land planning.

Key points of contention are whether the power relationship between states and cities is *zero sum* (whatever influence cities gain, states lose) and how much power cities really have, since they are not independent of the states where they are located. In broader terms, the rise of cities may result in redefining state sovereignty. Will sovereignty become limited, shared, or fractured, or will national governments continue to be seen as the supreme source of power and authority within national boundaries?[16]

Private Armies

Conventional accounts of war are organized around (1) military forces of states fighting one another or (2) government forces fighting civilian insurgents (rebels, terrorists, protesters). Overlooked in this framework is the long-standing presence of military forces organized and controlled by private sector actors.[17] In the past the most prominent private sector actors were identified as *mercenaries*, individuals hired to fight who do not belong to a government military force. Today, they are individuals on the payrolls of private military companies (PMCs).

PMCs are employed by both strong and weak states and perform a variety of functions. Over 20,000 private security personnel were present during the Iraq War in 2004, making them the second largest contingent of the "coalition of the willing." In 2018 it was reported that almost 27,000 contractors supported 14,000 troops in Afghanistan, 10,000 of whom were US citizens. Decades earlier a PMC was hired by Croatia with US support to deter Bosnian Serb aggression and ensure the success of the Dayton Peace Accords; since the United States was expected to be neutral in this dispute, it could not commit US forces for this purpose. In 1993 a PMC was hired by Angola to fight insurgent groups that government forces had proven too weak to defeat. Russian and Ukrainian pilots flew MiG fighters for both militaries in the Ethiopian-Eritrean civil war. PMCs are also employed by nongovernmental actors. CARE and the World Wildlife Federation have contracted with PMCs to protect their employees. Shell and BP have hired PMCs to protect their facilities in Nigeria and Colombia from rebels. PMCs are also used by international organizations for peacekeeping purposes as a result of the Somalia Syndrome. In 1993 US military personnel were killed in the Battle of Mogadishu, better known as the Black Hawk Down incident; soon after, the United States withdrew its forces from a Somali UN peacekeeping operation fearing future attacks.

Not all PMCs are *combat-active* (participate directly in combat missions). A second type of PMC is the military consultant firm, which provides governments with tactical and strategic military advice in such areas as the training, equipment, and use of military force. The main function of other PMCs is to maintain and operate military weapons systems, including signal interceptions, computer hacking and protection, and technical surveillance.[18]

The rise in prominence of PMCs in international politics is tied to several factors. With the end of the Cold War powerful states began to reduce the size of their militaries. Public opinion also became less supportive of the use of force. At the same time intrastate conflicts became more pronounced and typically involved weak governments struggling to control territory. Finally, the reductions in the size of militaries created a pool of trained professional soldiers from which PMCs could recruit.

Disagreement exists over the desirability of employing PMCs. The most frequently cited benefits are that they (1) provide a flexible surge military capacity, (2) offer specialized skills, and (3) are politically less costly than placing government forces in combat situations. Critics of PMCs make the following counter points: (1) as for-profit organizations, PMCs can be much more expensive than national forces; (2) the personnel they employ are often inadequately trained; (3) their legal status in war is unclear; and (4) they complicate problems of government oversight and accountability for their actions.

TRADITIONAL GLOBAL CHALLENGES

At the heart of the traditional agenda of international politics is fighting and winning wars. Multiple challenges present themselves during wartime. Situations may be misunderstood, and accidents happen. So too does the unexpected. In short, making policy always involves an element of uncertainty; the chosen response may be inadequate or make the problem worse. To improve our understanding of conflict situations, we need to broaden our perspectives to include the concepts of risk cascades and trauma states.

Risk Cascades

The full extent of the risks inherent in a response often go unrecognized, because state and international policy-makers typically focus on the initial crisis, problem, or challenge rather than placing it within a broader context. For example, at first the unrest in Syria caused by the Arab Spring movement was seen as a domestic problem, one that positioned President Assad against domestic opponents. Over time it became a breeding ground for terrorist groups and a window of opportunity for Russia to reinsert itself in the Middle East.

International consultant Seth Kaplan proposes that one way to place international problems and challenges in a broader context is the term **risk cascades**.[19] These are situations in which a primary event (such as a military coup, natural disaster, global financial crisis, terrorist attack, or election) sets in motion a series of secondary, tertiary, or more far-removed effects that broaden and deepen the negative consequences of the initial problem. The chain of interactions that emerge from the triggering event reflect the natural and political linkages among them.[20]

risk cascades
Situations in which a primary event sets in motion a series of secondary, tertiary, or more far-removed effects that broaden and deepen the negative consequences of the initial problem.

One international politics challenge that has repeatedly overwhelmed policy-makers is presented by fragile states. As you learned in Chapter 3, the social and political institutions in these states are so weak that relatively mild shocks or stress that could be contained in stronger states can set off events (risk cascades) that cross international borders. As was the case in Syria, the initial shock might be political protests based on long-standing grievances. Risk cascades could include the following (see Figure 11.2):

- Terrorists using the fragile state as a base of operations.
- Criminal gangs using it as a base from which to smuggle weapons and drugs, spreading violence and corruption across borders.
- Competitive or disruptive military operations by neighboring states seeking to contain the spread of instability.
- The loss of regional markets and access to natural resources resulting in increased poverty.
- Large-scale population movements across borders, which not only place increased financial burdens on other states but may also result in the spread of infectious diseases.

Figure 11.2 Risk
Cascade.

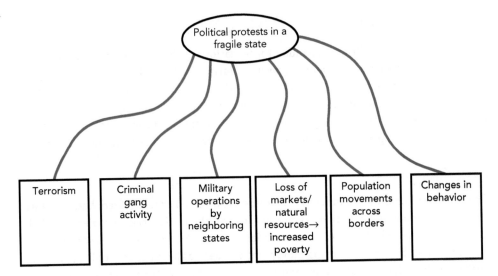

- Changes in politically acceptable behavior impacting religious, ethnic, and cultural relations at home and abroad.

Kaplan argues that a first step to reducing the onset of cascading risks is to better assess which risks are most likely and prioritize responses accordingly. Doing so is made difficult by two major factors. First, the risks might arise sequentially or in combination. Second, cascades are not static; they are complex systems that evolve and change over time. In one case terrorism may precede the onset of gang violence. In another terrorism may follow gang violence or be a response to foreign state's intervention. The correct response to one problem may only worsen a similar problem in another state or in the future.

Trauma States

Although each has a different focal point, to one degree or another post-conflict reconstruction, nation building, and peacebuilding all emphasize economic, political, social, and security challenges in their efforts to help societies recover from war. Post-WWII Germany and Japan are proof that these efforts can succeed. In many cases, such as Haiti (1915–34 and 1994–96), the Dominican Republic (1965–66 and 1916–24), Cambodia (1970–73), and Panama (1989 and 1903–36), success has proven to be temporary or partial. More recently even short-term successes have been hard to come by. Afghanistan is the prime example. According to Erik Goepner, a retired Air Force colonel and political scientist, a primary reason that post-conflict reconstruction efforts in Afghanistan have failed is the failure to recognize that Afghan society has become traumatized by endless war. Afghanistan has been at war for over forty years, dating back to the outbreak of civil war in 1978. Goepner defines Afghanistan as a **trauma state**, a country stuck in a vicious circle of war driving more war, which places severe limits on the potential for creating peace and promoting long-term social change.[21]

trauma state
A country stuck in a vicious circle of war driving more war, which places severe limits on the potential for creating peace and promoting long-term social change.

In trauma states violence has become pervasive, socially tolerated, making it an acceptable problem-solving tool and means of achieving everyday goals. In a situation in which violence becomes "normal," high rates of societal trauma can "eradicate previous norms and values" and "diminish the ability of individuals to work together in a productive and positive manner." States become locked into a vicious circle of war, causing trauma which then drives more war and produces more trauma. Data collected in Afghanistan show that adults have experienced an average of 7 traumatic events (including bombings, domestic abuse, beatings by members of the armed forces, forced displacement, and death of a loved one) while children have experienced between 5.7 and 6.6 such events. For comparison, European adults experienced less than 2 traumatic events, and US adults experienced between 1 and 3.

An employee of Doctors Without Borders in October 2015 inside what remained of the organization's hospital in Afghanistan that was destroyed in an airstrike killing forty-two people.

Najim Rahim / AP Images

One implication of this line of thinking is that military and national security officials need to assess the mental health status of a society before intervening in order to better anticipate the challenges that they will face. Similarly, strategies for post-conflict reconstruction need to involve a broader understanding of the society in which they are operating and include addressing societal mental health needs. Goepner acknowledges that this is not easy. Switching from an emphasis on military force to economic and diplomatic initiatives is a start, but it is no guarantee of success, as the relationship among aid, economic growth, and human development is not strong.

Others would build on Goepner's recommendation for treading carefully into traumatic state conflicts by citing the need for an even stronger long-term international commitment to post-conflict reconstruction in these states. The stakes in moving forward in one direction or the other are high. Afghanistan is not alone. Iraq, Libya, and Syria have been identified as other states whose societies have, to varying degrees, become traumatized by war.

NEW GLOBAL CHALLENGES

While international military conflicts are unlikely to disappear from the global political agenda, an ever-increasing number of global economic, environmental, and human rights issues are likely to gain importance as globalization continues. Two new challenges that are already the subject of debate include green growth and mass migration.

Green Growth

Green growth, by definition, is not a new idea. Its roots go back over twenty-five years to the Rio Summit, where the concept of sustainable development was introduced (see Chapter 8). Most observers interpret green growth as a subcategory of sustainable development. Sustainable development's broad agenda encompasses environmental concerns, economic and social progress, equity, peace, and justice, but **green growth** is more narrowly focused on creating the necessary conditions for economic growth in a manner that promotes biodiversity without adverse environmental consequences.[22]

Over the last decade green growth has become a leading concept in the field of economic development, central to the missions of a wide variety of international and regional organizations including the World Bank, the Organization for Economic Cooperation and Development (OECD), and the Asian Development Bank. It also led to the creation of a new international organization dedicated to achieving its goals, the Global Green Growth Institute (GGGI).[23]

A number of factors have contributed to the influence of green growth. One is the increased political importance of economic growth following the global economic crisis of 2008–09. A second is the perceived need to create global economic growth to promote the development of low-income countries and lift their citizens out of poverty. Finally, green growth is seen as central to addressing the problem of global climate change. It is recognized that no one green growth strategy is seen as capable of achieving all of green growth's goals; instead, policy initiatives must be geared to the social, economic, and political conditions of specific countries.

Along with the rise in the influence of green growth on formulation of economic development strategies have come voices of concern stating that the strong sense of optimism held by its advocates may be misplaced and overstated. Three challenges for the future stand out.

1. **Tradeoff between short-term and long-term growth**. The standard green growth perspective envisions a short-term reduction in economic growth followed by a higher long-term rate of growth.[24] This perspective raises questions of how long and deep it will be and who will be most affected by it. The roles played by states, international organizations, and multinational corporations may be crucial in promoting and harmonizing innovative policies that negate the short-term consequences of reduced economic growth and speed movement toward green growth.

2. **Impact on the poor**.[25] Can they benefit from green growth? Does green growth offer a rapid route out of poverty? It is taken as a given that economic growth is essential for large-scale poverty reduction, but what is the impact of green growth on the current condition of the poor? They are widely seen as the biggest losers from climate change, polluted local environments, and the loss of natural resources. The poor also experience great difficulties in trying to adapt their livelihoods to

green growth
Creation of the necessary conditions for economic growth in a manner that promotes biodiversity without adverse environmental consequences.

changing environmental conditions. Will they be able to benefit from a future upturn in economic growth? Related special concerns include pro-environmental pricing and regulation polices.

3. **Links between GDP and use of resources**. British anthropologist Jason Hickel[26] notes that recent computer-model studies of green growth strategies, all of which were based on optimistic assumptions, came to the same fundamental conclusion: global economic growth as measured by gross domestic production cannot be decoupled or separated from resource use. Technological innovation and taxes on resources do not save the environment. What is needed, Hickel argues, is the need to "liberate ourselves from our dependence on economic growth." We cannot consume more and produce more each year. We must learn to "share what we already have more fairly, rather than plundering the earth for more."

Mass Migration

Mass migration, the movement of people, has long been a central aspect of human development. A distinction is made between *internal migration*, which occurs within the borders of a country, and *international migration*, in which people move across borders. The care of internal migrants, referred to as **internally displaced people (IDPs)**, is the responsibility of the country's government. (IDPs were introduced in the Chapter 4 Regional Spotlight on Internally Displaced People in Africa.) The care of **international migrants** is less clear, but traditionally it has been the responsibility of the state to which they have travelled. Sometimes responding to large-scale international migration has required cooperation between the state that migrants left and the one to which they are moving. Such cooperation can involve activities from providing temporary or permanent welfare services or permanent residence or citizenship to returning them to their home country.

Increasingly it is recognized that effective responses to human migration are beyond the capacity of any single state or regional group. It requires a global response.[27] Consider the following recent cases involving mass migrations or forced repatriations.

internally displaced people (IDPs) Individuals who have moved away from their homes but remain inside the country.

international migrants People who have moved away from their homes and crossed national borders into another country.

- In 2012 an estimated 300,000 people fled Mali to neighboring states due to fighting between the Malian government and rebels and food shortages resulting from severe drought in the Sahel region of Africa.
- In 2015 over one million people sought to enter Europe by land and sea. Some 4,500 migrants died at sea. Most were fleeing Syria. Others came from Afghanistan, Iraq, Iran, and Pakistan. Some came from states in Africa or European states bordering Western Europe. (For more on the refugee flow into Europe see Chapter 4.)
- Since 2015 an estimated three million people have fled Venezuela due to the collapse of its economy and political chaos.
- In 2016 Pakistan returned 370,000 registered refugees and 250,000 undocumented migrants to Afghanistan, and Iran returned 2,300 refugees and 440,000 undocumented migrants to Afghanistan.

Mass exodus of Venezuelans into Colombia.

Schneyder Mendoza / EFE News Agency / Alamy Live News / Alamy Stock Photo

- In the last three months of 2017 over 630,000 people crossed into Bangladesh from Myanmar. They were Rohingyans seeking to escape from attacks by the Burmese military that the United Nations referred to as ethnic cleansing. (For more on this migration, see the Chapter 9 Regional Spotlight, "Genocide or Ethnic Cleansing in Myanmar?")

In the future, mass migrations due to war, domestic unrest, disease, and drought are expected to continue. It is anticipated that they will be joined by additional mass migrations due to environmental changes, including the flooding of coastal cities.[28]

At a minimum, to meet the challenges of international mass migration two issues must be addressed.

1. **A broader definition**. The definition of national interest must be broadened from a focus on security, economic, and national identity issues to include a concern for human interest and global interest.
2. **Elimination of silos**. Many policy discussions involving mass international migration take place in detached policy silos. Humanitarian aid is addressed in one policy silo, economic issues in another, and safety and security issues in yet another. To address mass migration effectively, these concerns must be brought together in a single setting.

Progress in addressing these two issues took place in 2016 when the UN General Assembly passed the New York Declaration for Refugees and Migrants. Governments expressed a commitment "to save lives, protect rights and share responsibility [for refugees and migrants] on a global scale."[29] Although this is a notable step forward, skeptics such as the Center for Migration Studies observed that the New York Declaration "falls short of creating a new framework for the protection of refugees and migrants around the world. Instead, it reaffirms the status quo, and, in some areas, weakens current protections for these vulnerable populations."[30] The Global Compact for Safe, Orderly and Regular Migration agreement adopted in 2018 attempted to address these concerns. It contains twenty-three objectives aimed at improving the management of migration at local, national, regional, and global levels.[31] These objectives address economic development issues as well as questions involving governance, human rights, and data collection (see Table 11.3). The nonbinding agreement, which does not create a new right to migrate, was signed by 164 countries in December 2018.

TABLE 11.3	Objectives for the Global Compact for Safe, Orderly and Regular Migration
1	Collect and utilize accurate and disaggregated data as a basis for evidence-based policies.
2	Minimize the adverse drivers and structural factors that compel people to leave their country of origin.
3	Provide accurate and timely information at all stages of migration.
4	Ensure that all migrants have proof of legal identity and adequate documentation.
5	Enhance availability and flexibility of pathways for regular migration.
6	Facilitate fair and ethical recruitment and safeguard conditions that ensure decent work.
7	Address and reduce vulnerabilities in migration.
8	Save lives and establish coordinated international efforts on missing migrants.
9	Strengthen the transnational response to smuggling of migrants.
10	Prevent, combat and eradicate trafficking in persons in the context of international migration.
11	Manage borders in an integrated, secure, and coordinated manner.
12	Strengthen certainty and predictability in migration procedures for appropriate screening, assessment, and referral.
13	Use migration detention only as a measure of last resort and work towards alternatives.
14	Enhance consular protection, assistance, and cooperation throughout the migration.
15	Provide access to basic services for migrants.
16	Empower migrants and societies to realize full inclusion and social cohesion.
17	Eliminate all forms of discrimination and promote evidence-based public discourse to shape perceptions of migration.
18	Invest in skills development and facilitate mutual recognition of skills, qualifications, and competences.

(Continued)

TABLE 11.3	(Continued)
19	Create conditions for migrants and diasporas to fully contribute to sustainable development in all countries.
20	Promote faster, safer, and cheaper transfer of remittances and foster financial inclusion of migrants.
21	Cooperate in facilitating safe and dignified return and readmission, as well as sustainable reintegration.
22	Establish mechanisms for the portability of social security entitlements and earned benefits.
23	Strengthen international cooperation and global partnerships for safe, orderly, and regular migration.

Source: Global Compact for Safe, Orderly and Regular Migration. https://refugeesmigrants.un.org/sites/default/files/180713_agreed_outcome_global_compact_for_migration.pdf.

Responding to the global challenges is an ongoing undertaking. It is one that has long puzzled and perplexed policy-makers and scholars. British Prime Minister Benjamin Disraeli returned from a meeting of the Great Powers at the Congress of Berlin in 1878 declaring that "peace for our time" had been achieved. By 1912 fighting had broken out in the Balkans, and in 1914 WWI began. Prime Minister Neville Chamberlin made a similar proclamation upon returning from the Munich Conference of major European powers in 1938. Less than one year later Adolph Hitler invaded Poland, setting WWII in motion. In 1989 scholar Francis Fukuyama invoked the phrase "the end of history" in his analysis of the end of the Cold War. He asserted the end of the Cold War might represent more than the passing of a particular period of history. It might signify "the end point of mankind's ideological evolution and the universalization of Western liberal democracy as the final form of human government."[32] Today it is not the triumph of democracy but the rebirth of authoritarianism that dominates headlines. As asserted at the beginning of this chapter and reinforced by statements such as these, in looking to the future our primary objective in *International Politics: Challenges and Responses* is not to make predictions about the future. It is to clarify our thinking about contemporary events and provide insight into how we think about responding to those events with an eye toward both the consequences for the present and the future.

Summary

- Trade wars are recurring but often unanticipated events in international politics.
- Creating images of possible alternative future international politics involves four steps: composing a plot, establishing a set of anchoring assumptions, identifying wild cards, and selecting a time frame.

- The *Global Trends 2035* report presents three alternative visions of future international politics: islands, orbits, and communities.

- Conservative internationalism and postcolonialism are two emerging alternative frameworks for studying international politics.

- Cities and private military armies are two new types of actors in international politics whose emergence might potentially lead to redefinitions of sovereignty.

- Trauma states and risk cascades are two concepts put forward for increasing our understanding of the dynamics of international conflicts.

- Green growth and mass migrations are two examples of global issues emerging out of the intersection of human rights, environmental concerns, and economics.

Key Terms

Conservative internationalism *(334)*
Green growth *(344)*
Internally displaced people *(345)*
International migrants *(345)*
Postcolonialism *(335)*

Risk cascades *(341)*
Risk management *(328)*
Trade war *(329)*
Trauma state *(342)*
Wild cards *(331)*

Critical Thinking Questions

1. Can risk cascades be used as a starting point help us understand the dynamics of trade wars? Why or why not?

2. What are the two most important wild cards to take into account in creating images of international politics? Explain your selections.

3. Which of the alternative futures in the Global 2035 report is most likely to occur and why?

4. Is conservative internationalism or postcolonialism a more useful framework for studying international politics? Explain your answer.

5. Do cities or private military armies represent the greater threat to the concept of sovereignty? Explain your answer. How should we think about sovereignty in the future?

6. How important is the concept of the trauma state for understanding conflict situations and the policies designed for them?

7. What is the proper role of non-state actors (businesses, international organizations, nongovernmental organizations, cities, individuals) in responding to mass human migrations?

Practice and Review Online
http://textbooks.rowman.com/hastedt-felice

Glossary

A

alliances Formal agreements among states to cooperate and promote their common interest.

Antarctic Treaty Regime A set of international agreements that regulate relations among states in the region to ensure that the area will be used exclusively for peaceful purposes.

B

bandwagoning A strategy in which secondary states join in alliances with the dominant state rather than try to unite together in opposition.

biodiversity The total variety of life found on Earth, including the genetic variety within each species and the ecosystems that species create.

bureaucratic politics model A perspective on policy-making that emphasizes the central role played by bureaucratic factors such as bargaining, vested interests, and standard operating procedures in formulating policies.

C

carbon tax A fee on fossil fuels designed as a market mechanism to reduce the emissions of carbon dioxide into the atmosphere.

causation An act, event, or process that produces an effect.

climate change Changes in weather patterns and global warming caused by human activity combined with the earth's natural processes.

Climate Change Convention A convention created at the Rio Conference in 1992 that established a general framework for nations to work together to mitigate and limit global warming; the objective is stabilizing atmospheric greenhouse gas concentrations at a level that would prevent dangerous human interference with the climate.

colonialism Period from the late fifteenth to the twentieth century when the European powers brutally conquered, settled and exploited large areas of the world.

Common Concern of Humankind A principle in international environmental law that signifies the need for collective action to protect areas of critical importance to all of humanity, even if those areas fall solely within a nation's jurisdiction.

Common Heritage of Humankind A principle in international environmental law that areas of the global commons should benefit all of humanity and not be unilaterally exploited by individual states; also known as the *Common Heritage of Mankind.*

comparative advantage Theory that each nation should produce those goods and services that it can produce most efficiently, then export them and use the revenues gained to import those goods that it produces less efficiently.

conservative internationalism A framework for studying international politics that occupies a middle ground between liberal internationalism and isolationism; emphasizes states as the central actors in international politics, protecting the national interest, practicing armed diplomacy, and prioritizing foreign policy goals.

constructivism A perspective for studying international politics that emphasizes contextual analysis and the need to determine the meaning of events and ideas from the setting in which they take place.

Convention on Biological Diversity (CBD) An international treaty requiring states-parties to develop national plans for the conservation and sustainable use of biological diversity and the equitable sharing of the benefits from genetic resources.

cooperation When states and other international actors work together for their mutual benefit or to address shared problems.

correlation Close links in time or location between two events.

covert action An attempt to further the interest of one state by secretly altering the internal balance of power in another state.

critical theory Social theory that takes as its starting point the need to critique and change established social and political systems rather than understand them.

cultural relativism The view that ethics differ from culture to culture and that judgments of right and wrong behavior are a product of particular societies.

cyberpower Information used in order to inflict harm, persuade, or more generally gain an advantage over an adversary.

D

democratic peace theory Theory asserting that democracies do not fight wars against other democracies.

deterrence Use of nuclear weapons to prevent an adversary from undertaking an unwanted action.

developing countries Some of the poorest nations in the world; also referred to as less-developed countries (LDCs), underdeveloped countries, and undeveloped countries.

diplomacy The practice of fostering relationships around the world in order to resolve issues and advance interests.

E

economic globalization The increased interdependence of the world's economies as a result of the growing flows of trade, investment, technology, and capital among states.

economic liberalism Theory that open and free trade and investments across borders with minimal state intervention will create a world in which all nations and individuals will be better off.

economic nationalism Theory that economic activity should be involved primarily with promoting and shielding national industries and the local economy from the vulnerabilities that emerge with global economic interdependence.

economic structuralism A perspective that draws heavily on Marxism and emphasizes the pursuit of wealth in international politics and the exploitive relations it creates.

environmental racism The disparate impact of environmental degradation and hazards on disadvantaged groups, including the disproportionate exposure to pollutants and the lack of access to clean air, water, and natural resources.

F

feminist theory A perspective that takes as its point of departure the gendered nature of political phenomena and the need to explicitly take gender into account in the analysis of international politics.

fragile states States that struggle to control violence, lack accountable government institutions, and have little economic stability, making them especially vulnerable to social, economic, and political shocks.

free riding A situation in which an alliance member does not contribute its fair share to the alliance's defense costs.

G

generational events Events that have a profound impact on the collective memory of a society, even for those who do not experience them personally.

genocide Acts intended to destroy, in whole or in part, a national, ethnic, racial or religious group.

Global Commons The areas and resources beyond the sovereignty of any state, including the oceans and seas, the atmosphere, biological diversity, and outer space.

global interest Goals that are in the interests of all states or benefit the international system as a whole.

grand strategy A plan that coordinates all of the power resources held by a state in order to achieve its fundamental foreign policy objectives and long-term goals.

great powers States that possess the ability to use their military, economic, and political resources to influence events on a global scale.

green growth Creation of the necessary conditions for economic growth in a manner that promotes biodiversity without adverse environmental consequences.

groupthink A key concept in small-group decision-making that holds that internal pressures for group consensus leads to a deterioration of rationality and morality.

H

hard power The power of coercion and command to accomplish foreign policy goals, generally by employing military and economic means.

Holocaust The planned genocide of approximately six million European Jews by Nazi Germany and its collaborators between 1941 and 1945.

horizontal history Events that occur at the same time as or relatively close to the event being examined.

human interest Values that promote the human condition; presented as an alternative to the national interest, which seeks to promote the global standing of states.

human rights Fundamental entitlements for all human beings designed to prevent and alleviate human suffering; based on moral principles including liberty, equality, and fraternity.

Human Rights Council (HRC) Established in 2006, the leading human rights body at the UN responsible for evaluating and monitoring member states' compliance with universal human rights.

human security Protecting individuals from situations of fear and want; considered to be more focused in its perspective on international politics than human interest.

hybrid war A form of warfare that combines elements of conventional warfare, irregular warfare, and cyberwarfare to create a highly flexible and resilient fighting posture that can adapt readily to changed circumstances.

I

interest group A set of people working together for a shared cause.

Intergovernmental Panel on Climate Change (IPCC) An international organization established in 1988 that is charged with assessing the science related to climate change.

internally displaced people (IDPs) Individuals who have moved away from their homes but remain inside the country.

International Bill of Human Rights Collective name for three core human rights documents:the Universal Declaration of Human Rights, the International Covenant on Civil and Political Rights, and the International Covenant on Economic, Social and Cultural Rights.

International Criminal Court (ICC) An international tribunal charged with prosecuting individuals for the international crimes of genocide, crimes against humanity, and war crimes.

international law The laws, rules, and customs that define the legal responsibilities of states in their conduct with one another.

international migrants People who have moved away from their homes and crossed national borders into another country.

International Monetary Fund (IMF) An international organization that has primary responsibility for monetary stability.

international organizations Formal institutions created by states to better realize common goals; final political power and authority reside with the member states.

international political economy (IPE) The study of the interaction and tension between (1) the market and the state and (2) the market and international economic entities—including MNCs, international organizations such as the IMF and the World Bank, and global and regional trade organizations such as the WTO.

international politics Relations between states, international organizations, and non-state actors such as individuals, corporations, terrorist groups, and humanitarian relief organizations.

J

just war A legal and philosophical concept that establishes the requirements for how and why war is started and how it is fought.

just war theory A theory that addresses two sets of questions: the proper criteria or right way to go to war (*jus ad bellum*), and the proper criteria or right way to fight a war (*jus in bello*).

L

Law of the Sea (LOS) Treaty An international convention finalized in 1982 that established the rights and responsibilities of nations on the world's oceans, including the protection and management of the environment and marine natural resources.

levels of analysis The focal points (individual, societal, state, or global) that can be used to study international politics.

liberalism A perspective for studying international politics which holds that states are capable of acting rationally in international politics in pursuing their national interests; emphasizes democratic government and free trade as the bases for cooperation.

M

methodology A set of rules, procedures, and principles used for studying a topic.

middle powers States that have limited power resources but are still powerful enough defend their interests and influence the policy positions of more powerful states and the outcome of events near them.

milieu goals Foreign policy goals that shape the global context in which all states act.

Millennium Development Goals (MDGs) An ambitious agenda for human development and sustainability for the global community approved by the member states of the UN in 2000.

multinational corporations (MNCs) Business firms that are headquartered in one country but have sales, production, research, or resource extraction activities in others.

N

national interest The fundamental goals and objectives of a state's foreign policy; typically including physical survival, economic well-being, and preservation of the form of government.

noise Competing or contradictory information that prevents policy-makers from recognizing signals.

nongovernmental organizations (NGOs) Voluntary, nonprofit organizations that operate independently of governments with the general purpose of bringing about progressive changes in international politics.

nonintervention The principle that states should not intervene in the affairs of foreign countries; based on the idea of separating morality and ethics from foreign policy.

nontariff barriers to trade Restrictions of imports or exports other than tariffs, such as import licensing, quotas, rules for valuing goods at customs, and inspections of imports.

North American Free Trade Agreement (NAFTA) Agreement established in 1994 that eliminated most tariff and nontariff barriers to trade and investment among Canada, Mexico, and the United States.

O

Office of the High Commissioner for Human Rights (OHCHR) Body that spearheads the UN's human rights efforts by supporting, administering, and monitoring human rights compliance and enforcement mechanisms.

P

Paris Climate Change Agreement A 2015 agreement that builds on the Climate Change Convention and aims to limit the rise of the world's temperature to 1.5 degrees Celsius.

peacekeeping The deployment of military and civilian personnel to prevent a return to violent conflict by monitoring conflict situations and separating combatants.

policy-making process The steps that a policy proposal must pass through in order to move from an idea to a formal policy; they include getting on the political agenda, formulating a policy option, making a decision, implementing the decision, and evaluating the decision.

poliheuristic model A two-stage model of decision-making in which policy-makers eliminate policy options on the basis of their beliefs in the first stage and conduct a more precise and reasoned evaluation of the merits of the remaining policy options in the second stage.

postcolonialism Theory that critically examines the ongoing legacy of imperialism and colonialism on both the colonizers and the colonized in order to highlight how ideas are created, defined, and evaluated.

post-conflict reconstruction The creation and strengthening of governmental and economic institutions to lay a foundation for peacebuilding.

power The ability to influence and determine the actions of others; can be viewed as a resource one possesses, a relationship, or a means to an end.

precautionary principle A framework for action stipulating that when an action may cause serious environmental threats and potentially irreversible damage, the lack of full scientific certainty should not be used to prevent implementation of measures to avert environmental degradation.

prospect theory A theory of decision-making that assumes individuals value losses and gains differently; they are more like to take risks to prevent possible losses than they are to seek potential gains.

proxy war Conflict in which an outside supporter (state or non-state actor) intervenes indirectly in order to influence the strategic outcome.

purchasing power parity (PPP) The conversion of the currency of one country to the amount needed to purchase the same basket of goods and services available in other countries; in practice the conversion is often to purchasing the same basket that a US dollar would purchase in the United States.

R

rational actor model A model of decision-making that is based on the assumption of informed choice in which all options are known and evaluated, and the option selected is the one most likely to realize the desired goal at a reasonable cost.

realism A classic perspective for studying international politics that starts from the assumption that it is a struggle for power carried out by states under anarchic conditions.

responsibility to protect (R2P) A global principle that reverses the traditional emphasis on sovereignty away from the right of states to act as they choose to require states to take responsibility for the welfare of their citizens in such areas as crimes against humanity, genocide, ethnic cleansing, and war crimes.

revisionist history Reinterpretation of the orthodox manner in which events have been explained and evaluated.

risk cascades Situations in which a primary event sets in motion a series of secondary, tertiary, or more far-removed effects that broaden and deepen the negative consequences of the initial problem.

risk management The procedure for identifying, assessing, and controlling potential threats.

S

signals Clues or pieces of information that are useful in addressing problems.

soft power The power of persuasion using information, culture, values, and ideas to accomplish foreign policy goals.

sovereignty The principle that no authority exists above the state; states decide what goals to pursue and how to pursue them.

state-based conflict A dispute between two actors, at least one of which involves the use of military force.

summit A face-to-face meeting between heads of government or political figures of high rank.

sustainable development goals (SDGs), adopted by the UN in 2015, are based on three pillars of sustainable development: economic development, social inclusion, and environmental sustainability.

T

terrorism Violence employed for purposes of political intimidation and the achievement of political goals.

theory A set of general principles used to explain, predict, and describe a class of events.

think tanks Policy or research institutes that conduct research on policy problems and make policy recommendations.

Track II diplomacy Unofficial and informal contacts between private sector groups and individuals to open lines of communication between adversaries and develop strategies for resolving a conflict.

trade war A conflict in which one state imposes economic restrictions on another, which then retaliates.

Tragedy of the Commons A theory that describes how individuals may exploit natural resources for their advantage without considering potential resource depletion and the need for long-term sustainability; highlights the conflict between individual and collective rationality.

transnational advocacy networks (TANs) Groups of activists from around the world who are linked together to promote change in policy issues that cross state boundaries.

trauma state A country stuck in a vicious circle of war driving more war, which places severe limits on the potential for creating peace and promoting long-term social change.

two-level game The need for policy-makers to simultaneously direct their attention to the domestic political context in which they operate as well as the international context for policies to succeed.

U

UN Conference on Environment and Development (UNCED) A conference held in Rio in 1992 that brought together the largest gathering of world leaders to date to reconcile economic development with protection of the environment.

UN Conference on Sustainable Development (UNCSD) A 2012 conference in Rio that launched international working groups to define and develop the UN's Sustainable Development Goals.

UN Conference on the Human Environment in Stockholm The UN's first major conference on the environment, held in 1972, represented a major turning point in the development of global environmental law and policy.

UN Human Rights System System composed of norms, institutions, and compliance procedures, which establish a framework for the global community to discuss and create policies to protect human dignity around the world.

United Nations (UN) An international organization founded in 1945 that provides a forum for members to discuss shared concerns and under certain circumstances take action to address global problems.

United Nations Environment Program (UNEP), The leading UN environmental organization, established at the Stockholm Conference, which sets the global environmental agenda and coordinates implementation of environmental agreements and sustainable development practices.

Universal Declaration of Human Rights (UDHR) Declaration adopted by the UN General Assembly on December 10, 1948, with forty-eight states in the affirmative, no states opposed, eight states abstaining, and two states not voting. The UDHR sets out fundamental universal human rights and has now been translated into over 500 languages. (Note: Whereas in 1948 there were 58 member states in the United Nations, today there are 193.)

Universal Periodic Review (UPR) Examination by the HRC of the human rights records of all member states of the UN.

universality In ethics this refers to the idea that there are certain truths that can be considered universal and applicable to all everywhere.

V

vertical history The sequence of events that preceded the event being examined.

W

Westphalian state system System based on principles of national sovereignty, the legal equality of states, and non-intervention in the domestic affairs of foreign states.

wicked problems Problems that are difficult or impossible to solve due to their complexity.

wild cards Unexpected developments that hold the potential for invalidating or contradicting expected outcomes; also referred to as *Black Swans*.

World Bank An international organization designed to provide states with an additional source of development funds beyond those that private banks could provide; also known as the International Bank for Reconstruction and Development (IBRD).

World Trade Organization (WTO) An international organization that has primary responsibility for managing international trade relations by establishing international rules for trade.

Notes

1: Thinking Critically about International Politics

1. For discussions of wicked problems see H. Rittel and M. Webber, "Dilemmas in a General Theory of Planning," *Policy Sciences* 4 (1973): 155–69; and E. Weber and A. Khademian, "Wicked Problems," *Public Administration Review* 68 (2008): 334–49.

2. See *Digital Globalization: The New Era of Global Flows*, McKinsey Global Institute, March 2016.

3. James Clapper, *Facts and Fears* (New York: Viking Press, 2018), 254.

4. Roberta Wohlstetter, *Pearl Harbor: Warning and Decision* (Stanford: Stanford University Press, 1962).

5. Marc Lynch, Deen Freelon, and Sean Aday, *Syria's Socially Mediated Civil War* (Washington, DC: United States Institute of Peace, *Peaceworks* No. 91, 2014).

6. Michael Hayden, *The Assault on Intelligence* (New York: Penguin Press, 2018), 182.

7. William Hitchcock, "The Myth of Ike's Nuclear Recklessness Could Lead US into War," *Washington Post*, August 11, 2017.

8. Walter Clemens, "Almost Back to Square One," *Bulletin of the Atomic Scientists* 60 (2004): 220–25.

9. Henry Kissinger, *The White House Years* (Boston: Little Brown, 1969), 54.

10. Elizabeth Saunders, *Leaders at War* (Ithaca: Cornell University Press, 2011).

11. Ernest May, *Lessons of the Past* (New York: Oxford University Press, 1973), 81.

12. May, *Lessons of the Past*, 71.

13. Robert Dallek, *Harry S. Truman* (New York: Times Books, 2008), 29.

14. Bill Clinton, *My Life* (New York: Alfred Knopf, 2004), 603.

15. Jean Edward Smith, *Bush* (New York: Simon & Schuster, 2016), 188.

16. Smith, *Bush*, 182.

17. Yuen Foong Khong, *Analogies at War* (Princeton: Princeton University Press, 1992), 6.

18. Steven Myers and Ellen Berry, "Putin Reclaims Crimea for Russia and Bitterly Denounces the West," *New York Times*, March 19, 2014; and Fiona Gaddy, "Putin and the Uses of History," *National Interest*, January 4, 2012.

19. Kongdon Oh and Ralph Hassig, "North Korean's Nuclear Politics," *Current History* 103 (2004): 273–79.

20. Khong, *Analogies at War*.

21. Stephen Rock, *Appeasement in International Politics* (Lexington: University of Kentucky Press, 2000).

22. Bush's speech can be found at http://www.aei.org/publication/president-george-w-bush-speaks-at-aeis-annual-dinner/.

23. May, *Lessons of the Past*, 81.

24. John Stoessinger, *Why Nations Go to War*, 9th edition (Belmont, CA: Wadsworth, 2005), 74.

25. Stoessinger, *Why Nations Go to War*.

26. Stoessinger, *Why Nations Go to War*, 76–77.

27. Khong, *Analogies at War*, 100.

28. Khong, *Analogies at War*, 108–8.

29. Bruce Cumings, "North Korea: The Sequel," *Current History* 102 (2003): 147–51.

30. Hayden, *Assault on Intelligence*, 19.

31. Francis Gaven, "History and Policy," *International Journal* (2007–08): 162–77.

32. Glenn Paige, *The Korean Decision* (New York: Free Press, 1968).

33. Robert Cox, "Social Forces, States, and World Order," *Millennium* 10 (1981): 126–55.

34. Dallek, *Harry S. Truman*, 105.

35. Dallek, *Harry S. Truman*, 106 and 108.

36. Alexander George, *Bridging the Gap* (Washington, DC: United States Institute of Peace, 1993).

2: The Theory Challenge

1. John Lewis Gaddis, "The Long Peace," *International Security* 10 (1986): 99–142.

2. For overviews of realism see Gideon Rose, "Neoclassical Realism and Theories of Foreign Policy," *World Politics* 51 (1998): 144–77; and Keith Shimko, "Realism, Neorealism, and American Liberalism," *Review of Politics* 54 (1992): 281–302.

3. Hans Morgenthau, *Politics among Nations* (New York: Knopf, 1948).

4. Mogenthau, *Politics among Nations*, 5.

5. See E. H. Carr, *The Twenty Years' Crisis* (London: Macmillan, 1939).

6. Jack Levy and William R. Thompson, "Hegemonic Threat and Great Power Balancing in Europe, 1495–2000," *Security Studies* 14 (2005): 1–30; and T. V. Paul, James J. Wirtz, and Michael Fortmann, eds., *Balance of Power: Theory and Practice in the 21st Century* (Stanford, CA: Stanford University Press, 004).

7. John Mearsheimer, *The Tragedy of Great Power Politics* (New York: Norton, 2001), and Robert Gilpin, "The Theory of Hegemonic War," *Interdisciplinary History* 18 (1988): 591–613.

8. Kenneth Waltz, *Theory of International Politics* (New York: McGraw Hill, 1979).

9. Mearshimer, *The Tragedy of Great Power Politics*.

10. See Andrew Moravcsik, "Taking Preferences Seriously: A Liberal Theory of International Relations," *International Organization* 51 (1997), 513–53; and Kenneth Oye, ed., *Cooperation under Anarchy* (Princeton: Princeton University Press, 1986).

11. Scott Burchill, "Liberal Internationalism," in *Theories of International Relations*, eds. Scott Burchill and Andrew Linklater (New York: St. Martin's, 1996), 28–66.

12. Immanuel Kant, *Kant's Political Writings*, 2nd edition, ed. Hans S. Reiss (Cambridge, UK: Cambridge University Press, 1991).

13. Michael Doyle, *Liberal Peace: Selected Essays* (New York: Routledge, 2011). Also see Bruce Russett and John R. Oneal, *Triangulating Peace: Democracy, Interdependence, and International Organizations* (New York: Norton, 2001).

14. Robert Keohane and Joseph Nye, *Power and Interdependence* (Boston: Little, Brown, 1977).

15. For an overview of economic structuralism see Elizabeth Matthews and Rhoda Callaway, *International Relations Theory: A Primer* (New York: Oxford University Press, 2017), 123–66.

16. Robert Cox, "Social Forces, States, and World Orders," *Millennium: Journal of International Studies* 10 (1981): 126–55.

17. Francis Fukuyama, "The End of History?" *National Interest* 16 (1989): 3–18.

18. See Immanuel Wallerstein, *The Modern World System I* (New York: Academic Press, 2004).

19. See Paul Baran, *The Political Economy of Economic Growth* (New York: Monthly Review Press, 1957); and Andre Gunder Frank, *Capitalism and Underdevelopment in Latin America* (New York: Modern Reader Paperbacks, 1969).

20. Ted Hopf, "The Promise of Constructivism in International Relations Theory," *International Security* 23 (1998): 171–200; Nicholas Onuf, *World of Our Making* (Columbia, SC: University of South Carolina Press, 1989).

21. Alexander Wendt, "Anarchy Is What States Make of It," *International Organization* 46 (1992): 391–425.

22. For discussions of constructivism and breakdowns of different schools of constructivism see Matthews and Callaway, *International Relations Theory*, 167–209; and Matt McDonald, "Constructivisms," in *Security Studies: An Introduction*, ed. Paul Williams, 2nd edition (New York: Routledge, 2008), 63–76.

23. For a survey of various feminist approaches see Sandra Whitworth, "Feminisms," in *Security Studies*, ed. Paul Williams, 107–119; Sandra Harding, *The Science Question in Feminism* (Ithaca: Cornell University Press, 1986); Lene Hansen, "Ontologies, Epistemologies, Methodologies," in *A Feminist Introduction to International Relations*, ed. Laura Shepard (New York: Routledge, 2009); and J. Ann Tickner, *Gender in International Relations* (New York: Columbia University Press, 1992).

24. Marysia Zalewski, "Well, What is the Feminist Perspective on Bosnia?" *International Affairs* 71 (1990): 342.

25. The *Journal of ERW and Mine Action*, now the *Journal of Conventional Weapons Destruction*, contains several articles on matters of gender and age.

26. Rebecca Grant, "Sources of Gender Bias," in *Gender and International Relations*, eds. Rebecca Grant and Kathleen Newland (Bloomington, IN: Indiana University Press, 1991), 8–26.

27. For an overview of books on the global politics of the Arctic see Jeffrey Mazo, "Cold Comfort," *Survival* 52 (2011): 151–60; Ronald O'Rourke, *Changes in the Arctic: Background and Issues for Congress* (Washington, DC: Congressional Research Service, January 4, 2018).

28. For a Russian perspective see the writings of Alexander Sergunin such as his "Is Russia Going Hard or Soft in the Arctic?" *Wilson Quarterly* 41 (2017).

29. Pavel Devyatkin, *Russia's Arctic Strategy* (Washington, DC: The Arctic Institute, February 13, 2018).

30. Anatol Rapoport, *Fights, Games, and Debates* (Lansing, MI: University of Michigan Press, 1960).

31. Douglas Nord, "The Challenge of Arctic Governance," *Wilson Quarterly* 41 (2017).

32. "Russia Plants Flag on North Pole," *Guardian*, August 2, 2007. Available at: https://www.theguardian.com/world/2007/aug/02/russia.arctic.

33. Roger Howard, *The Arctic Gold Rush* (New York: Continuum, 2009).

34. Tero Vauraste, "An Investment Model for the Arctic," *Wilson Quarterly* 41 (2017).

35. On China see Elizabeth Wishnick, *China's Interests and Goals in the Arctic* (Carlisle, PA: US Army War College, March, 2017).

36. Subhanakar Banerjee, ed., *Arctic Voices* (New York: Seven Stories Press, 2012), 7.

37. Clara Morgan, *The Arctic: Gender Issues* (Ottawa: Parliament Information and Research Service, October 24, 2008).

38. Heidi Sinevaara-Niskanen, "Vocabularies for Human Development: Arctic Politics and the Power of Knowledge," *Polar Record* 51 (2015): 191–200.

39. "The Waters of the Third Pole: Sources of Threat, Sources of Survival" (2010). Available at: https://www.chinadialogue.net/UserFiles/File/third_pole_full_report.pdf; and thethirdpole.net reports.

40. *Genderscape in the Brahmaputra River* (Hyderabad, India: South Asia Consortium for Interdisciplinary Water Resource Studies, January, 2018).

3: The Sovereignty Challenge: Who Is in Charge in World Politics?

1. Susan Strange, *The Retreat of the State* (New York: Cambridge University Press, 1996). For a contrary view see Michael Lind, "Revenge of the Nation-State," *National Interest* 146 (2016): 18–27.

2. Audrey Cronin, "ISIS is Not a Terrorist Group," *Foreign Affairs* 94, no. 2 (2015): 87–98.

3. On great powers see Kenneth Waltz, *Theory of International Politics* (New York, Random House, 1979) and Martin Wight, *Power Politics* (New York: Holmes and Meier, 1978).

4. John Mearshimer, *The Tragedy of Great Power Politics* (New York: Norton, 2001), 3.

5. T. V. Paul, *Accommodating Rising Powers* (New York: Cambridge University Press, 2016).

6. Dong-min Shin, "The Concept of Middle Power and the Case of the ROK," *Korea Yearbook 2012: Politics, Economy and Society* (Netherlands: Brill, 2012), 131–52.

7. Stewart Patrick, "Irresponsible Stakeholders?" *Foreign Affairs* 89, no. 6 (2010): 44–53.

8. Carl Meacham and Marcos Degaut, *Do BRICS Still Matter* (Washington, DC: Center for Strategic and International Studies, 2015).

9. Charles Call, "The Fallacy of the 'Failed State'," *Third World Quarterly* 29, no. 8 (2008): 1491–507.

10. Frances Stewart and Graham Brown, *Fragile States* (Oxford, UK: Centre for Research on Inequality, Human Security and Ethnicity, CRISE Working Paper 51, 2009).

11. The Fund for Peace, *The Fragile State Index*, https://fragilestatesindex.org/.

12. Anne-Marie Slaughter, "Sovereignty and Power in a Networked World Order," *Stanford International Law Review* 40 (2004): 283–327.

13. See Karen Mingst, Margaret Karns, and Alynna Lyon, *The United Nations in the 21st Century,* 5th edition (Boulder: Westview Press, 2017).

14. Thomas Weiss, Tatiana Carayannis and Richard Jolly, "The 'Third United Nations'," *Global Governance* 15, no. 1 (2009): 123–42; and Thomas Weiss, David Forsythe, Roger Coate, and Kelly-Kate Pease, *The United Nations and Changing World Politics,* 8th edition (Boulder: Westview Press, 2017).

15. Connie Peck, "The Role of International Organizations in Preventing and Resolving Conflict," in *Turbulent Peace,* eds. Chester Crocker et al. (Washington, DC: United States Institute of Peace Press, 2001), 561–83; and Louise Fawcett, "Regional Institutions," in *Security Studies, An Introduction,* ed. Paul Williams, 2nd edition (London: Routledge, 2013), 355–73.

16. Fawett, "Regional Institutions," 362.

17. On humanitarian, human rights, and conflict resolution NGOs see Pamela Aall, "NGOs, Conflict Management and Peacekeeping," in *Peacekeeping and Conflict Resolution,* eds. Tom Woodhouse and Oliver Ramsbotham (London: Frank Cass, 2000), 121–41. On development NGOs see David Lewis, *Non-government Organizations and Development* (London: Routledge, 2007).

18. Mary Anderson, "Humanitarian NGOs in Conflict Intervention," in *Turbulent Peace,* 637–48.

19. *World Investment Report, 2017* (New York: United Nations Conference on Trade and Development, 2017).

20. *A Military Guide to Terrorism in the Twenty-First Century* (Ft. Leavenworth, KS: US Army Training and Doctrine Command, 2007), Chapter 3.

21. Anthony Ceso, *Al-Qaeda's post 9/11 Devolution* (New York: Bloomsbury, 2014).

22. Andrew Kydd and Barbara Walter, "The Strategies of Terrorism," *International Security* 31, no. 1 (2006): 49–80.

23. Iraq's Vice President called a Referendum in Kurdistan, September 25, 2017, a "Declaration of War."

24. Slaughter, "Sovereignty and Power in a Networked World Order"; and David Lake, "The New Sovereignty in International Relations," *International Studies Review* 5 (2003): 303–23.

25. Garth Evans, "Limiting the Security Council's Veto Power," *Project Syndicate,* February 4, 2015.

26. This is along the lines of regional centers proposed by Connie Peck, *Sustainable Peace* (Lanham, MD: Rowman and Littlefield, 1998).

4: The Values Challenge: Deciding What to Do

1. David Easton, *The Political System* (New York: Alfred Knopf, 1953).

2. On the Nansen Passport see Otto Hieronymi, "The Nansen Passport: A tool of Freedom and Protection," *Refugee Survey Quarterly* 22 (2003): 36–47; and Katy Long, "Early Repatriation Policy: Russian Refugee Return 1922–1924," *Journal of Refugee Studies* 22 (2009): 133–54.

3. See Hans Morgenthau, "Another Great Debate: The National Interest of the United States," *American Political Science Review* 46 (1952): 961–88.

4. Secretary General Presents His Annual Report to General Assembly. Available at: https://www.un.org/press/en/1999/19990920.sgsm7136.html.

5. See for example, K.J. Holsti, *International Politics* (Englewood Cliffs, NJ: Prentice Hall, 1988), 124.

6. For differing perspectives see Peter Hough, *Understanding Global Security,* 3rd edition (New York: Routledge, 2013); and Michael Mandelbaum, *The Fate of Nations* (Cambridge: Cambridge University Press, 1988).

7. http://hdr.undp.org/sites/default/files/reports/255/hdr_1994_en_complete_nostats.pdf.

8. Arnold Wolfers, *Discord and Collaboration: Essays on International Politics* (Baltimore: Johns Hopkins University Press, 1962), 67–80.

9. Early advocates of this perspective include Harold and Margaret Sprout, *Towards a Politics of Planet Earth* (New York: Van Nostrand, 1971); and Dennis Pirages, *Ecopolitics* (North Scituate, MA: Duxbury Press, 1978).

10. Mark Amstutz, *International Ethics,* 4th edition (Lanham, MD: Rowman & Littlefield, 2013), 30–38; Gabriel Wollner, "The Third Wave of Theorizing Global Justice. A Review Essay," *Global*

Justice 6 (2013): 21–38; and Charles Beitz, "Cosmopolitanism and Global Justice," *Journal of Ethics* 9 (2005): 11–27.

11. Robert Putnam, "Diplomacy and Domestic Politics: The Logic of Two-Level Games," *International Organization* 42 (1988): 427–60.

12. Guosheng Deng and Scott Kennedy, "Big Business and Industry: Association Lobbying in China," *China Journal* 63 (2010): 125; and Scott Kennedy, "China's Porous Protectionism," *Political Science Quarterly* 120 (2005): 407–32.

13. C. Wright Mills, *The Power Elite* (New York: Oxford University Press, 1956).

14. See Jonathan Christensen, "Four Stages of Social Movements," *EBSCO Research Starters* (2009); and Greg Satell and Srdja Popovic, "How Protests Become Successful Social Movements," *Harvard Business Review*, January 27, 2017.

15. Robert Entman, *Projections of Power: Framing News, Public Opinion and US Foreign Policy* (Chicago: University of Chicago Press, 2004).

16. Matthew Baum and Yuri Zhukov, "Filtering Revolution: Reporting Bias in International Newspaper Coverage of the Libyan Civil War," *Journal of Peace Research* 52 (2015): 1–17; "Media Ownership and News Coverage of International Conflict," Paper presented at the 2013 annual meeting of the American Political Science Association.

17. Marc Lynch, et al., *Syria's Socially Mediated Civil War* (Washington, DC: United States Institute of Peace, 2014).

18. Craig Timber and Tony Romm, "New Report on Russian Disinformation," Prepared for the Senate Shows the Operation's Scale and Sweep," *Washington Post*, December 17, 2018, A1.

19. Margaret Keck and Kathryn Sikkink, *Activists beyond Borders* (Ithaca: Cornell University Press, 1998).

20. Ibid., 11–13.

21. Joe Hagan, "Domestic Political Explanations in the Analysis of Foreign Policy," in *Foreign Policy Analysis*, eds. Laura Neck, Jeanne Hey, and Patrick Haney (Englewood Cliffs, NJ: Prentice Hall, 1995), 117–44.

22. Daniel Kahneman and Amos Tversky, "Prospect Theory, an Analysis of Decision Making under Risk," *Econometrica* 47 (1979): 263–91; and Rose McDermott, James Fowler, and Oleg Smirnow, "On the Evolutionary Origin of Prospect Theory Preferences," *Journal of Politics* 70 (2007): 335–50.

23. Jack Levy, "Prospect Theory, Rational Choice, and International Relations," *International Studies Quarterly* 41 (1997): 87–112.

24. Alexander George, "The 'Operational Code': A Neglected Approach to the Study of Political Leaders and Decision-Making," *International Studies Quarterly* 13 (1969): 190–222.

25. Irving Janis, *Groupthink* (Boston: Houghton-Mifflin, 1982).

26. See Joanne Gowa, *"Ballots and Bullets": The Elusive Democratic Peace* (Princeton, NJ: Princeton University Press, 1999); Bruce Russett, *Grasping the Democratic Peace* (Princeton, NJ: Princeton University Press, 1993); and Dan Reiter and Allan Stam, *Democracies at War* (Princeton, NJ: Princeton University Press, 2002).

27. Michael Sussan, "Why the world's refugees should be given international passports," *Independent*, September 28, 2017. Available at: https://www.independent.co.uk/voices/
why-the-worlds-refugees-should-be-given-international-passports-a6670476.html.

28. "UN Refugee Summit talks end in abject failure," Amnesty International. Available at: https://www.amnesty.org/en/latest/news/2016/08/un-refugee-summit-talks-end-in-abject-failure/.

29. Michael Mazarr, "Preserving the Post-War Order," *Washington Quarterly* 40 (2017): 34.

30. See Garth Evans, *The Responsibility to Protect* (Washington, DC: Brookings, 2008); and Alex Bellamy, *Responsibility to Protect* (Oxford: Oxford University Press, 2014).

31. Alex Mintz, "Applied Decision Analysis: Utilizing Poliheuristic Theory to Explain and Predict Foreign Policy and National Security Decisions," *International Studies Perspectives* **6 (2005):** 94–98.

5: The Power Challenge: The Ability to Act

1. On Douhet see Giulio Douhet, *The Command of Air* (Washington, DC: Air Force History and Museum Program, 1998); Thomas Hippler, *Bombing the People* (New York: Cambridge University Press, 2013); and Bernard Brodie, *The Heritage of Douhet* (Santa Monica, CA: RAND Corporation, 1952).

2. Quoted in Matthew Evangelista, ed., *The American Way of Bombing* (Ithaca, NY: Cornell University Press, 2014), 10.

3. See the essays in Evangelista, ed., *The American Way of Bombing* (Ithaca: Cornell University Press, 2014).

4. The education data used here can be found at OECD, "Populations with tertiary education"; and UNICEF, 'Middle East and North Africa out of School Children Initiative.

5. Patricia Sullivan, "War Aims and Outcome," *Journal of Conflict Resolution* 51 (2007): 496–524; and Andrew Mack, "Why Big Nations Lose Small Wars," *World Politics* 27 (1975): 175–200.

6. Joseph Nye Jr., *Soft Power: The Means to Success in World Politics* (New York: Public Affairs Press, 2004); and *The Future of Power* (New York: Public Affairs Press, 2011).

7. *Global Trends: Paradox of Progress* (Washington, DC: National Intelligence Council, January 9, 2017).

8. Wuttikorn Chuwattananurak, "China's Comprehensive National Power and Its Implications for the Rise of China," paper presented at the CEEISA-ISA Joint International Conference, June, 2016.

9. *The Soft Power 30: A Ranking of Global Soft Power* (London: Portland Communications, 2016).

10. Clausewitz (1780–1831) died before his major book *On War* was published. Interpretations of it have long been contested and remain so today.

11. Bryan Early, *Busted Sanctions* (Stanford: Stanford University Press, 2015).

12. On cyberpower see Ben Buchanan, "The Life Cycle of Cyber Threats," *Survival* 58 (2016): 39–58; Lucas Kello, "The Meaning of the Cyber Revolution," *International Security* 38 (2013): 7–40; and Erik Gartze, "The Myth of Cyberwar," *International Security* 38 (2013): 41–73.

13. Herman Kahn, *On Escalation* (New York: Praeger, 1965).

14. David Sanger and Eric Schmitt, "Digital Weapons that Worked in Iran Miss the Mark against ISIS, Officials Say," *New York Times*, June 13, 2015, A5.

15. Martin Libicki, "The Convergence of Information Warfare," *Strategic Studies Quarterly* 11 (2017): 49–65.

16. Toby, Harnden, "Israel had 'doomsday plan' to win the 1976 war," *Sunday Times*, June 4, 2017. https://www.thetimes.co.uk/article/israel-had-doomsday-plan-to-win-1967-war-tqjrmng6d.

17. For these and other definitions of diplomacy see Chas. Freeman, Jr., *The Diplomat's Dictionary*, 2nd edition (Washington, DC: The United States Institute for Peace, 2010).

18. *Discover Diplomacy*, https://diplomacy.state.gov/discoverdiplomacy/.

19. For a critical history of the evolution of digital public diplomacy in the US State Department see Nicholas Cull, "The Long Road to Public Diplomacy 2.0," *International Studies Review* 15 (2013): 123–39.

20. Matthew Brown et al., "Bridging Public Health and Foreign Affairs," *Science and Diplomacy* (September 2014).

21. Robert Blackwell and Jennifer Harris, *War by Other Means* (Cambridge, MA: Harvard University Press, 2016); and David Baldwin, *Economic Statecraft* (Princeton, NJ: Princeton University Press, 1985).

22. Benjamin Cohen, *Currency Power* (Princeton, NJ: Princeton University Press, 2015).

23. Meghan O'Sullivan, *Shrewd Sanctions* (Washington, DC: Brookings, 1983), 12.

24. See Loch Johnson, ed., *Strategic Intelligence* (vol. 3): *Covert Action* (Westport, CT: Praeger Security International, 2007).

25. Bob Woodward, *VEIL: The Secret Wars of the CIA* (New York: Simon & Schuster, 1987).

26. Lawrence Freedman, "The Drone Revolution," *Foreign Affairs* 95 (2016): 154.

27. Sarah Kreps and Micah Zenko, "The Next Drone Wars," *Foreign Affairs* 93 (2014): 68–79.

28. Shashank Joshi and Aaron Stein, "Emerging Drone Nations," *Survival* 55 (2013): 53–78.

29. Kreps and Zenko, "The Next Drone Wars"; and Michael Boyle, "Is the US Drone War Effective?" *Current History* 103 (April, 2004): 137–43.

30. Joshi and Stein, "Emerging Drone Nations."

31. Micah Zenko, "Obama's Final Drone Strike Data," New York, Council on Foreign Relations, January 17, 2017. https://www.cfr.org/blog/obamas-final-drone-strike-data.

32. https://today.yougov.com/news/2013/10/28/americans-support-drone-attacks-only-without-civil/.

33. Dan Lamothe, "Retired generals cite past comments by Mattis while opposing Trump's proposed foreign aid cuts," *Washington Post*, February 27, 2017.

34. See Blackwell and Harris, *War by Other Means*, for discussions on Russia's use of economic power.

35. Rachel Stohl, "All the President's Drones," *The National Interest* 137 (2015): 31–36.

36. Lawrence Freedman, *Strategy: A History* (New York: Oxford University Press, 2013); and Richard Betts, "Is Strategy an Illusion?" *International Security* 25 (2002): 5–50.

37. Ionut Popescu, "Grand Strategy vs. Emergent Strategy in the Conduct of Foreign Policy," *Journal of Strategic Studies* 40 (2017): 1–23.

38. Quoted in Bruno Tertrais, "Drawing Red Lines Right," *Washington Quarterly* 37 (2014): 15.

39. Ibid., 19.

6: The Cooperation Challenge: Working Together

1. Report Card on International Cooperation, 2016–2017. https://www.lowyinstitute.org/publications/council-councils-2017-report-card-international-cooperation.

2. Report Card on International Cooperation, 2015–2016 (New York: Council on Foreign Relations, 2016).

3. *The Constitution of the World Health Organization*. http://www.who.int/governance/eb/who_constitution_en.pdf.

4. On the 1976 Ebola outbreak and for general articles on Ebola see Laurie Garrett, "The Return of Infectious Disease," *Foreign Affairs* 75 (1996): 66–79; Report of an International Commission, Ebola Hemorrhagic Fever in Zaire, 1976 *Bulletin of the World Health Organization* 56 (1978): 271–93; and David Fidler, "Epic Failure of Ebola and Global Health Security," *Brown Journal of World Affairs* 21 (2015): 179–97.

5. John Kinsman, "A Time of Fear," *Globalization and Health* 8 (2012): 1–12.

6. Fen Osler Hampson, *Multilateral Negotiations* (Baltimore: Johns Hopkins University Press, 1995); and Gilbert Winham, "Negotiations as a Management Process," *World Politics* 30 (1977): 87–114.

7. Fred Ikle quoted in Gordon Craig and Alexander George, eds., *Force and Statecraft*, 2nd edition (New York: Oxford University Press, 1990), 163.

8. Chester Crocker, "The Strategic Dilemma of a World Adrift," *Survival* 57 (2015): 7–30.

9. Daniel Drzner, "The System Worked," *World Politics* 66 (2014): 123–64.

10. Deepak Malhotra, "Without Conditions," *Foreign Affairs* 88 (2009): 84–90.

11. Stanley Foundation, "A Multistakeholder Governance Agenda, http://www.stanleyfoundation.org/spc/AgendaMultistakeholderGlobalGovernance.pdf. Stanley Foundation, Multistakeholder Coalitions. https://www.stanleyfoundation.org/publications/pdb/MultistakeholderPDB816.pdf.

12. Mark Mazower, *Governing the World* (New York: Penguin, 2012).

13. The data are from the Alliance Treaty Obligations and Treaty Project. They are discussed in John Duffield, "Alliances," in *Security Studies: An Introduction*, ed. Paul Williams, 2nd edition (New York: Routledge, 2013), 339–54.

14. Keren Yahli-Milo, Alexander Lanoszka, and Zack Cooper, "To Army or Ally?" *International Security* 41 (2016): 90–139.

15. Alexander Lanoszka, "Do Allies Really Ride Free?" *Survival* 57 (2015): 133–52.

16. Stephen Walt, *The Origins of Alliances* (Ithaca, NY: Cornell University Press, 1987).

17. Jan Melissen, *Summit Diplomacy Comes of Age* (Copenhagen: Netherlands Institute of International Relations, 2006).

18. Melissen, *Summit Diplomacy Comes of Age.*

19. On the iceberg theory see Alan Alexandroff and Donald Brean, "Global Summitry: Its Meaning and Scope," Part One, *Global Summitry* 1 (2015): 1–26.

20. Daniel Druckman and Peter Wallensteen, "Summit Meetings: Good or Bad for Peace?" *Global Summitry* 2 (2016): 71–92.

21. Peter Jones, *Track Two Diplomacy in Theory and Practice* (Stanford: Stanford University Press, 2015); Jean-Robert Leguey-Felleux, *The Dynamics of Diplomacy* (Boulder: Lynne Rienner, 2009).

22. Robert Keohane and Joseph Nye, *Power and Interdependence* (New York: Longman, 1977).

23. Robert Keohane and David Victor, "The Regime Complex for Climate Change," *Perspectives on Politics* 9 (2011): 7–23.

24. Klaus Aurisch, "The Art of Preparing a Multilateral Conference," *Negotiation Journal* 5 (1989): 279–88.

25. Hampson, *Multilateral Negotiations.*

26. Saadia Touval, "Multilateral Negotiation," *Negotiation Journal* 5 (1989): 159–73; and Hampson, *Multilateral Negotiations.*

27. Martin Daunton, "From Bretton Woods to Havana," in *Deadlocks in Multilateral Negotiations,* ed. Amrita Nariklar (Cambridge: Cambridge University Press, 2010), 47–78.

28. Melissen, *Summit Diplomacy Comes of Age,* 19–21.

29. Moises Naim, "Minilateralism," *Foreign Policy* 173 (2009): 134–35.

30. Stewart Patrick, "The New 'New Multilateralism': Minilateral Cooperation, but at What Cost?" *Global Summitry* 1 (2015): 115–34.

31. William Nordhaus, "Climate Clubs," *American Economics Review* 105 (2015): 1339–70; and Robert Falkner, "A Minilateral Solution for Global Climate Change?" *Perspective on Politics* 14 (2016): 87–101.

32. Miles Kahler, "Multilateralism with Small and Large Numbers," *International Organization* 46 (1992): 681–708.

33. For an overall assessment see Patrick, "The New 'New Multilateralism'."

34. Hilary Charlesworth, Christine Chinkin, and Shelly Wright, "Feminist Approaches to International Law," *American Journal of International Law* 85 (1991): 613–45.

35. Graham Allison, "China vs. America," *Foreign Affairs* 96 (2017): 86.

36. Gabrielle Lynch, "The International Criminal Court and the Making of a Kenyan President," *Current History* 114 (May 2015): 183–88.

37. For discussions of hard and soft law see Jon Birger Skjaerseth, et al., "Soft Law, Hard Law and Effective Implementation of International Environmental Norms," *Global Environmental Politics* 6 (2006): 104–20; Gregory Shaffer and Mark Pollack, "Hard vs. Soft Law: Alternatives, Complements, and Antagonists," *International Governance, Minnesota Law Review* 94 (2010): 706–99; and Kenneth Abbot and Duncan Snidal, "Hard and Soft Law in International Governance," *International Organization* 54 (2000): 421–56.

38. On the 2013 Ebola outbreak see Kevin Sack et al., "How Ebola Roared Back," *New York Times,* December 29, 2014; Congressional Research Service, "U.S. and International Health Responses to the Ebola Outbreak in West Africa" (Washington, DC: U.S Government Printing Office, October 29, 2014); and Laurie Garrett, "Ebola's Lessons," *Foreign Affairs* 94 (2015): 80–107.

39. For a Track III case study see Herman Kraft, "Track Three Diplomacy and Human Rights in Southeast Asia," *Global Networks* 2 (2002): 49–63.

40. Shaffer and Pollack, "Hard vs. Soft Law," 784–85.

41. William Tobey, "Peering Down from the Summit," *Global Summitry* 2 (2016): 93–113.

42. Tim Buthe and Walter Mattli, *The New Global Rulers* (Princeton, NJ: Princeton University Press, 2011).

7: The Security Challenge

1. http://www.ucdp.uu.se/.

2. Therese Petersson and Kristine Eck, Organized Violence, 1989-2017, Journal of Peace Research 55 (2018), 535-47.

3. Johan Galtung, "An Editorial," *Journal of Peace Research* 1 (1964): 1–4.

4. See Johan Galtung, "Violence, Peace, and Peace Research," *Journal of Peace Research* 6 (1969): 167–91; and "Cultural Violence," *Journal of Peace Research* 27 (1990): 291–305.

5. Randall Amster, *Peace Ecology* (Boulder: Paradigm Publishers, 2014).

6. Quincy Wright, *A Study of War* (Chicago: University of Chicago Press, 1983), 7.

7. Antulio Echevarria II, *War and Politics, Joint Forces Quarterly* (1995–96).

8. Hedley Bull, *The Anarchical Society* (London: Macmillan, 1983), 184.

9. For overviews of the development of peace studies see Peter Lawler, "Peace Studies," in *Security Studies: An Introduction,* ed. Paul Williams, 2nd edition (New York: Routledge, 2013), 77–89; Heikki Patomaki, "The Challenge of Critical Theory," *Journal of Peace Research* 38 (2001): 723–37; Houston Wood, *Invitation to Peace Studies* (New York: Oxford, 2016); and Nils Gleditsch et al., "Just the Study of War?" *Journal of Peace Research* 51 (2014): 145–58.

10. Istvan Kende, "The History of Peace," *Journal of Peace Research* 26 (1989): 233–47.

11. http://www.correlatesofwar.org/.

12. Thomas X. Hammes, "Insurgency: Modern Warfare Evolves into a Fourth Generation," *Strategic Forum* 214, January 2005.

13. Audrey Cronin, "The 'War on Terrorism': What Does it Mean to Win," *Journal of Strategic Studies* 37 (2014): 174–97.

14. Winifred Tate, "Paramilitary Forces in Colombia," *Latin America Research Review* 46 (2011): 192–200.

15. Seyom Brown, "Purposes and Pitfalls of War by Proxy," *Small Wars and Insurgencies* (27): 243–57.

16. Andrew Mumford, "Proxy Warfare and the Future of Conflict," *RUSI Journal* 158 (April 2013): 40–46; and "The New Era of Proliferated Proxy War," *The Strategy Bridge*, November 16, 2017. https://thestrategybridge.org/the-bridge/2017/11/16/the-new-era-of-the-proliferated-proxy-war.

17. Christopher Chivvis, "Understanding Russian 'Hybrid Warfare'," testimony before House Armed Service Committee, March 22, 2017. https://www.rand.org/content/dam/rand/pubs/testimonies/CT400/CT468/RAND_CT468.pdf.

18. Lionel Beehner, "How Proxy Wars Work," *Foreign Affairs Snapshot*, November 12, 2015. C. Anthony Pffaf and Patrick Granfield, "How (Not) to Fight Proxy Wars," *The National Interest*, March 17, 2018. http://nationalinterest.org/feature/how-not-fight-proxy-wars-25102.

19. Audrey Cronin, "How Al Qaeda Ends," *International Security* 31 (2006): 7–48.

20. James Sloan, "The Evolution of the Use of Force in UN Peacekeeping," *Journal of Strategic Studies* 37 (2014): 674–702.

21. Boutros Boutros-Ghali, *An Agenda for Peace* (New York: United Nations, 1992).

22. United Nations, General Assembly and Security Council, Report of the Panel on United Nations Peace Operations (A/55/305-S/2000/809), August 21, 2000.

23. Emily Paddon, "Partnering for Peace," *International Peacekeeping* 18 (2011): 516–33; and Mats Berdal and David Ucko, "The Use of Force in UN Peacekeeping Operations," *RUSI Journal* 160 (2015): 6–12.

24. Stephen Stedman, "Spoiler Problems in Peace Processes," *International Security* 22 (1997): 5–53.

25. James Dobbins et al., *The Beginners Guide to Nation Building* (Santa Monica: The Rand Corporation, 2007). For another breakdown see Nicole Ball, "The Challenge of Rebuilding War-Torn Societies," in *Turbulent Peace,* eds. Chester Crocker et al. (Washington, DC: US Institute of Peace Press, 2001), 719–36.

26. Ronald Paris and Timothy Sisk, "Conclusion," in *The Dilemmas of Statebuilding*, eds. Ronald Paris and Timothy Sisk (New York: Routledge, 2009), 304–15.

27. Thomas Schelling and Morton Halperin, *Strategy and Arms Control* (New York: Twentieth Century Fund, 1961).

28. Alexei Arbatov, *An Unnoticed Crisis: The End of History for Nuclear Arms Control* (Carnegie Moscow Center, June 2015).

29. Gregory Koblentz, *Strategic Stability in the Second Nuclear Age* (New York: Council on Foreign Relations, November 2014).

30. Vipin Narang, "Nuclear Strategies of Emerging Nuclear Powers," *Washington Quarterly* 38 (2015): 73–91.

31. Scott Sagan, "Why Do States Build Nuclear Weapons," *International Security* 21 (1996/97): 54–86; and Nuno Monteiro and Alexander Debs, "The Strategic Logic of Nuclear Proliferation," *International Security* 39 (2014): 7–51.

32. Vipin Narang, "Strategies of Nuclear Proliferation," *International Security* 41 (2016/17): 110–50.

33. Alex Wilner, "The Dark Side of Extended Deterrence: Thinking Through the State Sponsorship of Terrorism," *Journal of Strategic Studies* 40 (2017): 1–28.

34. Pavel Podvig, "Blurring the Line between Nuclear and Non-nuclear Weapons," *Bulletin of the Atomic Scientists* 72 (2016): 145–49.

35. Amy Woolf, "Conventional Prompt Global Strike and Long Range Ballistic Missiles," Congressional Research Service, Washington, DC, April 6, 2018.

36. "Austrian Pledge," Austrian Ministry of Foreign Affairs, December 9, 2014.

37. Andrey Baklitskiy "The 2015 NPT Review Conference and the Future of the Nonproliferation Regime," *Arms Control Today* 46 (July 2015): 15–18.

38. C. Anthony Pfaff, "Strategic Insights: Proxy War Norms," Strategic Studies Institute, US Army War College, December 18, 2017. http://ssi.armywarcollege.edu/index.cfm/articles/Proxy-War-Norms/2017/12/18.

39. Dominic Tierney, "Mastering the Endgame of War," *Survival* 56 (2014): 69–94.

40. Ibid.

8: Economic Challenges: Who Is in Charge of the Global Economy?

1. Robert O. Keohane and Joseph S. Nye, Jr., *Power and Interdependence* 4th edition, (New York: Pearson, 2011).

2. "The 1992 Campaign: Transcript of 2nd TV Debate Between Bush, Clinton and Perot," *New York Times*, Archives 1992. Available at: https://www.nytimes.com/1992/10/16/us/the-1992-campaign-transcript-of-2d-tv-debate-between-bush-clinton-and-perot.html (accessed May 29, 2019). Emphasis added.

3. Robert Whaples, "Where Is There Consensus among American Economic Historians? The Results of a Survey on Forty Propositions," *Journal of Economic History* 55, no. 1 (March 1995): 139–54. Available at: http://www.employees.csbsju.edu/jolson/econ315/whaples2123771.pdf (accessed June 1, 2019).

4. "Gore trounces Perot in Nafta debate: Vice-President's triumphant TV performance boosts White House hopes of congressional approval for pact," *Independent*, November 11, 1993. Available at: https://www.independent.co.uk/news/world/gore-trounces-perot-in-nafta-debate-vice-presidents-triumphant-tv-performance-boosts-white-house-1503459.html (accessed May 29, 2019).

5. "North American Agreement on Labor Cooperation: A Guide," United States Department of Labor. Available at: https://www.dol.gov/ilab/trade/agreements/naalcgd.htm (accessed June 2, 2019); Commission for Environmental Cooperation Website,

available at: http://www.cec.org/about-us/NAAEC (accessed June 2, 2019).

6. James McBride and Mohammed Alv Sergie, "NAFTA's Economic Impact," Council on Foreign Relations, October 4, 2017. Available at: https://www.cfr.org/backgrounder/naftas-economic-impact (accessed June 2, 2019).

7. United Nations Development Program, *Human Development Report 2016: Human Development for Everyone* (New York: UNDP, 2016), 3.

8. Ibid., 3–5.

9. World Bank, DataBank | Poverty and Equity Database, The World Bank Group, 2015, at https://databank.worldbank.org/data/reports.aspx?source=poverty-and-equity-database (accessed February 12, 2019).

10. William Felice, *The Global New Deal: Economic and Social Human Rights in World Politics* (Lanham, MD: Rowman & Littlefield, 2010), 5.

11. Oxfam Briefing Paper, *Reward Work, Not Wealth* (Oxford, UK: Oxfam International, 2018), 2.

12. Facundo Alvaredo, Lucas Chancel, Thomas Piketty, Emmanuel Saez, and Gabriel Zucman, *World Inequality Report 2018—Executive Summary* (World Inequality Lab, 2018), 6.

13. World Trade Organization, "Non-tariff barriers: Red tape, etc.," WTO website, available at: https://www.wto.org/english/thewto_e/whatis_e/tif_e/agrm9_e.htm (accessed June 8, 2019). (accessed May 29, 2019).

14. Alan Boyd, "ASEAN Free Trade Still a Distant Notion," *Asia Times*, September 6, 2017.

15. Felice, *The Global New Deal*, 28.

16. Mitsuru Obe, "TPP Deal Expected to Shake up Japan's Agriculture Sector," *Wall Street Journal*, October 6, 2015.

17. Milton Friedman, *Capitalism and Freedom* (1962 reprint; Chicago: University of Chicago Press, 1982).

18. Joel Cohen, *How Many People Can the Earth Support?* (New York: Norton, 1995), 272.

19. Robert Gilpin, *The Political Economy of International Relations* (Princeton, NJ: Princeton University Press, 1987), 27.

20. Felice, *The Global New Deal*, 32.

21. Ibid.

22. Gilpin, *Political Economy of International Relations*, 11.

23. McBride and Sergie, "NAFTA's Economic Impact."

24. "Zambia—Economy Still Dependent on Copper and Producing Few Jobs," *African Sustainable Conservation News*, September 21, 2015.

25. See for example: Sherry Keith and Robert Girling, "Bauxite Dependency: Roots of Crisis," *North American Congress on Latin America*, September 25, 2007. Available at: https://nacla.org/article/bauxite-dependency-roots-crisis (accessed May 29, 2019).

26. Gilpin, *The Political Economy of International Relations*, 33.

27. Ana Swanson and Jim Tankersley, "Mexico, Hitting Back, Imposes Tariffs on $3 Billion Worth of U.S. Goods," *New York Times*, June 5, 2018.

28. Ana Swanson, "U.S. and China Expand Trade War as Beijing Matches Trump's Tariffs," *New York Times*, June 15, 2018.

29. Associated Press, "China Gets US Tariff Delay but Movement on Tech Unclear," *New York Times*, December 3, 2018.

30. "What Is China's Belt and Road Initiative," *Economist*, May 15, 2017.

31. Jonathan E. Hillman, "How Big Is China's Belt and Road," *Center for Strategic & International Studies*, April 3, 2018.

32. Richard Fontaine and Daniel Kilman, "On China's New Silk Road, Democracy Pays a Toll," *Foreign Policy*, May 16, 2018.

33. Elizabeth C. Economy, "China's New Revolution: The Reign of Xi Jinping," *Foreign Affairs* Vol 97, No 3, May/June 2018.

34. Philip T. Hoffman, *Why Did Europe Conquer the World?* (Princeton, NJ: Princeton University Press, 2015), 2–3.

35. Andre Gunder Frank, *The Development of Underdevelopment* (Boston: New England Press, 1966).

36. United Nations Development Programme, *Human Development Report 2016* (New York: UNDP, 2016), 198–201.

37. International Labour Organization, *Trade Union Manual on Export Processing Zones* (Geneva, Switzerland: ILO, 2014), 3.

38. Ibid., 13.

39. Women's Environment and Development Organization (WEDO), *Mapping Progress* (New York: WEDO, 1998), 13.

40. J. Ann Tickner, *Gender in International Relation* (New York: Columbia University Press, 1992).

41. Felice, *The Global New Deal*, 1.

42. United Nations, *Millennium Development Goals Report 2015* (New York: United Nations, 2015), 3.

43. Ibid., 4–6.

44. United Nations, *Millennium Development Goals Report 2015* (New York: United Nations, 2015), 3–9.

45. The World Bank, "A Model from Mexico for the World," November 19, 2014.

46. The World Bank, "A Model from Mexico for the World."

47. Charles Kenny, *Getting Better: Why Global Development Is Succeeding—and How We Can Improve the World Even More* (New York: Basic Books, 2011), 166.

48. United Nations, *The Sustainable Development Goals Report 2017*. Available at: https://unstats.un.org/sdgs/report/2017/overview/ (accessed May 29, 2019).

49. Jonathan Tepperman, *The Fix: How Nations Survive and Thrive in a World in Decline* (New York: Duggan Books, 2016), 35.

50. Ibid., 41–43.

51. Ibid., 47.

52. Donald Trump, Campaign Rally, November 7, 2016. Available at *Politifact*: http://www.politifact.com/truth-o-meter/promises/trumpometer/promise/1410/renegotiate-nafta/ (accessed June 2, 2019).

53. McBride and Sergie, "NAFTA's Economic Impact."

54. "USTR Releases NAFTA Negotiating Objectives," Office of the United States Trade Representative, July 2017. Available at: https://ustr.gov/about-us/policy-offices/press-office/press-releases/2017/july/ustr-releases-nafta-negotiating (accessed June 3, 2019).

55. McBride and Sergie, "NAFTA's Economic Impact."

56. Guy Lawson, "First Canada Tried to Charm Trump. Now It's Fighting Back," *New York Times Magazine*, June 9, 2018.

Available at: https://www.nytimes.com/2018/06/09/magazine/justin-trudeau-chrystia-freeland-trade-canada-us-.html (accessed May 29, 2019).

57. McBride and Sergie, "NAFTA's Economic Impact."

58. Peter Baker, "Trump Signs New Trade Deal with Canada and Mexico after Bitter Negotiations," *New York Times*, November 30, 2018.

59. Glenn Thrush, "Trumps Says He Plans to Withdraw from Nafta," *New York Times*, December 2, 2018.

60. James Tobin, "Prologue," in *The Tobin Tax: Coping with Financial Volatility*, ed. Mahbub ul Haq, Inge Kaul, and Isabelle Grunberg (New York: Oxford University Press, 1996), x, xii.

61. James Tobin, "The Antiglobalisation Movement Has Highjacked My Name," *Der Spiegel*, September 3, 2001. Quoted in Robert Kuttner, *Can Democracy Survive Global Capitalism* (New York: Norton, 2018), 72.

62. Jared Bernstein, "The Case for a Tax on Financial Transactions," *New York Times*, July 22, 2015.

63. Jared Bernstein, "The Case for a Tax on Financial Transactions."

64. Kuttner, *Can Democracy Survive Global Capitalism?* 74.

65. Dwight D. Eisenhower, "The Chance for Peace," delivered before the American Society of Newspaper Editors, April 16, 1954.

66. Felice, *The Global New Deal*, 207–08.

67. United Nations Development Programme, *Human Development Report 1994* (New York: Oxford University Press, 1994), 50.

9: Human Rights Challenges: Protecting Human Dignity

1. Roosevelt quote from Blanche Wiesen Cook, *Eleanor Roosevelt: Volume One* (New York: Penguin Group, 1992), 18.

2. Telford Taylor, *The Anatomy of the Nuremberg Trials* (New York: Knopf, 1992), 171–72.

3. "Charter of the International Military Tribunal." Available at: http://avalon.law.yale.edu/imt/imtconst.asp#art6 (accessed May 31, 2019).

4. Taylor, *The Anatomy of the Nuremberg Trials*, 244–45.

5. Paul Gordon Lauren, *The Evolution of International Human Rights: Visions Seen*, 3rd edition (Philadelphia: University of Pennsylvania Press, 2011), 6.

6. Micheline Ishay, *The History of Human Rights: From Ancient Times to the Globalization Era* (Berkeley: University of California Press, 2004), 35–40; William Felice, "Economic and Social Rights," *The International Studies Encyclopedia*, (Oxford: Blackwell Publishing, 2010), 2.

7. Lauren, *The Evolution of International Human Rights*, 6–10; Felice, "Economic and Social Rights," 2.

8. Micheline Ishay, *The Human Rights Reader*, 2nd edition (New York: Routledge, 2007), 8–15.

9. Felice, "Economic and Social Rights," 3; Lauren, *The Evolution of International Human Rights*, 11–14.

10. Amartya Sen, "Democracy and Its Global Roots," *New Republic*, October 6, 2003.

11. Quoted in Sen, *Democracy and Its Global Roots*.

12. 'Thomas Jefferson to Virginia Delegates to the Continental Congress, August 1774: "A Summary View of the Rights of British America." Available at: https://www.loc.gov/teachers/classroommaterials/connections/thomas-jefferson/history3.html (accessed May 31, 2019).

13. "Declaration of the Rights of Man and Citizen," approved by the National Assembly of France, August 26, 1789. Available at: https://www.americanbar.org/content/dam/aba/migrated/2011_build/human_rights/french_dec_rightsofman.authcheckdam.pdf (accessed May 31, 2019).

14. William Felice, *The Ethics of Interdependence: Global Human Rights and Duties* (Lanham, MD: Rowman & Littlefield, 2016), 8.

15. Jack Donnelly, *Universal Human Rights in Theory and Practice* (Ithaca: Cornell University Press, 1989), 12.

16. William Felice, *Taking Suffering Seriously: The Importance of Collective Human Rights* (Albany: State University of New York Press, 1996), 17.

17. Felice, *Ethics of Interdependence*, 8.

18. Lauren, *The Evolution of International Human Rights*, 92.

19. Morgenthau quoted in Samantha Power, *"A Problem from Hell": America and the Age of Genocide* (New York: Basic Books, 2013), 8.

20. Kevork Bardakjian, *Hitler and the Armenian Genocide* (Cambridge, MA: The Zoryan Institute, 1985); also see Power, *"A Problem from Hell,"* 23.

21. The material on the UN Human Rights System is drawn from Felice, *The Ethics of Interdependence*, 9–10, 13–18.

22. Articles 1–21, *Universal Declaration of Human Rights*. Available at: http://www.un.org/en/universal-declaration-human-rights/ (accessed May 31, 2019).

23. Articles 22–28, *Universal Declaration of Human Rights*.

24. Felice, *Taking Suffering Seriously*, 31–32; Article 28, *Universal Declaration of Human Rights*; Roland Rich, "The Right to Development: A Right of Peoples," in *The Rights of Peoples*, ed. James Crawford (Oxford: Clarendon Press, 1988), 41.

25. Carol Morello, "US withdraws from U.N. Human Rights Council over perceived bias against Israel," *Washington Post*, June 19, 2018.

26. See: Office of the United Nations High Commissioner for Human Rights, *Human Rights Bodies—Complaints Procedures*. Available at: https://www.ohchr.org/en/hrbodies/tbpetitions/pages/hrtbpetitions.aspx (accessed March 24, 2019).

27. Human Rights Watch, *World Report 2018*. Available at: https://www.hrw.org/world-report/2018/country-chapters/burma (accessed May 31, 2019).

28. Nahal Toosi, "The Genocide the US Didn't See Coming," *Politico*, March/April 2018.

29. Antonio Guterres, "The Rohingya are victims of ethnic cleansing. The world has failed them," *Washington Post*, July 10, 2018.

30. Hannah Beech, "Myanmar's Military Planned Rohingya Genocide, Rights Group Says," *New York Times*, July 19, 2018. Available at: https://www.nytimes.com/2018/07/19/world/asia/myanmar-rohingya-genocide.html (accessed May 31, 2019).

31. Article II, Convention on the Prevention and Punishment of the Crime of Genocide, December 1948.

32. Upendra Baxi, "Voices of Suffering, Fragmented Universality, and the Future of Human Rights," in *The Future of International Human Rights*, eds. Burns H. Weston and Stephen P. Marks (Ardsley, NY: Transnational, 1999), 123; Walter Kaufmann, *The Portable Nietzsche* (New York: Viking Penguin, 1959), 160–61.

33. Julia Hausermann, "The Realisation and Implementation of Economic, Social and Cultural Rights," in *Economic, Social and Cultural Rights: Progress and Achievement*, eds. Ralph Beddard and Dilys M. Hill (New York: St. Martin's, 1992), 49.

34. Henry Shue, *Basic Rights: Subsistence, Affluence, and US Foreign Policy* (Princeton, NJ: Princeton University Press, 1980).

35. "The Maastricht Guidelines on Violations of Economic, Social and Cultural Rights," *Human Rights Quarterly* 20, no. 3 (1998): 693–94.

36. Felice, *The Global New Deal*, 164–65.

37. Joshua S. Goldstein, *Winning the War on War: The Decline of Armed Conflict Worldwide* (New York: Penguin, 2011).

38. Felice, *Ethics of Interdependence*, 87–88.

39. Office of the High Commissioner for Human Rights, "Born Free and Equal," Geneva 2012 (HR/PUB/12/06), 7.

40. Tanya Mohn, "The Shifting Global Terrain of L.G.B.T.Q. Rights," *New York Times*, June 21, 2018.

41. Amnesty International UK, "LGBTI Rights," May 31, 2018.

42. Pew Research Center, "Gay Marriage around the World," August 8, 2017. Available at: http://www.pewforum.org/2017/08/08/gay-marriage-around-the-world-2013/ (accessed May 31, 2019).

43. Joanna Slater and Vidhi Doshi, "India's Supreme Court Decriminalizes Gay Sex in Historic Ruling," *Washington Post*, September 6, 2018.

44. Felice, *Ethics of Interdependence*, 89–90.

45. Kathryn Sikkink, *Evidence for Hope: Making Human Rights Work in the 21st Century* (Princeton, NJ: Princeton University Press, 2017), 44–45.

46. These examples are from Sikkink, *Evidence for Hope*, 241–43.

47. Article II, *Convention on the Prevention and Punishment of the Crime of Genocide*, December 9, 1948.

48. Preamble, *Rome Statute of the International Criminal Court*, 1998. Available at: http://legal.un.org/icc/statute/99_corr/preamble.htm (accessed May 31, 2019).

49. Compiled by Philippe Sands, *East West Street: On the Origins of "Genocide" and "Crimes Against Humanity,"* (New York: Vintage, 2017), 362–64.

50. Sikkink, *Evidence for Hope*, 43–44.

51. Sikkink, *Evidence for Hope*, 243. Harold Hongju Koh, "Foreword: On American Exceptionalism," *Stanford Law Review* 55, no. 5 (2003): 1479–527.

52. Lauren, *The Evolution of International Human Rights*, 232–33.

53. Mandela quote from Lauren, *The Evolution of International Human Rights*, 314.

54. Chris Buckley, "Liu Xiaobo, Chinese Dissident Who Won Nobel While Jailed Dies at 61," *New York Times*, July 13, 2017.

55. American Anthropological Association, "Statement on Human Rights," *American Anthropologist* 49, no. 4 (1947): 539–43. Available at: https://lucian.uchicago.edu/blogs/around1948/files/2012/09/1947-Statement-on-Human-Rights-American-Anthropological-Association.pdf (accessed July 21, 2018).

56. See, for example, Philip Alston and Ryan Goodman, "Rights, Duties and Dilemmas of Universalism," *International Human Rights* (Oxford: Oxford University Press, 2013), 531–681.

57. Rosalyn Higgins, *Problems and Process: International Law and How We Use It* (Oxford: Clarendon Press, 1994), 96.

58. Abdullahi A. An-Na'im, *Human Rights in Cross-Cultural Perspectives: A Quest for Consensus* (Philadelphia: University of Pennsylvania Press, 1992), 3–6.

59. US Department of State, *Country Reports on Human Rights Practices for 2017: China*. Available at: https://www.state.gov/j/drl/rls/hrrpt/humanrightsreport/index.htm#wrapper (accessed July 24, 2018).

60. Amnesty International, *Human Rights in China 2017*. Available at: https://www.amnestyusa.org/countries/china/?gclid=EAIaIQobChMIusGH5oC43AIVBxIbCh337AImEAAYASAAEgJ3ePD_BwE (accessed July 24, 2018).

61. Human Rights Watch, *World Report 2018: China Events of 2017*. Available at: https://www.hrw.org/world-report/2018/country-chapters/china-and-tibet (accessed May 31, 2019).

10: Global Environmental Challenges: The Global Commons

1. Dr. Martin Luther King Jr., "A Christmas Sermon on Peace—1967." Available at: https://bsahely.com/2017/09/23/martin-luther-king-jr-a-christmas-sermon-on-peace-1967/ (accessed May 31, 2019).

2. Somini Sengupta, "2018 Is Shaping up to Be the Fourth-Hottest Year. Yet We're Still Not Prepared for Global Warming," *New York Times*, August 9, 2018.

3. David Hunter, James Salzman, and Durwood Zaelke, *International Environmental Law and Policy*, 3rd edition (New York: Foundation Press, 2007), 543–49.

4. Hunter, Salzman, and Zaelke, *International Environmental Law and Policy*, 550.

5. Hunter, Salzman, and Zaelke, *International Environmental Law and Policy*, 173–74.

6. Ronald Reagan, "Address before a Joint Session of the Congress on the State of the Union," January 25, 1984. Available at: http://www.presidency.ucsb.edu/ws/index.php?pid=40205 (accessed May 31, 2019).

7. World Commission on Environment and Development, *Our Common Future* (Oxford: Oxford University Press, 1987), 43.

8. Hunter, Salzman, and Zaelke, *International Environmental Law and Policy*, 187.

9. Pamela S. Chasek, David L. Downie, and Janet Welsh Brown, *Global Environmental Politics*, 6th edition (Boulder, CO: Westview Press, 2014), 322.

10. Garrett Hardin, "The Tragedy of the Commons," *Science* 162 (13 December 1968), 1243-1248.

11. "The White House and the Green House," *New York Times*, May 9, 1989. Available at: https://timesmachine.nytimes.com/timesmachine/1989/05/09/657689.html?action=click&contentCollection=Archives&module=LedeAsset&region=ArchiveBody&pgtype=article&pageNumber=30 (accessed August 5, 2018).

12. Eric Holthaus, "James Hansen's Legacy: Scientists Reflect on Climate Change in 1988, 2018, and 2048," *Grist*, June 22, 2018.

13. William Felice, *Global New Deal: Economic and Social Human Rights in World Politics*, (Lanham, MD: Rowman & Littlefield, 2010), 126. See also: Craig S. Smith, "150 Nations Start Groundwork for Global Warming Policies," *New York Times*, January 18, 2001, 7(A).

14. Intergovernmental Panel on Climate Change, *Climate Change 2007: Synthesis Report*, approved at IPCC Plenary XXVII, Valencia, Spain, 12–17 November 2007.

15. See https://www.nobelprize.org/nobel_prizes/peace/laureates/2007/ (accessed August 5, 2018).

16. Intergovernmental Panel on Climate Change, *Climate Change 2014 Synthesis Report; Summary for Policymakers*, 2014. Available at: https://www.ipcc.ch/pdf/assessment-report/ar5/syr/AR5_SYR_FINAL_SPM.pdf (accessed May 31, 2019).

17. Nathaniel Rich, "Losing Earth: The Decade We Almost Stopped Climate Change," *New York Times*, August 1, 2018.

18. UN Climate Change News, "UN Climate Change Launches First-Ever Annual Report," April 30, 2018.

19. Intergovernmental Panel on Climate Change, *Climate Change 2014 Synthesis Report; Summary for Policymakers*, 4. Available at: https://www.ipcc.ch/pdf/assessment-report/ar5/syr/AR5_SYR_FINAL_SPM.pdf (accessed May 31, 2019).

20. Felice, *Global New Deal*, 127.

21. Mark Landler, "U.S. and China Reach Climate Deal after Months of Talks," *New York Times*, November 11, 2014.

22. William Felice, The *Ethics of Interdependence: Global Human Rights and Duties* (Lanham, MD: Rowman & Littlefield, 2016), 139. See also: Gørild Heggelund, "China's Climate Change Policy: Domestic and International Developments," *Asian Perspective* 31, no. 2 (2007): 156.

23. Felice, *Ethics of Interdependence*, 139–40.

24. Coral Davenport, "Nations Approve Landmark Climate Accord in Paris," *New York Times*, December 12, 2015.

25. Louis Jacobson, "Yes, Donald Trump did call climate change a Chinese hoax," *Politifact,* June 3, 2016. Available at: https://www.politifact.com/truth-o-meter/statements/2016/jun/03/hillary-clinton/yes-donald-trump-did-call-climate-change-chinese-h/ (accessed May 31, 2019).

26. Ellen Knickmeyer, "Emails show cooperation among EPA, climate-change deniers," *Associated Press (AP)*, May 26, 2018. Available at: https://apnews.com/amp/64cd37b0503440c0b92e6ca075f87dd4 (accessed May 31, 2019).

27. Republican Platform, "America's Natural Resources: Agriculture, Energy, and the Environment," 2016.

28. Lisa Friedman, "College Republicans Propose an Unusual Idea from the Right: A Carbon Tax," *New York Times*, March 6, 2018.

29. John Schwartz, "Exxon Mobil Lends Its Support to a Carbon Tax Proposal," *New York Times*, June 20, 2017.

30. Schwartz, "Exxon Mobil Lends Its Support to a Carbon Tax Proposal."

31. Alliance for Market Solutions, "2018 Millennial Report," February 26, 2018.

32. NASA, "Global Climate Change: Vital Signs of the Planet." Available at: https://climate.nasa.gov/effects/ (accessed August 7, 2018).

33. Food and Agriculture Organization of the United Nations, *The State of World Fisheries and Aquaculture 2018, In Brief*, 12. Available at: http://www.fao.org/3/CA0191EN/CA0191EN.pdf (accessed May 31, 2019).

34. FAO, *Review of the State of World Marine Fishery Resources*, FAO Fisheries and Aquaculture Technical Paper No. 569 (Rome: FAO, 2011), 13–14. Available at: http://www.fao.org/docrep/015/i2389e/i2389e.pdf (accessed May 31, 2019).

35. Hunter, Salzman, and Zaelke, *International Environmental Law and Policy*, 754.

36. United Nations Convention on the Law of the Sea. Available at: http://www.un.org/depts/los/convention_agreements/texts/unclos/unclos_e.pdf (accessed May 31, 2019).

37. Hunter, Salzman, and Zaelke, *International Environmental Law and Policy*, 741.

38. United Nations Convention on the Law of the Sea. Available at: http://www.un.org/depts/los/convention_agreements/texts/unclos/unclos_e.pdf (accessed May 31, 2019).

39. U. T. Srinivasan, W. L. Cheung, R. Watson, and U. R. Sumaila, "Food Security Implications of Global Marine Catch Losses Due to Overfishing," *Journal of Bioeconomics* (2010) DOI: 10.10007/s10818-010-9090-9. Research Summary available from the PEW Environment Group at: http://www.pewtrusts.org/~/media/legacy/uploadedfiles/peg/publications/report/pegosdfoodsecuritypdf.pdf (accessed April 9, 2019).

40. Dick Russell, "Vacuuming the Seas: Where Countries Collide," *E Magazine*, July 1996, 28; Hunter, Salzman, and Zaelke, *International Environmental Law and Policy*, 758.

41. "Getting Serious about Overfishing," *Economist*, May 27, 2017.

42. Philippe Sands and Jacqueline Peel, *Principles of International Environmental Law*, 3rd edition (Cambridge: Cambridge University Press, 2012), 578.

43. The information on these five treaties is from Sands and Peel, *Principles of International Environmental Law*, 579–90.

44. "Getting Serious about Overfishing," *Economist*, May 27, 2017.

45. LOS Treaty ratification information available at: https://treaties.un.org/pages/ViewDetailsIII.aspx?src=TREATY&mtdsg_no=XXI-

6&chapter=21&Temp=mtdsg3&clang=_en (accessed May 31, 2019).

46. Hunter, Salzman, and Zaelke, *International Environmental Law and Policy*, 1004–05.

47. "The IUCN Red List of Threatened Species."

48. Center for Biological Diversity, "The Extinction Crisis." Available at: https://www.biologicaldiversity.org/programs/biodiversity/elements_of_biodiversity/extinction_crisis/ (accessed May 31, 2019).

49. Hunter, Salzman, and Zaelke, *International Environmental Law and Policy*, 7.

50. Sands and Peel, *Principles of International Environmental Law*, 450.

51. Gretchen Daily, "Introduction: What Are Ecosystem Services?" in *Nature's Services: Societal Dependence on Natural Ecosystems*, ed. G. Daily (Washington, DC: Island Press, 1997), 3–4.

52. *Millennium Ecosystem Assessment* (Washington, DC, 2005), 5, 16–22.

53. Vann Newkirk II, "Trump's EPA Concludes Environmental Racism Is Real," *Atlantic*, February 28, 2018.

54. Michael R. Anderson, "Human Rights Approaches to Environmental Protection: An Overview," in *Human Rights Approaches to Environmental Protection*, eds. Alan E. Boyle and Michael R. Anderson (New York: Oxford University Press, 1996), 1–4.

55. Fatma Zohra Ksentini, "Human Rights and the Environment," Final Report of the Special Rapporteur, UN Doc.E/CH.4Sub.2/1994/9 (6 July 1994).

56. Sands and Peel, *Principles of International Environmental Law*, 454.

57. Hunter, Salzman, and Zaelke, *International Environmental Law and Policy*, 1023–24.

58. Hunter, Salzman, and Zaelke, *International Environmental Law and Policy*, 1027–28.

59. Chasek, Downie, and Brown, *Global Environmental Politics*, 180–81.

60. Secretariat of the Convention on Biological Diversity, *Global Biodiversity Outlook 3* (Montreal: Progress Press, 2010), 9. Available at: https://www.cbd.int/doc/publications/gbo/gbo3-final-en.pdf (assessed May 31, 2019). See also: Chasek, Downie, and Brown, *Global Environmental Politics*, 181.

61. Hunter, Salzman, and Zaelke, *International Environmental Law and Policy*, 209.

62. The UN World Summit on Sustainable Development, *Johannesburg Declaration on Sustainable Development*, 4 September 2002, A/CONF.199/20. Available at: http://www.un-documents.net/jburgdec.htm (accessed May 31, 2019).

63. *Plan of Implementation of the World Summit on Sustainable Development*. Available at: https://sustainabledevelopment.un.org/milestones/wssd (accessed June 8, 2019).

64. Chasek, Downie, and Brown, *Global Environmental Politics*, 330. See also Felice, *Global New Deal*, 268–72.

65. Chasek, Downie, and Brown, *Global Environmental Politics*, 321.

66. United Nations, *Report of the United Nations Conference on Sustainable Development*, A/CONF.216/16 (New York: United Nations, 2012), 46–47.

67. Address by President Bill Clinton to the World Trade Organization, Geneva, Switzerland, 18 May 1998.

68. Felice, *Global New Deal*, 74.

69. "Principles of the Trading System," World Trade Organization. Available at: https://www.wto.org/english/thewto_e/whatis_e/tif_e/fact2_e.htm (accessed May 31, 2019).

70. *Rio de Janeiro Declaration on Environment and Development*, UN Doc.A/CONF.151/26 (June 13, 1992).

71. Sands and Peel, *Principles of International Environmental Law*, 218–19.

72. Sands and Peel, *Principles of International Environmental Law*, 222.

73. Chasek, Downie, and Brown, *Global Environmental Politics*, 42–46.

11: Looking Forward: New Policy Challenges And Responses

1. Peter Schwartz, *The Art of the Long View* (New York: Doubleday, 1991).

2. Norman Angell, *The Great Illusion* (New York: G. Putnam & Sons, 1911).

3. See Ronald Findlay and Kevin O'Rourke, *Power and Plenty* (Princeton, NJ: Princeton University Press, 2007); and Ka Zeng, *Trade Threats, Trade Wars* (Ann Arbor: University of Michigan Press, 2004).

4. Quoted in Josh Wingrove, "Economists Invoke Great Depression in Warning to Trump on Trade," Bloomberg, May 2, 1018.

5. Federal Reserve History, "Stock Market Crash of 1929."

6. National Intelligence Council, *Global Trends 2035* (Washington, DC: National Intelligence Council, January, 2017).

7. See Charles Laderman, "Conservative Internationalism: An Overview," *Orbis* 62 (2018): 6–21; and Paul Miller, *Armed Power and Liberal Order: A Conservative Internationalist Grand Strategy* (Washington, DC: Georgetown University Press, 2016).

8. Henry Nau, *Conservative Internationalism: Armed Diplomacy under Jefferson, Polk, Truman, and Reagan* (Princeton, NJ: Princeton University Press, 2015); and Henry Nau, "Why 'Conservative,' Not Liberal Internationalism?" *Orbis* 62 (2018): 22–29.

9. For discussions of postcolonial theory see Patrick Williams and Laura Chrisman, eds., *Colonial Discourse and Post-Colonial Theory* (New York: Columbia University Press, 1994); Pal Ahluwala, *Politics and Post-Colonial Theory: African Inflections* (New York: Routledge, 2001); and John McLeod, ed., *The Routledge Companion to Postcolonial Studies* (New York: Routledge, 2007).

10. Orientalism at the service of imperialism: A review article of Edward W. Said's Orientalism, (London: Routledge & Kegan, 1978).

11. Phillip Darby, "Pursuing the Political: A Postcolonial Rethinking of Relations International," *Millennium* 33 (2004): 1–32; Phillip Darby and J. Paolini, "Bridging International Relations and Postcolonialism," *Alternatives* 19 (1994): 371–97; Sankaran Krishna, *Globalization and Postcolonialism: Hegemony and Resistance in the Twenty-First Century* (Lanham, MD: Rowman and Littlefield, 2009); and Randolph Persuad and Alina Sajed,

eds., *Race, Color, and Culture in International Relations: Postcolonial Perspectives* (New York: Routledge, 2018).

12. See, for example, Simon Curtis, "Cities and Global Governance: State Failure or a New Global Order," *Millennium* 44 (2016): 415–77.

13. US Department of State, *2015 Quadrennial Diplomacy and Development Review* (Washington, DC: Atlantic Council, 2015).

14. A. T. Kearney, 2018 Global Cities Report. https://www.atkearney.com/2018-global-cities-report.

15. On cities as international actors see Michele Acuto, "City Leadership in Global Governance," *Global Governance* 19 (2013): 481–98; Deborah Avant et al., *Innovations in Global Governance* (New York: Council on Foreign Relations, September 2017).

16. Peter Engelke, *Foreign Policy for an Urban World* (Washington, DC: Atlantic Council, Issue Brief, October 2015); and Kristin Ljungkvist, *The Global City 2.0* (London: Routledge, 2015).

17. On private military corporations see Martha Minow, "Outsourcing Power: How Privatizing Military Efforts Challenges Accountability, Professionalism, and Democracy," *Boston College Law Review* 46 (2005): 989–1025, Thomas Adams, "The New Mercenaries and the Privatization of Conflict," *Parameters* 29 (1999): 103–116; Rita Abrahamsen and Michael Williams, "Selling Security: Assessing the Impact of Military Privatization," *Review of International Peacekeeping* 15 (2008): 131–46; and Deborah Avant, *The Market for Force* (Cambridge: Cambridge University Press, 2005).

18. For a typology see Robert Mandel, "The Privatization of Security," *Armed Forces and Society* 28 (2001): 129–51.

19. Seth Kaplan, "Risk Cascades and How to Manage Them," *American Interest* 12 (2017): 101–09.

20. Other studies utilizing the notion of cascading disasters include Gianluca Pescaroli and David Alexander, "A Definition of Cascading Disasters and Cascading Effect: Going beyond the 'Toppling Dominos' Metaphor," *Planet @ Risk*, 3 (2015); and Emily Simmons, *Recurring Storms, Food Instability, Political Instability and Conflict* (Washington, DC: Center for Strategic and International Studies, February, 2017).

21. Erik Goepner, *War State, Trauma State* (Washington, DC: Cato Institute Policy Analysis #844, June 19, 2018).

22. For an overview see Alex Bowen and Cameron Hepburn, "Green Growth: An Assessment," *Oxford Review of Economic Policy* 30 (2014): 407–23.

23. For an example of a discussion of green growth by an international organization see OECD, "What Is Green Growth and How Can It Help Deliver Sustainable Development?" www.oecd.org/greengrowth/whatisgreengrowthandhowcanithelpdeliversustainabledevelopment.htm.

24. Some argue that a "strong green growth" variation exists that promotes short- and long-term growth. See M. Jacobs, "Green Growth," in *Handbook of Global Climate Change and Economic Policy*, ed. R. Falkner (Oxford: Wiley-Blackwell, 2013), 197–214.

25. Stefan Dercon, "Is Green Growth Good for the Poor," *World Bank Research Observer* 29 (2014): 163–85.

26. Jason Hickel, "Why Growth Can't be Green," *Foreign Policy*, September 12, 2018. For a competing view see Linus Blomqvist, "Green Growth Is Still Possible," Bloomberg Blog, May 8, 2018.

27. Patrycja Sasnal, "Domesticating the Giant: The Global Governance of Migration," Council on Foreign Relations, June 18, 2018. https://www.cfr.org/report/domesticating-giant-global-governance-migration; and Kathleen Newland, "New Approaches to Refugee Crises in the 21st Century," Migration Policy Institute, Policy Brief, October, 2016.

28. See Cynthia Rosenzweig, ed., *Climate Change and Cities* (Cambridge: Cambridge University Press, 2011); and "The Three Degree World: Cities That Will Be Drowned," *Guardian*, November 3, 2017. https://www.theguardian.com/cities/ng-interactive/2017/nov/03/three-degree-world-cities-drowned-global-warming.

29. New York Declaration. http://www.unhcr.org/en-us/events/conferences/57e39d987/new-york-declaration-refugees-migrants.html.

30. Quoted in Maryknoll Office for Global Concerns, "Global Migration Crisis: New York Declaration." https://maryknollogc.org/article/global-migration-crisis-new-york-declaration.

31. Global Compact for Safe, Orderly and Regular Migration. https://refugeesmigrants.un.org/sites/default/files/180711_final_draft_0.pdf.

32. Francis Fukuyama, "The End of History," *National Interest* 16 (1989): 4.

Index